# EUROPEANIZATION AND THE SOUTHERN PERIPHERY

## Books of Related Interest

**Europeanised Politics?**
*European Integration and National Political Systems*
Klaus H. Goetz and Simon Hix, London School of Economics (eds.)

**The Barcelona Process**
*Building a Euro-Mediterranean Regional Community*
George Joffé, School of Oriental and African Studies, University of London, and Álvaro Vasconcelos, Director, Instituto de Estudos Estratégicos e Internacionais, Lisbon (eds.)

**The Euro-Mediterranean Partnership**
Richard Gillespie, University of Portsmouth (ed.)

**Immigrants and the Informal Economy in Southern Europe**
Martin Baldwin-Edwards, Mediterranean Migration Observatory, Athens, and Joaquin Arango, Instituto Universitario Ortega y Gasset, Madrid.(eds.)

**Southern European Welfare States**
*Between Crisis and Reform*
Martin Rhodes, European University Institute, Florence (ed.)

**Spain**
*The European and International Challenges*
Richard Gillespie, University of Liverpool, and Richard Young, University of Portsmouth (eds.)

# Europeanization and the Southern Periphery

*Editors*

Kevin Featherstone
and George Kazamias

FRANK CASS
LONDON • PORTLAND, OR

*First published in 2001 in Great Britain by*
FRANK CASS PUBLISHERS
Crown House, 47 Chase Side, Southgate, London N14 5BP

*and in the United States of America by*
FRANK CASS PUBLISHERS
c/o ISBS
5804 N.E. Hassalo Street
Portland, OR 97213-3644

*Website* www.frankcass.com



British Library Cataloguing in Publication Data

Europeanization and the southern periphery
1.European Union – Europe, Southern 2.Europe, Southern – Politics and government – 20th century
I.Featherstone, Kevin II.Kazamias, George
320.9'4

ISBN 0714681288

ISBN 0 7146 5087 0 (cloth)
ISBN 0 7146 8128 8 (paper)

Library of Congress Cataloging-in-Publication Data:

Europeanization and the southern periphery/editors,
Kevin Featherstone and George Kazamias.
p. cm
1.Europe–Relations–Mediterranean Region. 2. Mediterranean Region–Relations–Europe. 3. Europe–Economic integration. 4. Mediterranean Region–Economic integration. 5. Mediterranean Region–Economic conditions–1945–I. Featherstone, Kevin. II. Kazamias, G. A. (Georgios A.)

D973 .E925 2001
337.1'4–dc21

2001028423

This group of studies first appeared in a Special Issue on 'Europeanization and the Southern Periphery' of *South European Society & Politics*, 5/2 (Autumn 2000) ISSN 1360-8746, published by Frank Cass.



Printed in Great Britain by
Antony Rowe Ltd., Chippenham, Wilts.

# Contents

# BIOGRAPHICAL NOTES

**Carles Boix** is Assistant Professor in the Department of Political Science at the University of Chicago. His research and teaching interests include comparative political economy and comparative politics. He has authored several articles in the *American Political Science Review*, *American Journal of Political Science*, *British Journal of Political Science*, *Electoral Studies*, and *European Journal of Political Economy* and *World Politics*. His book *Political Parties, Growth and Equality* (Cambridge: Cambridge University Press, 1998) won the 1999 American Political Science Association Award for the Best Book in Political Economy.

**Quim Brugué** is Lecturer of Political Science at the Universitat Autònoma de Barcelona (UAB). He has been Visiting Fellow at Fitzwilliams College (University of Cambridge). He is currently Academic Coordinator of the Public Management Master Programme at the UAB. His recent work includes books on local government and public policy.

**Michelle Cini** is Jean Monnet Senior Lecturer in the Department of Politics, University of Bristol and was Jean Monnet Fellow in the Schuman Centre for Advanced Studies, European University Institute, 1999–2000. Her recent publications include 'Merger Control in the European Union', *Governance* 12/2 (1999) (with L. McGowan); *Competition Policy in the European Union* (with L. McGowan; Hants: Macmillan, 1998); and *The European Commission* (Manchester: Manchester University Press, 1996).

**Kevin Featherstone** is Professor of European Politics and Jean Monnet Professor of European Integration in the Department of European Studies, University of Bradford. His recent work includes 'Italy and EMU as a "*Vincolo Esterno*": Empowering the Technocrats, Transforming the State' (with Kenneth Dyson; *South European Society and Politics* 1/2 (Autumn) 1996); and *The Road to Maastricht: Negotiating Economic and Monetary Union* (with Kenneth Dyson; Oxford: Oxford University Press, 1999).

**Marco Giuliani** is Associate Professor in Comparative Politics at the University of Milano. His main research interests include the theoretical and empirical analysis of public policy-making (*Dizionario di politiche pubbliche*, edited in 1996 with G. Capano; *Decidere per l'ambiente*, 1998), and the relationship between Italy and the EU ('Italy', in D. Rometsch and W. Wessels (ed.), *The European Union and Member States* (1996); 'Italy and Europe: Policy Domains and Dynamics', in M. Fedele and R. Leonardi (eds.), *Italy: Politics and Policy* vol.2, 2000).

**Ricard Gomà** is Lecturer of Political Science at the Universitat Autònoma de Barcelona. In the past he has been Visiting Fellow at the Universities of Warwick and Bath. He is presently Academic Coordinator of Political Science and Sociology Studies at the UAB. His recently published books have been on local and regional government and public policies in Spain.

**David Hine** is a Fellow of Christ Church, Oxford. His research interests include Italian government and politics and European politics, including the politics of European integration. He is the author of *Governing Italy: The Politics of Bargained Pluralism* (Oxford: Clarendon, 1993; *Beyond the Market: The EU and National Social Policy* (London: Routledge, 1998) ed. (with H. Kassim); and *Italy: The Return of Politics* (Berghaus, Oxford, 2000) ed. (with S. Vassallo).

**P.C. Ioakimidis** is Professor of European Policy and Institutions, Department of Political Science, University of Athens. His recent work includes *The European Union and the Greek State* (Athens: Themelio, 1998 (in Greek)); 'The Model of Foreign Policy-Making in Greece: Personalities Versus Institutions' in St. Stavridis, Th. Couloumbis, Th. Veremis and N. Waites (eds.), *The Foreign Policies of the European Union's Mediterranean States and Applicant Countries in the 1990's* (London: Macmillan, 1999).

**George Kazamias** is Lecturer in the Department of European Studies, University of Bradford. He has written on Greek politics and contemporary history including '"The usual Bulgarian stratagems": The Big Three and the end of the Bulgarian occupation of Greek E. Macedonia and Thrace, Sept.–Oct. 1944', *European History Quarterly* 29/3 (1999); 'Greece and the Negotiation of Economic and

Monetary Union: preferences, strategies, and institutions' (with K. Featherstone and D. Papadimitriou), *Journal of Modern Greek Studies* (2000); and 'The Limits of External Empowerment: EMU, Technocracy and Reform of the Greek Pension System, 1996–98' (with K. Featherstone and D. Papadimitriou), *Political Studies* (2001).

**José M. Magone** is Lecturer in European Politics in the Department of Politics and Asian Studies, University of Hull. His work includes *The Changing Architecture of Iberian Politics: An Investigation on the Structuring of Democratic Political Systemic Culture in Semiperipheral Southern European Societies* (Lewiston, NY: Mellen University Press, 1996); *European Portugal: The Difficult Road to Sustainable Democracy* (Basingstoke/New York: Macmillan/St Martin's Press, 1997); and 'The Golden Mean of Domestic European Policy Coordination: The Case of Portugal', in H. Kassim, G. Peters and V. Wright (eds.), *National Coordination of European Union Policy* (Oxford: Oxford University Press, 2000, pp.141–60).

**George Pagoulatos** is Assistant Professor of Comparative Politics in the Department of International and European Economic Studies, Athens University of Economics and Business. His most recent work includes 'European Banking: Five Modes of Governance', *West European Politics* 22/1 (1999) and 'The Liberalization of Southern European Financial Systems', in K. Lavdas (ed.), *Junctures of Stateness: Political Boundaries and Policy Change in Southern Europe* (Aldershot: Ashgate, forthcoming 2001).

**Spyros Sofos** is Senior Research Fellow at the European Research Centre, Kingston University. His research focuses on issues of identity and nationalism in south-eastern Europe. He has co-edited (with Brian Jenkins) *Nation and Identity in Contemporary Europe* (London: Routledge, 1996), and written extensively on these topics. His two forthcoming monographs focus on issues of identity and politics in south-eastern Europe and a comparative study of Turkish and Greek nationalisms.

**Joan Subirats** is Professor of Political Science at the Universitat Autònoma de Barcelona and Visiting Professor at the University of California (Berkeley). He is the Director of the Public Management and Politics and Government Master Programmes at the UAB. He has recently published books on public policies and social capital in Catalonia and Spain, and on environmental policy.

**Mehmet Ugur** is Jean Monnet Senior Lecturer in Economics and European Integration at the University of Greenwich. His research and teaching interests include economic integration, European public policy and EU–Turkey relations. He has recently published *The European Union and Turkey: An Anchor/Credibility Dilemma* (Aldershot: Ashgate, 1999). He is currently the course co-ordinator for the MA in European public policy.

# Editors' Note

The idea for this volume stemmed from a panel convened at the conference of the European Community Studies Association (ECSA) in Pittsburgh in June 1999. Several of the contributors to this volume participated in that panel. Carles Boix, Marco Giuliani and George Pagoulatos each presented first drafts of the articles included here. The interest of the editors in the concept of 'Europeanization' has also been underlined by the establishment of the Research Unit on Europeanization, within the Department of European Studies at the University of Bradford. The new Unit has initiated a range of activities, and this publication is one of the early manifestations of its work.

The volume is asymmetrical in content as well as in title. It does not claim to provide a complete answer to the debate about the definition and constituent elements of the concept of Europeanization. Rather, it is concerned with the domestic adaptation of states on the southern periphery to the pressures emanating from the European Union (EU). It begins with a discussion of the concept of Europeanization and its relevance to the South. This is followed by case studies of existing member states (Portugal, Italy, Spain and Greece) and the applicant states from the region (Cyprus, Malta and Turkey). The adjustment processes are examined across different dimensions – political, economic and social. What is made clear are the multifarious ways in which actual or prospective EU membership impacts upon domestic polities, with both intended and unintended consequences. The articles examine the contours and bases of these asymmetrical effects and assess their overall significance.

Inevitably, in a project such as this, the support and tolerance of a number of collaborators were essential. The editors would like to thank first and foremost Susannah Verney, the editor of *South European Society and Politics*, for her continuous support and invaluable guidance. Without her, it is doubtful if this effort would have come to fruition. Thanks are also due to Anthony Green and Stewart Cass at Frank Cass, whose help and experience made possible the resolution of some complex problems.

KEVIN FEATHERSTONE
GEORGE KAZAMIAS
*Bradford, May 2000*

# Introduction: Southern Europe and the Process of 'Europeanization'

KEVIN FEATHERSTONE AND GEORGE KAZAMIAS

This volume presents a comparative study of the impact of the European Union (EU) on the states of southern and Mediterranean Europe. In doing so, it highlights different manifestations of a process of 'Europeanization', charting the varied impacts of EU obligations on state institutions and modes of governance, as well as wider state–society and state–economy relations. The focus is on the adaptation evident in the distinct institutional settings of each state. Europeanization via the structures of the EU entails more than a passive response to external pressures: the domestic and EU institutional settings are intermeshed, with actors engaged in both vertical and horizontal networks and institutional linkages. Thus, at the domestic level, Europeanization is both a cause and an effect of action and this volume explores these diverse features in the different national case studies. The mode of reaction of the different states highlights not only the importance they attach to Europe, but also their understanding of what 'Europe' is.

The setting of southern and Mediterranean Europe highlights a number of important themes relevant to an understanding of what is entailed by Europeanization in the EU context. These themes stem from a series of significant contrasts associated with the region:

- Between first and second generation EU member states (Italy compared to Greece, Portugal and Spain)
- Among current and applicant member states (the above contrasted with Cyprus, Malta and Turkey)
- Of large, medium and micro-states
- Of states often seen as constituting the EU's 'periphery' as opposed to its 'core'
- Between states possessing different foreign policy legacies and ties,

but largely sharing an historic vulnerability to external interference
- Of states that historically have had differing strengths of cultural identity with an hegemonic western Europe, but the domestic state traditions of which display both resilience and some commonality.

With these traits in mind, the region is a useful focus for an analysis of the different dimensions of Europeanization. It allows differentiation according to the length of EU membership; states inside and outside the EU; the size of state; and historically competing identities and ties.

Moreover, southern and Mediterranean Europe is often seen as a 'periphery' to the EU's 'core'. In its strongest form, 'periphery' here would refer to the Marxist critique of capitalism propounded by dependency theorists, such as Gunder Frank and Wallerstein in the 1970s. The assumptions of a conscious, cohesive and consistent exploitation are difficult to sustain empirically in this context, however. Within the international system, southern Europe is more accurately a 'semi-periphery'. While EU membership has exposed southern Europe to the effects of 'disciplinary neo-liberalism', to use Gill's (1995) term, it has mediated the full effects of globalization and it has provided substantial developmental support to these states.

Instead, 'periphery' is used here in a much weaker, descriptive sense. Southern and Mediterranean Europe can be identified as an EU 'periphery' in terms of a number of predominant traits: the economic inequality compared to northern EU states; the historically distinctive mode of the region's economic development and social stratification as a consequence of 'late industrialization' and the relatively greater importance of agriculture and services; the financial dependence on EU development aid; the structural power of Germany in shaping the EU's policy agenda in many areas; and the lesser bargaining strength of the 'south' in EU treaty negotiations. Against this background, the challenge of 'Europeanization' can be expected to be set more starkly. The contrasts in condition and aspiration are generally greater than between other EU states, while the region has displayed remarkably resilient and distinctive features of state tradition and political culture despite the pressures of the EU.

The articles in the rest of this volume offer case studies of the experience of 'Europeanization' in many of the states within the region. Few attempts have been made previously to compare and contrast these experiences, yet the value of doing so is high both in terms of deepening the understanding of Europeanization as a conceptual tool and of gauging patterns of domestic change within the region. Europeanization represents a process of major structural transformation within the region; indeed, perhaps it is *the* prime focus of change that these states have in common.

The empirical case studies stress key attributes of the southern experience of Europeanization. These can be summarised as dynamism, asymmetry and fragmentation. The terms of EU membership have undergone substantive change over time. When Greece joined the EU in 1981, there was little reason to predict the magnitude of the later commitment to a single European market or a single European currency. Moreover, individual programmes – like EMU – can undergo significant evolution in the implementation process, not least because of changing bargaining strengths between the key players. The impact may be uncertain and reversible. The effects of Europeanization are generally asymmetrical: varying between sectors and location affected by distinct institutional settings. Domestically, Europeanization – like 'modernization' theories before it – can be seen as having important fragmentation effects on domestic society, creating or strengthening social cleavages, based on competing economic interests. The restructured cleavages set new constraints, revise opportunities and stimulate a redefinition of both preferences and interests for the actors involved.

Europeanization did not begin, of course, with the EU. Indeed, to neglect the previous history of competing notions of international identity within the region, or of external interference in its development, would be to misunderstand the basis of the current setting. It is appropriate, then, to begin with a brief survey of how the south has viewed and experienced 'Europe' historically. Following this, the concept of Europeanization is discussed in terms of its current usage, in the context of the domestic ramifications of EU membership. This helps to outline a framework for how Europeanization is applied later in this volume, and sets the scene for those national case studies.

## EUROPEANIZATION AND SOUTHERN EUROPE'S HISTORICAL EXPERIENCE

Europeanization has taken on different meanings throughout modern history (Mjoset 1997). The different historical meanings of what is constituted by 'Europe' and who are 'Europeans' indicate the use of Europeanization as a basis of separation for social, cultural and religious identities and interests within the broad geographical area. Now, however, through European integration, a number of divides, most of them long-established, are being confronted. As a result, the concept of 'Europe' has become more heterogeneous. The states covered in this volume comprise former imperial powers (Italy, Spain and Portugal); countries with strong cultural links with Latin America (Spain and Portugal); countries with a dual (eastern and western) cultural identity (Greece, Cyprus, Malta and Turkey); and a country (Turkey) whose main land mass lies beyond the conventional borders of Europe in what was conventionally termed the Near East. Moreover, the religious affiliations of the region would, in past historical periods, not only have been mutually exclusive, but would also have created a decisive divide with the present 'core' EU states: uniquely for the EU, the population of Greece is predominantly Eastern Orthodox Christian; Turkey mainly Muslim; and Cyprus combines both affiliations. While the Catholic divide runs through parts of southern Europe, no country among those examined has any significant Protestant population. Nonetheless, the desire to join the 'European' paradigm has created and is still in the process of creating pressures that overcome many of these traditional divisions.

In the modern period, Europeanization has usually meant adaptation to (west) European norms and practices. In southern Europe in the nineteenth and twentieth centuries, 'modernization' was often defined as *west* Europeanization, acknowledging the 'pull' to convergence of the major powers of the region (Diamandouros 1994). Despite resistance by traditionalists, the Europeanization/modernization concept always enjoyed considerable currency. Indeed, as Tsoukalas writes (specifically in relation to Greek national identity), 'the struggle between tradition and modernity is not reducible to an opposition between [the] domestic and [the] imported' (Tsoukalas 1999: 13). Europeanization has typically engaged the support of domestic elites with internationally oriented identities and interests.

Moreover, the EU's role in this regard has been to represent an alternative mode of governance to the peoples of the south. With the quickening pace of integration, there emerged a credible and enforceable alternative in many policy sectors to the often-discredited national government machines. This was an historical innovation for the south: Europeanization had a specific form, with its own juridical order. Local politicians could be judged by their success as conduits to this modernization process. The resilience or underperformance of domestic institutions became starker.

## EUROPEANIZATION AS A CONCEPT

'Europeanization' as a term has been applied across a wide variety of contexts, with a range of different meanings attached to it, either implicitly or explicitly. The risk is that the more that it is 'stretched', the less will be its value (Sartori 1970). At its broadest, 'Europeanization' often appears to be used synonymously with 'integration'. Yet this seems an unduly constraining definition of the term: if 'Europeanization' is merely a loose synonym for 'integration', is the process structured in a 'top–down' fashion, 'bottom–up' or both? Moreover, some forms of Europeanization – in the sense of a transnational process of 'convergence' – may be found with little direct reference to the EU. Identities and interests change as a result of shifts in social norms, values and beliefs and these may occur in response to transnational or global pressures only loosely connected to the EU. The modern discourse on human rights, citizenship and the position of ethnic minorities and migrant workers seems in many respects to be such a case (Soysal 1994). Instances of policy transfer between subnational actors across Europe in areas lightly touched by EU obligations may be more borderline (Bennett 1991). Europeanization might also be related to the effects of 'globalization' (Hirst and Thompson 1996). It might be understood as a set of responses by European and/or national actors to wider systemic pressures and so ultimately a regional reaction to globalization (e.g. the impact of capital mobility; see Garrett 1996). Indeed, Europeanization has been interpreted as a challenge to US hegemony; a leadership replacement in reaction to the loss of dominance of the international system by Europe; and a means to build economic security and rearrange the state–economy relationship (Mjoset 1997).

Nonetheless, the deepening and widening of the EU integration process over recent decades has meant that the term 'Europeanization' has been used largely as a description of the EU's own processes and impacts. In this respect, the hijack is complete. This broad usage is accepted for the purposes of this volume. Transnational effects not linked in significant part to EU structures and processes are not explored here in any depth. Even with this more narrow perspective, there are important distinctions to be drawn and applications to be elaborated if 'Europeanization' is to have a clear set of meanings. In this context, Europeanization cuts across the domestic and EU levels of politics, though its usage is intended to stress the interdependence of forces between the two. Europeanization here has three dimensions, which are useful to separate at least in an abstract sense:

(1) The increase and expansion of institutionalization at the EU level (e.g. the development of the EU's competence and coordination in foreign and security policy).
(2) The adjustment evident in the institutional setting – incorporating the norms, rules, identities and interests of actors within a structured set of relationships – at the level of member states, consequent on EU obligations.
(3) The adjustment evident, in similar respects, in states that are not EU members, but which are closely linked to it.

This volume focuses on dimensions (2) and (3) above. It incorporates case studies of Europeanization as a process of domestic structural change in both southern European member states and states aspiring to join the EU as full members. In this context, Europeanization is examined in terms of the fit or misfit between the national setting and EU-level commitments, and the response of domestic actors to this process. Europeanization is assumed to be a two-way process, between the domestic and the EU levels, involving both top–down and bottom–up pressures.

As a process of structural change, the effects of Europeanization can be differentiated over time, as well as between settings. Empirical analysis can gauge the *extent* and *significance* of the adjustments involved. It also has a *dynamic* quality: its systemic effects are not *necessarily* permanent or irreversible. Thus, the course and progression of the changes wrought are unclear and uncertain. This is one major reason why Europeanization is not a new label for 'neo-functionalism' (E.B. Haas 1958). Moreover, cause and effect in the Europeanization process can be deceptive: relatively 'small' and technical EU obligations may have widespread domestic ramifications in certain settings and be a subterfuge for further changes. For example, EU transparency rules for financial accounts have had major implications for pension fund institutions in Greece.

Further, Europeanization can relate both structure and agency in ontologically complex ways. Actors can be of different types: individual, collective or corporate. Within the process of Europeanization, structure and agency are best understood as being inherently relational concepts (Bhaskar 1979; Giddens 1984; Checkel 1998). Agency within the Europeanization process is not only structured, but may also be structuring, as actors 'lead' (Dyson and Featherstone 1999: 776–82). In addition, the study of Europeanization does not fit easily 'the language of dependent and independent variables and the logic of regression analysis'

(Olsen 1996: 271). Transformation may occur on the basis of 'a multitude of co-evolving, parallel and not necessarily tightly-coupled processes' (Olsen 1996: 271).

In gauging the process of domestic adaptation, the conceptual framework of 'new institutionalism' is a useful starting point (Olsen 1996). The approach has different branches, but they each explain differences of policy by reference to sets of principles, norms and rules ('institutions' broadly defined) which structure and pattern relationships within the policy process (Hall and Taylor 1996). The conception of 'institutions' varies significantly between the different branches and this has implications for the characterization of the process and setting of Europeanization.

An increasing number of scholars have applied the framework of *rational choice institutionalism* to the European integration process (Scharpf 1988, 1997; Tsebelis 1994, 1995; Garrett and Tsebelis 1996; Featherstone, Kazamias and Papadimitriou 2001). Institutions here are seen in the most minimal or narrow sense. Drawing on rational choice assumptions, actors are assumed to have fixed preferences and they aim to maximize the satisfaction of their self-interest. Yet institutions structure the interactions, or bargaining game, between actors. Actors 'select their best available course of action under the circumstances, given their (institutionally shaped) preferences and perceptions' (Scharpf 1997: 32). The EU institutional setting – connecting both the domestic and the European levels – affects the range and sequence of alternatives on the choice agenda, provides information, and offers enforcement mechanisms that reduce uncertainty about others' behaviour. This allows 'gains from exchange' and leads actors to particular calculations and potentially better social outcomes (Hall and Taylor 1996: 945). Under this perspective, the institutional setting underpinning EU membership – both domestic and European – acts as an intervening variable between the power and preferences of individual actors and their subsequent choices.

In this context, the bargaining game can be seen as 'two-level' (Putnam 1988) or as involving 'nested games' (Tsebelis 1990). An expression of such strategic behaviour is when domestic actors seek to be bound by EU constraints in order to obtain reform at home: in such cases rational actors exploit the new strategic opportunities offered by EU-level institutions. Dyson and Featherstone (1996, 1999) noted how technocrats in Italy viewed EMU membership as an external constraint (a '*vincolo esterno*') which allowed them to impose fiscal and monetary discipline on the often-errant instincts of politicians in the old '*partitocrazia*'. Grande (1995) also identified a willingness of member governments to be bound by EU commitments. 'Blameshift' becomes a strategic option for rational actors in a multi-level institutional setting.

The conception of the institutional setting is broadest for *sociological institutionalism* (or 'social constructivism'). It includes not just formal rules, procedures or norms, but symbols, cognitive and normative beliefs that provide 'frames of meaning' guiding human action. Such a definition breaks down the conceptual divide between 'institutions' and 'culture' (Hall and Taylor 1996: 947). However, institutions do not simply affect the strategic calculations of individuals, but also their basic preferences and identity. 'Institutions' are thus a strong independent variable (Checkel 1999). Actors are constituted by the institutional setting, in that the latter defines their identity, understandings, preferences and interests. Rather than the utility-maximization of rational choice perspectives, scholars here emphasize a 'logic of appropriateness' and 'rule-governed action' (March and Olsen 1989). Relatively few studies have applied this approach to the EU, however. In a wider context, Checkel (1997) analyzed how international norms associated with the Council of Europe reached the domestic arena to empower actors. The approach is compatible with earlier studies which focused on shifts of loyalty from the domestic to the European level (the neo-functionalism of E.B. Haas 1958) and the cognitive and affective response to participation in EC institutions (Kerr 1973). Studies of EMU central bankers as an epistemic community (Verdun 1999) and of the role of ideas in shaping the Maastricht agenda (McNamera 1998) can also be seen as compatible with this approach.

A mid-position is adopted by *historical institutionalism* in relation to the interpretation of 'institutions'. The impact of the institutional setting grows over time, developing from a calculus to a more cultural form. In the short term, institutions structure the bargaining game and provide incentives to rational actors to rethink their strategies; over the longer term, institutions can have deeper effects on actors as strategies, initially adopted for self-interested reasons, get locked into the institutional setting (Checkel 1999: 547). Institutions can therefore be both an intervening and an independent variable. Institutions carry with them asymmetries in the power of actors and their access to the policy process. The 'historical' aspect is reflected in the attention given to path dependence, with specific contextual features of the institutional setting pushing development along a set of 'paths'. Such development involves both unintended consequences and inefficiencies. The continuity of historical development is punctuated, nevertheless, by 'critical junctures' in which substantial institutional change occurs and history moves onto a different path (see also Hay and Wincott 1998).

Historical institutionalism lends itself to studies in which domestic and/or EU institutions have an intervening effect on actor preferences and interests in the short term and a sufficiently stronger impact over the longer term to establish distinct paths of development in policies and institutions. In principle, such an approach follows the 'deepening' of the European integration process over time, with the strengthening of the institutional setting at the EU level. As European monetary cooperation intensified, for example, the relevant EU institutions – ECOFIN (the Council of Ministers comprising economics and finance ministers), the EC Monetary Committee and the Committee of Central Bank Governors – assumed a more distinct identity, beyond the sum of their parts, as actors sought to uphold their credibility with their partners, engaged in a shared learning process, and defended the policy territory of their institution from encroachment by other EU bodies (Dyson and Featherstone 1999). The monetary institutions created a distinct set of venues by which to route policy on EMU and this affected the nature and content of what was agreed at Maastricht in 1991. Political institutionalization at the EU level can be related to the slightly broader notion of the emergence of 'supranational governance' (Stone Sweet and Sandholtz 1998). The historical institutionalist approach has also been applied to the adaptation of domestic institutions to the need for EU coordination, showing the resilience of the domestic setting to new EU pressures (Bulmer and Burch 1998). In a more distinctive approach, Rometsch and Wessels (1996) went further and argued that there has been a 'fusion' of national and European institutions in the policy cycle, though only a partial convergence of political systems. Their volume charts the degree of adjustment shown by national institutions in the process of EU participation.

The three forms of 'institutionalism' identify different roles for agency and structure in the Europeanization process. They posit different types of constraint on actors and they have different understandings of how preferences are formed. These differences, which stem from contrasting conceptions of what 'institutions' are, also suggest distinct interpretations of what the EU institutional setting *is*. The choice of approach must be related to the empirical task in hand: different lenses will capture distinct aspects of a large and multi-faceted subject (Checkel

1999). A narrow notion of institutions can offer a parsimonious account of core elements of actor behaviour and policy outcomes, but the study of the cognitive and normative elements requires a focus on the broader institutional setting.

An alternative approach to the study of the structural impact of EU obligations is to focus on the degree to which it involves a transformation in the mode of governance affecting domestic and EU institutions. This approach raises different sets of questions. In a typically provocative analysis, Moravcsik (1994) argued that a major effect of EU participation is the empowerment of the government executive within the domestic polity: 'Integration redistributes political resources by shifting control over domestic agendas (initiative), altering decision-making procedures (institutions), magnifying informational asymmetries in their favour (information), and multiplying the potential domestic ideological justifications for policies (ideas)' (1994: 1). In sum, the 'democratic deficit' is exacerbated and national governments seek further integration in order to obtain yet more room for manoeuvre domestically.

Strikingly, few of the case studies presented in this volume offer empirical support to the stark thesis of executive empowerment. In Catalonia, Greece and Portugal, the conclusion is more one of the diffusion of executive power, whilst in Italy the effects are judged ambiguous and not necessarily attributable to European factors. The alternative diffusion thesis is often placed in a framework of 'multi-level governance'. Marks (1993: 392) argued that a centrifugal trend is leading to 'the emergence of "multi-level governance" [drawing] some previously centralized functions of the state up to the supranational level and some down to the local/regional level'. This thesis finds empirical support here in each of the four member states, though equal stress is given to the empowerment of the domestic civil society. Studied at the EU level, the multi-level governance framework typically identifies actors engaged in policy networks of a horizontal and vertical nature. In a more fulsome account, Kohler-Koch and Eising (1999: 268) have argued that 'we are currently witnessing a transformation towards a network mode of governance at the level of the European Community'. Given the peculiar characteristics of the EU polity (its multi-level structure; the combination of supranational and inter-governmental elements; the strength of the judiciary; the functional and technocratic style; the heterogeneity and fluidity of the actors involved, over the different policy phases), the emergence of a predominantly network mode of governance – as opposed to pluralism, statism and corporatism – is seen as inevitable. The focus here is more on how EU policies develop and the role of EU actors in the process, while this volume is concerned with domestic impacts and response.

Participation in EU institutions and processes may promote a policy convergence between member states. Andersen and Eliassen identify the EU 'as a system of transnational authority and policy-making', and they describe the effect, rather awkwardly, as 'Europeification' (1993: 255–6). In another comparative volume, Hanf and Soetendorp apply Europeanization to 'a process in which Europe, and especially the EU, become an increasingly more relevant and important point of political reference for the actors at the level of the member-states', and the latter engage in intergovernmental and transnational policy networks that reach from Brussels into the domestic sphere (1998: 1). Mény (1996) takes a wider perspective. He posits a convergence process in which there is a 'progressive emergence of a bundle of common norms of action, the evolution of which escapes the control of any particular member state and yet decisively influences the behaviour of public policy actors' (1996: 8–9). Evidence for convergence can be found at three levels: the emergence of a European political agenda (the process of problem definition shifts to the European level); the forms of interest representation (e.g. corporatism threatened by more open and competitive modes of representation); and the modes of operation of various actors. He does indeed find a convergence of public policies in Europe, but argues that in the absence of an arbitrating agency at the top, this constitutes a 'kind of co-operative federalism without a state' (1996: 17).

The key point here is that of causality, between structure and agency: convergence may occur as a loose transnational phenomenon and may be described as Europeanization; but for the EU to be identified as a prime agent, or facilitating structure, in this process requires evidence of direct causal effect. Convergence as a result of EU participation is far from being inevitable. Integration has significant asymmetrical effects. As the studies in this volume indicate, the impact of Europeanization in the southern member states has been incremental, irregular and uneven over time and between locations, national and subnational. Profound disparities remain, within and without the region.

The conception of the institutional setting of the EU thus must be sensitive to evidence of core–periphery differences between member states. The notion of small states being an appendix to larger ones has a long history in realist-inspired studies of international relations. But even a rational choice perspective in which actors are self-interested utilitymaximizers need not assume equal partners. EMU might be cited as a case in which a set of core states established an agreement that obliged the remaining states to sign up in order to minimize the losses they might suffer from being left on the outside (see Boix's contribution to this volume). A sociological institutionalist interpretation might highlight the diffusion of a new policy paradigm from the core to the periphery, as with the 'sound money, sound finance' principles of the EMU agreement. Essentially, most, if not all, the southern periphery states were 'importing' the policy paradigm against the background of isolated indigenous support for its key principles.

The engagement of the southern member states in EU bargaining processes also displays the inequality in the structural power between 'core' and 'periphery'. Individually, and even collectively, the southern states managed to have little distinctive impact on the elaboration of the 1991 EMU agreement (Dyson and Featherstone 1999; Featherstone, Kazamias and Papadimitriou 2000). Even on the issue they had defined as critical to their acceptance – that of extra 'cohesion' money – they had to settle for 'half a loaf'. They struggled to establish a bargaining coalition among themselves and, as a result, their overall influence remained very much inferior to that of the Franco–German axis.

This structural imbalance raises the general question of the autonomy that remains for periphery states in the process of Europeanization. The EU might be cast as a 'penetrative' agent, participating in the domestic political processes of such states and affecting the level of acceptance of its policies. This follows the early notions of penetration advanced by scholars of International Relations like Rosenau (1969: 46). In this perspective, the EU participates in the 'selection of goals, the allocation of costs, and the mobilization of resources and capabilities' in the domestic policy process (Siegel and Weinberg 1977: 46, quoted in Bennett 1991). Such an interpretation posits a maximalist view of the EU's power, somewhat akin to dependency theory. As with the latter, the requirements of evidence are daunting. Even where southern influence in the EU is low and divergence from the core is great, periphery state actors may prefer acceptance of EU policies in a calculation of the externalities involved in the choice before them. Moreover, the EU itself is not a separate, unitary actor over and above member states. Rather, 'Europeanization' denotes an interactive, iterative process between actors, domestic and European or both, and the EU level is occupied by varied and competitive actors.

Instead, the process of Europeanization in this context is better understood – like that of 'modernization' (Olsen 1996) – as involving a fragmentation effect on the periphery (Featherstone 1998). That is, the domestic response to the impact of the EU can be differentiated between actors which are more positive ('reformers') and those which are more resistant ('traditionalists'). Competing 'advocacy coalitions' can emerge on issues of reform defined, at least in part, by the EU (Sabatier 1998; Sabatier and Jenkins-Smith 1993; Featherstone, Kazamias and Papadimitriou 2000). Similarly, policy subsystems increasingly involve domestic actors enjoying privileges of technical information and expertise linked to EU networks. 'Epistemic communities' can emerge, bringing together technocrats, national and European (P. Haas 1992; Verdun 1999). Engagement in the EU advantages certain types of actor – notably technocratic reformers, businesses involved in external trade – relative to those that are dependent on traditional state protection. This restructuring of the power, preferences and interests of sets of actors constitutes the fragmentation effect of Europeanization. This differentiation follows that of the cultural dualism in southern Europe noted by Diamandouros (1994) and taken up by Ioakimidis in his study of Europeanization in Greece. Europeanization creates and reinforces domestic cleavages based on competing notions of reform, economic interest and identity. The impact is felt in social, cultural, economic and political terms as change and continuity are juxtaposed as domestic fault-lines across the domestic system. It is striking that many of the case studies in this volume make a direct connection between modernization and Europeanization, in terms of the domestic perception and understanding of the latter. Indeed, this linkage is drawn for both existing EU states and those that are current EU applicants.

## EUROPEANIZATION AS A CONCEPTUAL FRAMEWORK

While many use the term 'Europeanization', relatively few writers have sought to develop a conceptual framework for its empirical application. Ladrech (1994) provided one of the first definitions and this has been widely cited. He saw Europeanization as 'a process reorienting the direction and shape of politics to the degree that EC political and economic dynamics become part of the organizational logic of national politics and policy-making' (1994: 69). Inherent in this conception is the notion that actors redefine their interests and behaviour to meet the imperatives, norms and logic of EU membership. Whilst it has the strength of incorporating both 'politics' and 'policy-making', it remains a somewhat loose definition. It is generally compatible with the domestic dimension of earlier neo-functionalist theory. It is unclear how this helps the analyst to gauge the extent of Europeanization.

For others, Europeanization is most often placed within some type of institutional perspective. Olsen (1996) considered Europeanization as institution-building, drawing upon earlier perspectives on national integration and differentiation. This schema reflects the established concerns of comparative politics, but it probably remains too general to constitute an empirical framework in its own right (see also March and Olsen 1995). Schmidt (1997) extended the conception of Europeanization to the process of adaptation to the economic, institutional and ideational aspects of the integration process. This conception also suffers from being too general and underdeveloped. Is the process structured in a top–down, bottom–up fashion or both? Where is agency and structure in this process?

In a large comparative study, Caporaso, Green Cowles and Risse (forthcoming) similarly see Europeanization as political institutionalization. This 'involves the development of formal and informal rules, procedures, norms, and practices governing politics at the European, national, and subnational levels'. Their focus is on cross-level political interactions, interpreted within the framework of historical institutionalism (see above). They recognise different levels on which Europeanization may take place: institution building at the European level; the impact of EU membership at the national level; and as a response to globalization. This is a useful and broad perspective, though its specific application again depends on further interpretation.

In one of the most explicit frameworks developed to date, Knill and Lehmkuhl (1999) outline three mechanisms of Europeanization. By contrast to Caporaso *et al.*, their focus is exclusively top–down. Each mechanism involves constraints from the European level that may yield domestic institutional change. Other forms of Europeanization – as institutionalization at the EU level, as transnationalism between states – are not accounted for. The first mechanism they identify takes the form of 'positive integration' and is found when EU obligations prescribe an institutional model to which domestic arrangements have to be adjusted, with limited national discretion. They cite EU policy on environmental protection; health and safety at work; consumer protection; and some aspects of social policy. Europeanization here rests on the institutional 'goodness of fit' of domestic and European arrangements. The second mechanism is labelled 'negative integration' and occurs where EU legislation alters the domestic rules of the game. They cite the single market as an example. The impact is to alter the 'domestic opportunity structures' entailed in the distribution of power and resources between actors. Here, it is not a question of institutional fit or misfit, but rather 'the extent to which European policies have altered the strategic position of domestic actors' (ibid. 3). The third, and weakest, mechanism is where European policy alters the beliefs and expectations of domestic actors, which may in turn involve a change of preferences and strategies, as well as institutional adaptation. They see this mechanism as one of 'framing integration', affecting perceptions.

The typology builds on much of the existing literature. The first mechanism reflects a new (especially historical) institutionalist perspective on adaptation. The second can be related to multi-level bargaining games and rational choice. The third can be linked to sociological institutionalism and to the work of Schoen and Rein (1994) on frame reflection. Though the typology does not cover all aspects of what might reasonably be termed 'Europeanization' by political scientists, as a schema of domestic structural transformation it is useful and sensitive, empirically. It goes beyond locating *types* of change by identifying *mechanisms* inducing them. It offers a wide lens on the consequences of EU integration for the structural power of domestic actors: this is appropriate as empowerment effects need to be analyzed empirically. Indeed, the stress on domestic adaptation, highlighting a new institutionalist perspective, identifies the potential significance of divergences between different national settings. It is thus relevant to a comparative volume such as this.

## THE STRUCTURE AND SCOPE OF THIS VOLUME

While it is beyond the scope of this introduction to elaborate a typology of Europeanization in all its political manifestations, the individual articles that follow in this volume reflect much of the range and diversity of the domestic transformation considered above. As such, the discussions stress the related themes of *asymmetry*, *fragmentation* and *dynamism* in the Europeanization process. Europeanization is examined in the case studies across a range of dimensions. It is analyzed in terms of:

(1) a process of *institutional adaptation within government*, in relation to the coordination of EU policy and strategy (see contributions by Hine; Featherstone);

(2) a process of *transformation in the structural power of domestic actors*, in terms of:
   (a) the empowerment of executive and technocratic actors (Giuliani);
   (b) the empowerment of sub-national actors and institutions (Brugué *et al.*; Giuliani; Ioakimidis; Magone); and
   (c) the strengthening of civil society (Ioakimidis; Magone);
(3) an adjustment of the *domestic macroeconomic policy regime*, affecting state–economy relations (Boix; Cini; Featherstone; Pagoulatos; Ugur);
(4) an issue exerting a new dynamic within the *domestic party system* (Cini; Giuliani; Sofos);
(5) a pressure to *redefine national identity* (Cini; Sofos); and
(6) a strategic tool in the pursuit of *foreign policy interests* (Featherstone; Ugur; Sofos).

The case studies lead to the conclusion that there is limited scope for generalizations about the impact of Europeanization within the region. *A priori* assumptions are too often contradicted by the diversity of impacts found by detailed empirical analysis. This divergence testifies to the strength and importance of examining the domestic institutional setting in each of the southern states.

The diversity of content of Europeanization as a term as well as the different theoretical approaches referred to earlier is reflected in the individual articles that follow. The contents of the volume are organized in three unequal parts, focusing respectively on the impact of Europeanization on domestic structural transformation; macroeconomic policy regimes; and national identity. No attempt has been made to provide comprehensive cover of all three aspects for all countries covered. The emphasis has been chosen by the individual authors, reflecting the strong asymmetry of impact observable in the Europeanization project.

The first country studied in the section on domestic transformation is Italy. The process of government adaptation and reform in this country is the focus of Hine's article. He examines specifically the adaptation of the Italian central government to the European norms since the mid-1980s. Here the main problems were the dichotomy between policy formulation and policy implementation and institutional constraints, mainly the Italian government machinery's over reliance on the law as the solution to all problems. In this respect, Europeanization in Italy has meant a radical departure from long-established traditions, the continued existence of which would make adaptation problematic. Giuliani offers an alternative view of the Europeanization of the Italian political system. He argues that the main contribution of the Europeanization process was in the attitudinal change it effected, rather than on the specific reforms. This adaptation of practices (as opposed to structural reform) points toward consensus and cooperation as the way ahead at home and in Brussels.

Ioakimidis offers a survey of the EU's impact on the Greek state. He sees the EU as a major stimulus for advancing the economic, social and political modernization of Greece. Domestic political elites have 'internalized' the logic, norms, behaviour and culture associated with integration, equating Europeanization with modernization. Adaptation is thus intentional, rather than a passive response. Moreover, the pace of adaptation is quickening, with the deepening of the integration process represented by projects like EMU.

The subnational affects of Europeanization are explored in the distinctive context of Spanish decentralization. Brugué, Gomà and Subirats look at the development of multi-level governance from the perspective of Catalonia. They argue that government is ceasing to be a unidirectional, hierarchical, segregated and monopolistic action; rather, it is becoming a network of relationships with power and influence distributed among multiple actors. Self-governance in Catalonia has meant the *Generalitat* (the autonomous government) sharing power in a multi-level structure amidst a pluralist and interactive system of regulation. Europeanization has occurred alongside territorialization: the displacement of government towards both the EU and local governments.

The EU's impact on the modernization of public and regional administration is the focus of Magone's study of Portugal. The EU was an important factor reinforcing the consolidation of democracy in Portugal after 1974. Administrative modernization was the price to be paid for full participation in the EU. At the same time, the enhancement of the EU's role in distributing regional development aid has created an 'output legitimacy' for the integration process among the public. Europeanization has thus provided both a stimulus to reform and an alternative to the cynicism attached to domestic politics and politicians.

The Europeanization process extends beyond the current EU member states. Featherstone analyzes the impact of the EU on Cyprus during its 'pre-accession' phase. The processes of Europeanization are considered in terms of the structural transformation of state–economy relations (in which 'empowerment' is diffused and differentiated among domestic actors); and the adaptation of the state administration (to the demands of coordination; readjustment of competencies). Across a range of domestic reforms, EU pressure has been crucial to its pace, if not also its content. With the exception of the events of 1974, the stimulus from the EU represents the most far-reaching transformation of Cypriot society in four decades of independence. Indeed, it is against the background of the 1974 invasion that Europeanization takes on a distinctive role in Cyprus. Here, Europeanization plays a major role in the discourse of key actors on foreign policy (where the EU is seen as a vital foreign policy lever). Yet the high expectations of the EU to 'unblock' relations with Turkey poses important strategic risks should the EU fail to deliver.

Opening the macroeconomic policy section, Boix's article examines the relationship between globalization, European integration and the economic policies of the Spanish government during the period 1982–96. He finds that a combination of external pressures and domestic policy failures led to a significant shift in the policy priorities of the Gonzalez government. Global market pressures and the growing economic policy competence of the EU encouraged a shift of government priorities towards disinflation, in the absence of the option of devaluation. This shift was further aided by the inability to secure wage moderation because of the failure to secure corporatist pacts with the unions. Moreover, fiscal laxity (stemming from pressures to increase welfare expenditure and misjudgements about the economic cycle) left tight monetary policy as the only viable option. In short, the cognitive and normative beliefs held by domestic leaders were revised, in significant part as a result of the regime represented by the single European market and EMU.

Working in the same area, Pagoulatos argues that Europeanization has promoted the shift of Greece towards being a 'stabilization state'. The shift has been based on subjecting the economy to the EU's increasingly powerful external constraints (balance of payments loans; capital liberalization; the European Monetary System; and EMU) which has enabled the government to overcome domestic opposition from sectional interests and to follow a more pragmatic policy programme. In the process, the EU has become a Ulyssean mast for government leaders and a basis for their empowerment.

Perhaps it is not surprising that the section on national identity comprises three articles examining two candidate states. Ugur sees the links between the EU and Turkey as a non-credible '*vincolo esterno*', and in this respect an incomplete contract between the two sides. He examines the reluctance of Turkish elites to comply with European norms, particularly as regards democratization, but also in the field of economic liberalization and modernization. He further shows how both the EU and Turkey have used foreign policy problems (particularly the Cyprus problem and the Greek reaction to closer EU–Turkish relations) to mask Turkey's desire for a continued exceptionalism, a pick-and-mix approach in order to reconcile diverging internal views. The relationship between Europeanization and modernization in Turkey is developed in the study by Sofos. The challenge to the long-dominant Kemalist ideology from Europeanization is explored. Here, it becomes clear that the meaning of 'modernization' is closely contested, and a new form of social contract is needed. Closing the volume, Cini discusses the Europeanization of Malta both as an adaptation to European norms and rules and in terms of its impact on national identity. She looks at the impact of 'Europe' on Maltese politics; the differences between the Europeanization/modernization strategies of the political parties; and the resulting tensions between this process and the constructions of Maltese identity. This is an intriguing insight into the relationship between identity and Europeanization in a micro-state.

Taken together, we believe these articles present an innovative and rewarding attempt to examine the current contours of the EU's impact along its southern periphery and the domestic response to it. The individual articles exemplify the asymmetry, fragmentation and dynamism of the Europeanization process and in doing so they underline the importance of the distinct institutional settings to the nature of this process. The EU is set to undergo major changes in this first decade of the twenty-first century – 'deepening' alongside 'widening' – and these developments are likely to intensify the pressures on the southern states. Obligations will be greater and choices starker. The focus of this volume should become of increasing importance, both for the understanding of the domestic politics of each state and for the stability and cohesion of the EU process.

## REFERENCES


Andersen, S.S., and K.A. Eliassen (eds.) (1993): *Making Policy in Europe: The Europeification of National Policy-Making*, London: Sage.

Bennett, C. (1991): 'Review Article: What Is Policy Convergence and What Causes It?', *British Journal of Political Science* 21, pp.215–33.

Bhaskar, R. (1979): *The Possibility of Naturalism*, Brighton: Harvester.

Bulmer, S., and M. Burch (1998): 'Organizing for Europe: Whitehall, the British State and European Union', *Public Administration* 76 (Winter), pp.601–28.

Caporaso, J., M. Green Cowles, and T. Risse (forthcoming): 'Introduction', in the same authors' *Europeanization and Domestic Change*.

Checkel, J. (1997): 'International norms and domestic politics: bridging the rationalist-constructivist divide', *European Journal of International Relations* 3, pp.473–95.

—— (1998): 'The Constructivist Turn in International Relations Theory', *World Politics* 50/2, pp.324–48.

—— (1999): 'Social construction and integration', *Journal of European Public Policy* 6/4, pp.545–60.

Diamandouros, N. (1994): 'Cultural Dualism and Political Change in Post-Authoritarian Greece', *Estudios-Working Papers* 50, Madrid: Centro de Estudios Avanzados en Ciencias Sociales.

Dyson, K., and K. Featherstone (1996): 'Italy and EMU as a "Vincolo Esterno": Empowering the Technocrats, Transforming the State', *South European Society and Politics* 1/2, pp.272–99.

—— (1999): *The Road to Maastricht: Negotiating Economic and Monetary Union*, Oxford: Oxford University Press.

Featherstone, K. (1998): '"Europeanization" and the Centre Periphery: The Case of Greece in the 1990s', *South European Society and Politics* 3/1, pp.23–39.

Featherstone, K., G. Kazamias and D. Papadimitriou (2000): 'Greece and the Negotiation of Economic and Monetary Union: Preferences, Strategies, and Institutions', *Journal of Modern Greek Studies* 18/2, pp.381–402.

—— (2001): 'The Limits of External Empowerment: Greece, EMU and Pension Reform', *Political Studies*.

Garrett, G. (1996): 'Capital Mobility, Trade and the Domestic Politics of Economic Policy', in R. Keohane and H.V. Milner (eds.), *Internationalization and Domestic Politics*, Cambridge: Cambridge University Press, pp. 79–107.

Garrett, G., and G. Tsebelis (1996): 'An Institutional Critique of Intergovernmentalism', *International Organization* 50, pp.269–300.

Giddens, A. (1984): *The Constitution of Society*, Cambridge: Polity Press.

Gill, S. (1995): 'Globalization, Market Civilisation, and Disciplinary Neoliberalism', *Millennium: Journal of International Studies* 24/3.

Grande, E. (1995): 'Das Paradox der Schwaeche, Forschungspolitik und die Einflusslogik europaischer Politikverflechtung' [The paradox of weakness: Research Policy and the logic of influence of interlinked European politics], in M. Jachtenfuchs and B. Kohler-Koch (eds.), *Europaische Integration* [European Integration], Opladen: Leske and Budrich.

Haas, E.B. (1958): *The Uniting of Europe: Political, Social and Economic Forces 1950–57*, Stanford, CA: Stanford University Press.

Haas, P. (1992): 'Introduction: Epistemic Communities and International Policy Co-ordination', *International Organization* 46/1, pp.1–35.

Hall, P., and R. Taylor (1996): 'Political science and the three new institutionalisms', *Political Studies* 44, pp.936–57.

Hanf, K., and B. Soetendorp (1998): *Adapting to European Integration: Small States and the European Union*, Harlow: Addison Wesley Longman.

Hay, C., and D. Wincott (1998): 'Structure, Agency and Historical Institutionalism', *Political Studies* 46/5, pp.951–7.

Hirst, P., and G. Thompson (1996): *Globalization in Question: The International Economy and the Possibilities of Governance*, Cambridge: Polity.

Kerr, H. (1973): 'Changing attitudes through international participation: European parliamentarians and integration', *International Organization* 27, pp.45–83.

Knill, C., and D. Lehmkuhl (1999): 'How Europe Matters: Different Mechanisms of Europeanization', *European Integration Online Papers* 3/7.

Kohler-Koch, B., and R. Eising (eds.) (1999): *The Transformation of Governance in the European Union*, London: Routledge.

Ladrech, R. (1994): 'Europeanization of Domestic Politics and Institutions: The Case of France', *Journal of Common Market Studies* 32, pp.69–98.

March, J., and J.P. Olsen (1989): *Rediscovering Institutions: The Organizational Basis of Politics*, New York: The Free Press.

—— (1995): *Democratic Governance*, New York: Free Press.

Marks, G. (1993): 'Structural Policy and Multilevel Governance in the EC', in A. Cafruny and G. Rosenthal (eds.), *The State of the European Community II: The Maastricht Debates and Beyond*, Boulder, CO: Lynne Rienner.

McNamera, K. (1998): *The Currency of Ideas: Monetary Politics in the European Union*, Ithaca, NY: Cornell University Press.

Mény, Y. (1996): 'Introduction', in Y. Mény, P. Muller and J-L. Quermonne (eds.), *Adjusting to Europe: The impact of the European Union on National Institutions and Policies*, London: Routledge.

Mjoset, L. (1997): 'The Historical Meanings of Europeanization', *Arena Working Paper* 24, Oslo: University of Oslo.

Moravcsik, A. (1994): 'Why the European Community Strengthens the State: Domestic Politics and International Cooperation', *Center for European Studies Working Paper* 52, Cambridge, MA: Harvard University.

Olsen, J.P. (1996): 'Europeanization and nation-state dynamics', in S. Gustavsson, and L. Lewin (eds.), *The Future of the Nation-State*, Stockholm: Nerenius and Santérus Publishers.

Putnam, R. (1988): 'Diplomacy and Domestic Politics: The Logic of Two-Level Games', *International Organization* 42, pp.427–60.

Rometsch, R., and W. Wessels (eds.) (1996): *The European Union and Member States: Towards Institutional Fusion?* Manchester: Manchester University Press.

Rosenau, J.N. (1969): 'Towards the Study of National-International Linkages', in J.N. Rosenau (ed.), *Linkage Politics*, New York: The Free Press.

Sabatier, P. (1998): 'The Advocacy Coalition Framework: Revisions and Relevance for Europe', *Journal of European Public Policy* 5/1, pp.98–130.

Sabatier, P., and H. Jenkins-Smith (eds.) (1993): *Policy Change and Learning: An Advocacy Coalition Approach*, Boulder, CO: Westview Press.

Sartori, G. (1970): 'Concept misinformation in comparative politics', *American Political Science Review* 64/4, pp.1033–53.

Scharpf, F. (1988): 'The Joint-Decision Trap: Lessons from German Federalism and European Integration', *Public Administration* 66/3, pp.239–78.

—— (1997): *Games Real Actors Play*, Boulder, CO: Westview Press.

Schmidt, V.A. (1997): 'Discourse and (Dis)integration in Europe: The Cases of France, Germany and Great Britain', *Daedalus* 126/3, pp.167–99.

Schoen, D., and M. Rein (1994): *Frame Reflection*, New York: Basic Books.

Siegel, R.L., and L.B. Weinberg (1977): *Comparing Public Policies: United States, Soviet Union and Europe*, Homewood, IL: Dorsey Press.

Soysal, Y. (1994): *Limits of Citizenship: Migrants and Postnational Membership in Europe*, Chicago: University of Chicago Press.

Stone Sweet, A., and W. Sandholtz (eds.) (1998): *European Integration and Supranational Governance*, Oxford: Oxford University Press.

Tsebelis, G. (1990): *Nested Games: Rational Choice in Comparative Politics*, Berkeley: University of California Press.

—— (1994): 'The Power of the European Parliament as a Conditional Agenda-setter', *American Political Science Review* 88, pp.128–42.

—— (1995): 'Conditional Agenda Setting and Decision Making Inside the European Parliament', *Journal of Legislative Studies* 1, pp. 65–93.

Tsoukalas, C. (1999): 'European Modernity and Greek National Identity', *Journal of Southern Europe and the Balkans* 1/1 (May), pp.7–14.

Verdun, A. (1999): 'The Delors Committee: an Epistemic Community?', *Journal of European Public Policy* 6/2, pp.308–28.

# Europeanization and Domestic Structural Transformation

# European Policy-Making and the Machinery of Italian Government

DAVID HINE

## INTRODUCTION: THE ITALIAN DECISION-MAKING CULTURE AND EUROPEAN POLICY-MAKING

Each EU member state relates to the European Union in ways that reflect its own political and administrative culture.[1] Italy's relationship has from the outset been characterized by a strong commitment to European integration, linked to a corresponding willingness, at least nominally, to cede sovereignty across a broad front. However, while there is a high level of domestic consensus on the integration process, the *quality* of Italian participation in European policy-making has been widely criticized (Massai 1982; Chiti 1991; Franchini 1993). The domestic political management of the policy agenda and the weaknesses of the administrative system both appear to militate against timely and effective definition of Italian interests. At the other end of the policy process, Italy has had notorious difficulties of implementation. This has been evident both in the transposition of European directives into national law and in the wider approximation of policy to the requirements of harmonization programmes. Italy is a frequent defendant in the ECJ, and it has had numerous high-profile clashes with the Commission over state aids (Hine 1993: 286–90). The explanation of this combination of a strong commitment to integration, and a poor record of delivery, lies in well-known aspects of the political system: the long-standing difficulties of domestic political management in a fragmented, coalition-based, multi-party system, and the poor cross-departmental coordination that characterizes the public administration, and that itself stems from deep-rooted features of Italian public law.

Summarized in the simplest way, the culture of Italian public law could be said to consist of 'government by legally defined institutional competence'. Institutions are allocated explicit, circumscribed and precisely defined powers *through legislation*. Policy is supposed to emerge from formally defined pathways. Individual departments of government are highly compartmentalized and relations between them are governed by strict procedures. The idea of a unified, organically cohesive government in which interdepartmental boundaries are porous and flexible is alien to the Italian culture.

This outlook has been highly visible in the development of institutions dealing with European policy. There has been a self-conscious focus on the definition of procedure. The roles and relationships between the various actors are set down in law and in government decrees. The procedures they must follow, even at relatively early stages in the policy cycle, are fairly rigid. Moreover, because implementing legislation (the transposition of European directives into domestic law) is concrete and legally definable, while the formative phase of European policy-making is fluid and largely beyond the control of Italian law, the focus of debate has tended to fall on end-stage implementation (the so-called *fase discendente* or implementation phase) rather than first-stage policy formation (the *fase ascendente* or ascendant phase). The implementation phase fitted much better with the formalism of Italian decision-making culture. The European policy circuits at the formative stage are fluid and complex, Franco–German leadership for long traditionally held the upper hand, and package deals emerging from the decisional black box of heads of government summits became the norm. Parliamentary and party contributions to the formative phase have thus been modest, and because of the lack of a cohesive executive capable of defining and managing objectives, there has been, even in this phase, a tendency to try to formalize administrative procedures rather than exercise real political control over them.

A second culturally determined feature of the Italian approach to European policy-making has been a high level of agreement on Italian objectives, and a reluctance to see the European Community as working against Italy's fundamental interests. Italians have a predisposition to think of policy handed down from Europe as enlightened and benevolent, rather than as dangerous interference in national autonomy. Hence the task of the elected government is less to defend Italian interests *against* Europe than to ensure that the various parts of the state machinery understand what they are required to do *by* Europe (and are properly prepared, in particular as regards structural funds, to extract *from* Europe). Where Europe becomes politically controversial for the Italian government is therefore not so much in making choices which influence the eventual policy decided on by European institutions, but in ensuring that policy is implemented, and that Italy is in the best position to draw benefit from Europe's distributive policies.

These features of the Italian approach have come under great challenge over the last 15 years. Italian policy-makers have become seriously concerned about the country's capacity to respond both to developments in the EU agenda and to broader patterns of economic change that have integrated European markets. A more self-assertive stance has been called for as Italy's status in the European system has changed, as its net financial position in the EC budgetary system has deteriorated, as its interests have come under challenge in various ways by new member states, and as its domestic markets have become more exposed to European competition by integration and harmonization. There has also been a gradual realization that failures of domestic policy are a more serious handicap the more integrated Europe becomes. Poor education, poor transport and communications infrastructure, a complex regulatory environment for business planning and investment, inflexible labour markets, and uncertain standards of probity in public life provide testimony to the difficulties Italy has of harmonizing its practices with European standards. Equally, for a country that, despite prosperity, continues to qualify for a significant, albeit diminishing, share of structural payments, Italy has had far greater problems in managing the flow of funds than most. Administrative mechanisms for identifying and planning projects qualifying for assistance, and bringing them forward to deadlines, have been inadequate. And there have been serious problems of fraud in the management of CAP payments.

These pressures were greatly enhanced by the intensification of the European policy impact on member states that came from the internal market programme in the 1980s, and monetary union and the addition of two new pillars of EU action in the 1990s. The volume, scope and impact of European legislation has increased, and has made the political class much more aware of the costs of poor Italian preparation and input as policy is being made. Similarly, the difficulties of coping with the flow of legislation to be implemented in the descendant phase if the earlier phase has not taken Italian interests sufficiently into account have also been thrown into sharper relief.

## DEFAULT MODE: COORDINATION BY MINISTRY OF FOREIGN AFFAIRS

The mechanisms for making and implementing Italy's EU policies, and coordinating both processes, include:

- the Ministry of Foreign Affairs (MAE)
- the Italian permanent representation in Brussels (ITALRAP)
- the Presidency of the Council of Ministers (PCM)
- the special department for coordinating EC/EU policies (*Dipartimento per il co-ordinamento delle politiche europee* (DPCE)), located in the PCM
- individual ministerial departments in cases where there is one department which is more involved than all others, and where its specialist expertise is at a premium
- *ad hoc* working groups and commissions to deal with special problems, including other agencies of government such as the Bank of Italy or representatives of regional and local government
- the two chambers of the Italian Parliament.

Within the complex interactions that exist across this range of agencies, two relationships stand out as the key ones. The first is that between the MAE and the rest of the government machine, including the PCM. The second, within the PCM itself, is that between the DPCE and the remainder of the Prime Minister's office.

Locating the structures of power that these relationships imply in a comparative European framework is not easy. In so far as EU member states choose one of two routes to EU coordination (Chiti 1991: 235), these tend to consist of either:

- a decentralized system, in which the relevant department (i.e. that most closely involved, or perhaps first involved, in the issue in question) takes the lead in negotiations with other departments, and acts as temporary coordinator-in-chief, periodically benefiting, but only in a fairly light-touch manner, from the intervention and support of a central agency, normally the MAE; *or*
- a central agency, generally linked to the Prime Minister's office, which has final arbitrating authority over individual sectoral departments.

Initially, Italy opted for the first of these. In the early decades of membership, the default mode of EU policy-making was light-touch coordination through the MAE. There were successive versions of a grand interministerial committee grouping the ministers of Foreign Affairs, Industry, Agriculture and Finance, and subsequently the Treasury and Labour ministers, together with others on an *ad hoc* basis. At the administrative level, its work was prepared by a parallel committee of directors-general from the various ministries involved. Indeed, the inter-ministerial committee gradually faded out, meeting only to resolve difficulties not capable of being resolved at the administrative level. As a result, in practice, as individual departments developed some expertise in EC affairs, each came in its own field to play the lead role (Ronzitti 1987, 1990).

The one department that sought to maintain oversight over the whole range of policy was the Ministry of Foreign Affairs, in time taking over the generalized coordinating role played by the interministerial committee. This was a natural state of affairs in the sense that European policy – certainly in the first two decades of the EC's existence – was still seen as a matter of external relations. Foreign ministry staff were understandably anxious to stay in the policy-making loop when any issue of external relations was being decided, believing that they normally had a better perspective of the broader consequences of any particular outcome than other actors within government. As in most other member states, the permanent representation (ITALRAP) was established, organized, led and largely staffed by the MAE: it was the official channel of communication between EU institutions and the Italian state. Its role was similar to that of all other national representative delegations: not merely official channel of communication, but participant in COREPER, monitoring agency, early-warning device, information gatherer, bridge-builder to other delegation, and coordinator and clearing house for Italian representative missions across the policy spectrum (Papisca 1985; Pocur *et al.* 1988).

As one of Italy's more self-confident departmental corps, with a clear sense of collective purpose and mission, MAE staff also had the psychological foundations necessary for such a role. Over time, it developed into the repository of accumulated experience and understanding of EU politics, including Commission and Council procedures, and national government attitudes and values. Even today, when direct links between individual sectoral departments and established policy communities in Brussels are the norm, the MAE retains a role as the main coordinator of communication channels in all subsectors. It is also a key player in its own sectors. These include foreign and defence policy – and of course EU institutional reform and EU enlargement. The Ministry has worked hard over the years at developing its European capabilities and, of the major European states, Italy is probably the one whose foreign policy is most dominated by European issues. Europe occupies a good part of the time of the Minister, of his *cabinet* and of the general secretariat that heads the Ministry. One junior minister is also dedicated full-time to European affairs.[2]

Despite the MAE's efforts to play the central coordinating role, its position was never likely to survive unchallenged in the face of the more complex needs posed by faster and deeper European integration from the late 1980s onwards. A study by the Department for the Public Service (Presidenza del Consiglio dei Ministri 1994: 72) concluded that in most EC sectors, the national interest was in practice being defined at the policy formulation stage by individual ministerial departments, and that this resulted in a sectoral, if not overtly interest group-driven, perspective. It also concluded that Italian involvement in the formulation stage was largely reactive. Italy, it claimed, rarely influenced the internal workings of the Commission until well on in the negotiating process.

The weaknesses being identified were not aimed exclusively at the role of the MAE, but rather at the failure to adapt by the wider governmental and parliamentary framework. But they underlined clearly the dangers of relying for national coordination on the grossly overstretched resources of a single ministry. As elsewhere, the pressures on resources when major initiatives are in progress left no spare capacity (IGCs, preparation for the period when Italy held the Presidency, monetary union, enlargement, etc.). Unless the MAE were to be transformed from a normal foreign ministry into a super-ministry with vastly enhanced resources and given a special political status within the Council of Ministers, including real authority over other departments, there was never much prospect that it could impose real policy leadership in the ascendant phase, let alone real administrative authority in the implementation phase. The intensity of Italy's relationships within the EC had by the 1980s far outstripped that of bilateral relationships between Italy and non-EC countries. They had implications that descended deep into domestic politics. They required complex legislative and administrative follow-up. And they were beginning to have far-reaching consequences for domestic economic management.

If the MAE could not provide the political authority or resources to impose a coherent strategy, the obvious direction in which to look was the Prime Minister's office, and this led, from the mid-1980s, to efforts to move from the first to the second of the models identified above: the development of a strong coordinating capacity in the Prime Minister's office. Similar developments had already taken place in two other large member states, the UK and France, where the European secretariat of the Cabinet Office and the SGCI respectively had acquired precisely this role (Guyomarch, Machin and Ritchie 1998: 53–60; Seldon 1990: 103–21). In both cases existing institutions, already well-established and recognized by other actors as authoritatively cited at the heart of the governmental machine, had been adapted to play a key role in European coordination. The problem in the Italian case, however, was that there was no similarly prestigious and authoritative pre-existing agency to which to turn. Resources for intelligence gathering, programme monitoring, early warning and dispute resolution were poorly developed, making the Prime Minister's office a much less suitable location for effective intervention, and making the building up of such a capacity a long and tortuous one, with considerable potential for confusion of goals and motives.

## THE PRESIDENCY OF THE COUNCIL OF MINISTERS AND THE DEPARTMENT FOR EUROPEAN POLICY COORDINATION

The main vehicle by which the Prime Minister's office came to play a role in EC policy was through the establishment of a minister without portfolio attached to the Prime Minister's office, with special responsibilities for coordinating EC policies. This minister, although 'without portfolio' (i.e. lacking a formal ministerial department), has since 1983 headed the Department for European Policy Coordination (DPCE) *inside* the Prime Minister's office, and gradually has acquired resources and roles by the powers delegated by prime ministerial decree at the start of each new government.

The emergence of the DPCE has to be understood in relation to the Prime Minister's more general status and powers, the constitutional and administrative weaknesses of the office, and attempts to introduce improvements. The most general level at which reform has been attempted has been the constitutional framework and the party system. There have been no fewer than three major bicameral parliamentary commissions of inquiry into the Constitution since 1983. However, none has come up with recommendations that have generated enough broad cross-party support to make progress. Even the pressure that followed the corruption scandals in the early 1990s failed to achieve this. There was a reform of the electoral system, though to date it has had perverse consequences in terms of the number of parties getting into Parliament.[3]

In contrast, it has been easier to introduce remedial intervention at the level of the Prime Minister's office and his formal powers *vis-à-vis* other departments of government, where only ordinary law rather than constitutional amendment is needed. The main achievement in this respect is the 1988 reform of the Prime Minister's office (Law No.400/1988). The measure aimed to give the prime minister new formal coordinating powers and improve staffing levels. In some respects it simply formalized what had been developing pragmatically and informally over several years, and many critics were doubtful that it would add much to what had already been done earlier in the decade in the absence of wider constitutional reform (Fusaro 1989: 374–86). This is not the place to make a definitive judgement, though the fact that the law has been followed up with extensive prime ministerial decrees fleshing out particular aspects in detail, and that prime ministers do appear to make use of the powers it creates, suggests that it has not been without impact. It has also put the issue of the staffing of the Prime Minister's office on a more rational footing. The office, although substantial in terms of total staff, was traditionally large only through the accumulation of an odd assortment of administrative roles which had landed in the office over the decades. Its core staff was not well-suited to the exercise of an effective coordinating role in critical areas like budgetary policy or EC policy. Staff could be seconded from other departments without cost, but this was done in an unsystematic way, and frequently on an explicitly partisan basis. The lack of institutional memory created by improvisation and high prime ministerial turnover was widely recognized as a serious weakness, and the 1988 legislation did at least something to address this.

Ironically, however, it did not do so in the case of the DPCE. The 1988 reform legislation built on trial-and-error experimentation during the 1980s. An early recommendation was that the prime minister's support staff units should be divided between *offices* that supplied particular support services for the prime minister (legislative support, economic advice, a press office etc.) and *departments* that would be established in those policy areas (regional issues, EU coordination, social affairs) where the main activity was inter-sectoral and cross-departmental coordination. In practice, the office/department distinction proved not to be at all clear cut, nor were the implications fully thought through. Some 'departments' might well have been defined as 'offices'. More importantly, some 'departments' were to be headed by ministers without portfolio. They were to be headed by elected politicians rather than the prime minister's chosen aides. They thus operated at some distance from direct prime ministerial command and, like other ministers in the complex and brittle structure of Italian government, could only be removed by a dissatisfied prime minister by putting at risk the stability of the wider coalition. In this sense their relationship to the prime minister was very different from that of an appointed policy adviser or administrative staff aide, especially as many were not from the prime minister's own party. The flaw in the minister without portfolio formula, in short, was that the departments headed by them, albeit formally located in the Prime Minister's office, were not necessarily flexible and immediate instruments at the direct service of the prime minister. In fact, several departments developed formal structures, and politically became more like quasi-ministries. The personal and close collaborative link between the prime minister and his departmental head was undermined, and the departments themselves started to acquire formal administrative tasks enshrined in law.

The obscure issue of Italian public law concerning the exact status under which each department of the Prime Minister's office received its charter and had its role defined thus became a real issue having a bearing on the philosophy of prime ministerial coordination powers. Defining the role by presidential decree (requiring the approval of the Council of Ministers and consultation with Parliament) implied a set of enduring public interest roles not set up to suit the personal preferences and purposes of the prime minister of the day. Defining it by prime ministerial decree (issued on the personal authority of the current prime minister, but alterable by simple decree of his successor) implied a very different role: one in which the department in question served the prime minister of the day very closely, and depended for its effectiveness on his personal political authority.

This problem was especially acute in the case of the minister heading the DPCE. The post was established in 1980, and the DPCE itself in 1981. The first formal definition of the role was set down in prime ministerial decrees dated 25 July 1980 and 9 January 1981, and in a prime ministerial circular of 12 September 1981. The minister's tasks included helping the prime minister to prepare Italian positions on upcoming draft Commission legislation, as well as tasks in the field of assessment of the domestic impact of EU policies and in the implementation of EC law into domestic law. Significantly, however, after early skirmishes with the MAE, the external and policy-formulating roles associated with the ascendant phase of EC policy (data-gathering, linking

EC institutions with the Italian regional authorities, representing Italy in EC decision-making arenas) were largely shorn from the DPCE's brief. After only a year of existence, a new definition of the role was produced (DPCM 140, 24 May 1982), leaving functions mainly concerned with the implementation phase of policy. In this early skirmish on who controlled the ascendant phase of Italy's EC policy, therefore, the narrowing of the DPCE's role represented a clear victory for the MAE in its efforts to maintain control of this aspect of the coordination role (Franchini 1997: 571–2).

This, and the prime minister's unwillingness or inability to appoint political heavyweights to the DPCE, weakened it as an effective tool of coordination in EC matters. Subsequent developments, though complex, confirmed this tendency. The regular appointments of ministers without portfolio to head the DPCE, most of whom had no special personal or party link with the prime minister, generated a clear separation of the DPCE from the core functions of political leadership exercised through the prime minister. Lacking any special political support to enhance its role at the policy formulation stage, the Department came to concentrate increasingly on implementation rather than formulation.

There were in any case strong objective pressures pushing the Department in this direction. They came from growing worries at the difficulties Italy was encountering in transposing Community directives into domestic law, especially in relation to the 1992 internal market programme. The backlog of unimplemented legislation, and the list of cases being brought by the Commission against Italy, put the country at the bottom of the league table for implementation. Equally seriously, with the emergence of a new Community approach to structural funds, the administrative problems Italy was encountering in making use of these funds were also growing at an alarming rate.

Legislation passed in 1987, the so-called Fabbri Law, employed new mechanisms to speed up the use of structural funds and clear the backlog of EC directives. These included a new rotating fund to be administered by the Treasury to receive and disburse EU transfer payments, and a new form of administrative delegation enabling individual departments to issue decrees giving force to Community directives. The 1987 legislation also contained other strategies to improve coordination. It assigned to CIPE, the inter-ministerial committee for economic planning, the tasks of setting out guidelines for Italy's overall EC policy, speeding up the spending of EC funds, and monitoring the implementation of EC directives. The DPCE was also given other new roles. These included regular reporting to Parliament and subnational government on EC matters and coordination of the presentation to Parliament of bills implementing Community directives, particularly in the area of the internal market. The Minister was also to head, and his Department supply the secretariat for, a grand consultative committee of senior civil servants drawn from all government departments to monitor the implementation process.

In short, the Fabbri Law represented a clear enunciation of the philosophy of the 'department as independent quasi-ministry', rather than the 'department as personal tool of the incumbent prime minister'. By focusing the department's work on the formal roles associated with the execution of statutory legislative and financial exercises, rather than the definition of Italian interests in the formulation phase, there was however a high degree of probability that the DPCE would remain a rather limited and politically isolated tool of policy coordination. It is true that the Fabbri Law gave the European minister roles that in principle could help overcome this: chairmanship of the grand consultative committee and participation in the Italian delegation to all internal-market councils. In practice, however, the grand consultative committee proved too unwieldy ever to meet and was abolished in 1992, and the DPCE, lacking real resources of its own to stay on top of the details of a wide range of sectoral briefs, found that its presence in Italian internal-market delegations made rather little difference to the quality of Italian preparation for such exercises.

The Fabbri Law proved inadequate in various other ways. The legal complications of giving each government department administrative discretion in implementing EC law proved greater than had been foreseen, and the inertia of the departments proved far stronger than the drafters of the legislation had allowed for. The measure had also been intended to define the Department's sources of personnel, budget and operating procedures. Hitherto, having no establishment and no budget, it had operated on resources lent to it by the Prime Minister's office, and on staff seconded from elsewhere in the administrative system. Here too, however, the outcome was a disappointment. Differences of view over whether to allow the DPCE to develop further in the direction of a quasi-ministry, or to bring it back within the ambit of the PCM, led to a further three-year delay before the ministerial decree fleshing out staffing and budgetary issues was published.

Thus, the worst of both worlds prevailed. The Department was allocated more and more specific tasks endowing it with a distinct identity, structure and set of administrative and legislative tasks, resulting in a status, among all the departments headed by ministers without portfolio, most clearly resembling an independent government department. Yet at the same time little was done to give the DPCE permanent staff, administrative authority and other resources to control the ministries nominally under its coordinating powers. The Department continued to be staffed by the time-honoured principle of secondment from other parts of the public sector, and finding top-quality staff in this way, for a department with little prestige and an uncertain future, was difficult from the outset. Staff morale and self-confidence remained low. The DPCE was never closely linked in with ITALRAP, the majority of whose staff continued to be seconded from the MAE, and continued to lack heavyweight political leadership (Franchini 1997: 574–6).

## THE *LEGGE COMUNITARIA*

Although the outcome of the iterative process of defining the DPCE's role in the 1980s satisfied very few of the participants, the last phase of that process, leading in 1989 to a revision of the Fabbri Law, was in some respects a significant success. The new framework legislation for the Department, the so-called La Pergola Law, set up a procedure for dealing with the implementation of EC law that became known as the *legge comunitaria*. It established a special timetabled parliamentary session – mirroring procedures introduced in the field of budgetary legislation. There was henceforth a fixed timetable for the annual passage of all Community legislation requiring transposition into national law. The government was to submit a package proposal to Parliament between 31 January and 1 March every year, containing timetabled deadlines for legislative implementation, and granting the government the authority to complete the process through legislative decree, or other forms of administrative or regulatory implementation (Mencarelli 1999: 277–331). This delegated authority covered not just new measures, but the power to remove from the statute book legislation incompatible with the supremacy of Community law.

Without doubt, the new approach was successful in clearing the backlog, at least in a formal sense. However, although, thanks to the seven *leggi comunitari* passed during the 1990s, the backlog has been cleared quite successfully (879 EU directives were transposed into domestic law in this period (Mencarelli 1999: 285)), there have recently been suggestions that Parliament is being persuaded to legislate in a more timely manner because the legislation itself is delegated legislation simply passing discretionary authority back to the sponsoring department, without actually solving the real implementation issue. Moreover, the implementation of several hundred items of EC legislation into national law in the space of only a few years has generated formidable legal and constitutional difficulties that government law officers have faced with what appears to be mounting alarm.

## THE DPCE'S STATUS IN THE 1990S: AN UNRESOLVED DILEMMA

In any case, in the years since the *legge comunitaria* became a routine part of Italy's European machinery, the authorities have had further opportunities to reflect on the sort of capability best suited for the core executive, and the past decade has seen a complex interweaving of efforts to adjust and improve the EC coordination machinery with wider efforts to enhance the prime minister's status and power.

The fundamental uncertainty has continued to lie in the fact that, for all its success in meeting the legislative crisis, the quasi-ministry formula does not encourage a proactive role for the DPCE in the formulation phase before EC policy is defined. It was this uncertainty which explained the delay in laying down the delegated legislation concerning the structure and staffing of the DPCE, as required by the 1987 Fabbri Law. The legislation, as we have seen, took a further three years to materialize, and when it was introduced it came in an ambiguous way, revealing the uncertainties in the minds of the authorities about precisely what sort of institution they wanted to create. The original model set out in the Fabbri Law envisaged something not far short of an autonomous ministry, with defined functions, to be established by a presidential decree, involving approval by the full Council of Ministers and consultation with Parliament. What was introduced in 1990 (DPCM, 30 April 1990) in contrast was issued under the authority of Law No.400/1988, dealing with the Prime Minister's office.[4] The difference might seem insignificant to the uninitiated, but it revealed a good deal about the concerns of the main protagonists. Establishment by the legislative decree route implied something permanent and autonomous. Establishment by simple prime ministerial decree left the door open to later modifications should these prove expedient.

The reason why the authorities wanted the door left open was that many remained unconvinced by the semi-detached status implied by the quasi-ministry model, yet no-one had any better proposal to press, outside the context of a more general strengthening of the Prime Minister's office. In 1990, it was anticipated that following the 1992 general election a strong prime minister – probably Bettino Craxi – would come to office ready to exploit the potential of the 1988 reform of the Prime Minister's office. Instead, the 1992 election ushered in four years of highly provisional and uncertain government, mainly headed (Berlusconi's brief débacle apart) by 'technocrat' prime ministers (Amato, Ciampi and Dini) before a government with a definable parliamentary majority re-emerged in 1996. The ambiguity of the formula for the DPCE remained. Each new prime minister issued a decree delegating approximately the same range of powers to a minister without portfolio in charge of the DPCE. None of the individuals appointed (Costa, Palladin or Comino) was closely associated with his respective prime minister (only Comino was even a party colleague), and none was a high-profile personality. In effect, with each new government, prime ministers delegated authority to an individual who was expected to exercise the sort of cross-departmental coordinating role performed by a ministry like the Treasury or Interior, yet with none of the contacts, traditions, status and authority of those ministries. Such a role would require the minister to carry authority with his senior ministerial colleagues in a way that was quite unthinkable given the DPCE's low ranking in the ministerial hierarchy. The minister was therefore detached from the prime minister, and performed certain functions enshrined in law, yet was deprived of full portfolio status, and publicly down-graded by the need, at the start of each new government, for the prime minister to issue a decree defining his powers.

Had the rate of prime ministerial turnover been lower, and had incumbent prime ministers and their advisors had more time, the status of the DPCE and its minister might have received more studied attention. But three prime ministers were technocrat caretakers, and the fourth, Berlusconi, had only entered politics four months before taking office. The DPCE was therefore not an immediate priority. Only Ciampi's team, a few weeks before demitting office, started to address the issue by seeking to bring European policy more fully under the prime minister's *personal* control, but in essence the issue was left in abeyance from 1990 to 1996. The *legge comunitaria* was working reasonably well. The Treasury was dealing with the one 'European' issue, the budget deficit, that really counted in the short term. Thus, while most prime ministers and all would-be architects of the Prime Minister's office during the 1990s probably wanted to strengthen the prime minister's role in EU affairs, and while there was considerable doubt about whether the DPCE formula in its quasi-ministry form was the right one, the issue was not sufficiently high on a crowded reform agenda to be tackled until the election of a government with a secure enough parliamentary majority to face the full range of issues surrounding the prime ministerial role.

Such a government seemed to be in prospect when Romano Prodi came to office in 1996, and in anticipation of this wider reform package Prodi abandoned the quasi-ministry model in favour of direct control of the DPCE by the Prime Minister's office. No minister without portfolio was appointed, and instead Prodi divided the formal responsibilities previously performed by the minister between Piero Fassino, the under-secretary of state for the coordination of EU policies at the MAE, Giorgio Bosi, under-secretary of state in the Prime Minister's office in charge of relations with Parliament, and the Treasury and Budget Minister, Carlo Azeglio Ciampi. Responsibility for coordinating parliamentary management of the *legge comunitaria* passed into the hands of the under-secretary for relations with Parliament, reflecting the belief that the procedure had become or was becoming a matter of ordinary parliamentary routine. The Treasury, meanwhile, took on responsibility for the structural funds coordination role. The DPCE staff continued to perform the functions of linkage with sectoral ministries in preparation for the *legge comunitaria*, but the external political projection of those functions, especially *vis-à-vis* Parliament, were now in the hands of Bogi, or of the prime minister directly.

Prodi's decision not to nominate a minister without portfolio reflected several overlapping concerns. One was a response to pressure to reduce the size of the government. There had been much criticism over many years that Italian governments were too large and unwieldy to operate cohesively (Fabbrini 1999). Large governments generally reflect multiple partisan pressures for political patronage; to assemble a small government is therefore a sort of political virility symbol. A second, more important consideration was that the absence of a separate head of the DPCE enhanced the prime minister's own European role, which in the period 1996–98 was of crucial importance, covering, as it did, the last two years of the economic and monetary convergence programme, and the conclusion of the Amsterdam IGC. Both issues had such a strong resonance in domestic Italian politics that there was advantage in projecting the image of a cohesive troika of prime minister, foreign minister and treasury minister working in close harmony to deliver first-wave membership of EMU (Hine and Vassallo 1999: 43–8). A third consideration was that sacrificing the post of minister fitted a broader reform project emerging in the Department for the Public Service, where Franco Bassanini was appointed with a wide-ranging brief to press through a major overhaul of both central and regional government. The essence of this programme combined an inherently federalist design with an ambitious programme to reduce the number of ministries in Rome, and strengthen the coordinating role of the Prime Minister's office (Gilbert 1999: 162–80).

The path to institutional reform is rarely a unilinear one in Italy, however. With the collapse of Prodi's government in October 1998 the pendulum swung back once again to a preference for the nomination of a minister in charge of European policy coordination within the Prime Minister's office. Massimo D'Alema, the new prime minister, had to assemble a far more heterogeneous coalition than his predecessor, and could not afford to cut back on the patronage offered to his various coalition allies (Fabbrini 1999: 150–55). His relationship with the centrist Lamberto Dini, Minister of Foreign Affairs, was also less close than Prodi's, and in the aftermath of successful Italian entry into EMU, and with Amsterdam concluded, the nexus of interest between prime minister and foreign minister was bound to weaken. Institutionally, moreover, it was less obvious to D'Alema than to his predecessor that prime ministerial authority was best served by not appointing a politician to head the DPCE. Indeed, Prodi himself had come under considerable criticism from Parliament for a decision which, in the eyes of the special committees of the two chambers dealing with EU affairs, had downgraded the status of their work. By failing to appoint a minister without portfolio, Parliament was in their view deprived of the main vehicle of liaison between executive and legislature, whose focus in Parliament (unlike the ministers of foreign affairs, the treasury and the minister without portfolio for relations with Parliament) was exclusively on these commissions.[5]

D'Alema therefore restored the practice of appointing a minister without portfolio to head the DPCE, choosing Enrico Letta from the People's Party.[6] Significantly, however, he did not give up on the aspiration harboured by Prodi of more thorough-going reform of his office. He appointed Franco Bassanini as his main under-secretary, with a brief to press ahead with further legislative decrees issued under the authority of the primary legislation Bassanini had put on the statute book the previous year during the Prodi government. A key element of this was a renewed attempt to reassert prime ministerial control over European policy by explicitly identifying the role of the prime minister himself in the process. Thus, the initial decree delegating authority to the incoming minister spoke as in the past only of a *generalized* capacity for the minister in the formative stage of European policy-making, constrained by 'existing legislation', allocating general oversight role to the Foreign Ministry[7] (i.e. the decree did not touch the existing powers of the Minister for Foreign Affairs, or seek to redraw the powers of the prime minister in the EU area). However, in July 1999, in pursuit of Bassanini's plans to concentrate power in a smaller number of ministries and in the Prime Minister's office, two important new legislative decrees were issued (dec. leg. 30 luglio 1999, nn. 300 and 303). Their effect, at least formally, is to shift power decisively in the direction of the Prime Minister's office, and away from the MAE.

The main features of the new measures are that, first, the EU roles explicitly allocated to the MAE are henceforth limited to management of the Italian position in relation to second pillar issues (CFSP) and the EU's external relations and to EU treaty revision mechanisms. The MAE is to retain a general coordinating role in relation to the 'coherence of the international and European activities of individual ministries with the broader objectives of [Italian] foreign policy' (art. 12.2). However, this general role is further circumscribed by art. 3 of dec. leg. 303, which now allocates to the prime minister the task of 'promoting and coordinating action to ensure Italy's full participation in the European Union, and the development of the process of European integration'. The DPCE, meanwhile, is assigned not only the role of coordination of implementation, but is to be used by the prime minister 'in accord with the MAE' to coordinate departments of government, regional authorities and private actors in defining Italy's policy in the formative stage of EU policy-making. The words 'in accord with the MAE' remain in the text, without doubt as a reassurance to the MAE, but while the Ministry itself is allocated specific powers only on second pillar and treaty revision issues, the Prime Minister's office (or at least the minister without portfolio for the DPCE) 'coordinates departments ... in the formative stage of policy-making'. Although it is too early to pass judgements on the impact of the new arrangements, and the distinctions have to be read carefully, there is no doubt that the intention, in the context of the two decrees passed in 1999, is to shift responsibility firmly in the direction of the Prime Minister's office and the prime minister personally.

## CONCLUSION

At least on paper, therefore, Italy has now adapted its central government machinery to place the primary responsibility for policy coordination, arbitration and strategic guidance in European policy with the prime minister, or at least the Prime Minister's office, rather than with the Ministry of Foreign Affairs. This now applies at both the formulation and the implementation stages. It has taken an extraordinarily long time, but this is probably less significant than that there also remains a major concern that what has been achieved could still be not much more than legislative aspiration, and that as long as cohesion and purpose in public policy goals continue to be pursued through formalistic mechanisms, rather than through the development of shared attitudes towards the role of programmatic political leadership, the adaptation will not be effective.

The reason why the process has proved so tortured is that it has been difficult for the actors to develop a clear, long-term view of the problems to be resolved, and because the powerful need at any stage along the road to make the system work (which requires a minimum of inter-institutional collaboration) has tended to overwhelm the incentive to take a long-term view of how the system could be changed. The most immediate and urgent problems for a long time were thought to be those of implementation, which required legislative-drafting and administrative skills, and improved systems of legislative management. Other aspirations, linked to the formulation stage, could be set out in imprecise outline, but ignored in practice in the absence of sufficient administrative resources to make them work. This applied in particular to the great range of tasks nominally allocated to the DPCE after 1990, which for practical purposes were not pursued. And it applied in general to the role of the Prime Minister's office which, after the 1988 reform, was supposed to enjoy not just the general responsibilities for policy leadership and coordination allocated to it by the Constitution, but also specific responsibilities in the European field allocated by art. 5.3.a of Law No.400/1988. These responsibilities were simply allowed to run alongside those already inherent in the roles performed by the MAE, and no specific resources were allocated to help the prime minister to fulfil them, other than those few endowed on the DPCE, which were all concentrated on implementation anyway. To tackle the MAE head-on would have jeopardized the regular working relationship with that ministry which the prime minister and his office needed in a system where the capacities of the core executive were (and remain) comparatively weak.

When the immediate implementation crisis started to resolve itself, it was possible to tackle more systematically the problem of leadership in policy formulation. But this was caught up in the wider political and constitutional uncertainties of the early and mid-1990s, and the high rate of prime ministerial turnover. It was also prejudiced by uncertainty over the fundamental issue of the desirability of the quasi-ministry model. Hence, the contrasting solutions adopted by Prodi and D'Alema. The price paid by the Prime Minister's office for these uncertainties has been high. A strong European profile is important for countries with a middle-ranking status like Italy, and the ability to exercise strong leadership over national policy towards the EU has become an important domestic asset for all European prime ministers. In this policy sector, as in many others, the reliance of the Italian government machinery on law and procedure rather than on real resources and political cohesion has remained a powerful constraint on effective institutional reform.

## NOTES

1. This article is part of a wider study of policy coordination by the core executive in Italy, undertaken in the context of the ESRC's 'Whitehall Programme' project on core executive coordination in Western Europe, directed by Prof. J.E.S. Hayward and the late Dr V. Wright. The author is grateful to the ESRC for financial support for research for this article. The article does not represent a complete account. The changing role of the Italian Parliament in European policy-making, and therefore the implications for democratic accountability, are not analyzed in detail. Nor is it possible, in the space available, to test the new structures and procedures empirically against the outcomes of particular policy case studies, though the wider study covers policy-making in relation to air transport, EU-budget policy and the Italian management of policy towards IGCs.
2. The largest and most important internal directorate in the Ministry is that dealing with European affairs. Under a reorganization implemented in July 1999, this directorate is divided into six divisions:
   - Internal EU economic affairs including the internal market, monetary and budgetary policy, structural policy, and a range of sectoral economic policies
   - EU external relations
   - Aid and EU development activities
   - The Common Foreign and Security Policy
   - Justice and Home Affairs
   - Legal and Institutional Affairs.

   (The author is grateful to Ministro Nelli Feroce (MAE) for direct provision of this information.)
3. It would be wrong to suppose that the last decade has left the prime minister's political

status unaltered. It is clear that voters do want stronger executive leadership, and this has strengthened prime ministers against their parliamentary majorities. The overwhelming economic imperative of meeting the convergence criteria for monetary union also helped. But in the absence of fundamental constitutional reform, Italy continues to labour under a fragmented and complex multi-party coalition. Intracoalition coups, and changes of parliamentary majority such as that which ended the tenure of Romano Prodi in mid-legislature in 1998 and led to the installation of Massimo D'Alema, continue to weaken the office (Fabbrini 1999: 139–60).

4. This legality of the use of the 1988 legislation, as opposed to the 1987 Fabbri Law, was in fact questioned by public lawyers (Franchini 1997: 575–6).
5. The tensions between the Fourteenth Commission of the Chamber of Deputies (dealing with EU policies) and the Prodi government were palpable during 1996 and 1997, and were only resolved in 1998 with the appointment of Piero Fassino as the single member of the government charged with liaison with the Commission. See especially the papers relating to the government's regular six-monthly reporting sessions to the Commission, *Atti parlamentari* (XIII legislatura – sedute del 20 aprile e del 21 aprile 1998) pp.342–3.
6. Letta, not a member of Parliament nor a member of D'Alema's party, was nevertheless a rising star on the Catholic left, strongly in tune with the centralising philosophy of Franco Bassanini's reforms begun under Prodi. Letta was promoted in October 1999, in the cabinet reshuffle of that month, to become Minister of Industry, and to be replaced in the October 1999 reshuffle by Patrizia Toia from the same party.
7. Thus Art 1 of the decree began:

   'Within the limits posed by the competencies allocated to the Minister of Foreign Affairs, the Minister (Enrico Letto) is delegated to exercise the functions of policy-definition (*indirizzo*) … legislative initiative, and supervision (*verifica*), and all other functions assigned by existing legislation to the prime minister, in relation to:

   a. activities inherent in implementing Community policies both at a general level, and by sector, ensuring this is done in a timely and coherent manner, and activities inherent in the participation of the Italian state in the making of Community policy …'

   (d.p.c.m. 10 Nov. 1998, author's translation).

## REFERENCES

Bender, B. (1991): 'Governmental Processes: Whitehall, Central Government and 1992', *Public Policy and Administration* 6 (Spring), p.1.

Chiti, Mario P. (1991): 'Il coordinamento delle politiche comunitarie e la riforma degli apparati di governo' ['The coordination of community policy and the reform of the government apparatus'], in *Associazione per gli studi e le ricerche parlamentari. Quaderno n.1 Seminario 1989–90* [Association for parliamentary study and research. Working Paper No.1 Seminar 1989–90], Milan.

—— (ed.) (1997): *Pubblica amministrazione e integrazione europea* [Public Administration and European Integration], Rome: CNR.

'Decreto del presidente del consiglio dei ministri' [Decree of the president of the council of ministers], 10 Nov. 1998, published in *Gazzetta Ufficiale della Repubblica Italiana* [Official Journal of the Italian Republic] No.272, *serie generale*, 20 Nov. 1998.

'Decreto Legislativo 30 luglio 1999' [Legislative Decree 30 July 1999] Nos.300 and 303, 'Ordinamento della Presidenza del Consiglio dei Ministri, a norma dell'art. 11 della l. 15 marzo 1997, n.59' [Structure of the Presidency of the Council of Ministrers, relating to art. 11 of 15 March 1997, No.59], published in *Gazzetta Ufficiale della Repubblica Italiana* [Official Journal of the Italian Republic], 1 Sett. 1999, *supplemento ordinario n. 167*.

Fabbrini, S. (1999): 'Dal governo Prodi al governo D'Alema: continuità o discontinuità?' [From the Prodi government to the D'Alema government: continuity or discontinuity?] in D. Hine and S. Vassallo, *Politica in Italia 1999* [Politics in Italy], Bologna: Il Mulino.

Franchini, C. (1993): *Amministrazione italiana e amministrazione comunitaria* [Italian administration and Community administration], Padova.

—— (1997): 'Il dipartimento per il co-ordinamento delle politiche comunitarie' [The Department for the coordination of Community policies], in M.P. Chiti (ed.), *Pubblica amministrazione e integrazione europea* [Public Administration and European Integration], Rome: CNR.

Fusaro, C. (1989): 'La leggi sulla presidenze del consiglio dei ministri, primi adempimenti a otto mesi dell'entrata in vigore' [The law on the presidency of the council of ministers, first accomplishments in the eight months since its entry into force], *Quaderni costituzionali*, 9/2.

Gilbert, M. (1999): 'Le leggi Bassanini: una tappa intermedia nella riforma del governo locale' [The Bassanini laws: an intermediate stage in local government reform] in D. Hine and S. Vassallo, *Politica in Italia 1999* [Politics in Italy], Bologna: Il Mulino.

Grotanelli de' Santi, G., and F. Francioni (ed.) (1984): *National and Supranational Powers in the Shaping of Community Policies*, Milan: Giuffrè.

Guyomarch, A., H. Machin and E. Ritchie (1998) *France in the European Union*, Basingstoke and London: Macmillan.

Hine, D. (1993): *Governing Italy: the Politics of Bargained Pluralism*, Oxford: Oxford University Press.

Hine, D., and S. Vassallo (1999): *Politica in Italia 1999* [Politics in Italy], Bologna: Il Mulino.

Massai, A. (1982): 'Il co-ordinamento interno delle politiche comunitarie' [The internal coordination of the community policies], *Quaderni costituzionali* 2/2.

Mencarelli, A. (1999): 'Riflessioni sulla legge comunitaria come legge organica in senso materiale' [Reflections on the community law as organic law in material sense], in S. Labriola (ed.), *Il parlamento repubblicano (1948–1998)* [The parliament of the Republic (1948–1998)], Milan: Giuffrè.

Papisca, A. (1985): 'La Présidence du Conseil des ministres des Communautés européennes: Rapport national sur l'Italie' [The Presidence of the Council of Ministers of the European Communities: National Report on Italy], in C. O'Nuallain (ed.), *The Presidency of the European Council of Ministers*, London: Croom Helm.

Pocur, F., *et al.* (1988): 'Italie', in H. Siedentopf and J. Ziller (ed.), *Making European Policies Work: The Implementation of Community Policies in the Member States*, ii (national reports), London: Sage.

Presidenza del Consiglio dei Ministri – Ministero per la Funzione Pubblica (1994): *La riforma della pubblica amministrazione: Vol. IV. La pubblica amministrazione e l'Europa* [The Reform of the public administration: Vol. IV. The public administation and Europe], Rome.

Ronzitti, N. (1987): 'European Policy Formulation in the Italian Administrative System',

*International Spectator*, 22.
—— (1990): 'The Internal Market, Italian Law, and the Public Administration', *International Spectator*, 25.
Seldon, A. (1990): 'The Cabinet Office and Coordination 1979–87', *Public Administration* 68.

# Europeanization and Italy: A Bottom–up Process?

MARCO GIULIANI

## INTRODUCTION

'In many ways, today, Italy is a 'new Italy'' (Prodi 1999: 49). It is difficult to disagree with the former Italian Prime Minister, now president of the European Commission. 'U-turn', 'earthquake', 'revolution', 'metamorphosis' and 'new-season' are among the widely used expressions to portray the radical changes that have taken place in this last decade. Whereas old stereotypes are certainly hard to die, when new ones begin to appear (*Economist* 1999) this probably indicates that some real transformations have already happened.

A brief review indicates the general point (Vesperini 1998):

- the party system now has little to do with its traditional image of immobilist, polarized pluralism;
- old political conventions have been completely upset;
- electoral laws – from the municipal to the national level – have been reformed in a majoritarian direction;
- almost the whole political elite has been replaced;
- there has been a gradual reorganization of the governmental structure, both in vertical and horizontal terms;
- new or revised procedures have altered the relationship between the executive and the parliament in the law-making process;
- decentralization and federalization are now more than empty catchwords;
- the introduction of independent authorities and a clearer distinction between political and administrative responsibilities have modified some of the traditional attributes of the bureaucracy;
- privatization and liberalization have begun to affect the country's so-called economic constitution;

- substantive reforms have been introduced in crucial policy sectors such as welfare; and
- an extraordinary recovery in the public accounts permitted Italy to join the Monetary Union in the first wave of countries.

Europe is widely quoted as one major factor behind all this. As clearly stated by the Italian Commissioner, Mario Monti (1998: 13): 'Italy is changing. The deep influence of European integration is the major agent of change.' On one side, the 'European model' – whatever this means – has inspired the introduced reforms. On the other, the factual and cognitive constraints set by the EU have favoured – if not indirectly compelled – many of these transformations.

The funny thing is that the Europeanization of Italy is normally considered both an element and a cause of the new framework: Italy is more 'European' because of the increasing EU integration and, at the same time, is more integrated because of its renewed European attitude. To be sure, the unclear distinction between what has to be considered exogenous and what is endogenously controlled – or between independent and dependent variables – is not peculiar to Europe. The same applies to several supposed causes: the kickback city scandals have certainly undermined the political elite, but the investigations were so effective because parties were already unstable; the fiscal crisis demanded a sound budgetary policy, but the executive chose to make the fulfilment of EMU requirements its first priority; the electoral law first applied in 1994 seemed to represent the watershed of the new Italy, but many reforms were introduced earlier, whereas the new electoral system has not produced the expected results, for example in terms of the reduction of the number of political parties.

From a methodological standpoint, acknowledging the extent of the variation is not sufficient for identifying the cause. '*Post hoc, propter hoc*'; but too many things happened at the same time, and to disentangle the role of single variables – EU constraints (Dyson and Featherstone 1996), the new internal institutional settlement (Fabbrini 1998), the globalization of the economy (Regini 1999), the mass disaffection (Morlino and Tarchi 1996), etc. – is not an easy exercise.

This article pursues the following line of reasoning. The next section contrasts two different meanings of the concept of Europeanization: the one that can be found in the specialized literature of political science, and the one that prevails in the political debate in Italy. Bearing in mind this double interpretation, the core of the article is devoted to an empirical investigation of the indications of Europeanization that can be found in Italy. This synthetic exploration begins at the polity/institutional level, and then continues at the policy/cognitive one. After this empirical and analytical journey, it is hoped that the reader will be better equipped to understand the crucial relationship between the 'new Europe' that emerged from Maastricht and Amsterdam and the 'new Italy' outlined by Prodi.

## EUROPEANIZATION/NORMALIZATION

Literally, 'Europeanization' indicates the fact that national features give way to a common supranational character: in different domains the fading of the former and the gradual appearance of the latter should be made out. As Schmidt (1997a) puts it: 'All member-states are now enmeshed ... in a European politico-administrative system that turns national political officials into European decision-makers, national administrations into implementers of European decisions, and nationally organized interests into European lobbies.' It is beyond the aim of this article to review the many variations in the use of this concept, but a few general notes will be useful to this argument (see Morisi and Morlino 1999).

In the political science literature, Europeanization is often defined in four ways variously combined: institutions, political dynamics, cultures and policies. These are typically identified as the major targets of the shift in governance which is affecting Europe's political systems (similarly, Knill and Lehmkuhl 1999).

Whereas it is difficult to imagine that the EU influence reaches the fundamental structures of power inside the nation-state – directly modifying its party system, form of government or electoral system – the actual functioning of the European democracies (i.e. the balance between those powers) has certainly been affected (Schmidt 1997b). This does not necessarily imply a high level of institutional homogeneity, since national 'institutional spheres are affected differently and they are likely to attend to, interpret and respond to European developments differently and in non-synchronized ways' (Olsen 1995: 34).

Rometsch and Wessels (1996) take the EU challenge seriously, looking for an improbable institutional 'fusion' of the political structures formally involved in the national–EU relationships, but the empirical evidence shows little convergence at this level. A more promising approach is the one chosen by Caporaso, Cowles and Risse (2000), which, exploring the goodness of fit between EU and domestic structures, referred explicitly to the 'formal and informal norms, rules, regulations, procedures and practices' of each.

Another way of looking at the same phenomenon is to refer to the dynamics which take place in the European-wide, multi-level system of governance (Hooghe 1996). In this perspective, the same dichotomy between the domestic and the supranational loses much of its interest: public and private actors interact 'freely' in non-hierarchical and non-market webs, posing entirely new problems of political steering (Mayntz 1998). The same structure of opportunity modifies their behaviour, extending their capacity of cooperation and conflict, of using their exit and voice options, or of loyally defending some form of boundary.

Thirdly, Europeanization may be approached from a cultural side. Though political cultures do not change overnight, the European Community is now almost 50 years old, so that it is possible to perceive the slow penetration and diffusion of a set of European values and identities. After all, in certain circumstances, the mass publics as well as the elites are less subject to inertial phenomena than are institutions. The issue of the legitimizing arguments – the public discourse (Schmidt 1998) – used by the European governments in order to assure the necessary collective support for the integration project pertains to the same conceptual universe.

Finally, fulfilling the original ambition of its founding fathers and Delors' prophecy, the EU spreads its influence upon national policies. 'In fact, European integration is at its very core an endeavor of transforming or harmonizing member states' policies' (Conzelmann 1998: 1). International jurists are certainly at ease with the direct authority exercised by the EU with its regulations and directives, as well as with the increasing role exercised by the European Court of Justice (Stone Sweet and Brunell 1998). Data regarding transposition effectiveness or infringement procedures are certainly important benchmarks for evaluating the actual degree of Europeanization, but policy analysts often prefer to go beyond the formal framework in order to assess how the context, the content, the processes and the outcomes of the domestic policy-making have changed because of EU membership (Andersen and Eliassen 1993). In other words, policy change may occur even in areas that are (still) not among the EU's direct competencies. The modified environment alters the 'preferences, alliances, strategies [and] the range of ideas available to policy-makers' (Borrás, Font and Gómez 1998: 27), thus producing convergence through a sort of spill-over effect that modifies the relationship between public and private actors (Leonardi 1995; Falkner 2000).

In the next pages the article refers implicitly to all these different meanings of the concept of Europeanization in order to evaluate the Italian case, but before turning to this empirical assessment, note that the common use of this same term in the domestic political debate normally transcends the arguments presented hereto.[1]

In the rhetoric of political disputes, concepts do not have to be presented neatly, but it is clear that in the transition phase which Italy has been experiencing since the early 1990s, Europeanization mostly meant 'normalization'. The 'new Italy' has to be more European, in the sense of losing its eccentric, extraordinary, astonishing and unique features that have certainly fascinated many Italianists but probably not many Italians.

The quest for normality mainly takes two different roads. On one side is found the idealization of foreign experiences, especially regarding the supposed effects of their institutional setting. In this case, a generic reference to the working of the 'major European democracies' is enough to support very different projects – from the reform of the electoral system to the introduction of a (semi-)presidential government, etc. In this perspective, the variety of possible 'models' does not seem to represent a problem: it is the *a quo* term that matters (the pressures for reforming the present institutional system), not the *ad quam* (the potentially imported setting). The EU bears no responsibility for this kind of xenophilia, if not for the fact that it amplifies the contiguity between nations and induces the comparisons.

The second path taken in the political debate by the idea of 'Europeanization as normalization', is the claim for a new role of the country on the international (especially European) scene. As a matter of fact, Italy has long been considered an awkward partner (Sbragia 1992). The governmental instability hindered the credibility of its political elite, both in the domestic and in the international arena, so that the simple fact of 'surviving without governing' (Di Palma 1977) has often been regarded as part of the Italian miracle. Accordingly, Italian executives have always played a minor role in its external relations, with a foreign policy the subordinate character of which appeared in the major critical circumstances as well as in the many micro-decisions.[2]

Though with irregular successes, recovering an international political standing and autonomy consistent with their belonging to the elitist G-7 club became a priority for the governments of the 1990s. The stubborn run after the EMU requirements probably has many origins, but it is one of the most evident exercises (and successes) of Italy's strategy and aspiration in the international arena. In this field, the globalization of governance does not leave many alternatives for large countries like Italy. As Giuliano Amato once said: '[B]ehind the corner there isn't simply the exit from [the core of] Europe, the shelter in an impossible autarchy, but the danger of becoming a Disneyland at its service' (Pesole 1994: 170).[3]

The Europeanization of Italy certainly goes through this wider process of gaining an international credibility: the acquisition of a greater confidence by the major public and private financial organizations (e.g. IMF or Moody's), the pursuit of autonomous strategies in case of international crisis (e.g. Lebanon or Kosovo), the conception of independent alliances in diplomatic relations (e.g. regarding the reform of the UN Security Council), the promotion of Italian experts and politicians to the leadership of crucial international organizations (e.g. Masera at the EIB, Ruggiero at the WTO, I. Visco at the Economic Department of the OECD, Prodi at the EU Commission), etc. It is somehow curious, but revealing, that while the EU experiences at its core some of the most deplorable features of Italian politics – such as the anticipated resignation of its executive (the Commission) because of corruption and financial scandals – the Italian representatives are generally appreciated for their work in that same institution.[4]

As argued in the following pages, as far as Italy is concerned the 'theoretical' and 'political' declinations of the concept of Europeanization seem to share a common destiny. In both cases, changes at the highest and most visible level – a formal restructuring of the executive, renewed institutions and procedures to govern the relationships with the EU, a neat improvement in the implementation of EU directives or decrease in the number of infringement proceedings, the unambiguous adoption of a definite 'model of democracy', the simplification of the party system, etc. – have been rare. At the same time, the more positive record achieved in less palpable spheres – the public consciousness of the potential drawbacks of easy-spending policies, the redefinition of crucial policy networks, the kind of discourse that governs the selection of ideas for policy-making in several sectors, the professional behaviour of members of the 'new' politico-administrative elite – seems to be more appreciated abroad than in the domestic arena. For many observers, the gap between 'hard' and 'soft' reforms demonstrates the poor consolidation of the new Italy portrayed by Prodi, thus suggesting a tame Europeanization of the country (Verzichelli 1999; Fabbrini 1998; Pasquino 1999; Ferrera and Gualmini 1999). I would rather be more optimistic. Informal mechanisms, practices, dynamics and discourses at the meso level – the kind of factors on which new institutionalists have reoriented their attention – may guarantee sufficient stability by transforming policy networks governing crucial decision-making processes. At a macro level, the present formal institutional architecture may reveal itself not so 'unfit' for the future governance of the EU. But I return to this point in the conclusions.

## DOMAINS OF EUROPEANIZATION

One of the recurrent observations regarding Italy's EU membership is that its political system is ill-suited for the EU. Leaving aside those political factors that have contributed to its well-known 'originality', there are many features that clash with the typical Brussels dynamics and its institutional framework. The incomplete decentralization of the responsibilities left the regions in a limbo of duties with poor representation. The absence of ministerial coordination produced incomprehension and political tensions. Complex law-making procedures slowed the adaptation to the *acquis communautaire*, without increasing internal democratic scrutiny. The juridical tradition conflicted with the flexibility of the EU approach, while the inefficient domestic bureaucracy hardly coped with Brussels' technocrats. The secluded 'emergencial' policy style failed to adapt itself to the EU's open problem-solving ambitions, reducing the anticipation capabilities of the Italian representatives.[5] No member state has adjusted itself to the new EU framework without problems (Mény, Muller and Quermonne 1996), but many observers agree that Italy's integration turned out to be particularly problematic.

Bearing in mind the distinctions suggested in the preceding section, I try to revise this general picture in order to assess its eventual modification. As the introductory remarks of the article reminded us, too many 'constant' features of Italy changed in a short time span. Even if this analysis confirms the null hypothesis that no change derives from EU membership, it will not have been a useless exercise. For the sake of simplicity I trace a rough line between politics and policy domains, and then explore in greater detail how both these arenas have been affected by EU membership. In each case, I first advance (in the section title) a *tentative* hypothesis regarding the presumed effect of Europeanization in a specific field, and then discuss (and possibly validate or reject) it empirically.

### *Politics*

A first distinction within the political domain can be drawn between changes affecting the internal distribution of power (here, A1–A4), and variations regarding Italy's external relationships (B1–B3). In the first case, the main interest is in party dynamics, in the confrontation between legislative and executive powers, in the internal control of the public administration and in centre–periphery relationships. In the second, the link between the government in Rome and the work of its representatives in Brussels and Strasbourg is referred to, as are the specialized institutions which work on EU affairs both in the parliament and in the executive.

*Hypothesis A1: Party dynamics have been moderated and reoriented.* If labels do teach us something regarding a political system, the Italian democracy has certainly received its fundamental imprinting from its party system. None of the institutional reforms introduced in this last decade to modify its essential features derives from EU membership, though they have all been normatively legitimized with reference to a hypothetical European standard.[6] In this confrontational environment, Europe has seldom represented a contested issue. Since the communists criticized the EMS, more than 20 years of full bipartisanship has passed. Party platforms register continuously the convergence of every party – from the 'Democratici di Sinistra' to 'Alleanza Nazionale' – the full integration of Italy in Europe.[7]

As Pasquino (1999) underlines, party elites found it convenient to superficially align themselves according to the prevailing euro-enthusiasm of the population. Its positive attitude may well be the plain result of misinformation (Eurispes 1993) or the ultimate hope of sceptical citizens (Martinotti and Stefanizzi 1995), but it has long represented a relevant political resource. The absence of dissenting voices discouraged any real evaluation of the EU, which remained constantly outside the hottest internal political debates (Giuliani 2000). Even in the European elections, candidates usually pay lip service to EU issues, in order to return rapidly to more divisive topics.

Paradoxically, people have shown they are more discerning than parties. In fact, in the last few years there has been a gradual reorientation in the political preferences of citizens towards the Union. Until the 1970s, the most enthusiastic supporters were mainly centre or right-wing citizens; clearly, the communist party's original anti-EC stance influenced its electorate's attitudes. The 1980s and the first half of the 1990s represented the apex of bipartisanship: political orientation had almost no influence upon the public perception of the EU. The last years have witnessed the inversion of the original relationship, and Europe has gradually become a positive value among left and centre-left voters. Conversely, centre-right and right-wing citizens – as elsewhere in Europe – begin to share a critical disposition towards the Community institutions (Biorcio 1998). This may remain the only relevant reorientation in party dynamics around the European issue.

*Hypothesis A2: The executive has strengthened its autonomy vis-à-vis the legislature, and has become more hierarchically organized.* Internal reformers have pursued both transformations at the highest institutional level (e.g. in the special bicameral committee that aimed to revise the Italian Constitution). The Europeanization process has probably given new force to their arguments, since enjoying sufficient degrees of freedom is commonly recognized as a prerequisite for effective action in Brussels. Nonetheless, the attainment of concrete progress along these dimensions is ambiguous, and its direct attribution to European factors is even more questionable.

I return later to the specific instruments used by governments to cope with their EU obligations. Parliamentary procedures do not assign outstanding legislative powers to the Italian executive. Private members' bills largely outnumber the amount of government projects, and though their approval rate is obviously lower, they still represent a consistent share of the aggregate of approved bills (Della Sala 1998). Comparatively speaking, Italian governments traditionally have been unable to guide the ordinary law-making process, and their performance has certainly not improved in the last few years (Döring 1995; Capano and Giuliani 2001).

Government bills systematically have been delayed or amended by parliament, and even the extensive (albeit ineffective) use of temporary decrees could not help in increasing the steering capacity of the executives during the 1990s. It is thus difficult to argue that the institutional autonomy formally held by the executive in its EU bargaining spilled over into the internal law-making arena.

There is a second type of instruments potentially used by the executive. The absence of administrative reserve (i.e. a constitutionally defined domain subject to direct regulations) compels governments to play a difficult legislative game 'against' parliament. However, through the usual channels, they can ask for the delegation of specific powers. In this way, they obtain the formal authority to intervene with a larger autonomy in different sectors. This opportunity – the employment of which was introduced initially thanks to the so-called *leggi comunitarie* –

has been used quite extensively in the last years. Beside the implementation of EU directives, two major fields have been characterized by this procedure. On the one hand, the delegation of legislative jurisdiction has been employed to force the smoother introduction of far-reaching reform projects, from pension policies to decentralization and administrative reforms, from labour to health policies. In each case, these were the structural actions that the European Commission and the IMF repeatedly requested. On the other hand, governments have increasingly introduced simplification and delegation measures in accordance with the EU SLIM project.[8]

Vassallo (2001) has argued convincingly that the executive has gradually learned how to use the larger degrees of freedom assured by the delegation procedure, especially in order to avoid the traps of the ordinary law-making process. Since 1987, the attainment of delegated powers entitled the government to act autonomously on more than 300 issues: almost 60 per cent of them concerned the incorporation of EU directives.

As far as the internal organization of the executive is concerned, the typical collegial style of government has not been deeply modified, and Italian premiers still have the problem of controlling dissenting voices inside their government. Formal and informal attempts to strengthen their relative position have been tried since the early 1980s, but they have not been particularly effective. Since the government led by Amato (1992–93), the leadership of premiers has been only moderately contested by other ministers. Their technical character or their electoral investiture, combined with the crisis of the party system, has tended to consolidate their authority inside the government (Fabbrini 2000). Nonetheless, no Italian chief executive was afforded even half of the prominence enjoyed by the British Prime Minister or German Chancellor. The lack of a pivotal role probably pushed the Italian *Presidente del Consiglio* to look for other instruments in order to strengthen his personal leadership, such as, for example, a more resolute use of the media. Europe had no influence on this, although it helped to reveal with greater emphasis one of the traditional weaknesses of the Italian executive.

*Hypothesis A3: Technical bodies have increased their role inside the public administration*. The Italian public administration is known for its poor performance. The economic and social costs of its ineffectiveness are widely reckoned. Whereas the participation of Italian bureaucrats in EU affairs has not modified their deep-rooted attitudes, there have been a few indirect effects of Europeanization.

First of all, the former minister for the civil service, Bassanini, tried to use the familiar logic of the *vincolo esterno* to force the internal adaptation of the Italian administration to international standards of performance. He proposed to his European colleagues the adoption of a sort of 'administrative Maastricht', with the fulfilment of tangible bureaucratic requisites at precise deadlines. At the same time, he advanced in four steps a comprehensive set of improvements that try to emulate the most successful European experiences in administrative reform (Capano 2000). Both projects will face severe implementation problems for very different reasons – the mostly symbolic nature of the first, and the far-reaching character of the second – but, at the same time, they both clearly reveal the end of the autarchic approach to resolving administrative problems for Italy.

Secondly, the increased familiarity with foreign and EU experience has brought the introduction of yet unknown technical structures inside the Italian public administration. Here, this refers mainly to the extensive introduction of independent authorities, which began in 1990 with the adoption of an anti-trust law modelled explicitly upon the corresponding EU authority inaugurated in the same period. Thereafter, independent technical bodies have been replicated in several sectors: telecommunications, energy, privacy, bank control, etc (Morisi 1997).

Finally, and more informally, Prodi and D'Alema have somehow institutionalized the habit of establishing specific expert committees and *fora* in crucial reform sectors such as welfare, macro-economic adjustment, labour policy, poverty, etc. These committees – which have only consultative powers but in reality do influence government policy activity – are composed mainly of university professors and think-tank experts traditionally open to European and international experiences. Their increasing contribution in the selection of 'ideas' capable of becoming 'solutions' represent a further channel of indirect Europeanization of the public machinery.

*Hypothesis A4: Regions are gaining an autonomous role in EU affairs.* Regions have law-making jurisdiction and autonomy on specific topics: environment, health, etc. It should have been sufficient to allow them the possibility of representing their own needs and preferences at the European level, but the Italian Constitution retains every activity related to foreign representation for central institutions, namely the government. This severe obstacle has long hindered their capacity to act directly at the Brussels level, thus reducing even their local performance on issues tackled by EU policies (such as structural funds). Given the new European structure of opportunities, regions and municipalities have tried recently to bypass some of the rigidities which have hampered their achievements in the recent past (Morisi 1999), but their networking potential still cannot be compared to that of many foreign counterparts.

The transformation of the regional system into a federal state entered the political agenda already in the early 1990s with the electoral successes of the *Lega Nord*, but it acquired relevance in the governmental agenda only with the Prodi government. In the last five years, more than 200 norms and regulations that decentralized functions and competencies to local levels of government have been introduced: almost half of them affected regional powers, including the introduction of a larger (albeit still marginal) fiscal autonomy (Vesperini 1998). This policy somehow conforms to the idea of 'Europe of the regions' – though regional governments have seen their external powers only marginally modified – but its inspiration has to be sought in internal events such as the success of autonomist parties and growing discontent with the central government.

*Hypothesis B1: There has been a reorganization of ministerial competencies around European issues.* Two processes could indicate a formal restructuring of competencies because of the Europeanization process: on the one hand, the powerful institutionalization of an *ad hoc* minister for EU affairs and, on the other, a complete reorganization of competencies modelled upon the works of the European Council(s) of Ministers. None of the two have been realized, however.

First of all, the number of senior and junior ministers, as well as the assignment of their portfolios, still depends on a complex balance between the parties (and factions) which support the government. Only the entirely technical executive led by Dini drastically reduced the number of senior and junior positions available (to 19 and 31 respectively), whereas D'Alema – leading a seven-party government – appointed the highest number of ministers (almost 100, divided between senior and junior positions). In this context, a comprehensive revision of competencies is out of the question.[9]

Secondly, regarding the *ad hoc* ministry for EU policies, its authority is still in flux. On the one hand, it has always been exposed to competition from the powerful economic department of the ministry for foreign affairs. On the other, its status and autonomy changed from time to time, and Prodi even abolished it before being compelled to assign its competencies to a junior minister of the Foreign Office (Giuliani 2000). The formal reintroduction of a senior position in the current executive has not yet produced radical changes, with the new Minister often confined to the 'second rank' of the government. In a parliamentary debate, an MP of the committee for EU policies polemically addressed the executive wishing that 'the new Minister will hopefully be able to co-ordinate the other members of the government ..., because they often give precedence to matters which are different from the problems of EU norms and regulations'.[10]

*Hypothesis B2: There has been a reorganization of parliamentary competencies around European issues.* The Union is mainly an arena for executives. The relative weight of the European Parliament is growing, but generally speaking that of national parliaments is not. The more Brussels acquires an active role, the less MPs are able to verify the accountability of their national representatives involved in EU policy-making. Each parliament has established institutions and procedures to bridge the national democratic deficit implied by multi-level governance: Italy is certainly not an exception in this respect.

Whereas the Senate has long established its own *ad hoc* committee for European Affairs (*Giunta per gli affari europei*), the lower House only introduced a special committee for EU policies in 1990, and transformed it into a permanent committee in 1996. The change is not merely symbolic. Until the XII legislature, the committee had mainly to coordinate the parliamentary examination of the *legge comunitaria* (the 'annual' Community law for the cumulative transposition of EU directives). Currently it has a sort of super-ordinate status (almost like the one enjoyed by the budgetary and constitutional committee), since it has to review all the bills under discussion in order to ascertain their 'EU congruity'.

Both committees (and chambers) are saturated by the formal competencies connected to the descending phase of EU policy-making, and lament their impossibility of influencing the ascending one (Camera Deputati 1999c). Every six months, through an official report, the government had to inform parliament of its record and projects in EU affairs. Though it has mostly been a symbolic and useless account, at the beginning of 1999 the government was successful in approving an article in the Community law for 1998 that placed that report in an annual cycle. Several MPs protested that the government 'wanted to reduce the controlling powers of the Parliament' (Camera Deputati 1999b), but that did not change the outcome of the vote. The often-requested special parliamentary session devoted to EU policies may increase the formal efficiency of the descending phase, but it is doubtful if it can improve the accountability of the executive in these matters.

*Hypothesis B3: Politico-administrative elites have changed their European attitude.* Italian elites have never been against Europe or the integration process. They may have cultivated 'third ways' in foreign policy, but without conceiving them as real alternatives to the 'European adventure' (Padoa Schioppa 1998). Nonetheless, with the usual notable exceptions, politicians and top civil servants have never been particularly fond of Europe. The European Parliament has often been conceived of as the golden retirement exile for decadent politicians, or the first political training for inexperienced outsiders. Italy has always deplored its second-rank role in the European Commission, without recognizing that it lacked competent top civil servants wishing to permanently invest their professional lives in the Brussels Babel. Members of the government seemed to prefer the heated atmosphere of internal partisan quarrels to the pragmatic style of EU councils.

In the past, the highest position in the EU Commission was not worth a second-rank Minister in the national government (e.g. Colombo), national elections were a sufficient stimulus even for a Commissioner (e.g. Ruffolo), and a rarefied presence in Strasbourg was the unavoidable side effect of double mandates. There are tiny signals that something is changing. First of all, the simple awareness of the EU's persistent role in internal matters has grown considerably. A few years ago, laypeople, entrepreneurs, civil servants and even MPs failed to recognize the EU's systematic influence in the domestic arena (Radaelli 1988; Censis 1989). Secondly, the two Commissioners chosen by the government led by Berlusconi in 1994 convinced insiders and policy-makers of their competencies. Thirdly, strategic posts in crucial policy sectors are now covered by Italian officers, and there is a growing rotation of top jobs among the internal private and public sectors, research centres and EU appointments. Finally, albeit still cautiously, politicians are beginning to chose Brussels instead of Rome: in 1998 Bonino preferred to retain her role in the European Commission than to enter the executive led by D'Alema (though she proposed herself as a candidate put forward not by political parties, but by a committee of citizens for the Presidency of the Italian Republic), and then led a party list in the 1999 European elections, whereas Prodi – not without hesitations – chose not to guide the new Democratic Party in order to take the leadership of the EU Commission.

### *Policy*

This section reviews synthetically the major changes that have affected the internal policy-making dynamics. An in-depth survey is beyond the aims of this article, since it examines different sectors and/or different types of policy (Borrás, Font and Gómez 1998; Falkner 2000). The investigation turns on two main topics. First, it analyzes the procedures adopted in order to cope with EU obligations. Simple quantitative comparisons allow assessment of the actual working of these procedures (C1). Secondly, attention is paid to some qualitative features of the main policy reforms discussed and adopted in the last few years: content, involved actors, underpinning ideas, etc (C2).

*Hypothesis C1: There has been a gradual convergence towards the normative performance of the main EU partners*. Italy is known for its delayed and reactive EU policy-making. Compared to that of the major European member states – those who should represent the benchmark for policy influence and activism – Italy has long been passive in the ascending phase and reluctant in the descending one (Giuliani 1996). In order to cope with a normative burden which increased from year to year, and respond to the intensifying scrutiny of the European Commission and the sharpening 'attention' of the Court of Justice, Italy chose to introduce a radical innovation in its internal procedures for the ratification of EU directives: the so-called *legge comunitaria* (Annual Community law), noted above.

Now, a decade since its first introduction, its success can be evaluated in reducing the normative gap. With the *legge comunitaria*, the government commits itself to submit a bill every year to transpose cumulatively all unsatisfied obligations stemming from EU legislation. Unfortunately, some technical shortcomings of the instrument itself, combined with the endemic instability of the political system, hampered the conceived automaticity and produced a few perverse political effects.[11] Instead of looking at the overall total of European directives dealt with by the Annual law – which is by no means representative of the number of EU norms introduced in the Italian body of laws – its outcome is considered directly, comparing the data published by the European Commission.

The most general indicator is the quota of directives actually transposed. Since 1992 – the earlier record was even worse – Italy has always remained among the last three member states for incorporation of EU norms, and the situation did not change after the EU's enlargement. Figure 1 shows the Italian rate of transposition of European directives from 1992 to 1998, compared to the EU average and to the best performing country.

Further data show that the other member states often 'choose' not to respect the deadlines of EU directives. They may strategically delay their incorporation in order to favour (or not displease) national interests, or to take advantage of their free rider status. A comparative analysis of the data for those countries indicates a great variation in the rate of transposition, both diachronically and through different sectors. Italy's incapacity is more evenly distributed, the figures indicating a possible lack of strategy.

To be fair it should be said that, as Figure 1 shows, starting in the mid-1990s, there has been a gradual improvement in the Italian record: the rate of transposition has increased since 1994 (albeit slowly), and the gap between Italy and the best performers has been partially reduced.[12]

FIGURE 1
RATE OF TRANSPOSITION OF EU DIRECTIVES

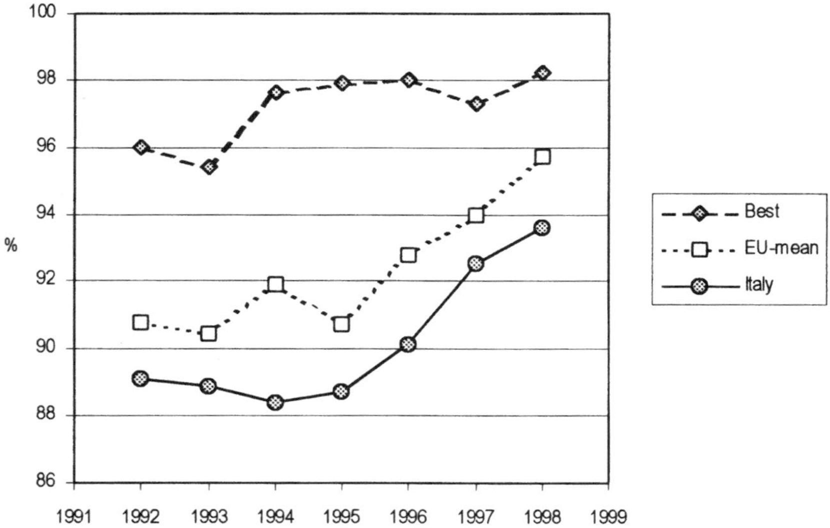

*Source*: Own elaboration on EU Commission data, 'Relazione annuale sul controllo del diritto comunitario' (several years)

However, the percentage of incorporated directives does not tell the whole story. A second possible indicator – which partially takes into account even the implementation stage – is the amount of infringement proceedings opened against Italy, at each stage, in the last seven years. Comparison of these figures with the average record of the other 14 member states (see Figure 2) still shows a systematic lack of observance of EU norms (treaties, regulations and directives), and a delay, compared to those of the other EU partners, both of which tend to grow from stage to stage. Even the number of ECJ rulings against the member states – including those with an economic sanction – is against Italy.[13]

Finally, we turn to a subgroup of EU norms which has always been considered strategic for the integration of Europe, namely the Internal Market measures. At the beginning of the 1990s, the Italian Annual Community law attained its best performance precisely in this field. DG XV constantly monitors the progress shown by member states through its 'Single Market Scoreboard'. Thus, an updated evaluation of Italy's efforts can be made.

Data displayed in Figure 3 represent the percentages of non-compliance to Internal Market directives in three different periods: November 1997, November 1998 and November 1999. While the tag portrays the final situation at the end of the last year, the lines show the

FIGURE 1
RATE OF TRANSPOSITION OF EU DIRECTIVES

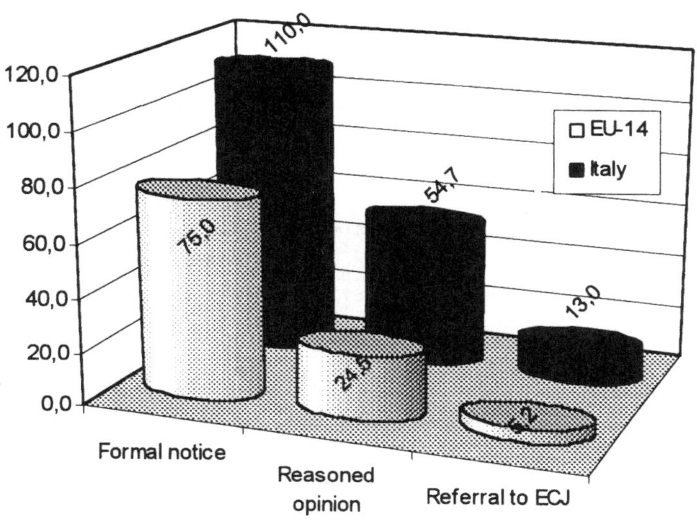

progress (or small regress in some cases) made in the relevant interval by each member state.

Although in 1998 Italy still had the poorest record among the 15 member states, the situation changed slightly during 1999: for the first time Italy was not in the group of the five worst countries as regards incorporation of Internal Market directives. A further positive indicator is observable in the consistent improvement of its transposition ratio (represented by the length of the line in the diagram). Though there are still problems in a few areas (such as social policy and telecommunications), the overall judgement on the Italian performance is not as bad as in the past. The actual progress is confirmed by the satisfaction exhibited by the national business community and monitored by the same DG XV in its *Single Market Scoreboard* (EU Commission 1999a: 18). The Italian score is still not comparable in absolute terms to

FIGURE 3
PERCENTAGE OF NON-INCORPORATED INTERNAL MARKET DIRECTIVES (1997–99

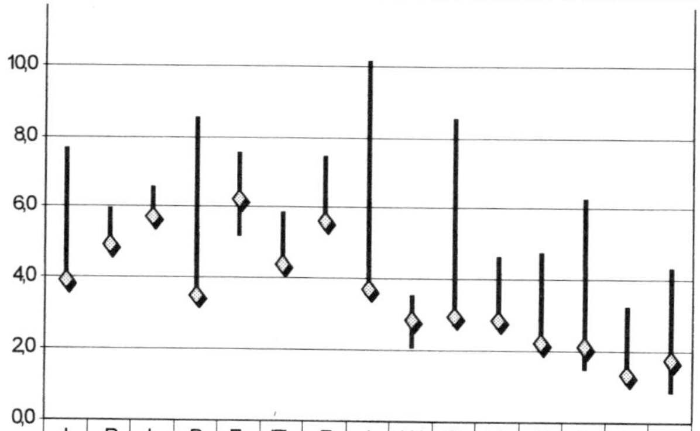

| | I | P | L | B | EL | IRL | F | A | UK | D | NL | E | S | DK | FIN |
|---|---|---|---|---|---|---|---|---|---|---|---|---|---|---|---|
| Nov. 1997 | 7,6 | 5,9 | 6,5 | 8,5 | 7,5 | 5,4 | 7,4 | 10,1 | 3,5 | 8,5 | 4,6 | 4,7 | 6,2 | 3,2 | 4,3 |
| Nov. 1998 | 5,7 | 5,6 | 6,2 | 5,2 | 5,2 | 5,8 | 5,5 | 4,2 | 2,1 | 2,7 | 3,8 | 2,7 | 1,5 | 1,5 | 0,9 |
| ◇ Nov. 1999 | 3,9 | 4,9 | 5,7 | 3,5 | 6,2 | 4,4 | 5,6 | 3,7 | 2,8 | 2,9 | 2,8 | 2,2 | 2,1 | 1,3 | 1,7 |

*Source*: DG XV, 'Single Market Scoreboard', Nov. 1999.

that of Denmark or Finland, and even its progress is not so impressive as that of Austria, Germany or Belgium, but, for the first time, there is a consistent group of countries which exhibit an even slower adaptation to the integration of markets.

*Hypothesis C2: The content, actors and discourse of the 'new' policy-*

*making displays a European influence*. If the quantitative test portrays some timid progression away from the inertial legacies of the past, it is a long way from suggesting a concrete Europeanization of policy-making processes. Actually, on a closer qualitative inspection, things look different, at least in part. It certainly cannot be maintained that the data hereto presented are meaningless, and that there will not be any real integration of Italy in EU policy-making without more incisive progress at that level; however, the overall picture may appear rosier from a different perspective.

The most significant turn produced directly by EU membership has obviously been joining in the first wave of states entering the euro-zone (Sbragia 2000; Dyson and Featherstone 1999; Vassallo 2000). A sequence of hard choices (Sbragia 1999), deemed impossible for a country like Italy, has characterized macro-economic policy since the Amato government. The unexpected outcome, together with its durability and sustainability, would not have been possible 'simply' through a mix of cuts and increased taxation. It required a complex restructuring of strategic policy areas that is still continuing. For this reason, European influence spilled over different policy sectors such as pension, health, labour and industry, cohesion and, generally speaking, every high-spending policy sector (Ferrera and Gualmini 1999; Verzichelli 1999; Pierson 1999; Di Palma, Fabbrini and Freddi 2000). EMU served as the catalyst for a sequence of planned and accomplished reforms that range from welfare to administrative reorganization, from budgetary procedures to decentralization. The Europeanization of policy-making has been both the source and the target of these efforts.

Though the path-dependency of these kinds of processes constrains the magnitude and degree of success of the attainable reforms, there are visible signs of discontinuity with the policy strategies normally followed in the near past. Pension policies – once more a focus of political debate – have been reformed three times in the 1990s: the current contribution formula, retirement age and standardization of public and private sectors draw the Italian pension system nearer to that of other EU nations. The introduction and strengthening of selectivity measures (much in the vein of north European welfare models) has amended the health policy and inaugurated new assistance programmes and tax benefits (Ferrera 1999). Privatization and liberalization have been central for the economic strategies of the centre-left governments, while territorial pacts, flexibility and tax incentives (well-known European catchwords) deeply characterize their labour policies. Even the use of structural funds, the second major shame area of Italy's EU membership, seems to have registered substantive improvements (EU Commission 1999b; Graziano 1999; Dipartimento Politiche Comunitarie 2000). Now, the increased political credibility of the country even permits a more active role of the governmental elite at the European level.[14]

To summarize, all the major policy areas have been subjected directly or indirectly to European influence. Their content, the range of alternatives taken into account, the way solutions are publicly defended echo policy processes occurring in other countries and in the EU itself. Issues like the Dutch model of welfare reform, the Irish strategy of debt reduction, the Scandinavian dual taxation schemes or the logic of the EU subsidiarity principle – once confined to academic debates – now pragmatically influence the choices of policy-makers. Policy emulation is not less difficult and delicate than autarchic decision-making, but it is the systematic attention to comparative benchmarks which represents the major innovation in the policy arena.

I believe that these transformations which have EU constraints as catalysts, but which have been pushed through the window of opportunity offered by the overall crisis of the Italian political system, find their explanation at a micro rather than macro level. Reforms have been discussed, suggested and implemented by a 'new' constellation of actors that tends to resemble more an epistemic community than a partisan coalition. External experts, academic consultants, leading internal technocrats and think-tank specialists have been increasingly 'internalized' in those policy processes (Radaelli 1999). I cannot elaborate further on this point here, but the composition of these networks is certainly more cosmopolitan and open to European influences than policy-makers have usually been in the past. They have taken the opportunity of a reduction in the veto powers of political parties to act as brokers of ideas and discourses that are in good currency beyond the Italian borders. Task forces have flourished around the executive, often with the implicit goal of evaluating the feasibility of policy emulation. Certainly, Brussels does not have all the answers for every policy problem, but it probably represents a useful crossroads in this regard.

The qualitative influence of Europeanization has taken this indirect cognitive path, rather than the main route of structural and juridical adjustment. External constraints and a 'new' market for policy ideas created the conditions for political learning (Pierson 1999) which is not issue-specific. In the peculiar political climate of the early 1990s, there were not the internal conditions to oppose such a process, and a wide variety of actors supported it, though for very different reasons (Della Sala 1999). Its institutionalization passes through a change in the way policy-makers, private entrepreneurs and public opinion perceive policy and political problems, but eventually it may even alter long-established political dynamics.

## CONCLUSION

The adjustment to European pressures and policy models has been hitherto realized without any substantial reform of the institutional framework. Indeed, the situation is quite the contrary. There have been feedbacks from the policy arena to the political one, pragmatically affecting the functioning of Italian democracy. The performance and credibility of the Italian political system will remain under the close scrutiny of the financial organizations and the EU partners. For some observers, the exceptional period has already come to an end and there will not be any 'new Italy' without constitutional corrections. From my viewpoint, bottom–up cognitive processes may steadily alter the actual functioning of national institutions without modifying their architecture (at least if policy actors do not decide to enter into a stubborn prisoner's dilemma game). In any event, the general surprise of the achievements of the last few years, epitomized by the unexpected entry into Monetary Union, overcame two of the most widely used stereotypes regarding Italy: its innate eccentric character, and the famous adage from 'Il Gattopardo' about the unchanging changes.

I have tried to argue that the Italian political system has adjusted itself to Europe more in its practices than in its structures. Europeanization – both in the sense of normalization and openness towards EU influence – has been the outcome of changes that have happened at the level of actors, rather than at that of institutions.[15] A consensual but ideologically divided parliament still struggles against a collegial executive that leads an under-professionalized bureaucracy in a context of contested regionalism. However, substantial reforms that permitted entry into the euro-zone have been adopted; regions are beginning to spend their structural funds more efficiently; the politico-administrative elite is reorienting its professional preferences; policy ideas circulate at a faster pace both from and to Europe; policy networks have been extended to cosmopolitan actors and groups; and even the formal respect for EU norms begins to show some progress.

The Europeanization process came up against the sovereignty of member states, compelling them to modify several of their political attributes. At the same time, Europeanization modified the Union itself. Its deepening and widening – the new competencies and the new members – have rendered the EU more complex and political than ever before. The risk of it being monopolized by a single country (e.g. the germanization of the Union) or by an historic axis (e.g. Paris–Berlin) has never been so distant. The EU is (and will become increasingly) a power-sharing polity. The minimization of external decision-making costs (those potentially deriving to outsiders in case of closed and secluded processes) will continue to be a central concern in EU policy-making: during the past, the main reason was the defence of national sovereignties; in the future, it may well be the deliberate political strategy chosen by cooperative elites that recognize the dangers of a confrontational style.

If this is true, consensual attitudes will represent valuable political resources, and cooperative dispositions will become an unavoidable ingredient of future EU politics. Behind the appearances, Italy has a long tradition of both. Consensualism institutionalized itself under a polarized surface, and has not experienced relevant retreat during the recent majoritarian mood: the propensity for mediation and compromise, the inclination for rhetoric and heresthetics, the predilection for creative solutions and arcane bargaining are still at the core of everyday policy and politics. These elements, which are not necessarily associated with ineffectiveness, immobilism or corruption, might turn out to be pivotal and appealing features in the future EU. In that case, Italy will be ready.

## NOTES

*A first version of this article was presented at the Conference of the European Community Studies Association, Pittsburgh, 2–5 June 1999. The financial support of the Nuffield Foundation, Murst and CNR is gratefully acknowledged.*

1. The lack of a tradition of Italian political science studies on these topics (Giuliani and Radaelli 1999) is probably among the causes of the discrepancy between the theoretical and the political debates.
2. There are certainly notable exceptions to this general statement (e.g. the first enforcement of the majority rule in the European Council of Milan that opened the way to the SEA), but they do not contradict the overall picture of a political system unable to act according to its international economic rank. For an historical overview, see Varsori (1998).
3. Much in the same vein, though with different arguments, Panebianco (1991) suggested the absence of any alternative scenario to belonging fully to the European world, and Cotta (1998) stressed the compelled commitment to this project using (and stretching)

Hirschman's category of 'loyalty'.

4. I am referring specifically to the work done in the former European Commission by Mario Monti and Emma Bonino, but also to the team of experts guided by Padoa Schioppa at the ECB responsible for the transition to the euro.
5. For a closer investigation of these dynamics, see e.g. Giuliani (1996). In a comparative perspective, Schmidt (1997b) extends the analysis to political cultures and to the process of interest intermediation, though her macro approach extends by far the validity of some stereotypes.
6. After all, since the beginning of the Fifth Republic in France, Italy remained the unique western representative of centrifugal democracies in Lijphart's original typology (1968).
7. The electoral platform of 'Rifondazione comunista' in 1996 deplored the absence of a labour/social dimension in the EU projects, and not the monetary union *per se*.
8. There have been three 'delegations' for simplification in the X legislature (1987–92), eight in the XI (1992–94), eight in the XII (1994--6) and already 35 in the first two years of the XIII legislature (1996–98).; See Camera dei Deputati (1998), and different chapters in Vesperini (1998). For the first time since 1948, in 1999 the number of delegated norms exceeded that of ordinary laws (Camera dei Deputati 1999a).
9. Actually, there have been several projects in that direction. Recently, Bassanini proposed a reorganization of the executive based on nine ministers only, but the only ministerial fusion already accomplished involved that of the treasury and budgetary departments.
10. Camera Deputati (1999b); a further sign of 'low-profile' is given by the constant turnover of EU ministers: though apparently animated by reform ambitions at the beginning of their mandate, they often strive for a different position at the first reshuffle.
11. For these technicalities see Giuliani (2000). In any event, it must be underlined that neither the parliamentary procedures (i.e. the navette system) nor harsh political conflicts have delayed the progress of the governmental bill (which normally consists of far-reaching delegation powers seldom employed by the government itself). The degree of bipartisanship is quite surprising: only the 1992 *legge comunitaria* has been approved with less than 90 per cent of votes in favour; more recently the 1994 law had only 13 votes against and the 1995–97 only one (!), whereas the 1998 law received nine votes against (out of a possible total of 630 MPs, with 315 the minimum quorum).
12. The progress has been confirmed even in 1999: actually, in the last year Italy obtained the highest improvement in the rate of transposition among the 15 member states (Dipartimento politiche comunitarie 2000)
13. Of the proceedings for infringements started in 1993, 12.5 per cent were against Italy; the percentage rose to 41.9 per cent for infringements started in 1994, and to 42.9 per cent for those started in 1995. Later infringements have still not reached the ECJ stage. See also Mendrinou (1996) with data for the 1978–93 period.
14. The Italian Commissioner Monti criticized some normally untouchable EU partners; the former Treasury Minister Ciampi proposed new structural reforms for fighting the economic stagnation at the Ecofin council; the Italian representation managed to obtain most of the expected benefits from the bargaining around the Agenda 2000 project; the adoption of the Italian concerted style through 'social pacts' has been suggested even at the EU level, etc.
15. For a similar account of how the EU affected the decentralization process in France, see Ladrech (1994).

## REFERENCES

Andersen, S., and K. Eliassen (1993): *Making Policy in Europe. The Europeification of National Policy-making*, London: Sage.

Biorcio, R. (1998): 'Gli italiani e l'Europa' [Italians and Europe], in Abacus, *Italia al Macroscopio* [Italy under the macroscope], Milan: Feltrinelli, pp.15–39.

Borrás, S., N. Font and N. Gómez (1998): 'The Europeanization of National Policies in Comparison: Spain as a Case study', *South European Society & Politics* 3/2, pp.23-44.

Camera dei Deputati (1998), 'Rapporto sull'attività legislativa nel 1998' [Report on the legislative activity in 1998], Rome: http://www.camera.it/ primapagina/ primapagina/ files/raffronti.doc.

—— (1999a), 'Rapporto sull'attività 1999' [Report on the legislative activity in 1999], Rome: http://www.camera.it/primapagina/primapagina/files/rapporto99.pdf.

—— (1999b), 'Dichiarazioni di voto finale sul disegno di legge della Legge comunitaria 1998; Seduta n. 472 del 27.1.1999 C 5459' [Final voting declaration on the EC bill for the year 1998], Rome.

—— (1999c), 'Relazione della XIV Commissione permanente sul disegno di legge della Legge Comunitaria 1999 – N. 5619-A.' [Report of the XIV Permanent Committee on the EC bill for the year 1999 – N. 5619-A.], Rome.

Capano, G. (2000): 'Le politiche di riforma amministrativa nella transizione italiana: dall'improbabile riforma alla riforma permanente' [Administrative policies in the Italian transition: from an improbable reform to a permanent one], in G. Di Palma, S. Fabbrini and G. Freddi (eds.), forthcoming pp.153–98.

Caporaso, J., M. Cowles and T. Risse (2000): *Europeanization and Domestic Change*, Ithaca NY: Cornell UP, forthcoming.

Censis (1989): Data in *Note e Commenti*, 25/ 9–10.

Conzelmann, T. (1998): 'Europeanization of Regional Development Policies? Linking the Multi-level Governance Approach with Theories of Policy Learning and Policy Change', *EIoP Paper* 4.

Cotta, M. (1998): 'Le élite politiche nazionali di fronte all'integrazione' ['National political élites and the EU integration'], *Il Mulino* 3, pp.445–56.

Della Sala, V. (1998): 'The Italian Parliament: Chambers in a Crumbling House?', in P. Norton (ed.), *Parliaments and Governments in Western Europe*, London: Frank Cass, pp.73–96.

—— (1999): 'Monetary Integration and the Italian Social State', paper presented to the meeting of the EMU and European Model of Society Group, Brussels, 25–24 June 1999.

Di Palma, G. (1977): *Surviving without Governing. The Italian Parties in Parliament*, Berkeley, CA: UCLA Press.

Dipartimento politiche comunitarie (2000): *L'Italia in Europa 1999–2000* [Italy in Europe 1999–2000], Rome: Presidenza del Consiglio dei Ministri, http://www.politichecomunitarie.it/facciamo/relazione2000/Indice1.htm.

Döring, H. (ed.) (1995): *Parliaments and Majority Rule in Western Europe*, New York: St Martin's Press.

Dyson, K., and K. Featherstone (1996): 'Italy and EMU as a "Vincolo Esterno": Empowering the Technocrats, Transforming the State', *South European Society and Politics* 1/2, pp.272–99.

—— (1999): *The Road to Maastricht. Negotiating the EMU*, Oxford: Oxford University Press.

*The Economist* (1999): 'A canny breed, those jolly Italians', 27 March 1999, p.35.

EU Commission (1999a), 'The Single Market Scoreboard', DG XV, Brussels: http://europa.eu.int/comm/internal_market/en/update/score/index.htm.

—— (1999b), 'Ninth Annual Report on the Structural Funds (1997), Brussels: http://europa.eu.int/comm/regional_policy/document/raka/raka_en.htm.

Eurispes (1993): *Rapporto Europa* [Report on Europe], Rome: Koinè edizioni.

Fabbrini, S. (1998): 'Due anni di governo Prodi. Un primo bilancio istituzionale' [The Prodi executive first two tears. An institutional account], *Il Mulino* 4, pp.657–72.

—— (2000): 'Parlamento, governo e capo del governo nella transizione italiana (1992–1998)' [Parliament, government and head of government in the Italian transition], in G. Di Palma, S. Fabbrini and G. Freddi (eds.), forthcoming pp.45-78.

Falkner, G. (2000): 'Policy networks in a multi-level system', *West European Politics* 2, 23/4.

Ferrera, M. (1999): 'Targeting Welfare in a Soft State: Italy's Winding Road to Selectivity', in N. Gilbert (ed.), *Targeting Social Benefits*, New Brunswick: Transaction.

Ferrera, M., and E. Gualmini (1999): *Salvati dall'Europa?* [Rescued by Europe?], Bologna: Il Mulino.

Di Palma, G., S. Fabbrini and G. Freddi (eds.) (2000): *Condannata al successo? L'Italia nell'Europa integrata* [Condemned to succeed? Italy in an integrated Europe], Bologna: Il Mulino.

Giuliani, M. (1996): 'Italy', in D. Rometsch and W. Wessels (eds.), *The European Union and Member States*, Manchester: Manchester University Press, pp.105–33.

—— (2000): 'Italy and Europe: policy domains and dynamics', in M. Fedele and R. Leonardi (eds.), *Italy: Politics and Policy*, vol.2, Dartmouth: forthcoming.

Capano, G. and M. Giuliani (eds.) (2001): *Il processo legislativo in Italia: continuità e mutamento* [The Italian law-making process: continuity and change], Bologna: Il Mulino, forthcoming.

Giuliani, M., and C. Radaelli (1999): 'Italian Political Science and the European Union', *Journal of European Public Policy* 2, pp.517–24.

Graziano, P. (1999): 'L'europeizzazione delle politiche di coesione: il caso italiano' [The europeization of cohesion policies: the Italian case], *Quaderni di scienza dell'amministrazione e politiche pubbliche* 6, Università di Pavia.

Hooghe, L. (ed.) (1996): *Cohesion Policy and European Integration. Building Multi-level governance*, Oxford: Oxford University Press.

Knill, C. and D. Lehmkuhl (1999): 'How Europe Matters. Different Mechanism of Europeanization', *EIoP Papers 3/7*.

Ladrech, R. (1994), 'Europeanization of Domestic Politics and Institutions: The case of France', *Journal of Common Market Studies* 32/1, pp.69–88.

Leonardi, R. (1995): *Convergence, Cohesion and Integration in the European Union*, London: Macmillan.

Lijphart, A. (1968): 'Typologies of Democratic Systems', *Comparative Political Studies* 1, pp.3–44.

Martinotti, G. and S. Stefanizzi (1995): 'Europeans and the Nation State', in O. Niedermayer and R. Sinnott (eds.), *Public Opinion and Internationalized Governance*, Oxford: Oxford University Press, pp.163–89.

Mayntz, R. (1998): 'New Challenges to Governance Theory', Florence: Jean Monnet Chair Paper, IUE, now in *Rivista Italiana di Scienza Politica* 1 (1999).

Mendrinou, M. (1996): 'Non-compliance and the European Commission's Role in Integration', *Journal of European Public Policy* 3/1, pp.1–22.

Mény, Y., P. Muller and J.-L. Quermonne (eds.) (1996): *Adjusting to Europe. The impact of the European Union on national institutions and policies*, London: Routledge.

Monti, M. (1998): *Intervista sull'Italia in Europa* [An interview on Italy in Europe], Rome: Laterza.

Morisi, M. (1997): 'Le autorità indipendenti in Italia come tema di ricerca' [Italian independent authorities as a case study], *Rivista Italiana di Scienza Politica* 27/2, pp.225–72.

—— (1999): 'La rappresentanza politica tra Unione europea e sistemi nazionali: un'angolazione italiana' [Political representation between the European Union and the national systems: an Italian perspective], in F. Morata, *L'Unione europea* [The European Union], Rome: Edizioni lavoro, pp.ix–xxvii.

Morisi, M. and L. Morlino (1999): 'Europeanization and Representation in Italy', paper for the conference on 'The Impact of Increased Economic Integration on Italy and the Rest

of Europe', Georgetown University, 30.4 (2 May 1999).
Morlino, L. and M. Tarchi (1996): 'The dissatisfied society: The roots of political change in Italy', *European Journal of Political Research* 30 (July), pp.41–63.
Olsen, J. (1995): *European Challenges of the Nation-State*, Oslo: ARENA Working Paper, n.14.
Padoa Schioppa, T. (1998): 'Che cosa ci ha insegnato l'avventura europea' [What did it teach us, the European adventure], *Il Mulino* 6, pp.987–1001.
Panebianco, A. (1991): 'Gioco di simulazione. Quattro scenari per il Duemila' [Simulation game. Four scenarios for the third millennium], *Il Mulino* 6, pp.1015–21.
Pasquino, G. (1999): 'The Impact of Europe on Italian Institutions', paper for the conference on 'The Impact of Increased Economic Integration on Italy and the Rest of Europe', Georgetown University, 30.4 (2 May 1999).
Pesole, D. (1994): *La vertigine del debito* [The debt vertigo], Rome: Editori Riuniti.
Pierson, P. (1999): 'Lo stato sociale nell'era dell'austerità permanente' [Welfare state in permanent austerity], *Rivista Italiana di Scienza Politica* 29/3, pp.393–439.
Prodi, R. (1999): *Un'idea dell'Europa* [An idea of Europe], Bologna: Il Mulino.
Radaelli, C. (1988): 'Europeismo tricolore' [The Italian Europeanism], *Relazioni internazionali* 4, pp 92–98.
Radaelli, C. (1999): 'Networks of Expertise and Policy Change in Italy', *South European Society & Politics* 3/2, pp.1–22.
Regini, M. (1999): 'L'Europa fra de-regolazione e patti sociali' [Europe between deregulation and social pacts], *Stato e Mercato* 1.
Rometsch, D. and W. Wessels (eds.) (1996): *The European Union and Member States*, Manchester: Manchester University Press.
Sbragia, A. (1992): 'Italy/EEC. An Undervalued Partnership', *Relazioni Internazionali* 2, pp.78–86.
—— (2000): *Italy pays for Europe: political leadership, political choice, and institutional adaptation*, in J. Caporaso, M. Cowles and T. Risse (eds.), forthcoming.
—— (1999), 'Hard Currency and Hard Choices: Italy and EMU', paper for the conference on 'The Impact of Increased Economic Integration on Italy and the Rest of Europe', Georgetown University, 30.4 (2 May 1999).
Schmidt, V. (1997a): 'Discourse and (dis)integration in Europe: The cases of France, Germany, and Great Britain', *Daedalus* 3, pp.167–97.
—— (1997b): 'European Integration and Democracy: the differences among member states', *Journal of European Public Policy* 4/1, pp.128–45.
—— (1998): 'Democracy and Discourse in an Integrating Europe and a Globalizing World', IUE Seminar paper, 20 October, now in *Rivista Italiana di Scienza Politica* 2 (1999).
Stone Sweet, A. and T. Brunell (1998): 'Constructing Supranational Constitution: Dispute resolution and governance in the European Community', *American Political Science Review* 92/1, pp.63–81.
Varsori, A. (1998): *L'Italia nelle relazioni internazionali dal 1943 al 1992* [Italy in international relations from 1943 to 1992], Rome: Laterza.
Vassallo, S. (2001): 'Le leggi del governo' [Governmental laws], in M. Giuliani and G. Capano (eds.), forthcoming.
—— (2000): 'La politica di bilancio. Le condizioni e gli effetti istituzionali della convergenza' [The budgetary policy. Conditions and institutional effects of convergence], in G. Di Palma, S. Fabbrini and G. Freddi (eds.), pp.287–323.
Vesperini, G. (1998): *I governi del maggioritario* [Executives in the majority era], Rome: Donzelli.
Verzichelli, L. (1999): *La politica di bilancio* [The budgetary policy], Bologna: Il Mulino.

# The Europeanization of Greece: An Overall Assessment

P.C. IOAKIMIDIS

## THE CONCEPT OF EUROPEANIZATION

The aim of this article is to examine the processes of Europeanization in Greece. As Featherstone has pointed out: 'Europeanization is a term that can be stretched in different directions at the cost of some debasing of its meaning' (Featherstone 1999: 1). Europeanization is seen as the process that is transforming the political systems of the EU member states and beyond, namely the political systems of the states aspiring to accede to the EU in eastern Europe.[1] Europeanization as a process describes the impact of EU membership or prospective membership (Friiss and Murphy 1999) upon political systems, society and economy in general. Ladrech, who has promoted the wide circulation of the term in academic discourse, sees Europeanization 'as an incremental process reorienting the direction and shape of politics to the degree that EC political and economic dynamics become part of the organizational logic of national politics and policy-making' (Ladrech 1994: 69). Europeanization is a process of 'internalization of environmental inputs' by the political and societal systems of EU member states, and, as such, it entails a steady redefinition of functions, relationships, boundaries, values and cultural traits, regulatory patterns that shape the internal dynamics of the political system. It involves the redefinition of boundaries between the state and society as well as of relationships within state structures and within society.

The position is, however, that Europeanization is experienced differently by member states depending on factors such as the specific state formation, the patterns of policy-making, the political culture, but also the balance of power between state and society on the one hand and national and subnational units on the other. It depends also on the expectations, significance and functional role a given member state accords to the European integration process and the EU in particular.

Thus, it is one thing, for instance, to view the EU as a framework for projecting an international role (i.e. Britain) or maximizing a position of power (i.e. France), and entirely another to regard the EU as an external power source and stimulus for advancing economic, social and political modernization, as in the case of Greece. In the latter case, there is a predetermined tendency on the part of the political elites of the member state to transplant into their political system the logic, norms, patterns of behaviour and regulation, even the culture, associated with European integration. This is because they tend to see all these elements as integral components of the modernization process. The case of Greece conforms precisely to this model.

More generally, it has been suggested that Europeanization penetrates more deeply the unitary, statist political systems, rather than the federally, decentralized structured ones. As Schmidt argues (1999: 2): 'the EU's quasi-federal institutional structures have had a greater impact on member states with unitary institutional structures, by altering the traditional balance of powers among branches and levels of government, than to those with federal institutional structures, where the traditional balance of powers has been largely maintained.'

Europeanization can therefore be conceptualized into two basic types: (1) responsive Europeanization, and (2) intended Europeanization. Responsive Europeanization refers to cases where no or little conscious effort is being made by the political actors to introduce into the political system the logic, norms and dynamics of the EU. Europeanization in these cases comes somehow spontaneously, as a response to the pressures and penetrative impact of European integration upon the political system. Europeanization does not, in other words, form a substitute for modernization and change and is not projected as such by the political actors. Europeanization results from the interactive osmosis between the national political system, institutions and various elites (political, administrative) on the one hand and the EU system and processes on the other. Europeanization does not represent an alternative model for the organization and functional arrangement of the political system; nor does it offer a source of legitimization for political, social and economic change. Responsive Europeanization is in a sense a political process, in so far as it is not being embraced by political actors and is not embedded into a political and ideological design for political change.

The case of intended Europeanization is clearly different. As already said, intended Europeanization stands for modernization. That is, there is a strong intention and thus a purposefully framed scheme by the political actors to transfer into their political systems the logic, dynamics, organizational traits, behavioural and regulatory patterns associated with European integration (governance patterns). This is because they aim at transforming their systems by making them 'modern' which (to them) means 'European'. As a result, in addition to responsive Europeanization, which operates practically in all EU member states and beyond, there is the purposeful action by the political elites to copy the European model (intended Europeanization). Consequently, Europeanization becomes a political or even an ideological programme for change, a slogan for political reform.

These characteristics indicate the very political nature of the process of intended Europeanization for the countries concerned. It must be clear that, in contrast to responsive Europeanization, intended Europeanization is much broader in the scope of its implications in terms both of its territorial and thematic penetration.

The cases of Greece, Spain and Portugal, as well as those of eastern European countries seeking EU membership, seem to conform to the model of intended Europeanization. Indeed, the so-called 'Copenhagen Criteria' for accession can be seen as a well-prepared programme for the Europeanization of these countries, imposing upon them a model of governance reflecting the values, norms and principles upon which the EU system and those of its member states are constructed (Friiss and Murphy 1999: 218–19).

Placed in a wider context, the study of the Europeanization process raises inevitably the question of the relationship between the EU on the one hand and the nation-state, society and subnational units, like the regions, on the other. Space does not permit a detailed examination of the subject here. The present research, however, clearly supports the thesis that Europeanization works towards the direction of weakening the relative power, role, control and autonomy of the central state institutions, while at the same time strengthening the power and autonomy of the subnational units, actors and society as a whole. The strengthening includes also the ability of those units to form networks through which they participate, alongside state institutions (government administration) in the process of policy formation at a European-wide level. In other words, Europeanization seems to lead to what has been termed the model of 'multi-level governance', according to which 'decision making competencies are shared by actors at different levels rather than monopolized by state executives' (Jorgensen 1997).

## THE EUROPEANIZATION OF GREECE

Greece acceded to the EC in 1981, after being an associate member for almost 20 years, since 1961, the year in which the (first) association agreement ('Athens agreement') between Greece and the EC was signed. Although the association agreement never functioned properly, Greece opted in 1975, a year after the collapse of the seven-year dictatorship, for full membership. The application for accession was filed by Constantine Karamanlis, the then Prime Minister, who saw EC membership as the paramount factor for achieving political stability, consolidating democracy, strengthening external security, as well as securing the conditions (financial resources, large market, etc.) for the modernization of the Greek socioeconomic system (Tsoukalis 1979).

Modernization was interpreted, of course, to mean 'westernization', or more precisely 'Europeanization'. However, at the time when Greece was seeking to join the EU, the effort did not enjoy widespread support among Greek political elites. Greece's drive to join the EC was supported by the conservative New Democracy party and small centre groups and the Eurocommunists, but was fiercely opposed by the rising political force in Greek politics, PASOK (the Panhellenic Socialist Movement) and the orthodox Communist party, KKE. Nevertheless, Greece succeeded in concluding the accession negotiations in 1979 and thus adhered to the EU as a full, institutional member in January 1981, before, that is, the advent of PASOK to power in October 1981. Once in power, however, PASOK came to gradually accept the EC, as it evolved into the EU, as the underlying framework for the modernization and Europeanization of Greece. So, by the early 1990s, all Greek political forces, save the KKE, had emerged as keen supporters of Greece's membership of the EU and ardent advocates of deeper integration along federal lines (Tsalicoglou 1995; Ioakimidis 1998).

To understand the Greek stance towards the EU, however, as well as the process of Europeanization, it is imperative to take into consideration the salient features of the Greek state and social formations. One of the striking features of the state morphology at the time of Greece's accession was the gigantic size of the state apparatus and the over-centralized nature of the state and political system in general. The state occupied a hegemonic position in practically every aspect of Greek society. The gigantism of the state was exemplified in (1) the over-employment in the public sector; (2) the high amount of public expenditure as a share of GNP; and (3) the extensive regulatory role performed by the state and the latter's overwhelming participation in economic activities (Tsoukalas 1986).

Over-employment in the public sector constituted one of the main traits of the state's gigantism. The number of public sector employees amounted in 1981 to 351,028 people, rising to 615,956 people in 1992, or 17 per cent of the total Greek population. This meant that one in six Greeks or one in three employed in the tertiary sector were working in the public sector. As Tsoukalas observed, 'public sector employment coveted by the overwhelming majority of the Greek population dominated the labor market' (Tsoukalas 1981: 36). The clientelistic nature of Greek politics was an important factor for swelling employment in the public sector.

The level of public expenditure reflected also the gigantism of the Greek state. Total public expenditure amounted in 1981 to 49.6 per cent of Greek GDP, much higher than the EU average, while public debt rose from 17.6 per cent of GDP in 1970 to 28.3 per cent in 1981, and 112 per cent in 1986. The huge public deficits incurred by the steadily expanding activities of the Greek state were described as 'the blight of the Greek economy' (Agapitos 1996).

The state's extensive regulatory role over the economy constituted a further strong expression of state gigantism with particular importance for the country's position in the integration process. According to all indicators in almost all sectors, the Greek state was considered to have developed a powerful role in the economy. In the areas of production (regulation for product production) and the labour market, Greece was viewed as the most tightly regulated country in the EU. The regulatory rules imprinted in tens of opaque bureaucratic provisions, laws or texts, governed the allocation of state subsidies, grants and aids in every form (to business, exports, economic activities, transfers, etc.). Hence, a study published in 1993 located the existence of six different categories of (state) grants given directly by the state budget to state businesses, foundations, educational institutions, payments for loan forfeiture, etc. (Patsouratis 1993).

The direct state involvement in economic activities through setting up and operating (public) business and the overt or covert business control constituted for Greece a particular dimension of state regulatory role and a further facet of its gigantism. From the early 1960s until the country's entry into the EC, one of the constant and ideologically indisputable elements of economic policy had been the increasingly entrepreneurial expansion of the public sector. Irrespective of the ideological identity of governments, statism had been the main trait of all the post-war governments' economic policy. It is characteristic that even the conservative (rightist) governments were accused of following, as part of their main ideological trait, statist, paternalistic policies. Particularly after 1974 and despite the fact that Greece had submitted its application for accession to the EC, the conservative government of ND began a massive process of state expansion in the area of entrepreneurial activity with, among others, the nationalization of significant segments of the economy (Olympic Airways, Commercial Bank, etc.). Furthermore, the expansion of the entrepreneurial activity of the public sector was accomplished through the functioning of an opaque network of patron–client relations and 'dependencies'. The net effect was that at the time of Greece's entry into the EU as a full member, the state was regarded as the greatest entrepreneur and employer, controlling an unspecified number of businesses in practically all areas of economic activity.

Besides its indirect involvement in economic activity, the Greek state exercised decisive regulatory powers through the asphyxiating control of the banking system. The banking system was actually in the hands of the state, which distributed loans and other banking favours for purely political, clientelistic purposes.

Overall, the huge economic state interventions driven by clientelistic, political motives gave rise to a paternalistic, regulatory model, clearly at odds with the economic logic of the EU. It must be stressed in this respect, however, that the gigantic character of the Greek state did not mean a powerful or effective state. It was rightly described as 'a colossus with a feet of clay' in terms of its organizational and functional capabilities (Sotiropoulos 1993). Gigantism resulted from a varied set of peculiar socioeconomic conditions, the most important of which was the patron–client system operated by the political parties. It would not be, therefore, an exaggeration to suggest that the state was used by political parties as a means of distributing favours in order to maximize their electoral appeal.

The state's predominant position in the Greek socioeconomic system also manifested itself in the over-centralization of powers, functions and competencies in the state apparatus located in Athens with very little regional powers and autonomy. Athens controlled practically everything at regional level. Moreover, greater Athens was the residence of almost 45 per cent of the total Greek population and the location of almost 70 per cent of the total economic activities. Greece was rightly considered as the most centralized unitary state in Europe in the early 1980s. Coupled with the unstable regional environment within which Greece found itself, the hegemonic position of the Greek state left little room for the development of an articulate civil society in Greece.

The Europeanization process in Greece must be seen against this political background. Given the peculiar situation described, as regards state–society relations and the formation and multiple roles of the Greek state, it is not surprising that the Europeanization process seems to have had more pervasive consequences in Greece than elsewhere. More specifically, this research leads to the conclusion that Europeanization has deeply penetrated into the Greek political system and has brought about redefinitions in at least four different, but interrelated, levels (Ioakimidis 1998): regulatory, functional, territorial, and institutional.

The cumulative effect of these redefinitions has been the birth of the dynamic process for rebalancing relations between state and society in favour of the latter. The boundary between state and society has been changing as a result of EU membership in the direction of limiting the scope of the state and widening that of society. The rebalancing process results in enhancing the civil society, a phenomenon exemplified in:

(1) loosening the state's grip on the social institutions and reinforcing the latter's autonomy;
(2) widening existing opportunities or creating new possibilities for the participation of interest groups in the policy-making process at national and European levels;
(3) loosening Athens' grip on the regions through a process of regional decentralization largely spurred by EU membership;
(4) weakening the dominant position of the party system in Greek society and, as a consequence, diminishing the role of the traditional patronage system as a factor shaping state–society relationships; and
(5) 'de-externalizing' foreign policy by broadening its scope and agenda and bringing new actors into the process of policy formulation and implementation.

Inevitably the Europeanization process, with its far-reaching consequences, has given rise to new types of political conflicts and ideological cleavages. Thus, the old ideological conflict between right and left has largely been replaced by a new pattern of conflict between the Europeanists/modernizers on the one hand and the traditionalists on the other, a conflict that cuts cross political parties. The traditionalists are in a sense seeking to contain the impact of the Europeanization process (Lyrintzis *et al.* 1996). They tend to see Europeanization as a force threatening the country's traditional cultural identity. They therefore resist the adaptation of the political and socioeconomic systems to the logic and requirements of European integration. Albeit in diminishing numbers, the traditionalists carry considerable weight in the political process largely because they appeal to 'losers', which the Europeanization process inevitably produces. This is especially so, after the advent of Costas Simitis to power, as Prime Minister of the PASOK government in 1996. Simitis, indisputably one of the most pro-European figures in Greek politics, upon assuming power initiated a vigorous programme for Greece's Europeanization by, among other things, seeking to achieve the so-called 'convergence criteria' for the accession of Greece to the euro. Meeting the convergence criteria (reducing public deficits to three per cent of GNP, reducing inflation, etc.) involved a radical reform of the Greek public finances and economy, something which has unavoidably created a large number of 'losers' among those who depended on the state for their economic survival.

## REDEFINING THE REGULATORY REGIME

The impact of EU membership upon the state's economic role has manifested itself in two specific developments: first, it has fostered a considerable reduction in state economic activities and the gigantic size in general of the Greek state; secondly, it has altered radically the regulatory pattern of the Greek economy, from one tightly controlled by the state into one conforming with the EU's regulatory regime.

The reduction of the size of the state resulted primarily from the need imposed by the EU to curtail public expenditure as a means of trimming excessively high budget deficits. For a considerable period of time after entering the EU, Greece, under the PASOK government, pursued a wild expansionary fiscal policy in order to satisfy the pressing social demands as well as demands of its electorate. Consequently, the total volume of public expenditure increased from 30 per cent of GNP in 1980 to 42 per cent in 1985, while employment in the public sector had also expanded dramatically.

This expansionary policy was clearly at odds with the contractionary fiscal policies pursued by the rest of Europe and with the macroeconomic policy guidelines recommended by the European Commission to the EU member states. Until at least 1985, Greece simply conspicuously ignored these guidelines. The net effects of this reckless fiscal policy were uncontrollable public deficits, rapidly rising public debt and a bloated public administration with a steadily increasing number of employees in the public sector (Christodoulakis 1994). Nevertheless, because of the rapidly worsening fiscal position, Greece was forced in 1985 to seek the EU's assistance in order to face the consequences of this situation, especially in the balance of payments which exhibited huge deficits. The EU responded positively to the Greek request for assistance, but only after imposing a tough programme for economic stabilization and reforms involving, among other things, a drastic reduction in public deficits, expenditure and employment. It involved, that is, the drastic curtailment of the gigantic size of the Greek state. The EU stabilization programme of 1985 heralded the opening of the process for reversing the trend towards the steady expansion of the Greek state (Kazakos 1991: 17). Although this programme was abandoned in 1987 in the face of mounting social pressures, it contributed to raising political awareness of the need to carry out widespread economic reforms in the public sector in order to enable Greece to adapt to EU requirements and the internal logic of integration.

Without doubt, the most drastic EU intervention in the Greek economy came with the adoption of the Maastricht Treaty which set out the 'convergence criteria' along with the multilateral surveillance mechanism for supervising the economies bent on joining economic and monetary union (EMU). All these have subjected the economies of EU member states to a systematic macroeconomic discipline through the implementation of the so-called 'convergence programmes' for meeting the criteria, a discipline supervised by the European Commission.

Greece, eager to join EMU but without any real hope of doing so under the prevailing chaotic conditions in the Greek economy, submitted its convergence programme to the EU in 1993, which was then revised in 1994. The aim of the programme was to meet the convergence criteria by reducing public deficit, public debt, interest rates and achieving monetary and fiscal stability. This was in essence a programme for restructuring the Greek public sector with two key novel elements: first, the supervision of the implementation of the programme by the EU itself, and secondly, the fact that failure to implement it carried a heavy penalty, notably the exclusion of Greece from EMU, the group of states that was expected to form the hard core of policy-making in the EU.

The first task of the Simitis government in 1996 was to reduce sharply the huge budget deficit, the highest in the EU. The deficit indeed fell 12.5 per cent in 1993 to 0.9 per cent in 1999. However, curbing the public deficit involved primarily the reduction of public expenditure, the reduction of employment in the state and the termination of state financial support through state aids and subsidies to public firms and enterprises. It entailed, in other words, a radical reduction in the size of the Greek state and a thorough redefinition of the state's economic role. Indeed, this seems to have been accomplished to a significant degree by 1999. The budget deficit of 0.9 per cent was an unprecedented figure in Greek post-war history, while employment in the public sector also began to decline. The same applies to state aids and subsidies to Greek state enterprises, most of which were either privatized or closed down as heavily indebted and unprofitable. Indeed, privatization has gathered momentum in recent years as a means of rationalizing the economic role of the Greek state (Christodoulakis 1998).

In addition to spearheading the reduction in the size of the state and altering its economic role in a fundamental way, EU membership brought about a complete overhaul in the regulatory regime governing the private economy in Greece. Prior to EU accession, the Greek economy was tightly controlled by the state through a plethora of legal and bureaucratic regulations, which left little room, if any at all, for competition and unhindered economic activity. Moreover, as noted, the state had in its hand, almost in its entirety, the banking system and thus it was in a position to determine the distribution of loans and financial favours on purely political grounds, flagrantly ignoring economic logic.

EU membership gradually led to the complete liberalization of the banking system. New private banks were set up while, by applying the second EU banking directive, an increasing number of European and foreign banks began to establish branches in Greece. Furthermore, the state was forced to introduce EU legislation aiming at securing transparency in the transactions between the state and public enterprises. This, coupled with the introduction into the Greek economy of the plethora of EU directives underpinning the internal single market, directives designed to establish a competitive regulatory regime for the whole of the European economy, the liberalization of the banking system and the general reduction of the economic role of the state, resulted in shaping a new competitive regulatory regime for the Greek economy congruent with that of the wider European economy and the single market.

## REDEFINING STATE FUNCTIONS AND COMPETENCIES

According to established theories of European integration, EU membership involves first and foremost a transfer of competencies and functions from the state level to the central EU level. The transfer is presumed to be always upwards, one-directional, from the state to the EU. The parallel hypothesis is that because of this upward transfer of competencies and functions the state is steadily and irreversibly losing powers and stripped of its functions.

The Greek case reveals, however, that EU membership could involve not only an upward transfer of functions or a surrender of competencies to Brussels, but also a downward flow of competencies from the EU (i.e. to an individual state). This is because the EU could develop policies on the basis of legal competencies acquired by a process which does not necessarily involve subtraction of competencies from a given state or simultaneously from *all* member states. When the EU acquires, through the intergovernmental conferences for the revision or expansion of the Treaties, new competencies in policy areas, this by no means implies that the competence in question is taken away from all member states. For it is possible that a given individual state might not have developed or exercised at all a specific competence. The case of environmental policy is a very characteristic example. The EU constitutionally assumed this competence in 1987 through the Single European Act as a concurrent power, a power shared between the EU and the state. Greece had not, however, by that time developed any coherent environmental policy and so there was very little, if anything, at the state level to be transferred to Brussels (Kazakos 1999b).

Environmental policy is not the only example as far as Greece is concerned. Indeed, empirical research suggests that, because of EU membership, the Greek state, while forced to abandon a host of economic functions and activities, was at the same time led by the EU's impact and dynamics to assume new functions and develop policies that otherwise it might not have developed at all. The EU, in other words, imposed upon the Greek state an array of new competencies and new functions.

More specifically, research suggests (Ioakimidis 1998: 85–128) that the Greek state developed at least six new policy functions as a direct response to the need to adjust its performance to the EU's policy *acquis*. These policies were:

- structural policy
- policy for vocational training
- policy for the protection of the environment
- policy for research and technology

- consumer protection policy
- policy for cross border cooperation.

The Greek state had, of course, before its accession to the EU, pursued certain incoherent activities in the above policy areas. But these activities could hardly be described as 'policies' in any meaningful sense. Indeed, my own research suggests that without the impact of the EU, the Greek state would not have gone so far as to shape coherent policies, as it did, probably in all six areas mentioned and certainly not in some of them (border cooperation, consumer protection, vocational training). The Greek experience therefore indicates a downward flow of policy competencies, from the EU to the state. The state is forced in certain cases to assume functions and to shape policies, choices and performance which it would not have assumed in the absence of the EU's impact. This can be seen as the Europeanization of the policy mix performed by the state, Europeanization that springs from the interactive policy exchanges between the EU and the member states on one hand, and an individual member state on the other.

## TERRITORIAL REDEFINITION OF POWERS

Given the over-centralized character of the Greek state and political system in general prior to Greece's EU membership, it is not surprising to discover that the territorial impact of the Europeanization process has been considerable in the Greek case. Indeed, it would not be an exaggeration to say that EU membership has been the factor that contributed to altering fundamentally the territorial distribution of political power, political activities, choices and resources (Ioakimidis 1996; Verney and Papageorgiou 1993).

The most important component of the EU's integration process that has affected the redefinition of power relationships between the Greek centre and the periphery has been the structural and cohesion policy which was inaugurated by the EU in 1985 with the adoption of the so-called 'Integrated Mediterranean Programmes' (IMPs) and culminated in 1988 in the new structural policy (the Delors package). As in other member states covered by the structural policy (Hooghe 1996), the implementation of the cohesion and structural policy in Greece has generated the dynamics and conditions for introducing a systematic policy of regional decentralization and reinforcing the powers and autonomy of the regions.

The basic principles of the new structural policy, and especially those of 'programming' and 'partnership' stipulating the active involvement of the regions in all stages of policy-making and policy-implementation, have compelled the Greek state and the governing political elites to cede considerable chunks of power, resources and autonomy to the regions, so as to make possible the implementation of the EU's structural and cohesion policy. Admittedly, the PASOK government which took office in October 1981 had projected as one of its main programmatic objectives 'the radical decentralization of the over-centralized Greek state'. However it is widely held that decentralization would have remained either an empty promise or, at best, it would not have gone as far as it did, if it had not been for the impact primarily of the EU's structural policy (Ioakimidis 1996a; Verney and Papageorgiou 1993; Christopoulos 1999).

Thus, although the first legislative measures for promoting regional decentralization were adopted in 1982 with the setting-up (on paper) of the so-called 'prefecture councils', it was not until 1986 that a set of far-reaching reforms was introduced. Included in these reforms were the division of the country into 13 administrative regions (in order to 'facilitate the planning, elaboration and coordination of policies for regional development') and the establishment of the second level of local administration (i.e. the provision for electing the heads of the *nomos* (prefects) instead of appointing them by the government of the day).

These reforms were followed in 1994 by a new package of measures which completed the required institutional framework and structures for the operation of the second degree of regional administration. In October 1994 the first elections at the level of *nomarchies* (prefectures) were held. The first elected *nomarchs* (prefects) took office in January 1995. This marked a decisive step in Greece's political organization. The regional reforms were extended in 1997 through the adoption of the so-called 'Kapodistrias plan'. This plan sought to confront the problem of widespread fragmentation in the local administration system comprising as it did no fewer than 363 *demoi* (municipalities) and 5,550 *koinotites* (communities), by promoting their amalgamation into a smaller number of units. In spite of some original hostile reactions, the 'Kapodistrias reforms' were eventually carried out, thereby leading to the rationalization of the regional administrative system.

Although, as noted, all these reforms towards a more decentralized political system were carried out by the PASOK governments, as part of their programmatic policy, most, if not all of them, were introduced as a response to the requirements and impact of EU membership. The 1986 reforms came about after Greece had discovered that it was not in a position to implement the IMPs because it lacked the decentralized regional structures required by the EU as partners in the execution of the structural policy. Hence, the division of Greece into 13 regions (*peripheries*) occurred with a considerable degree of autonomy and resources as the basic administrative units for developmental purposes. The implementation of the new structural policy (the Delors packages of 1988 and 1993) was effected through the Community Support Frameworks (CSFs) which contained two basic parts, one with developmental priorities of a national dimension (big infrastructure projects) and one composed of 13 regional development programmes specifically tailored to the regions' developmental needs and priorities. These programmes evolved into the most important instruments for the economic invigoration of the regions, thus contributing immensely to the implementation of decentralization and regional autonomy.

But besides the reforms designed and carried out by the governing elites as a response to the EU pressures, EU membership has contributed in a more direct way to enhancing regional power, autonomy and sense of identity. Thus, because of the EU structural policies, the Greek regions have gained financial resources, access to policy making at national and supranational levels, communication channels with the organs of the EU and their counterparts in other member states, networks of influence, and exchange of experiences (Ioakimidis 1996a).

More importantly perhaps, the regions' involvement in the process of framing and implementing the CSFs has altered profoundly their policy agenda. While prior to the arrival of the EU structural policy and financial resources, regional authorities used to deal almost exclusively with a limited range of issues (waste collection, street cleaning, etc.), the implementation of structural policy through the CSFs has forced them to confront wider developmental issues and choices. On the other hand, the setting-up of the Committee of the Regions by the Treaty on EU provided the institutional forum at the EU level for the regions to air their views and build alliances with their counterparts in other member states.

On the whole, the Europeanization process has indeed had a substantial impact on the territorial distribution of power by shifting the balance in favour of the regions. In a unitary, over-centralized state like that of Greece, the territorial transformation in the balance of political power, resources and relationships represents an important move towards the democratization of the political process.

## EUROPEANIZATION AND THE INSTITUTIONS

The effects of the Europeanization process on the institutional structures of an individual political system is one of the most contested aspects of the whole process of European integration. The commonly held view is that EU membership tends to strengthen the executive and bureaucratic branches of the political system, to weaken the role of national parliamentary institutions and the domestic legislative process, and thus to challenge the democratic bases of the political process (Andersen and Eliassen 1996). Wessels and Rometsch speak of a process of deparliamentarization of the political system of the EU member-states, a process accelerated by European integration because 'national parliaments to a varying degree [have] lost in decision making competencies in all member states, whereas the national governments with the help of the bureaucracy could strengthen their position and extend their scope of competencies' (Wessels and Rometsch 1996: 362).

The Greek case suggests, however, that the Europeanization process and EU membership in general can play a decisive role in strengthening democratic institutions and widening the scope of the democratic process by bringing into it new social and political actors. Similarly, the Europeanization process can give rise to new institutional structures, bodies and channels of democratic expression, where the democratic structures and processes appear weak and deficient and the political elites are anxious to bolster them by 'importing' institutional formations from Europe as part of their strategy of intended Europeanization.

Of course, when referring to Greece one needs always to bear in mind that in 1975 Greece sought EU accession primarily as a means of consolidating the newly established (1974) democratic institutions. Indeed, it is convincingly argued that EU membership contributed significantly to underpinning political, democratic stability in Greece, a country plagued by instability and authoritarian rule until at least 1974, the year of the collapse of the military regime (Verney 1990; Ioakimidis 1994). Accordingly, the EU is credited with playing a pivotal role in assisting the consolidation of democratic institutions and processes. As a result, the EU is seen not only by Greece, but also by Spain, Portugal and even the east European countries seeking EU membership, as a powerful force for building democracy and a pluralistic society. It is regarded as exporter of democratic governance.

The EU's role in assisting the process of building democracy in Greece was mainly the effect of a systemic and cultural spillover. However, on a more concrete disaggregated level, the Greek experience shows that in addition to fostering regional decentralization, the Europeanization process has affected in a dynamic way the process for strengthening the formal as well as the operational autonomy and independence of public and social institutions. The case of the Bank of Greece is perhaps the most important example. The Bank, tightly controlled by the government until 1995, gained almost full institutional independence and operational autonomy in shaping monetary policy by being forced to comply with the EU rules in the context of the convergence programme for acceding to the EMU. These provide for central bank independence as a prerequisite for joining the single currency, the euro. As pointed out, along with the central bank, the commercial banks also acquired considerable independence by adopting the EU's regulatory regime.

More interestingly perhaps, from the perspective of state morphology, EU membership fostered the conditions for enhancing the managerial and operational independence of the public administration, particularly the civil service more directly involved in or exposed to EU policy *vis-à-vis* the government and the political parties. First of all, because the handling of the EU policy agenda required specialized skills, technocratic knowledge and expertise, the recruitment of civil servants, at least in the departments dealing with EU matters, became more transparent and based on objective criteria, rather than on the patron-client system and party patronage. Similarly, the grip of government and party politicians on the administration declined, while the latter's ability and manoeuvre to influence policy outputs increased through its participation in the EU policy formulating process (Tsinisizelis 1996).

Although Greece has not yet succeeded in setting up an efficient system of European policy-making and policy coordination, public administration as a whole seems to have profited considerably from its interaction with the EU policy-making process and other administrations of the EU member states. The interaction has offered resources, experiences, skills, channels of communication and opportunities for travelling to an administration suffering traditionally from low pay and low morale. This, however, does not imply that the administration as a whole has grown capable of coping with the negotiating pressures emanating from the EU. Precisely because of the incapacity of the established administration to deal efficiently with the EU negotiations, new specialized administrative units have been created recruiting personnel from the private sector, something which contributes to the overall modernization of the administration.

Moreover, the Europeanization process has encouraged in several ways (institutional, financial, etc.) the formation of an increasing number of social associations, especially non-governmental organizations (NGOs). Statistical data show that the number of social associations financed by the European Commission quadrupled between 1996 and 1998. Included in these new groups is the Economic and Social Committee which was founded in 1994 as a matching institution to the EU's Economic and Social Committee (ESC) to contribute to economic and social policy-making.

Coupled with the proliferation of new social associations and interest groups is the equally important phenomenon of gradually opening the national policy-making process to society. Indeed, the Greek state was forced as a consequence of EU pressures to invite social associations and interest groups to participate in the process of elaborating the developmental and structural policy to be supported by the EU. It is characteristic that while in the drawing up of the first Regional Development Plan covering the period 1988–93 only 23 regional and social bodies took part, in the second plan for the period 1993–99 no fewer than 71 social and regional bodies were involved (Ministry of National Economy 1993). It must be pointed out here that one of the effects of the Europeanization process is that the Greek state has begun to draw up developmental plans of an enforceable, operational nature as the basis for concluding the CSFs with the European Commission. What is interesting in this context is that the widening of the policy-making process to actors other than solely the executive bureaucratic institutions eventually embraced even the domain of foreign policy. Thus, apart from other governmental departments, like the ministries of national economy, agriculture and environment, which by virtue of their involvement in EU negotiations have begun to have a substantial bearing on foreign policy, other social and economic actors (economic associations, universities, etc.) have also been drawn into the process of seeking to influence foreign policy outputs; so much so that one can speak of a tendency towards de-externalizing the foreign policy-making process, in the sense that a wider range of actors are by now involved in the process rather than only the Ministry of Foreign Affairs, as was previously the case (Ioakimidis 1999).

The broadening of the policy-making process with the inclusion of an increasing number of actors in it clearly refutes theoretical hypotheses arguing that participation in the EU leads to the bureaucratization of the national policy-making process. The Greek experience tends rather to support the opposite thesis, namely that participation in the EU tends on the whole to debureaucratize the policy-shaping process, making it more democratic. This is especially true as the vast majority of pressure groups and social associations, including the Federation of Greek Industrialists (SEV) and the trade union confederation, GSEE, feel that the EU is affording them greater opportunities and better channels of influencing policy both at national and supranational levels. This, of course, explains why an increasing number of interest groups, including even the Church of Greece, seek to establish representation offices close to EU organs, namely in Brussels. Thus the Greek case seems to bear out the thesis that 'negotiations in Brussels offer new opportunities to certain interests otherwise marginalized in national decision making' (Mény *et al.* 1996: 5).

By contrast, this is not the case with the Greek parliament. Parliament had not (at least until the early 1990s) shown any visible interest in the EU policy-making process. From the early 1990s, however, parliament has begun to take a wider interest in Europe and for that it set up a special committee on European affairs consisting of members of both the national parliament and the European Parliament. The new interest owes much to two basic factors: first, the deepening Europeanization of all Greek political parties (with the exception of the Communist Party, KKE) and especially the metamorphosis of PASOK from a fiercely anti-European movement in the 1970s and early 1980s into a pro-federalist, integrationist force in the 1990s; and secondly, the new emphasis placed by the Treaties of Maastricht and Amsterdam on the role of national parliaments in the EU policy-making process. However, in spite of the new heightened interest in EU matters, the Greek Parliament has not yet established a workable system for screening EU legislation.

## CONCLUDING REMARKS

The overall conclusion one can draw from the analysis of the case of Greece in the EU is that Europeanization has been a powerful force for redefining the role, functions and powers of the state and altering the balance of power between the state on the one hand, and society and the regions on the other.

Contrary to the claims of state-centric approaches to European integration (Moravcsik 1998), the redefinition has clearly shifted powers, functions and resources away from the state to society in general and the regions in particular. There has been, in other words, a rebalancing of powers and a redefinition of boundaries between the state and society in favour of the latter. The state has certainly lost its unchallenged ability to impose its grip upon society and control the economy. Similarly, the party system has been forced to lessen its control upon the state and progressively shed the habit of using the latter as a means of promoting electoral objectives through the patronage system. Although it is widely claimed that new forms of opaque links have been forged between the state, the leading political parties and some strong private firms (*diaplekomena symferonta*, interlinked interests), it is true that a clear distinction has been established between the party system and the state system.

Viewed from the perspective of the state–society relationship, it is also evident that EU membership operates as a very effective force supporting the process of building a civil society in Greece. The absence of civil society has been identified as one of the fundamental shortcomings of Greece's social organization (Mouzelis 1997). By weakening the omnipotence of the state, the Europeanization process has actually emerged as a formidable factor assisting the process of shaping civil society in Greece. More than that, as noted above, the EU has helped the birth of numerous social associations and 'citizens' movements which, according to Diamandouros (1997: 37), form the basis for the construction of civil society in Greece and the improvement of the quality of democracy (also Tsoukalis 1997: 169). One should also not underestimate the role EU membership has played in the creation of new institutions for the protection of the citizen (Ombudsman) as well as in conferring new rights upon the Greek citizens (European citizenship, protection of minority rights, protection of personal data, etc.). The EU has been a source for the empowerment of civil society, not least through its substantial financial transfers amounting to about 4.5bn euros per year and the new regulatory patterns it has 'imposed' upon the Greek economy and society.

The Greek experience of internalizing Europeanization seems therefore to refute the sweeping assumptions of state-centric theories about the impact of EU membership upon state–society relationships and interactions. On the contrary, as the preceding analysis demonstrates, in the Greek case EU membership has been an important factor for rebalancing relations between the state and society in favour of the latter. And as an increasing number of societal and regional authorities feel that they have better chances of influencing policy outputs at the European level and thus tend to advance their participation in various policy networks, the assumption of the multi-level governance school that 'decision making competencies are shared by actors at different levels rather than monopolized by state executives' (Marks, Scharpf, Schmitter and Streeck 1996: 346) seems to hold true.

## NOTE

1. The term European Union (EU) is used throughout this text to denote the current EU and its earlier manifestations, European Economic Community (EEC) and European Community (EC).

## REFERENCES


Agapitos, G. (1996): Δημόσιος Τομέας το <<σαράκι>> της ελληνικής οικονομίας' [Public Sector: The Blight of the Greek Economy], *Oikonomikos Tachydromos*, no 51 (19 Dec. 1996).

Andersen, S.S., and K. Eliassen (1996): *The European Union: How Democratic is it?* London: Sage.

Christodoulakis, N. (1998): *Το νέο τοπίο της ανάπτυξης* [The new landscape of development], Athens: Kastaniotis.

—— (1994): 'Fiscal Developments in Greece 1980–93: A Critical Review', *European Economy* 3.

Christopoulos, D. (1999): 'Regionalism in Greece', in P. Wagstaff (ed.), *Regionalism in the European Union*, Exeter: Intellect.

Diamandouros, P.N. (1997): 'Greek Politics and Society in the 1990's', in T.G. Allison and K. Nikolaidis (eds.), *The Greek Paradox, Promise vs Performance*, Cambridge MA: MIT Press.

Featherstone, K. (1999): 'The British Labour Party from Kinnock to Blair: Europeanizm and Europeanization', paper presented to ECSA Biennial Conference, Pittsburgh, 2–5 June.

Friis, L., and A. Murphy (1999): 'The European Union and central and eastern Europe: Governance and boundaries', *Journal of Common Market Studies* 37, p.2.

Hooghe, L. (ed.) (1996): *Cohesion Policy and European Integration: Building Multilevel Governance*, Oxford: Oxford University Press.

Ioakimidis, P.C. (1994): 'The EC and the Greece Political System: An overview', in P. Kazakos and P.C. Ioakimidis (eds.), *Greece and EC Membership Evaluated*, London/New York: Pinter Pub./St Martin's Press.

—— (1996): 'EU Cohesion Policy in Greece: The Tension between Bureaucratic Centralism and Regionalism', in L. Hooghe (ed.), *Cohesion Policy and European Integration: Building Multilevel Governance*, Oxford: Oxford University Press.

—— (1998): *Ευρωπαϊκή Ενωση και 'Ελληνικό Κράτος* [The European Union and the Greek State], Athens: Themelio.

—— (1999): 'The Model of Foreign Policy-Making in Greece: Personalities Versus Institutions', in St. Stavridis, Th. Couloumbis, Th. Veremis and N. Waites (eds.), *The Foreign Policies of the European Union's Mediterranean States and Applicant Countries in the 1990's*, London: Macmillan.

Jorgensen, K.E. (ed.) (1997): *Reflective Approaches to European Governance*, London: Macmillan.

Kazakos, P. (1991): *Η Ελλάδα ανάμεσα σε προσαρμογή και περιθωριοποίηση* [Greece between Adjustment and Marginalization], Athens: Diatton.

—— (1999): 'The "Europeanization' of Public Policy: The impact of European integration on Greek environmental policy', *European Integration*, pp.369–91.

Ladrech, R. (1994): 'Europeanization of domestic politics and institutions: The case of France', *Journal of Common Market Studies* 32.

Lyrintzis, Ch., H. Nikolakopoulos and D. Sotiropoulos (eds.) (1996): *Κοινωνία και Πολιτική 'Οψεις της Γ' Ελληνικής Δημοκρατίας* [Society and Politics, Aspects of the Third Greek Republic 1974–1994], Athens: Themelio.

Marks, G., F.W. Scharpf, P.C. Schmitter and W. Streeck (1996): *Governance in the European Union*, London: Sage.

Mény, Y., P. Muller and J.-L. Quermone (1996): 'Introduction', in ibid. (eds.), *Adjusting Europe, The Impact of the European Union on National Institutions and Policies*, London: Macmillan.

Ministry of National Economy (1993): *Σχέδιο Περιφερειακής Ανάπτυζης 1994–1999* [Regional Development Plan, 1994–1999], Athens.

Moravcsik, A. (1998): *The Choice for Europe*, London: UCL Press.

Mouzelis, N. (1997): '*Ο συνήγορος του πολίτη και χαμένη ευκαιρία*' [The Ombudsman and the missed opportunity], *To Vima*, 27 April.

Patsouratis, V.A. (1993): *State Grants, Subsidies and Transfer Payments*, Athens: IOBE.

Schmidt, V.A. (1999): 'The EU and its Member -States: Institutional Contrasts and their Consequences', MPIfG Working Paper 99/7.

Sotiropoulos, D.A. (1993): 'A Colossus with Feet of Clay: The State in Post-Authoritarian Greece', in H.J. Psomiades and S.B. Thomadakis (eds.) (1993), *Greece and the New Europe and the Changing International Order*, New York: Pella.

Tsalicoglou, I.S. (1995): *Negotiating for Entry: The Accession of Greece to the European Community*, Aldershot: Darmouth.

Tsinisizelis, M. (1996): 'Greece', in W. Wessels and D. Rometsch (eds.), *The European Union and Member States: Towards Institutional Fusion?* Manchester: Manchester University Press.

Tsoukalas, C. (1981): *Κοινωνική Ανάπτυζη και Κράτος η συγκρότηση του δημόσιου χώρου στην Ελλάδα* [Social Development and the State. The Structure of Social Space in Greece], Athens: Themelio.

—— (1986): *Κράτος, Κοινωνια, Εργασία στη Μεταπολεμικη Ελλάδα* [State, Society, Labour in Post-War Greece], Athens: Themelio.

Tsoukalis, L. (ed.) (1979): *Greece and the European Community*, London: Saxon House.

—— (1997): 'Conclusion: Beyond the Greek Paradox', in T.G. Allison and K. Nikolaidis (eds.) (1997), *The Greek Paradox, Promise vs Performance*, Cambridge MA: MIT Press.

Verney, S. (1990): 'To be or not to be within the European Community: The party debate and democratic consolidation in Greece', in G. Pridham (ed.) (1999), *Securing Democracy: Political Parties and Democratic Consolidation in Southern Europe*, London: Routledge.

Verney, S., and F. Papageorgiou (1993): 'Prefecture Councils in Greece: Decentralization in the European Community Context', in R. Leonardi (ed.), *The Regions and the European Community*, London: Frank Cass.

Wessels, W., and D. Rometsch (1996): 'Conclusions: European Union and national institutions', in ibid. (eds.), *The European Union and Member States: Towards Institutional Fusion?* Manchester: Manchester University Press, 1996.

## OTHER SOURCES

Allison, T.G., and K. Nikolaidis (eds.) (1997): *The Greek Paradox: Promise vs Performance*, Cambridge MA: MIT Press.

Anderson, J.J. (ed.) (1999): *Regional Integration and Democracy: Expanding on the European experience*, Oxford: Rowman and Littlefield.

Bache, I. (1998): *The Politics of European Union Regional Policy, Multilevel Governance or Flexible Gatekeeping?* London: Sheffield.

Chrysanthakis, Ch. (1998): *Η Θεσμική μεταρρύθμιση της πρωτοβάθμιας τοπικής αυτοδιοίκοισης Το σχέδιο Ιωάννης <<Καποδίστριας>>*[The Institutional Reform of the First Level of Local Administration: The 'Ioannis Kapodistrias' Plan], Athens: An. Sakkoulas.

Hanf, K., and B. Soetendorp (eds.) (1998): *Adapting to European Integration, Small states and the European Union*, London: Longman.

Ioakimidis, P.C. (1989): 'Οι συνέπειες της εσωτερικής αγοράς και Ελλάδα' [The consequences of the internal market programme for Greece], in P. Kazakos, (ed.),

*1992. Η εζέλιζη της Εσωτερικής Αγοράς στην Ευρώπη και η Ελλάδα* [1992. The Evolution of the Internal Market in Europe and Greece], Athens: Ionian Bank.

—— (1993): *Ενωση Θεωρια Διαπραγμάτευση Θεσμοί και Πολιτικές* [European Political Union: Theory, Negotiation, Institutions and Policies], Athens: Themelio.

—— (1993): 'Η Ελημική Διοίκηση και η διαμόρφωση της Ευρωπαϊκής Πολιτικής' [The Greek Administration and European Policy Making], in L. Tsoukalis (ed.), *Η Ελλάδα στην Ευρωπαϊκή Κοινότητα: Η πρόκληση της προσαρμογής* [Greece in the European Community: The Challenge of Adjustment], Athens: EKEM/Papazisis.

—— (1993): 'Greece in the EC: Policies, Experiences and Prospects', in H.J. Psomiades and S.B. Thomadakis (eds.), *Greece: The New Europe and Changing International Order*, New York: Pella Inc.

—— (1997): *Η Ελλάδα στην Ευρωπαϊκή Ενωση 1981–1996: Επιλογή Βιβλιογραφίας Προοπτικές εζευρωπαϊσμού στην Ελλάδα* [Greece in the European Union 1981-1996: A Bibliographical Selection – Prospects of Europeanization in Greece], Athens: Themelio.

—— (1995): 'The Evolution of the Third Greek Presidency in the European Union', in P.C. Ioakimidis, St Stavridis and A. Mitsos, *The Greek Presidency of the European Union*, Center for Mediterranean Studies, University of Bristol, Occasional Paper 12.

—— (1996): 'Contradictions Between Policy and Performance'. in K. Featherstone and K. Ifantis (eds.), *Greece in a Changing Europe: Between European Integration and Balkan Disintegration*, Manchester, NY: Manchester University Press.

Ioakimidis, P.C., St Stavridis and A. Mitsos (1995): *The Greek Presidency of the European Union*, Center for Mediterranean Studies, University of Bristol, Occasional Paper 12.

Kazakos, P. (1999a): "Ο Εζευρωπαϊσμός της Δημόσιας Πολιτικής Η Εθνική Περιβαλλοντική Πολιτική ανάμεσα σε εσωτερικούς παράγοντες και υπερεθνικές δεσμεύσεις' [The 'Europeanization' of public policy: the national environmental policy between the pressures of domestic factors and supranational obligations], *Elliniki Epitheorisi Politikis Epistimis* 13.

Kazakos, P., and P.C. Ioakimidis (eds.) (1994): *Greece and EC Membership Evaluated*, London: Pinter.

Keating, M. (1998): *The New Regionalism in Western Europe*, London: Edward Elgar.

Lavdas, K.A. (1997): *The Europeanization of Greece: Interest Politics and the Crises of Integration*, London: Macmillan.

Legg, K.R., and J.M. Roberts (1997): *Modern Greece, A Civilization on the Periphery*, London: Westview Press.

Marks G., L. Hooghe and K. Blank (1996): 'European Integration from the 1980s: State–Centric v. Multi-level Governance', *Journal of Common Market Studies* 34, p.3.

Papageorgiou, F., and S. Verney (1993): 'Regional Planning and the Integrated Mediterranean Programmes', in R. Leonardi (ed.), *The Regions and the European Union*, London: Frank Cass.

Sandholtz, W., and A.S. Sweet (eds.) (1998): *European Integration and Supranational Governance*, Oxford: Oxford University Press.

Scharpf, F. (1999): *Governing in Europe, Effective and Democratic?* Oxford: Oxford University Press.

Sotiropoulos, D.A. (1996): *Populism and Bureaucracy, The Case of Greece under PASOK, 1981–1989*, London: University of Notre Dame Press.

Verney, S. (1994): 'Central State–Local Government Relationships', in P. Kazakos and P.C. Ioakimidis (eds.), *Greece and EC Membership Evaluated*, London: Pinter.

—— (1996): 'The Greek Socialists', in J. Gaffney (ed.), *Political Parties and the European Union*, London: Routledge.

# Multilevel Governance and Europeanization: The Case of Catalonia

QUIM BRUGUÉ, RICARD GOMÀ AND JOAN SUBIRATS

## MULTILEVEL GOVERNANCE IN CATALONIA: THE FRAMEWORK OF ANALYSIS

### *From monopoly to multilevel: territorial complexity on politics and policies*

The classic form of understanding processes of government was based until recently on the maintenance of two clear divisions. This was the division between the public and private spheres and, within the public sphere, the asymmetrical distribution of political responsibilities between different levels of government, with absolute predominance of the nation state. Recently, both divisions have been subject to processes of redefinition. On the one hand, the segregated coexistence between the state and the market, subject to tensions of relative size, gives way to new dialectics between public and private regulations (market but also social, communitarian and informal) competing for the same areas of influence and societal configuration. The ability to govern is no longer a unidirectional, hierarchical and monopolistic process flowing from public decision-makers to citizens. Citizenship demands new spaces for involvement and engagement, both in the definition of problems and policies and in the management of programmes and services; spaces which should conform to relational logics, in which the actors stop working on the basis of formal hierarchies and contribute to the organization of deliberative, non-authoritative channels for the resolution of social conflict (Kooiman 1993). On the other hand, the quasi-monopoly of the nation state collapses and is transformed into a complex institutional framework, with new territorial balances in favour, often, of supranational and intranational levels.

Over the last two decades, Catalonia has been fully subject to both tendencies. On the one hand, Catalan civil society had already, since 1980, occupied relevant *public spaces* (education and health cooperatives, cultural production, and a network of organizations for youth leisure activities). Since the 1980s, the enormous advance of the public sector has not meant the weakening of the social initiative, although the actual terms of the relationship have shifted dramatically: the public initiative has ceased to be subsidiary. It has assumed predominant roles and universal coverage; the private initiative has fallen within the framework of public regulation and has been resituated against a background of collaboration. On the other hand, the progressive recovery of self-governance has meant the irruption of a Catalan national perspective in policy-making. Nevertheless, this fact has not led, in general, to the creation of new, clear, stable, well-defined areas of sovereignty, but rather the presence of the *Generalitat* of Catalonia (the autonomous government), in areas of government that are shared both upwards and downwards. The *Generalitat* is placed specifically within a double, pluri-national context, comprising the Spanish state and the EU, and shares its internal presence with a strengthened system of local governments. In synthesis, Catalonia represents a multilevel, territorially organized system of governance, whose operation takes placed within a framework of pluralist and interactive public, market, social and community regulations.

In Spain, analyzing territorial complexity requires reference to two simultaneous dynamics, 'Europeanization' and 'territorialization', understood respectively as relocation processes of government towards the EU and towards autonomous communities and local governments. Furthermore, both are projected onto differentiated dimensions of the political system: on the dimension of identities, institutions and actors ('polity-politics') and on the dimension of decision powers ('policy-making') (Marks and Scharpf 1996).

The territorial dimension in Spain is currently more developed than

TABLE 1
TERRITORIAL COMPLEXITIES IN SPAIN: MULTILEVEL POLITY, POLITICS AND POLICIES

| | Polity-politics | Policymaking |
|---|---|---|
| Europeanization: | Low and homogenous | Medium and uneven |
| Territorialization: | Medium and very asymmetrical | Strong and less asymmetrical |

the European dimension. As we show in Table 1, political powers and political identities have undergone a process of decentralization that is stronger and deeper than the process of Europeanization. Furthermore, both processes find greater expression in policy-making (decision powers over the policy agenda) than in the symbolic-institutional sphere (identities and collective action). Decentralization in this latter dimension is linked closely to the national or regional character of the autonomous community. In nations like Catalonia, the Basque Country or Galicia, the territorial element has a reasonably strong impact on the politics-polity; in regional communities, the state maintains indisputable centrality. In policy-making, territorialization stands at higher levels, with asymmetries that are of lesser significance than the symbolic ones, with a tendency towards certain convergence, and which are only partly related to the national or regional character of the communities. In the territorial framework, local governments have policy-making and management powers that are clearly inferior to those of the autonomous communities.

Adopting a Catalan perspective, it can be stated that the government of the *Generalitat* is a major actor in policy formulation, with the Spanish state and the EU playing restricted and selective roles, and with a weak, though growing, need to share the formulation of policies with local governments. All this takes place within a framework of less symbolic and media relevance, in that the state maintains an important degree of centrality in the perception of the citizenship towards the political reality.

Finally, it is necessary to point out that the imbalances between the symbolic centrality of the state and the multilevel distribution of policy-making can have far-reaching consequences. On the one hand, the EU's symbolic shortfall can operate as a brake or a delegitimizing factor for possible new advances in the supranational integration of public policies (e.g. in European employment or cohesion policies). On the other hand, Catalan self-government will not easily be able to continue growing without a strategic ability to participate directly and on an equal basis in the definition of pluri-national political projects, whether they be on a Spanish or a European scale (Guibernau 1997).

After considering the breakdown in traditional conceptions of government and the tensions between nation state resistances and the territorial overspill of public decisions, we continue with the development of an analytical framework by considering the impact of three levels on the policy-based governance of Catalonia: the EU, the state and the local level.

*Strategic Europeanization*

Multilevel tension with regard to the build-up of policy-making capacities is a constituent element of European politics. The logic of diversity, enshrined in multiple state and territorial agendas makes the construction of European government responsibilities difficult. However, the logic of convergence, as expressed in the multiple attempts at EU policy harmonization, makes the emergence of new, localized policy capacities difficult. Since the end of the 1980s, *subsidiarity* has opened the way, even in the legal ambit, towards a possible logic of synthesis in the territorial distribution of government roles. Nevertheless, such a notion generates an epistemic conflict between two alternative interpretations. First, the traditional interpretation leads to a rigid pattern of sectoral distribution of responsibilities in favour of levels on a more reduced territorial scale. Its resulting profile is thus a set of monopolies and exclusions from public policy. Secondly, the innovative interpretation leads to an intrasectoral distribution, the multilevel confluence of powers over the majority of policies based on criteria of roles division (Leibfried and Pierson 1996).

We believe that, in effect, the innovative interpretation of subsidiarity has great explanatory potential. Thus, it is possible to differentiate between three major types of public role in each policy sector: *strategic regulation* (the setting of the policy paradigm), *policy formulation* (options on e.g. fields of priority action, amount of resources to be allocated, rates of coverage, etc.) and *service delivery* (organizational and management models). As a general thesis, it can be established that the EU takes responsibility for the setting-up of transnational regulative regimes of a strategic nature, while the tasks of formulating and implementing policies are distributed among central and territorial governments depending on each state model.

TABLE 2
A BIDIMENSIONAL MODEL OF POLICY INTEGRATION AT EU LEVEL

| | | Nature of integration |
|---|---|---|
| Level of integration | Strategic | Integral |
| High Europeanization | EU multilevel governance | Harmonization of policies |
| Low Europeanization | Exchange of policy ideas | Transference of policy paradigms |

Yet this general framework presents at least two complications. First, as it is presented in the bidimensional model of Table 2, the

Europeanization of policies understood as the integration of strategic elements currently shows a strong uneven development. In fact, the action of the EU is today open to a range of options. A number of policy sectors are still weakly Europeanized: policy ideas are exchanged or transferred on a basis of intergovernmental networks, without any relevant EU role. Furthermore, when the policy impact of the EU level is determinant, it sometimes leads to harmonization – that is, to the full integration of most sectoral decisions (agriculture or monetary policies). Only in the remaining policy fields, when Europeanization is strategic, do multilevel governance models emerge fully. Secondly, in the case of Spain, there is a comparatively under-consolidated multilevel allocation of public roles, due both to the tension derived from pluri-nationality and to the irruption of municipalities into many policy areas that had traditionally been away from the local level.

### *Uneven autonomization*

In terms of the real impact of the different levels on fiscal revenue, policy formulation and public spending, we can consider the existence of two

TABLE 3
DUAL AND COMPLEX MODELS OF FISCAL AND SPENDING AUTONOMY

| | Taxation: Level of autonomy | | Decision-making and public spending: Level of authonomy | |
|---|---|---|---|---|
| Dual model: | High<br>Basque country<br>Navarra | Low<br>Catalonia pre-1997 | High | Low |
| | ← Tendency | | | |
| Complex model: | | | Catalonia and ACs in art. 151* | ACs in art. 143* |

AC = autonomous communities.
* Arts. 151 and 143 refer to two constitutional provisions which make a distinction in terms of level of autonomy.

major ideal types of decentralized state. Both are shown in Table 3: the *dual* type, in which there is a clear sectoral distribution of fiscal and spending powers; and the *complex* type, in which there is a general multilevel confluence of financial and decision-making powers over each tax and in each policy area. Each type allows for varying levels of politico–financial autonomy at regional and local levels. Spain's position is not homogenous: in decision-making and spending, the scheme tends to be complex, with different but large-scale levels of autonomy; in the area of taxation, the model, up until 1997, was clearly dual and with few levels of autonomy, with the exception of the Basque country and Navarra.

As far as Catalonia is concerned, the above adds two key elements of qualification with regard to what we have discussed up to now. On the one hand, we notice that the relevant autonomous powers are focused on public spending and on the sovereignty of decision over a major part of this spending; the limited fiscal autonomy acts as a restrictive factor. On the other hand, the system of multilevel governance, of which Catalonia is an example, implies an interactive, reflexive and highly political logic, with little margin for any general regulation in legal-rational terms.

### *Restricted localization*

Multilevel governance in Catalonia has an internal nature that is just as complex as its position within pluri-national frameworks. The Catalan system of local powers contains a high density of territorial and institutional structures. In these structures lie tensions with multiple direct effects upon the governance of Catalonia.

Within the framework of the development of the Keynesian welfare state (KWS) (Esping-Andersen 1990; Pierson 1996), European local governments polarized around two major models. The first is municipal administration of welfare, particular to Anglo-Saxon and Scandinavian countries, in which local institutions performed large-scale operational roles: municipalities become the executive wings of the universal public services of the KWS. The second is the residual model of local government, as evidenced by the major continental states, in which local institutions designed programmes of community development and networks of social assistance, but – with little responsibility for the administration of resources – remained at the margins of the large-scale services of the welfare state. Nevertheless, there existed two common elements which permit us to uphold the idea of a *common contribution* of the local level in Europe, under Keynesian conditions of welfare:

(1) a relatively simple agenda, centred around urban and social policies, with no significant contribution to employment, economic growth or the environment; and
(2) the adoption of purely operational roles, carrying out policies framed at higher levels, with no form of involvement in strategic roles in any key policies of the KWS.

Throughout the 1980s and 1990s, new lines of change were projected on the European models of local government. In the first place, Thatcherism had a devastating impact – both because it was neo-liberal but also because it was centralist – on the service provision of British local government. Secondly, continental local governments benefited from new internal decentralizing dynamics. Finally, southern Europe burst onto the scene of European municipal debate as a result of democratic transitions. In synthesis, a look at the present situation allows us to sustain the claim that the traditional Anglo–continental division has today been replaced by a new map, as shown in Table 4, on which appears at least four European models of local government. In continental and Anglo-Saxon regimes there is a predominance of elements of internal coherence between democratic dimensions (formation of policy and community identity) and provision ones (administration of resources and economies of scale), although these elements tend to go in contrasting directions. In Germany, local governments have a powerful profile; in the UK, they are in a state of decline. In Scandinavian and Mediterranean models, however, there is a strong potential for internal tension, deriving from the persistent community deficit of the former and the lack of resources of the latter (Batley and Stoker 1991).

TABLE 4
MODELS OF LOCAL GOVERNMENT IN THE EU: DEMOCRATIC/OPERATIONAL DIMENSIONS

| | Democratic dimension | | Operational dimension | |
|---|---|---|---|---|
| | Policy-making powers | Collective local identity | Resource management powers | Scale (economical) suitability |
| Scandinavian | High | Weak | High | High |
| Central Continental | Medium | Strong | Strengthened | Growing |
| Anglo-Saxon | Limited | Weak | Weakened | High |
| Latin-Med | High | Strong | Low | Minimal |

Adopting an internal perspective of analysis, it can be stated that Catalonia adheres fully to the basic characteristics of a local Mediterranean regime: a hyper-fragmented municipal map, rooted in feelings of collective belonging, with generalized responsibilities for public intervention in favour of the community, but with little technical or economic power and with a relatively weak position in the multilevel distribution of public resources. To this one should add two points: the problem of superimposing models at a secondary level (*comarcal* and provincial) and the problem of the homogenous consideration, from an institutional perspective, of a territory that is entirely heterogeneous from a socioeconomic and demographic perspective. All this leads to a dense system of local authorities with two emerging elements of great interest:

(a) increasingly complex agendas, with the presence of new economic, employment and environmental policies, and
(b) growing strategic roles, that is, a particular contribution of the municipal level to the collective generation of welfare.

Having developed a framework of analysis, we assemble and explore a series of data which allow us to qualify the considerations made up to this point in relation to the multilevel system of governance in Catalonia.

TABLE 5
THE MULTILEVEL STRUCTURE OF GOVERNANCE IN CATALONIA: KEY ASPECTS

| | No. of units | Share of expenditure in Catalonia (%) | Fiscal autonomy | Key policies | Involvement in multilevel policy-making |
|---|---|---|---|---|---|
| Pluri-national context: | | | | | |
| EU | 15 states | 1.2 | Low | Monetary<br>CAP<br>Cohesion | Medium-high |
| Spain | 17 AA.CC. | 37 | Very high | Social security<br>Labour market | High |
| Catalonia (autonomous community) | 1 | 48.5 | Medium | Health<br>Education | High |
| Local governments: | | | | | |
| Provinces | 4 | 2 | Very low | Social infrastructure | Low |
| *Comarques* | 41 | 0.5 | Very low | Personal social services planning<br>Economic promotion | Low |
| Munici-palities | 944 | 11 | Medium | | Medium |

We outline certain elements in Table 5, where an overall view of the multilevel system of governance in Catalonia is made available, by considering its key variables. All of them are assessed in more depth in the remainder of this article.

## GOVERNANCE IN CATALONIA: THE MULTILEVEL DISTRIBUTION OF PUBLIC RESOURCES

The political science literature usually considers public spending and public employment figures excessively inconsistent as principal indicators of government capacities. There is no doubt that they are relevant indicators, but they must be handled critically; their explanatory limits should be taken into account. A particular level of government manages economic and human resources when it produces services and implements transfer programmes. All this is very important, but governing neither begins nor ends here. Governing is, above all, deciding on the binding distribution of costs, opportunities and values between social groups. The task of governing involves the power to effect taxation and policy content. Sometimes, the level that designs the regulatory regime (finance options, objectives, rates of coverage, intensity of protection) also internalizes programme management. Often, however, this is not the case. Instead, there is an interfunctional split between institutional levels.

The capacity of *Generalitat* to manage resources is greater than its tax-raising and policy formulation powers. In many policy areas, the EU and the Spanish state govern in Catalonia via legislation, although this is later translated into autonomic and/or local public spending and employment. In other words, the *influence* of the EU and the Spanish state in Catalonia is greater than its *presence*. In contrast, the *presence* of the *Generalitat* is greater than its effective *influence* on governance. As far as local powers are concerned, the levels of influence and presence are balanced. It is true that the *Generalitat*'s regulatory potential acts as a limiting factor to local government; but it is also true that both fiscal autonomy and the possibility of operating beyond their legal competencies increases the social influence of local governments in Catalonia.

### *External multilevel structure: Catalonia in the context of the EU and the Spanish state*

*Multilevel distribution of public spending*. The presence of Community Structural Funds, the EU's instruments of investment, in Catalonia grew consistently between 1988 and 1996. If we take the average of the years

TABLE 6
CATALONIA AND THE STRUCTURAL FUNDS: RESOURCES 1994–99
(MILLION ECUS)

| Objective | ERDF | ESF | EAGGF | FIFG | Total | % |
|---|---|---|---|---|---|---|
| 1 | — | — | — | — | — | — |
| 2 | 843.9 | 226.5 | — | — | 1070.4 | 58.7 |
| 5b | 36.0 | 23.4 | 88.6 | — | 147.9 | 8.1 |
| 3 | — | 408.9 | — | — | 408.9 | 22.5 |
| 4 | — | 102.2 | — | — | 102.2 | 5.6 |
| 5a | — | — | 69.7 | 24.3 | 94.0 | 5.1 |
| Total | 879.9 | 661.0 | 158.3 | 24.3 | 1823.4 | 100 |

*Source*: Vallvé (1999: 36).

1994–96 we see that EU investment in Catalonia is 2.38 times the investment in 1988. This figure represents an incremental change that is staggered rather than steadily growing, because of the impact in Catalonia of two cycles of reforms arising from EU cohesion policies following the Single European Act (1988–89) and the signing of the Maastricht Treaty (1993–94).

Table 6 shows the amount of resources made available to Catalonia from the Structural Funds for the period 1994–99. As we can see, the objectives of regional policy (2 and 5b) account for 66.8 per cent of the total resources; however, the objectives of social and employment policy (3 and 4) and rural structural adaptation (5a) account for the remaining 33.2 per cent. The overall figure of ECU 1,823.4m represents around 0.7 per cent of Catalonia's gross domestic product.

The presence of the Spanish state in Catalonia in terms of public resources grew between 1986 and 1996. Nevertheless, it is necessary to qualify this growth. The figures for spending and state investment in Catalonia for the years 1996 and 1997 are, respectively, 1.8 and 2.25 times those for the period 1986–88. However, since 1991–92 a situation of stagnation and decline can be observed. At the beginning of 1991, the investment of the state in Catalonia was 54,807m pesetas per year; the average for the last three years was of 47,858m. The explanation is due largely to the investments linked to the Olympic Games of 1992. These investments hugely expanded the presence of the Spanish state in the implementation of infrastructural policies in Catalonia. After the Games, the levels of state financing of policies in Catalonia tend to diminish, but not significantly. The pacts of CiU with PSOE in 1993 and with PP in 1996 could be the main explanatory factor.

TABLE 7
DISTRIBUTION OF HUMAN RESOURCES BETWEEN THE STATE AND THE *GENERALITAT*: EVOLVING PATTERN

| | Spanish state | *Generalitat* |
|---|---|---|
| 1978 | 89,818 | 0 |
| 1988 | 25,633 | 86,942 |
| 1991 | 25,546 | 102,329 |
| 1993 | 26,221 | 107,241 |
| 1996 | 24,022 | 109,149 |

*Source*: Boletín Estadístico MAP 1996.

*The state and the autonomous government in Catalonia: multilevel distribution of human resources.* Another important variable which allows us to analyze the multilevel distribution of public powers and, above all, of the implementation of policies is human resources in one or other administration. In Catalonia, over the last 20 years there has been a spectacular fall in state public employment figures, from 89,818 in 1978 to 24,022 in 1996. This fall contrasts with the increase in regional and local public employment, from little more than 15,000 in 1978 (all at municipal level) to 161,241 in 1996, of which over 109,000 are in the *Generalitat*. Thus, the volume of human resources in the public sector in Catalonia is currently 185,263, of whom 87 per cent are in Catalan administrations (with a relationship between the *Generalitat* and local governments of 2.1 : 1) and 13 per cent are in the administration of the state (Table 7).

There is no doubt that the figures in Table 7 are easily analyzed from an institutional point of view; they express the extent to which the *Generalitat* has strengthened its leadership in Catalonia. However, a sectoral analysis of the figures helps qualify these conclusions. The level of public occupation against the volume of resources managed greatly increases in policies which are intensive in service provision (especially education and health) which, in Catalonia, correspond to the *Generalitat*. For this reason, if the action of government by means of regulative instruments at the hands of the state and the EU (e.g. the labour market or the environment) has little impact on spending indicators, it has even less on public employment. To this fact, we must add that the social security system run by the state, which is intensive in terms of economic resources, has a smaller impact in public employment.

In synthesis, there are four aspects to highlight in the recent evolution of the relative presence of European and state levels of government compared with the *Generalitat*:

(1) The Government of Catalonia rapidly gained ground over the state. Between 1989 and 1991, the figures of regional spending and investment were respectively 2.36 and 3.5 times those of the state; they have now increased up to 2.83 and 6.25 above the state.
(2) In relative terms, the Catalan governance system today contains a higher presence of the European level. During the years 1988 and 1989 regional investment in Catalonia was 12 times EU investment, whereas today that figure has been reduced to six.
(3) The increase in EU spending, linked to the stagnation and decrease in state spending, currently situates these two areas at similar levels of investment presence in Catalonia: both are around 47,000m pesetas per year.
(4) The structure of public occupation has been transformed radically in favour of Catalan administrations. In 1978 the relationship of state : *Generalitat* : local government was in the ratio: 87 : 0% : 13%. Today it is: 12% : 60% : 28%.

*State and the autonomous government in Catalonia: multilevel distribution of fiscal powers.* A key indicator, often forgotten, of real incidence on a multilevel governance system is the degree of fiscal sovereignty at each institutional level. In Catalonia, the *Generalitat*'s financial autonomy can be measured by determining the percentage of the volume of total revenue it derives from its own tax-raising powers. The rest, in the form of transfers, comes from state and European funds over which the *Generalitat*, in principle, has no power of fiscal decision-making. However, the autonomy of spending can be, and indeed is, greater than the autonomy of taxation. The degree of sovereignty over spending is determined by adding the previous percentage, the percentage of revenue represented by transfers that are free from any degree of specific targeting. With the granting of 15 per cent of the IRPF (income tax) (1994), financial autonomy was not increased in a strict sense, as the regulation of the tax continued to be monopolized by the state. However, the model accompanying the granting of 30 per cent of the IRPF (1997) implied a qualitative shift: the newly granted percentage comes with new fiscal legislative powers at the regional level.

In fact, the high degree of conflict in the debate on fiscal autonomy, in Catalonia and in the Spanish state as a whole, can be marked by two independent parameters: on the one hand, the level of fiscal autonomy; on the other, the level of inter-territorial redistribution of resources derived from the fiscal model (Table 8). From a centralist perspective

TABLE 8
FISCAL MODELS ACCORDING TO PARAMETERS OF AUTONOMY AND REDISTRIBUTION

| | Level of inter-territorial redistribution | |
|---|---|---|
| Level of fiscal autonomy | High | Low |
| High | Fiscal agreement with a clause of cohesion or solidarity | Economic agreement (Basque country and Navarra) |
| Low | Dependence with fiscal deficit | Dependence with fiscal balance (regions under the national average of income) |

(nourished in retrospect by anti-cohesion nationalist perspectives) there is an attempt to connect indivisibly fiscal unity with inter-territorial distribution of resources. The existence of the Basque model with little regional contribution to the central state also adds to this view. Nevertheless, it is necessary to state that there is no reason why it should be impossible to combine sovereignty with solidarity in the fiscal sphere. A model of bilateral fiscal agreement between Catalonia and the state, with an agreed component of contribution to cohesion (or solidarity), could alter radically the current situation of dependence, with a permanent fiscal deficit, without necessarily moving towards the Basque model.

Beyond the debate on models, the following data provide some pieces of interesting evidence (Table 9). The *Generalitat*'s fiscal autonomy has been reduced progressively in proportion to the expansion of its powers of spending. Thus in 1985, 27.6 per cent of the *Generalitat*'s resources came from its own taxes. This figure dropped to 17.42 per cent in 1990 and then to 15.06 per cent in 1996. In other words, the Catalan government increased its presence in policy-making against a background of dependent financing, via transfers. In ten years, these went from contributing 72 per cent of the budget to contributing 84.5 per cent. In contrast, the proportion of targeted transfers, which reduce the autonomy of spending, progressively declined: in 1985, these represented 85.93 per cent of the total; in 1990 the proportion had fallen to 53.58 per cent and in 1995 to 51.15 per cent. Thus, the overall level of spending autonomy received the *negative impact* of the fall in the proportion of self-generated resources (those arising from own tax-raising powers), and the *positive impact* of the increase in the proportion of transfers free from any target. Overall, in 1985 autonomy of spending

TABLE 9
THE EVOLUTION OF THE *GENERALITAT'S* REVENUE STRUCTURE
(MILLION PESETAS)

| | 1985 | 1989 | 1993 | 1994 | 1995 |
|---|---|---|---|---|---|
| Self-determined tax revenue | 20,250 | 15.837 | 30.108 | 28.071 | 32.343 |
| Transferred taxes | 86,000 | 97.105 | 216.721 | 197.501 | 211.851 |
| Total tax revenue | 106,250 | 112,942 | 246,829 | 225,572 | 244,194 |
| Non-targeted transfers | 35,461 | 315,064 | 528,672 | 569,125 | 623,678 |
| Targeted transference | 216,628 | 356,677 | 580,184 | 628,593 | 653,241 |
| Total transfers | 252,089 | 671,741 | 1,108,856 | 1,197,718 | 1,276,919 |
| Financial revenue | 26,074 | 30,000 | 93,000 | 107,000 | 99,500 |
| Total | 384,413 | 814,683 | 1,448,685 | 1,530,290 | 1,630,405 |

*Source*: *Nota d'Economia* n.53, DEF.

was 36.86 per cent; in 1990 it had increased to 53.51 per cent and in 1996 it was at 53.55 per cent.

### *The internal multilevel structure: relations between the Generalitat and local governments*

*The high density of Catalan levels of government*. There is a high internal density of levels of government in Catalonia. The *Generalitat* (leaving aside for the moment the EU and the state) shares the public landscape of Catalonia with four provincial governments, 41 *comarcal* councils and more than 900 municipalities, which make up the multifaceted territorial model of the country. This model is the historical expression of a political situation in which Catalan democratic forces managed to establish the *Generalitat* – *comarques* – municipality system laid down in the 1979 Statute of Autonomy of Catalonia, but in which centralist forces imposed the continuation of the state–provincial structure.

Beyond the initial inability of the former in simplifying the model at the expense of the latter, this multilevel internal density is today a fact and, while taking into account a general feeling that the system is too multilevelled, it is possible to make both positive and negative analyses of the situation. On the positive side, it responds to a certain policy-based allocation of responsibilities at each level; it answers in the widest and most pluralistic form to the demands and needs of the Catalan population; it generates a certain institutional competitiveness which can contribute to an improvement in services and an increase in management efficiency; and it increases the political pluralism and the capacity for institutional representation of the different sensibilities in Catalan society. On the negative side, it generates an overlapping of institutions and responsibilities which can be translated into increases in costs and inefficiencies of all types; it can create increases in intergovernmental and interparty conflict; and it can create an incentive to search for areas of public intervention connected to needs for institutional or party legitimization, which are not always reasonable from the point of view of the citizen's needs or problems.

An analysis of the last 20 years almost supports in part both the positive and the negative aspects of this complex and fragmented intergovernmental reality within Catalonia. In policy-making, it has produced both reasonable logics of specialization and very fertile structures of multilevel agreement (employment, housing). Within the party system, the alternation of political majorities of different colours at different levels has been maintained and reinforced. However, at the same time, it has led to conflicts of concurrence that are entirely avoidable (social welfare, urban planning etc.) and party-based institutional conflicts (such as metropolitan government) which could have been solved by alternative systems. Even so, it is most important to emphasize that the high multigovernmental density in Catalonia cannot be qualified as good or bad within the parameters of a supposed legal-organizational rationale. It is the expression of a complex process, and only from political persuasion could it be modified towards other parameters. Finally, it reflects, within Catalonia, European-wide trends towards a more complex political landscape.

*The* Generalitat *and levels of local government: multilevel distribution of public spending*. Beyond the previous considerations, we can state that recent years have seen both a tendency towards inflexibility as well as some dynamics towards change in the relative importance of the different levels of internal Catalan government, with regard to their respective shares of public resources. Table 10 shows two things: first, the *Generalitat* maintains and reinforces its predominant role in relation to the local governments in the internal distribution of public resources in Catalonia (with a relationship of 7 : 3); and secondly, the weakening of the provincial governments (from six to three per cent of Catalan public spending) has not happened to the advantage of any particular local level, and the new *comarcal* councils have maintained a low budgetary profile up until now. Table 11 shows how the multilevel asymmetries are

TABLE 10
THE DISTRIBUTION OF *GENERALITAT*/LOCAL GOVERNMENT RESOURCES
(MILLION PESETAS)

| | *Generalitat* | Provincial governments | *Comarcal* councils | Municipalities |
|---|---|---|---|---|
| 1983 | 319.800 (67%) | 29.426 (6%) | — | 128.145 (27%) |
| 1986 | 451.180 (63%) | 49.526 (7%) | — | 213.100 (30%) |
| 1991 | 1.211228 (67%) | 69.887 (4%) | 17.988 (1%) | 495.586 (28%) |
| 1995 | 1.718911 (70%) | 85.833 (3%) | 31.400 (1%) | 627.600 (26%) |

*Sources*: *Anuaris Estadádistics de Catalunya*, IEC, various years; Fundació Jaume Bofill 1989.

reproduced within local government in Catalonia. The aggregate of the two supramunicipal levels does not exceed 15 per cent, while the municipal councils are consolidated as the central institution of the Catalan system of local institutions with a participation of 85 per cent in total local public spending.

In general, Catalonia's multilevel internal organization continues to consolidate itself as a model with a strong tendency towards the centralization of power resources, with a local system of high institutional density, still weak and strongly oriented towards the municipal level. The hyper-fragmented, small-scale municipal map of Catalonia has already exhausted, in most of its municipalities, its effective governance potential. Nevertheless, the municipal authorities of large and medium-sized cities, and the *comarcal* level in non-metropolitan areas, shows great potential for growth in their respective governance roles. Both combine strong elements of local collective identity and high degrees of functionality in the provision of wide-scale services. The problem here lies in the fact that the simultaneous strengthening of cities and non-metropolitan *comarques* should generate a more balanced model of relationships between the *Generalitat* and the local sphere, which at present does not appear to be part of the Catalan government's political agenda (Figure 1).

TABLE 11
DISTRIBUTION OF RESOURCES AT LOCAL LEVEL
(MILLION PESETAS)

| | Provincial governments | | *Comarcal* councils | | Municipal councils | |
|---|---|---|---|---|---|---|
| 1988 | 54.900 | (15.8%) | 2.200 | (0.6%) | 291.900 | (83.6%) |
| 1995 | 85.800 | (10.7%) | 31.400 | (4.3%) | 627.600 | (85.0%) |

*Sources*: *Anuaris Estadádistics de Catalunya*, IEC, various years; Fundació Jaume Bofill 1989.

FIGURE 1
LEVELS OF LOCAL GEOVERNMENT IN CATALONIA:
IDENTITY AND FUNCTIONALITY

| | High identity<br>*Potential for strengthing* |
|---|---|
| SMALL MUNICIPALITIES | CITIES AND NON-METROPOLITAN *COMARQUES* |
| Low functionality | High functionality |
| PROVINCIAL GOVERNMENTS | METROPOLITAN GOVERNMENT AGENCIES |
| | Low identity |

## CATALAN GOVERNANCE: THE MULTILEVEL DETERMINATION OF PUBLIC POLICIES

The relative position of the different levels between which governance in Catalonia is fragmented has been analyzed, until now, in terms of public spending, human resources and taxation. We have considered the *Generalitat* as the axis of a multilevel complexity: in its double pluri-national context and in relation to the internal system of local powers. All this has provided information of great interest concerning the structure of political power in Catalonia. But this information reveals far more about the operational aspect of this structure than it does about its strategic aspect. In order to cast some light on this latter aspect a policy perspective needs to be taken. We discuss the level that predominates in each of the functions of government, and then we derive degrees of impact of each of these levels on each group of policies. This provides a much more accurate overview of the real structure of political power in Catalonia in terms of its territorial distribution.

### *The EU, the state and the Generalitat: building multilevel patterns of policy-making*

We need to make clear the multilevel allocation of public roles – strategic regulation, formulation and service delivery – in each policy area. Table 12 aims to show which is the predominant institutional actor in the performance of each of these functions, within some of the main policy areas in Catalonia today. In the first three policy areas, the EU performs intensive roles of strategic regulation, while the state predominates as the policy formulation level and the *Generalitat* principally plays an

TABLE 12
MULTILEVEL POLICY-MAKING IN CATALONIA (I)

| | Predominant institutional actor | | |
|---|---|---|---|
| Policy sector | Strategic regulation | Formulation | Provision |
| Telecommunications | EU | State | State |
| Employment | EU | State | *Generalitat* |
| Environment | EU | *Generalitat* | *Generalitat* |
| Social protection | EU | State | State |
| Immigration | EU | State | State/*Generalitat* |
| Housing | State | State/*Generalitat* | *Generalitat* |
| Education | State | *Generalitat* | *Generalitat* |
| Health | State | *Generalitat* | *Generalitat* |
| Language | *Generalitat* | *Generalitat* | *Generalitat* |

operational role. In the middle group, Europeanization is quite low, but the functions at regional level continue to be limited by the action of the state: both levels play key roles. Finally in the last three policy areas, the *Generalitat* predominates as the actor of government, with quasi-monopolistic powers of policy definition and service provision.

The analytical framework that has been developed up to this point allows the policy areas in Catalonia to be divided into three groups – economic, social and emerging policies – and the degree of impact of each institutional level to be established (see Table 13). For the four levels (EU, state, *Generalitat* and local governments) the performance of legislative powers and the formulation of policy contents grants a high degree of involvement. Furthermore, for the state and territorial levels, figures of public spending and human resources are taken into account. The development of management tasks, or in the case of the EU of symbolic action or non-legislative determination of frameworks of action, grants a medium degree of intervention. Finally, low involvement should be understood as the development of residual roles (low degree of involvement).

The most significant conclusions are the following. Policy formulation relating to the economy is made along an EU–state axis, with a reduced presence of the *Generalitat*. Policies of the welfare state are more widely fragmented, though they are far from being symmetrical: the Catalan government emerges as predominant, with a continuation of a significant role played by the state and a reduced impact of European and local levels. The European social dimension continues to have a low level of impact on the key areas of the welfare state in Catalonia. On the other hand, it displays degrees of greater impact on traditional but less central areas (health and safety) in emerging areas that had been underdeveloped

TABLE 13
MULTILEVEL POLICY-MAKING IN CATALONIA (II)

| Policies | Degree of level of involvement in policy-making | | | |
|---|---|---|---|---|
| | EU | State | Generalitat | Local governments |
| Economic | | | | |
| Fiscal | High | High | Medium | Low |
| Industrial | High | High | Medium | Medium |
| Energy | High | High | Low | Low |
| Employment | Medium | High | Medium | Medium |
| | High | High | Medium | Medium/low |
| Welfare state | | | | |
| Health | Medium | Medium | High | Low |
| Education | Low | Medium | High | Low |
| Social protection | Medium | High | Low | Low |
| Housing | Low | Medium | High | Medium |
| | Medium/low | Medium/high | High | Low |
| Emerging policy areas | | | | |
| Language | Low | Medium | High | Low |
| Environment | High | High | High | Medium |
| Immigration | High | High | Medium | Medium |
| Telecoms | High | High | Low | Low |
| Gender equality | Medium | Medium | High | Medium |
| | Medium/high | High | Medium/high | Medium/low |

(gender equality) and in areas that are more directly linked to European cohesion policies (programmes against social exclusion in deprived areas). Finally, it is the emerging public policy areas that exhibit the highest levels of intergovernmental confluence, and it is here that multilevel decision-making is greatest (Gomà and Subirats 1998).

Overall, the thesis of territorial complexity as a key element of Catalan governance is verified entirely. No institutional level manages to situate itself exclusively in the area of maximum impact, but even so the high profile of the EU, the state and the *Generalitat* expresses the relevance of these three levels in the complex policy-making process in Catalonia. Local governments are situated behind them, with a certain degree of non-residual presence in the policies considered. Nevertheless, this should not lead us to false conclusions. Beyond the policy areas that we have looked at, the Catalan system of local governments is already unfolding strategic roles of a new type in the areas of economic development (strategies for endogenous development), personal social services (anti social exclusion and community development) and urban policies (urban regeneration, community-oriented urban planning). Thus, they are also fully incorporated within the fragmented scenario of governance in Catalonia. We investigate this phenomenon further below.

### *The expanding contribution of local authorities to multilevel governance*

Previous sections note the weak position of the system of local authorities within the Catalan governance model in terms of the management of public resources. We also noted local degrees of impact on policy areas below the other levels of government. Nevertheless, we noted that the situation is changing rapidly, and that local governments in Catalonia are beginning to make very significant contributions in policy areas which until recently were unexplored by or excluded from the local agenda.

Until the end of the 1980s, the agendas of Catalan municipalities in effect were comparatively close to the model of the low-intensity municipal welfare state of the countries of southern Europe. Beyond general basic services (infrastructure, security, transport systems, cleaning, waste collection etc.), local public intervention was structured around:

(1) an urban dimension, combining the dual roles of, on the one hand, macro-regulation of land-use by means of planning and, on the other, micro-interventions in the physical renewal of highly deprived areas; and
(2) a social dimension, also with a dual internal structure: the provision of universalistic cultural services, and the establishment of a network of personal social services.

In parallel to all this, an emergent selection of economic, sociocultural and territorial processes began to have a major effect on the agenda of local policies: agendas expand, local governments acquire an unexpected relevance in the regulation of new social conflicts, and the municipalities find channels of strategic positioning in the framework of complexity.

*Dimensions of change and impacts on local agendas: the economic-employment dimension*. The effects of structural economic crisis on the territory has created almost devastating effects in Catalan industrialized metropolitan areas. At the centre of these effects, the lack and precariousness of employment constitutes, for many parts of the population, the defining axis of a new daily reality. Beyond this, no-one seems to know how to reactivate the now-exhausted seeds of growth: the political responses to the crisis, at a state and regional level, display very clear limits. In synthesis, the industrial and labour crisis, added to the centrality of the territorial factor in the emerging models of development, become the key factors in the emergence of economic policies onto local agendas. If up until now the economic sphere had been excluded from the municipalities' action programmes, in the new context these municipalities find themselves impelled first to design imaginative responses to the problem of unemployment, and later to elaborate strategies of local development which offer new horizons of economic growth for their own communities.

*The sociocultural dimension.* In this sphere, two phenomena take place which have a direct effect on the specific contribution of local government to the provision of welfare. First, social inequality adopts a pluri-dimensional character and there appear new needs that cannot be translated into the basic logic of the traditional model of welfare. Secondly, the political culture of welfare gains a new dimension. Welfare is already not just the response to a set of homogenous needs to be dealt with from the central state, but also the response to a set of risks and expectations connected to community life. It stops being merely a need for social protection, and becomes the result of developing a series of cohesive relationships within a local community.

*The urban-development dimension.* The model of the massive expansion in population and housing, and the degeneration of the inner city, came to a terminal crisis at the hands of the deindustrialization process. The end of this crisis, at the end of the 1980s, involved the unfolding of complex processes concerning the redefinition of space. In particular, the *new*, diffuse post-industrial cities present a series of emerging characteristics: a multinuclear structure; a variety of relationships with enormously heterogeneous densities, intensities and time frames; a process of accelerated change into directional centres of the global economy; and a series of new urban social divisions. These factors all increased the potential for the economic fragmentation of space and the increase in prosperity became compatible with a greater spatial division between social classes. The town planning agendas of the Catalan local governments are submitted to a series of new pressures. These pressures are expressed in new policies tending towards giving the urban system greater efficiency; designing structures for sustainable and equitable expansion; and establishing the regeneration of highly deprived inner city areas and urban peripheries (Brugué and Gomà 1998).

*The expression of impact: complexity of agendas, strategic roles and relational style.* The accumulation of contextual changes recreates the conditions for a much more significant policy contribution by the municipalities. The multiple transition towards an economic model that values the territory more, towards collective identities of a more community-based nature and towards a diffuse urban system with new social division translates into:

(1) *A more complex local agenda.* On the one hand, there is a movement towards policies that were traditionally on the margins of local regulation, such as economic promotion, employment, the environment or telecommunications. On the other, there is a deepening in the level of intervention in already-consolidated sectors: new personal social services and new urban regeneration policies.

(2) *New strategic local roles.* The complexity of agendas could not have been accompanied by a redefinition on the nature of policy roles. Instead, we observe that the processes of extension and deepening in the local agenda parallel a process of functional restructuring: local governments begin to define economic, social and territorial models for their cities, against a background of alternatives, based on diverse political and ideological values.

(3) *A relational style of local policy design.* The strict reading of the previous point could lead one to think that our reasoning is unrealistic and that it would be difficult to set autonomous policy contents on a local scale in a country as small as Catalonia and in a world tending towards globalization and the concentration of power resources. In effect, it is not a case of moving from the subordination of local governments to a new political centrality of this level within a structure of hierarchical but inverted logics. It is, in short, not a case of continuing to structure the action of local governments against a logic of hierarchies of any type. The possibility that local authorities might make strategic contributions to the development and welfare of their cities must be understood within the context of the *relational style* of government. This is a style that implies governing by means of networks of interdependent decision-making actors, who are non-hierarchical and legally established. It has more to do with the influence than with the execution of authority. In short, it is the relational, multilevel logic at local level that operates as the context and extent of the strategic logic.

## CONCLUSION

Our intention in this article has been to put together some elements of analysis in relation to the real multilevel power structure in Catalonia. We have done this from a relational conception of political power, taking the view that government is ceasing to be a unidirectional, hierarchical, segregated and monopolistic action, and is becoming a network of relationships by means of which powers of influence are more or less evenly distributed among multiple actors. From this perspective, we have suggested a multilevel pattern in Catalonia. There are two ideas that deserve emphasis: first, the *Generalitat* has a predominant presence in the multilevel scenario of governance in Catalonia. However, this predominance has major limitations of different natures: the difficulties of direct dialogue with the EU – an increasingly relevant constraint, as the Europeanization of policies develops – its fiscal dependency on the state, and the continued predominance of the Spanish state in the symbolic sphere. Secondly, the emerging multilevel governance system in Catalonia continues to display a persistent institutional weakness: that of local government. Their relative position in terms of their available resources has not improved. Nevertheless, they are beginning to play strategic roles in some relevant policy-making areas.

## REFERENCES


Batley, R., and G. Stoker (1991): *Local Government in Europe: Recent Trends and Changes*, London: Macmillan.

Brugué, Q., and R. Gomà (1998): *Gobiernos Locales y Políticas Públicas* [Local Governments and Public Policies], Barcelona: Ariel.

Esping-Andersen, G. (1990): *The Three Worlds of Welfare Capitalism*, Cambridge: Polity Press.

Guibernau, M. (1997): *Nationalisms*, London: Macmillan.

Gomà, R., and J. Subirats (1998): *Políticas Públicas en España* [Public Policies in Spain], Barcelona: Ariel.

Kooiman, J. (1993): *Modern Governance. New Government–Society Interactions*, London: Sage.

Leibfried, S., and P. Pierson (1996): *European Social Policy. Between fragmentation and integration*, Washington: Brookings.

Marks, G., and F. Scharpf (1996): *Governance in the European Union*, London: Sage.

Pierson, P. (1996): *Dismantling the Welfare State?*, Cambridge: Cambridge University Press.

Vallvé, J. (1999): *La Política Regional a la Unió Europea* [The Regional Policy of the European Union], Barcelona: Mediterrània.

## SOURCES OF STATISTICAL INFORMATION

Catalan Statistics Institute, *Anuari Estadístic* [Statistical Yearbook], different issues.
*Catalunya 1977–1987* [Catalonia 1977–1987], Fundació Jaume Bofill.
Catalan Government Economy Department, *Nota d'Economia.*
Catalan Government Health Department, *Planificació Sanitàri* [Sanitary Planning].
Spanish Public Administrations Department, *Boletín Estadístico* [Statistical Bulletin], different issues.
Statistics from the Catalan Government Education Department, from the Personal Social Services Department of the Barcelona Provincial Government and from the Delegation of the Spanish Government in Catalonia.

# The Transformation of the Portuguese Political System: European Regional Policy and Democratization in a Small EU Member State

JOSÉ MAGONE

## EUROPEAN PUBLIC POLICY AND DEMOCRATIZATION THEORY

One of the most neglected aspects of European integration studies has been the democratization effects on the semi-periphery of the European continent. The forthcoming central and eastern European enlargement may gain some insights from the integration experience of the southern European countries, in general, and Portugal, in particular. The restructuring of the EC/EU after 1985 represents an historically important, new qualitative stage of the European integration process. Suddenly, the integration of European public policy in the creation of the Single European Market (SEM) and the Economic and Monetary Union (EMU) set in motion a process of convergence of the member states' policy-making structures and cultures, both with each other and in relation to the EU. The transnationalization of policy-making already existed as a phenomenon in the origins of the EC, but it gained a more integrated, long-term and lasting impact. The work of Jacques Delors and others in integrating several emerging policy areas around the projects of SEM and EMU were an excellent opportunity for the new democracies of the southern semi-periphery, namely Spain, Portugal and Greece, to use it to push forward their interests related to economic and social cohesion.

Beyond the input of these new democracies aiming to achieve concessions in economic and social cohesion policies, they further regarded the technocratic EC as a means to consolidate the structures of their weak democracies. These paradoxical expectations of the southern

European countries in relation to the EC/EU were contradictory to the evaluation of most other west European democracies. The EC/EU's technocratic approach was regarded as a means to improve the democratic quality, efficiency and transparency of their own administrations. According to Whitehead (1991), this process can be called 'democratization by convergence'. The adjustment of the administrative, legal and political structures to the EC/EU was evaluated as the only way to strengthen democratic structures in these countries. Such a linkage between democratization and European integration has been the EC's policy since the Birkelbach Report of the European Parliament in 1962 and it was enshrined in the treaties. The EC was not content with a mere formal democratic structure from future members. Beyond that it asked for sustainability and the ability to absorb and honour the *acquis communautaire*. One could say that the Portuguese case, along with those of the other southern European members, deviated from that of the first enlargement in 1973. For the first time, the supranational EC was asked to design policies which would assure economic and social cohesion across the EC. The policies of cohesion have to be regarded as a means of democratizing the new member states by creating the necessary structures so that these economically and socially disadvantaged populations were able to enjoy the same equality of opportunities in the access to the forthcoming SEM and EMU.[1] This article argues that European regional policy through the Common Support Frameworks (CSF) was a crucial means of democracy-building and structuring in the Portuguese case. The policy formulation, making and implementation of national policies became increasingly subsumed in long-term European programmes. This not only had a lasting modernizing effect, but it also subsequently paved the way to strengthen the democratic structures of the country at local, regional and national levels.

## ESTABLISHMENT OF DEMOCRATIC GOVERNANCE: THE EU'S IMPACT

After the very difficult transition to democracy between 1974 and 1976, Portuguese political elites had to transform the poorest country in western Europe from a formal to a sustainable democracy which would overcome the past traditions of patrimonialism based on clientelism, patronage, closed-mindedness and repression. The revolutionary *intermezzo* did not facilitate this task. Portugal was economically bankrupt, most of the larger enterprises were nationalized and the country had lost a huge colonial empire. This was complicated by a constitutional settlement which defined Portugal as moving towards a classless society and which was still extremely constrained by the military, which had the right to monitor the democratization process for a further five years until 1982. The party ideological climate was very conflictive. No party was able to achieve a strong majority in the new Assembly of the Republic, creating further instability in an already unstable political system. Between 1976 and 1985, Portugal experienced nine governments which lasted for 328 days on average. This created major problems to transform a system of authoritarian governance into a system of democratic governance (Magone 1997b).[2] Indeed, in these first ten years of democracy and beyond, authoritarian and patrimonial forms of behaviour continued to coexist with new democratic forms of behaviour based on citizen-friendly policies, accountability and transparency. The lack of governmental and parliamentary stability prevented a thorough reform of public administration. Instead, reforms were delayed to a later date because of emerging problems such as the stabilization of the economy and the demilitarization of the constitution. This so-called 'post-Salazarism' (a term coined by Joaquim Aguiar) would remain a major feature of the transformation of the Portuguese political system into a democratic governance system (Aguiar 1983, 1984). After the explosion of mass participation during the revolution and the occupation of the political field by the military, the politicians avoided consulting the population or actually engaging in debate with civil society. This democratic governance system in the making still neglected the weak civil society.

The Europeanization of public administration had already started in the early 1980s and became an important priority after 1986, in view of preparing for the Portuguese presidency of the EU Council of Ministers in 1992. The integration of the Portuguese bureaucratic structures into the COREPER mechanisms and the committees of the Commission steadily changed the nature of governance in the Portuguese case. This integration of bureaucratic structures led to the opening-up of the previously closed-minded authoritarian bureaucratic structure. Moreover, this convergence and cooperation with other national administrative structures was a gateway to introduce reforms within its own structures. This process did not happen overnight, but it has remained continuous throughout the 1990s (Magone 2000).

Indeed, simultaneously with EC membership, Portugal experienced more political and economic stability. The emergence of a charismatic leader, Anibal Cavaco Silva of the PSD, in 1985 gave political stability to the Portuguese political system until 1995. Moreover, in 1995 the PS government under António Guterres, instead of returning to past ideological habits of destroying the achievements of its predecessor, built on the positive results of Cavaquismo.[3] This is probably the main reason why in the 10 October 1999 elections Guterres was able to win once again with a relatively strong majority. Cavaco Silva will remain an important figure in Portuguese history in relation to European integration because he laid the foundations for a restructuring of the Portuguese administration and economy. He used the support of the EC/EU to develop long-term development plans which would have at their core the improvement of the education sector, the efficiency of the agricultural sector, administrative reform and sound macroeconomic policies. The 'decade of reforms' was possible because Cavaco Silva was able to rely on an absolute majority from 1987 to 1995.[4]

Quite crucial in this respect was the introduction of a vast programme to modernize the public administration. Particularly, the upgrading of civil servants' qualifications, decentralization of the civil service to the regions and the establishment of programmes to train civil servants in a more citizen-friendly approach based on accountability and transparency were emphasized in the reform of public administration. A secretariat for this modernization (*Secretariado para a modernizacao da administracao* (SMA)) was established to promote and supervise this reform. These efforts of administrative modernization were continued by the Guterres government. This transformation of the administration is partly because of the domestic necessity to improve its efficiency, but to a certain extent is related to the growing pressure coming from the EC to respond quickly to European public policy thrusts. The administration had to increase its efficiency in view of facilitating the absorption, implementation and monitoring of the structural funds. This was naturally not achieved overnight (Magone 1997a: 53–7). Between 1986 and 1989, several cases of fraud were discovered related to phantom vocational training courses (Eisfeld 1989). This possibility of fraud was reduced in subsequent generations of the CSF. Indeed, this is also a response to demands coming from northern European countries to prevent the loss of structural funds. European regional policy in the form of the structural funds became one of the central policies pushing the Portuguese political system towards a democratic governance system. In the Portuguese case, Europeanization meant not only modernization, but also democratization of policy-formulation, policy-making and policy implementation processes. The design of European public policy did not only require transparency and accountability of the policy process, but it was designed to mobilize citizens to play a role in shaping their concrete reality in a European democratic convergence towards SEM and EMU.

### *European regional policy as a central policy*

This transformation from authoritarian to democratic governance is related naturally to the fact that modern political systems are subject to a growth in complexity in society, administration and policy-making (Luhmann 1998: 134–44). It means that it is a transition from a closed-minded to an open-minded model of decision-making, the latter being based on accountability and transparency. Obstacles to this transformation may lead to a democratic political system with a semi-open-minded attitude, particularly when it is under strain to produce output legitimacy in terms of policies and improvement of the population's living conditions. The centrality of a citizen-friendly approach as the basis of modern democracies limits the possibilities of political elites to return to closed-minded forms of behaviour. Political learning becomes an essential element of democratic governance (Bermeo 1992: 274–5). Political learning does not involve simply the ability to adjust to new situations, but to recognize reflexively past mistakes and change policy accordingly. The integration of Portugal into the EC/EU was a major factor in structuring Portuguese democratic governance towards an open-minded, reflective, citizen-friendly, transparent and accountable political and administrative behaviour. This did not materialize soon after membership, but developed gradually as a response to the pressures coming from European public policy, learning from the experiences of other member states and the slow development of national, regional and local civil societies. Although the EU is still regarded today as having a democratic deficit and being essentially a technocratic supranational institution (Bach 1999), one cannot deny it is in a process of growing democratization and able to learn from past experiences (e.g. the EU's response to the resignation of the Santer Commission in 1999). According to Scharpf (1998), the EU cannot hope to gain an input legitimacy in the short term, in the sense of a government *by* the people (Chryssochoou 1996; Weiler 1997), but for the moment can only achieve an output legitimacy in a sense of a 'government *for* the people'. In this sense, one has to understand the EU's democratizing effects as coming from agreed European public policy-making, promoting a multilevel system of governance.

As a consequence, the Europeanization of the member states, meaning essentially the adjustment and convergence of public administrations and policy-making to decisions taken at a supranational level, tells only partly what is happening presently in the relationships between the supranational level and the member states (Ladrech 1994; Featherstone 1998). In reality the process is one of a double convergence and adjustment between the Euro-polity in the making and the member states. This institutional and structural adjustment has a different outlook in the different member states because of their different trajectories to democracy. Portugal as a late-comer to this club was very fortunate to join the EU, when Jacques Delors pushed the EU towards the path of democratic output legitimacy, forcing member states to adjust accordingly. Indeed, some founding countries such as Italy had difficulties adjusting to the EC's change of approach between 1985 and 1995. The crucial element of this silent revolution in the relationships between the EU and the member states took place between the agreement on the Single European Act (SEA 1986) and the approval of the second Delors package (Edinburgh summit 1992).

One of the most important EU policies emerging from this silent revolution was European regional policy, which was able to profit from an integration of certain funds of CAP, the European Social Fund (ESF) and the European Regional Development Fund (ERDF). Until 1988, there was lack of political will to transform the structural funds into a strategic instrument of social and economic cohesion. The lack of an overall aim and ambition as well as financial constraints produced only modest results (Armstrong 1995: 34–41). The first efforts were made after Greece's entry into the EC in 1981, with the integrated Mediterranean programmes which were designed to prepare Greece, southern regions of Italy and France to the forthcoming Iberian enlargement. According to Lord Cockfield, the Commissioner responsible for the implementation of the Single European Market during this period, the first Delors Package in 1988 was designed to gain the support of the southern European countries for the SEM. This shows that the Europeanization of political systems has to be put in the context of the changing architecture of both the institutions and interactions between the EU's supranational level and the member states (Cockfield 1994: 45–6; Tondl 1998).[5]

From then on, the Portuguese political system adjusted gradually to the principles and priorities set by the European policy-making process. This was possible because what was once (before 1986) a lukewarm support for European integration by the population soared to overwhelming support at the end of 1989, when CSF1 was approved and came into force.[6] Meanwhile, ten years of integrated European regional policy led to a substantial change of democratic governance in Portugal.

### *European regional policy and a change in the rationale of public administration*

The adjustment of public administration to the emerging pressures coming from European regional policy became a major priority. Between 1987 and 1989, Portugal had to submit a Regional Development Plan to the Commission in time to allow it to negotiate a CSF, which would define the EU's financial participation in this process. For this purpose, structural adjustments were undertaken to respond more quickly to problems that may appear between the EU and the Portuguese administration. The new democratic political system had a very fragmented and inefficient structure to deal with regional policy. Indeed, until 1983 the decision-making process was concentrated in the Ministry of Finance and Planning, while the decentralized implementation structures, the five so-called Regional Coordinating Commissions (*Comissões Coordenadoras Regionais* (CCR)) founded in 1979, were under the control of the Ministry of Internal Administration. This changed with the coming to power of the Central Block (*Bloco Central*) government, a coalition between the PS and the PSD. This coalition was designed to prepare Portugal for forthcoming EC membership. In 1984, the General-Secretariat for Regional Development (*Secretariado Geral para Desenvolvimento Regional*) was created in the Ministry of Internal Administration. Subsequently a Interministerial Commission for Planning and Regional Development (*Comissão Interministerial para o planeamento e desenvolvimento regional*) was established to coordinate the policies of the different government departments with a view to achieving the maximum impact on regional development. At a later stage, the General-Secretariat was upgraded to a General-Directorate of Regional Development within the Ministry of Planning and Territorial Organization, which remains in place today. At the same time, a basic document on the regional development policy and the means and instruments to implement it was approved by the Portuguese Council of Ministers. This document was still very general and did not go into detail, but in any case it stated that the regional instruments had to be adjusted to the needs of the different regions of Portugal. Closer to membership and following a request from the European Commission, the Portuguese government in 1985 sent a first version of the 1986–90 programme for regional development, which was (in comparison to the regional development plans of the other countries) very generic and broad and characterized by a lack of reliable statistics (Pires 1998: 42–4).

This showed clearly the main problem of the Portuguese public administration which was still struggling against many decades of underdevelopment imposed by an authoritarian regime, which tended to abuse statistics or even neglect to collect reliable figures. The main problem was to present reliable statistics about the five administrative regions in continental Portugal, Acores and Madeira (Oliveira 1996: 393).[7] The programme of regional development was designed to assure Portugal's access to the ERDF. After negotiations with the European Commission a more detailed programme, the National Programme of Community Interest as Incentive for the Productive Activity (*Programa Nacional de Interesse Comunitário de Incentivo para a Actividade Produtiva* (PNICIAP)), was approved, which assured Lisbon's eligibility for regional development funds (Pires 1998: 45–6).

This first major experience with the EC/EU's decision-making processes led after 1987 to a better preparation of the regional development plans to avoid delays in the decision-making process. The negotiation process became more smooth in the first and second CSF. Also, in terms of the aims and objectives of the CSF1 (1989–93) and CSF2 (1994–99), one can see a concentration around a smaller number of objectives. CSF1 contained six axes within Objective 1 funding, comprising economic infrastructure, productive investment, human resources, agrarian development, industrial reconversion and regional development. In CSF2 this was reduced to four axes (human resources and employment, competitiveness factors of the economy, quality of life and social cohesion, and regional economic base). Moreover, the operational programmes were reduced from 60 to 14. This naturally helped to debureaucratize the whole structure by concentrating the funds among fewer operational programmes. Moreover, the Cavaco Silva government regarded CSF2 as the last chance for Portugal to receive structural funds from the EU, in view of the forthcoming enlargement to central and eastern Europe as well as the need for structural funds coming from the eastern Bundesländer in Germany. This led to a very active participation of the whole Portuguese administration. Further, after the Portuguese presidency in the first semester of 1992, the government was very keen to consult groups from civil society to counteract the criticisms about the way CSF1 was decided in 1989.[8] Indeed, in CSF1 the Portuguese government was under time pressure to elaborate a consistent regional development plan comprising the whole territory. The Portuguese government also decided to submit the regional development plan before it was even known what amount of funding would be allocated to the individual countries. Portugal was the only country making this early submission. This was naturally both a strategic choice to achieve an early approval of the CSF2, but at the same time it was intended to show public opinion how efficiently the government was working on behalf of the Portuguese people. Institutionally, the government decentralized many of its implementation structures to the CCRs and to the municipalities. At the same time it increased its coordination efforts at all levels of the political system. At governmental level, a Governmental Commission for the Coordination of the Community Funds under the chairmanship of the Ministry of Planning and Administration of the Territory was established, while at the administrative level several controlling and coordinating positions were created to assure an optimal use of the funds. The monitoring committee on the structural funds, consisting of 50 members from the central, autonomous regional governments of Acores and Madeira and the CCRs and 12 members from the EU institutions, was not changed at all (Pires 1998: 160–66). This speedy process towards submission was criticized by the Portuguese Economic and Social Council (*Conselho Economico e Social* (CES)) in its opinion of 30 July 1993, highlighting that, apart from the fact that civil society was only sparsely represented and involved in the whole decision-making process, the government had to think also about a sustainable strategy after 1999, so that the achieved gains would not be lost again (CES 1996: 177–87).

The changeover from a social democratic to a socialist administration after the October 1995 elections did not change the overall approach towards the modernization of the administration. Indeed, the socialist government under Guterres emphasized the aspect of continuity in policy-making. In the government programme, adopted by the Assembly of the Republic in November 1995, administrative reform towards decentralization, transparency and accountability is a major aspect. This is linked to the idea of development based on the population's active participation. One of the big objectives is the creation of administrative regions, which would bring the decision-making process closer to the citizens (Assembleia da Republica 1996: 20–29). The 8 November 1998 referendum led to the rejection of this ambitious project of the Socialist

Party. The only alternative left to the Guterres government was to decentralize public administration and improve the interfaces between the elected local governments and the extended regional arms of the public administration, the five CCRs. The recent submission of the economic and social development plan under the heading 'A Strategic Vision to Win the Twenty-First Century 2000–2006' to the European Commission (in the context of negotiating the CSF for the next six years) makes it crucial to further decentralize, coordinate and improve the administrative structures in order to maximize the impact of the structural funds in Portugal (MEPAT 1999).[9]

One of the major problems that the Portuguese public administration has had to face until now was to overcome the deficiencies inherited from 48 years of authoritarian patrimonial approaches to public policy. In the first decade of membership in the EU, this led to a very passive, receptive attitude of Portuguese policy-makers in the process of negotiations with the European Commission. Changes to the CSF had to be agreed after consultation of the monitoring committee on the implementation of the structural funds by the responsible Commissioner himself. It took a long time before these adjustments could be made. Also, the ideology of partnership between the public and private sectors took a long time to materialize, if at all, because of the lack of tradition of cooperation between the state and civil society as well as lack of cooperation between firms (Syrett 1993, 1994; 1997: 104–11). The first decade could be seen also as a means to educate the management in small and medium-sized enterprises to modernize the culture of their firms in the light of the forthcoming SEM and EMU. The rhetoric did not match the reality. In spite of that, after 1995 all these efforts to recreate the Portuguese economic strategy began to pay off. The transnationalization of cooperation of Portuguese businesses created a dynamic, daring and self-confident economy. A process of internalization and administrative learning led to the establishment of a more citizen-friendly and transparent political system. At the same time the experience of the CSF has led to a simplification of procedures of approval, implementation and adjustment of projects. Although Portugal had to internalize within a decade a reflexive mode of policy-making and overcome the legacy of authoritarian governance, one can come to an overall positive verdict. There are still many problems to overcome, but the transition to democratic governance, reinforced by being part of a community of democratic countries and monitored by a supranational institutional framework, transformed the country in public administrative terms.

### *European regional policy and regional development*

One of the major obstacles towards economic and social development in Portugal was and still is the low level of qualifications of the Portuguese working population. Education has remained the single most important issue in the transformation of the Portuguese political system from authoritarian to democratic governance. Still today, the sixth periodic report on development of the regions of the EU acknowledges that, in spite of the progress made, the Portuguese structure of qualifications is dominated by low-skilled workers and is still by far underdeveloped in comparison to the economies of the north (European Commission 1999a: 132). In 1992, almost half of the working population was unskilled or semiskilled (see Table 1).

The competitive advantage of the Portuguese economy was (until the establishment of the SEM) in the low-paid, labour-intensive textiles, clothing and footwear industries, even if some technological innovation and modernization efforts were made in this period. One of the main tasks of Portuguese governments was to upgrade the quality of the economy by supporting the research and development efforts of small and medium-sized enterprises. Central to this was the need to change the culture of enterprises towards the SEM, because the competitive advantage began to be challenged in the 1990s by similar products coming from central and eastern Europe as well as south-east Asia. Change became an imperative to make economic and social development in Portugal more sustainable.

After 48 years of reluctant education policies (Cortesão 1982), education sciences and the education sector became the central element of any strategy of development (Stoer 1986). Indeed, by 1960, 40.3 per cent and, by 1970, 33.6 per cent of the population was still illiterate. In 1991, 15.3 per cent of the population was illiterate. The percentage of

TABLE 1

DISTRIBUTION OF DEPENDENT WORKERS BY LEVEL OF QUALIFICATIONS, 1992

| Professional category | % |
|---|---|
| Higher management | 2.2 |
| Medium management | 2.2 |
| Lower management | 4.1 |
| Highly skilled professionals | 39.2 |
| Semiskilled professionals | 17.4 |
| Unskilled professionals | 11.4 |
| Apprentices | 10.9 |
| Unknown level | 8.5 |

*Source*: Soares 1993: 175.

people who could read and write but who had achieved no school degree was 21.1 per cent in 1960, but this was reduced to 2.4 per cent in 1991 (Barreto and Preto 1995: 89). Today illiteracy is a phenomenon found among the older echelons of the population in the most disadvantaged regions of inner Portugal. In the same period, the rate of schooling has increased exponentially to respond to the needs of a democratizing society. Indeed, between 1974–75 and 1990, pre-school education has increased between 35 and 40 per cent; in the secondary sector it increased by 169 per cent; and in higher education by 158 per cent (Grilo 1995: 186). This exponential growth was naturally a major pressure on government to improve the quality of this sector.

A specific programme for the development of education in Portugal (*Programa Especifico para o desenvolvimento da educacão em Portugal* (PRODEP)) was negotiated with the EU within the CSF. It has now been running for ten years and led to major successes in improving this crucial area of Portuguese development strategy. Indeed, the European Commission has included the results of PRODEP in its list of success stories of the structural funds. PRODEP I (1989–93) and PRODEP II (1995–99) were financed 63–75 per cent by the EU, while the other 25–40 per cent was met by the Portuguese government and the private sector. Most of the 1.13bn ECUs of PRODEP I were directed towards improvement of school infrastructures, teacher training and cooperation between businesses and schools. Over 4,000 new courses were approved with the EU's support between 1989 and 1993 (European Commission 1999b). PRODEP is designed to give more structure to the growing demand of Portuguese society for education courses.

In the 1970s and 1980s, the education sector had major difficulties in meeting the demands of society. The emergence of new private universities complementing the public institutions led to a more diversified education sector. Although in the early 1990s the quality of the new private universities was very low, this changed in the second half of the 1990s because of the Portuguese government's willingness to introduce quality audit inspections. In spite of all that, Portugal has one of the highest drop-out rates in higher education. The positive results of PRODEP for the improvement of the Portuguese economy will only be measured in a long-term perspective, in spite of the fact that it helped to stabilize an important policy area for Portuguese society, which is extremely attached to a meritocratic understanding of equality of opportunities in a democratic political system (Grilo 1996: 432–4).

One of the main aims of the structural funds was to improve the industrial sector. A specific programme for the development of Portuguese industry (*Programa Especifico para o desenvolvimento da industria portuguesa* (PEDIP)) was designed to increase its competitiveness. According to evaluation studies of PEDIP I (1989–93), most of the regions outside the Lisbon–Porto axis were not very successful in developing projects in time and so absorbing the share of funds allocated to them. Multinationals located on the coast were the most successful enterprises in submitting projects during this phase. It is difficult to assess the results of PEDIP II (1994–99). Adjustment and lessons were learned from the previous programme, at least, by targeting more efficiently small and medium-sized enterprises. According to a study on PEDIP, one of the major aspects that undermined an even more successful implementation of the programme was the lack of decentralization and coordination between the different tiers of decision-making. The bureaucratization and lack of flexibility in terms of changing projects has been regarded as further negative aspects of PEDIP I. In PEDIP II, efforts were made to overcome this weakness. Another aspect was the will to achieve a balance in the support for projects originating outside Lisbon and Porto. Although there were other weaknesses, in general terms the implementation has been regarded as successful. The main aspect of this success is the introduction of innovation, technological development and better adjustment to markets by Portuguese firms (Rebelo 1996: 57–64; Eaton 1994). Although the Portuguese industrial sector is still characterized by low investment in research and development and is highly dependent on foreign direct investment, the European funds helped to make it more confident and stable. The traditional footwear and clothing industries still make up the dominant export sectors, but PEDIP I and II may help change this image in the longer term perspective (Corkill 1999a: 158–65). After 1997, following a long period of decline of foreign direct investment (FDI), the Portuguese economy was able to become attractive for the international economy. Most of the FDI went to the banking services sector, property and business services (European Commission 1999a: 119). According to a study by Michael Emerson and Daniel Gros, Portuguese export products from the industry sector come from clothing, vehicles, electricals, footwear and textiles, accounting for 53 per cent of Portuguese exports. They assume that enlargement to central and eastern European countries (CEECs) will increase the competition within the EU because the CEECs export structure is similar to the Portuguese one. The five goods exported by Portugal account for 33 per cent of the CEECs export structure (Emerson and Gros 1998: 19). In spite of all that, it is not the enlargement which is an imminent threat to Portuguese exports, but the Asian countries and other emerging economies. The Portuguese traditional industries of clothing, textiles and footwear also made considerable progress in terms of technological innovation in the past decade by simultaneously keeping products at a lower price (Emerson and Gros 1998: 23–9).

In terms of the structure of the economy, Portugal is becoming increasingly similar to other member states, with a booming tertiary sector of services, and declining industrial and agricultural sectors. In particular, the agricultural sector was reduced radically during the Cavaco Silva era through a 'Specific Programme for the Development of Agriculture in Portugal' (*Programa Especifico para o Desenvolvimento da Agricultura em Portugal* (PEDAP)) co-financed by the EU. A substantial reduction of farm enterprises and people working in the agricultural sector was important to increase the efficiency of Portuguese agriculture (Avillez 1994).[10]

The structural funds were also essential in bringing Portugal closer to the EU by co-financing road and railway programmes. Indeed, the recent Expo-98 was used to improve the transport infrastructure in and around Lisbon. The construction of a second bridge assuring access to Lisbon from the south was an important project for commuters between Lisbon and the outskirts at the other side of the Tagus river. Moreover, before

TABLE 2

GDP PER CAPITA IN POWER PURCHASING POWER IN RELATION TO EU AVERAGE (=100)

| Region | 1980 | 1988 | 1989 | 1990 | 1991 | 1992 | 1993 | 1994 | 1995 | 1996 |
|---|---|---|---|---|---|---|---|---|---|---|
| Norte | 44 | 54 | 57 | 52 | 53 | 56 | 60 | 62 | 62 | 62 |
| Centro | 42 | 45 | 45 | 48 | 49 | 52 | 55 | 58 | 60 | 61 |
| Lisboa e Vale do Tejo | 69 | 84 | 86 | 78 | 82 | 81 | 86 | 89 | 89 | 89 |
| Alentejo | 49 | 39 | 40 | 54 | 51 | 50 | 54 | 56 | 58 | 60 |
| Algarve | 48 | 56 | 54 | 63 | 65 | 69 | 71 | 70 | 70 | 71 |
| Acores | – | 43 | 45 | 43 | 44 | 46 | 49 | 50 | 50 | 50 |
| Madeira | – | 43 | 45 | 41 | 45 | 47 | 51 | 52 | 55 | 54 |
| **Portugal** | **53** | **61** | **63** | **60** | **62** | **63** | **68** | **70** | **70** | **70** |
| Regional disparity* | 27 | 45 | 46 | 35 | 38 | 35 | 37 | 39 | 39 | 39 |

* Between wealthiest and poorest region

*Source*: Data for 1980 from COVAS (1997: 184); European Commission (1999a: 224).

the millenium ended, the Portuguese were able to travel comfortably from Lisbon to destinations in southern Portugal, without having to cross the river by boat to gain access to the southern railway system. Another achievement was the improvement of the railway connections between the coast and inner Portugal by substantially reducing travel time. All these transformations can be regarded as important in achieving economic and social cohesion within Portugal and between Portugal and the other member states.

According to EU figures, the Portuguese GDP per capita improved considerably following accession; however, the cohesion among the regions of Portugal, including Madeira and Acores, has not improved. The disparity in GDP per capita remained stagnant throughout the 1990s. Apart from Madeira and Acores, Alentejo remained a problematic region because of its seasonal unemployment and also its peripheral status in the economy (see Table 2). Although Portugal remains the economy most exposed to asymmetrical shocks coming from the implementation of EMU, the long preparation towards it is helping the country to adjust accordingly and minimize the effects. Portugal, along with Finland, Greece and Denmark, is regarded as being one of the less prepared economies for EMU by looking at similarity of trade structure, correlation of GDP growth rate, correlation of industrial production growth, correlation of unemployment rate, intra-industry trade intensity and exports to the EU as a percentage of GDP (Emerson and Gros 1998: 45–6). Against this, it must be recognized that Portugal was able to profit from the structural funds and reverse substantially many of the disadvantages generated by the period of authoritarian governance.

### *European regional policy and civil society*

On 8 November 1998, the Socialist project of creating eight administrative regions and a more decentralized decision-making process closer to the citizen was rejected in a referendum. Although only slightly less than half of the voting population took part, two thirds voted against and only one third voted for the project. Although unsuccessful, the Guterres government managed to initiate a major debate about the advantages and disadvantages of decentralization in Portugal. The division was not along party or ideological lines: one could find supporters and opponents on both the left and the right. Ex-president Mário Soares campaigned vehemently against regionalization, while the socialist government was very keen to promote the idea as part of its 1995 party manifesto (Magone 1998b: 508–9; Corkill 1999b). The implementation of administrative regions is enshrined in the constitution, but because of the divisions among the parties it was difficult to find an all-party agreement.

The whole project had been designed to overcome the lack of horizontal coordination at regional level. Decentralized central services did not cooperate at regional level, representing a waste of financial resources. Regionalization was regarded as the best way to create an elected regional political system which would act in cooperation with the decentralized services to the benefit of the respective region. Presently, unelected district assemblies were established which are not able to fulfil this role. Regionalization was also designed to foster and coordinate intermunicipal cooperation (Pereira 1995; MEPAT 1997: 31–47)

Civil society had been engaged in the debate. The Assembly of the Republic asked major interest groups and local authorities for their views on regionalization. According to the responses given, most actors seemed to be divided about the idea. Many of the associations asked regarded the public consultation premature, pending the referendum (Assembleia da Republica 1997).

One of the aspects of European regional policy is to mobilize non-governmental political, social and economic actors for the elaboration of common projects. In the case of Portugal, during the previous period of authoritarian governance was very keen to do the opposite and prevent the input of civil society into the policy-making pròcess. After many decades of repression, the establishment of such interest groups at local and regional level is still in the making. The best case is the horizontal Community initiative INTERREG, which supports cross-border cooperation over the Portuguese and Spanish borders. INTERREG I (1990–93) allocated 384.5m ECU to the Spanish–Portuguese cross-border regions and INTERREG II (1994–99) allocated 552m ECU (Cavaco 1996: 432). These funds were used to overcome their status on the 'double' periphery of these regions in relation to the SEM (Covas 1993, 1995, 1997: 175–92). Most of the funds were invested in infrastructure, but since 1993–94 cross-border interest groups have been created to make the emerging cross-border regional civil society more sustainable. An example here is the Interregional Trade Union Councils (ITUCs) created along the Portuguese and Spanish border and part of a European-wide network of 38 ITUCs. This network is part of the European Trade Union Confederation (ETUC) and it is very keen to create cross-border regional institutions. In 1997, a European Employment Service (EURES) was founded which will assist cross-border workers to become better informed about their rights within the context of the SEM. The EURES was established between the Portuguese region of Norte Portugal and the Spanish region of Galicia. Other ITUCs in Alentejo–Extremadura, Beiras–Castilla–Leon and Algarve–Andalusia hope to achieve such a EURES for their regions as well (Magone 1999, p.139). Although these initiatives are still in their infancy, they represent the beginning of a new attitude of Portuguese and Spanish interest groups. In spite of the centralism in Portugal, civil society has become a major way forward in enriching this transformation from authoritarian to democratic governance. According to the Commission, INTERREG III will allocate to Portugal 394m euro, while 900m will go to Spain (including Spanish–French cross-border cooperation and Spain–North Africa cooperation) (European Commission 1999b). This cross-border cooperation represents an important step forward, not only by creating a European civil society where it matters – in the upgrading of living standards – but more than that it gives responsibility to civil society at local and regional level to change destinies that were decided in the past by central bureaucratic structures in Lisbon and Madrid. It is too early to make an assessment of the impact of European integration on the civil societies of Portugal and Spain, but the need to create an input legitimacy for the European integration process will probably increase the European Commission's efforts to make the involvement of civil societies at different levels of the political system a central part of the policy-making process.

## CONCLUSION

This contribution highlights the fact that the European integration process was an important reinforcing factor in transforming Portugal from an authoritarian to a democratic governance system. Integration into the EU led to a structuring and strengthening of the democratization efforts initiated by the public administration since 1974. It was particularly after accession that administrative modernization became a major issue to cope with the growth in complexity of society and the relationship to the EU policy-making process. At the same time, the membership of Portugal along with that of the other southern European countries reinforced the transformation of the EU from a mere supranational institution to a multilevel governance system. European regional policy became more sophisticated and integrated after the accession of Spain and Portugal. Aspects of social and economic cohesion became complementary to that of competitiveness. The ideology of the European social model based on solidarity and economic and social cohesion became an important key to mobilize social and political actors in shaping the political system (Hooghe 1998). At the same time it created output legitimacy for the European integration process. For Portugal, the past decade and a half of membership has induced a qualitative change of democracy. Indeed, the democratic governance system became more consolidated. The recent rejection of the regionalization proposals cannot be regarded as negative, but as a very positive event because it initiated a debate about how to improve democracy at regional and local level. In spite of a still existing democratic cynicism in Portuguese society in relation to politics and politicians, the Europeanization of Portugal has to be twinned with democratization. In this context, democracy has to be conceptualized as an open system subject to change; not a static position, but a continuing process (von Beyme 1994: 9).

## NOTES

1. Naturally this remains a long-term goal. The economic argument has until now neglected this aspect of empowering semi-peripheral citizens to change their living standards (e.g. Belloni 1994)
2. This diachronic approach is influenced by Gunther's excellent article (1996).
3. Cavaquismo derives from the name of Prime Minister Anibal Cavaco Silva and refers to his policies and charismatic style during his decade in office.
4. Anibal Cavaco Silva wrote a succinct book on the achievements of his government (see Silva Cavaco 1995); most of it is related to the liberalization of the economy.
5. The European Commission was on the defensive after the empty chair policy of Charles de Gaulle in 1965. Any social cohesion policies had to be legitimized in economic terms. This approach became quite important during the reform of the structural funds. An alliance between the southern European states and the European Commission helped to legitimize a reinforcement of economic and social cohesion policies. On the change of approach since the 1960s, see the excellent study by Cram (1997: 36–9).
6. While before 1986 the Portuguese were only moderately supportive of the EC, this changed completely after accession. Both in terms of the assessment of benefits and in support of the EU, Portugal has remained continuously among the most positive of the member states (Eurobarometer 1998, nr.49: 33).
7. In the Eurostat annual statistical yearbook on the regions, figures for Portugal existed only in 1987 for the whole of Portugal and in 1988 for the individual regions.
8. The Community allocation for the Portuguese CSF1 was 6,958bn ECUs (Pires 1998: 96). Between 1986 and 1988, Portugal was entitled to receive 1,119bn ECUs. It was only able to absorb 1,083bn, losing out on 116m ECU. Most of the funds were only absorbed by 1995 (Pires 1998: 58; Cabral 1994). A delay in absorption happened also in CSF1. In CSF2, after the approval of the Delors II Package, the amount was raised to 13,980bn ECUs plus 2,601bn coming from the new Cohesion Fund (Pires 1998: 244).

9. Agenda 2000 Portugal will receive a total of 19,029bn euros over the six-year period under the heading of Objective 1 and an ex-Objective 1 region in a transition regime (mainly for the region of Lisbon and Vale do Tejo). The number of Objectives was limited from six to three to achieve a higher, more integrated and concentrated use of the structural funds. Portugal will receive 10.36 per cent of the agreed overall sum for structural funds of 183,564bn euros, most of it to be spent on Objective 1 regions. Apart from the southern European countries, Germany is a major recipient of structural funds with a share of 15.34 per cent, directed particularly towards the eastern Länder (inforegio news, lettre d'information nr.65, June 1999).
10. While in 1970 31.7 per cent of the working population was still in the agricultural sector, in 1992 this declined to 11.6 per cent; the industrial sector remained quite stable with a slight increase from 32.3 to 33.2 per cent and the services sector soared from 36 to 55.2 per cent (Ferreira da Almeida *et al.* 1996: 319).

## REFERENCES


Aguiar, J. (1983): *A Ilusão do Poder. Análise do Sistema Partidário Portugues* [The Illusion of Power: An Analysis of the Portuguese Party System], Lisboa: Dom Quixote.

—— (1984): *O Pós-Salazarismo* [Post-Salazarism], Lisboa: Publicacões Dom Quixote.

Armstrong, H.W. (1995): 'The Role and Evolution of European Community Regional Policy', in B. Jones and M. Keating (eds.), *The European Union and the Regions*, Oxford: Oxford University Press, pp.23–62.

Assembleia da Republica (1996): *Programa do XIII Governo Constitucional. Apresentacão e Debate* [Programme of the 13th Constitutional Government. Presentation and Debate], Lisboa: Assembleia da Republica.

—— (1997): *Consulta Pública sobre a Regionalizacão. Relatório/Parecer* [Public Consultation on Regionalization. Report], Lisboa: Assembleia da Republica.

Avillez, F. (1994): 'Portuguese agriculture and the Common Agriculture Policy', in J.S. Lopes (ed.), *Portugal and EC Membership Evaluated*, London: Pinter, pp.31–50.

Bach, M. (1999): *Die Bürokratisierung Europas, Verwaltungseliten, Experten und politische Legitimation in Europa* [The Bureaucratization of Europe: Administrative Elites, Experts and Political Legitimacy in Europe], Frankfurt a.M.: Campus.

Barreto, A., and C.V. Preto (1995): 'Indicadores da Evolucão Social' [Indicators of Social Evolution], in A. Barreto (ed.), *A Situacão Social em Portugal, 1960–1995*, [The Social Situation in Portugal, 1960–1995], Lisboa: Instituto de Ciencias Sociais, Universidade de Lisboa, 1995 pp.61–162.

Belloni, F.P. (1994): *The Single Market and Socio-economic Cohesion in the EC: Implications for the Southern and Western Peripheries*, Centre for Mediterranean Studies, Occasional Paper no.8.

Bermeo, N. (1992): 'Democracy and the Lessons of Dictatorship', *Comparative Politics*, 24/3 (April), pp.273–91.

Cabral, A.J. (1994): 'Community regional policy towards Portugal', in J.S. Lopes (ed.), *Portugal and EC Membership Evaluated*, London: Routledge, pp.133–45.

Cavaco, C. (1996): 'As regioes de fronteira: perspectivas de desenvolvimento e de cooperacao transfronteirica' [The Border Regions: Perspectives of Development and Transborder Cooperation], in A.C. Fernandez and C.V. Bernardo (eds.), *Portugal-España, Ordenacion Territorial del Suroeste Europeo* [Portugal-Spain. Territorial organization in the European Southwest], Badajoz: Universidad de Extremadura.

Cockfield, Lord (1994): *The European Union, Creating the Single Market*, London: Wiley & Son.

Chryssochoou, D.N. (1996): 'Europe's Could-Be Demos: Recasting the Debate', *West European Politics* 19/4 (October), pp.787-801.

Conselho Economico e Social (CES) (1996): 'Parecer do Conselho Economico e Social sobre o Plano de Desenvolvimento Regional-PDR, Aprovado no Plenário 30 de Julho 1993' [Opinion of the Economic and Social Council on the Plan of Regional Development-PDR, Aproved by the Plenary on 30 July 1993], in *CES, pareceres e Reunioes do Conselho Económico e Social (Setembro de 1992 a Fevereiro de 1996)* [ECS. Opinions and Meetings of the Economic and Social Committee (September 1992 to February 1996], Lisboa: CES, pp.177-93.

Corkill, D. (1999a): *The Development of the Portuguese Economy, A Case of Europeanization*, London: Routledge

—— (1999b): 'Portugal's 1998 Referendums', *West European Politics* 22/2 (April) pp.186–92.

Cortesao, L. (1982): *Escola/Sociedade, Que Relacão?* [School/Society, What relationship?], Porto: Edicoes Afrontamento.

Covas, A. (1993): *Uniao Europeia e Coesao Interterritorial, A Regiao e a Uniao Europeia em Perspectiva* [European Union and Interterritorial Cohesion, The Region and the European Union in Perspective], Evora: Universidade de Evora.

—— (1995): 'La cooperation transfrontalière entre régions sous-developées: le cas d'Alentejo (Portugal) et d' Extremadure (Espagne)' [Crossborder Cooperation between Underdeveloped Regions: The case of Alentejo (Portugal) and Extremadura (Spain)], *Pole Sud* 3 (Autumn), pp.72–78.

—— (1997): *Integracao Europeia, Regionalizacão Administrativa e Reforma do Estado-Nacional* [European Integration, Administrative Regionalization and Reform of the Nation-State], Oeiras: Instituto Nacional de Administracão.

Cram, L. (1997): *Policy-Making in the European Union, Conceptual Lenses and the Integration Process*, London: Routledge.

Eaton, M. (1994): 'Regional Development Funding in Portugal', *Journal of the Association for Contemporary Iberian Studies* 7/2 (Autumn), pp.36–46.

Eisfeld, R. (1989): 'Portugal in the European Community 1986–88. The Impact of the First Half of the Transition Period', *Iberian Studies* 18/2, pp.156–65.

Emerson, M., and D. Gros (1998): *Impact of Enlargement, Agenda 2000 and EMU on Poorer Regions – The Case of Portugal*, Brussels: Centre for European Policy Studies, Working Document 125.

European Commission (1999a): *Sixth Periodic Report on the Social and Economic Situation and Development of the Regions of the European Union*, Luxembourg: Office of the Official Publications of the European Communities.

—— (1999b): 'The Community Initiatives in 2000-06: indicative allocation of funds among the Member States, 13 October 1999', IP 99/744 in Internet site of DG XVI: www.inforegio.org

Featherstone, K. (1998): "Europeanization" and the Centre Periphery: The Case of Greece in the 1990s', *South European Society and Politics* 3/1 (Summer), pp.28–39.

Ferreira da Almeida, J., A. Firmino da Costa and F.L. Machado (1996): 'Recomposicão Socioprofessional e Novos Protagonismos' [Socioprofessional recomposition and new protagonisms], in A. Reis (ed.), *Portugal, 20 Anos de Democracia* [Portugal. Twenty Years of Democracy], Lisboa: Temas e Debates, pp.307–30.

Grilo, E.M. (1995): 'Ensino Formal e as Suas Condicões' [Formal Education and its conditions], in *Portugal. Hoje* [Portugal. Today], Lisboa: Instituto Nacional de Administracão, pp.179–97.

Grilo, M. (1996): 'O Sistema Educativo' [The Education System], in A. Reis (ed.), *Portugal. 20 Anos de Democracia* [Portugal. Twenty Years of Democracy], Lisboa: Temas e Debates, pp.406–35.

Gunther, R. (1996): 'The Impact of Regime Change on Public Policy: The Case of Spain', *Journal of Public Policy* 16/2, pp.157–201.

Hooghe, L. (1998): 'EU Cohesion Policy and Competing Models of European Capitalism', *Journal of Common Market Studies* 36/4 (Dec.), pp.457–77.

Ladrech, R. (1994): 'Europeanization of Domestic Politics and Institutions: The Case of France', *Journal of Common Market Studies* 32/1 (March), pp.69–88.

Luhmann, N. (1998): *Die Gesellschaft der Gesellschaft* [The Society of Society], Bd.1. Frankfurt a.M.: Suhrkamp.

Magone, J.M. (1997a): *European Portugal: The Difficult Road to Sustainable Democracy*, Basingstoke/New York: Macmillan/St Martin's Press.

—— (1997b): 'Portugal: Das Grundprinzip demokratischen Regimeaufbaus' [Portugal: The Rationale of democratic regime building], in W.C. Müller and K. Strom (eds.), *Koalitionsregierung in Westeuropa. Bildung, Arbeitsweise und Beendigung* [Coalition government in Western Europe: Formation, Working Methods and Termination], Wien: Zentrum für angewandte Politikforschung, pp.663–703.

—— (1998a): 'Integracão Europeia e a Construcão da Democracia Portuguesa' ['European Integration and the Construction of Portuguese Democracy'], Penelope, 18, pp.123–63.

—— (1998b): 'Portugal', in *Political Data Yearbook 1998, Special issue of European Journal of Political Research* 34/3–4, pp.402–11.

—— (1999): 'European Integration and Iberian Transborder Cooperation: A Case Study of the Transregionalisation of Multi-level European Union Governance', paper presented at the Political Studies Association annual conference, University of Nottingham, 23–25 March.

—— (2000): 'The Golden Mean of Domestic European Policy Coordination: The Case of Portugal', in H. Kassim, G. Peters and V. Wright (eds.), *National Coordination of European Union Policy*, Oxford: Oxford University Press.

Ministério do Equipamento e do Planeamento do Território (MEPAT) (1997): *Descentralizacao: Regionalizacao e Reforma Democrática do Estado* [Decentralization: Regionalization and Democratic State Reform], Lisboa: MEPAT.

—— (1999): *Portugal: Plano Nacional de Desenvolvimento Económico e Social 2000–2006. Uma Visão Estratégica para Vencer o Século XXI* [Portugal: National Plan for Economic and Social Development 2000–2006. A Strategic Vision to Win in 21st century], Lisboa: MEPAT (Internet site: http://www.mercurio.min-plan.pt).

Oliveira, C. (1996): 'A questao da regionalizacão' [The question of regionalization], in C. Oliveira (ed.), *Historia dos Municipios e do Poder Local* [History of Municipalities and Local Power], Lisboa: Temas e Debates 1996, pp.494–509.

Pereira, A. (1995): 'Regionalism in Portugal', in B. Jones and M. Keating (eds.), *The European Union and the Regions*, Oxford: Oxford University Press, pp.269–80.

Pires, L.M. (1998): *A Politica Regional Europeia e Portugal* [European Regional Policy and Portugal], Lisboa: Fundacão Calouste Gulbenkian.

Rebelo, S. (1996): *European Union Regional Policy and Industrial Development in Portugal. A Case Study of the Specific Industrial Development Programme for Portugal-PEDIP*, Hull: unpublished MA dissertation, University of Hull.

Scharpf, F. (1998): *Governing in Europe. Effective and Democratic?* Oxford: Oxford University Press

Silva Cavaco, A. (1995): *A Década de Reformas* [The Decade of Reforms], Lisboa: Bertrand.

Stoer, S.R. (1986): *Educacão e Mudança Social em Portugal, 1970–1980, Uma Década de Transicão* [Education and Social Change in Portugal, 1970–1980: A Decade of Transition], Porto: Edicoes de Afrontamento.

Syrett, S. (1993): 'Local Power and Economic Policy: Local Authority Economic Initiatives in Portugal', *Regional Studies* 28/1, pp.53–67.

—— (1994): *Local Development: Restructuring, Locality and Economic Initiative in Portugal*, Aldershot: Avebury.

—— (1997): 'The Politics of Partnership:The Role of Social Partners in Local Economic Development in Portugal', *European Urban and Regional Studies* 4/2, pp.99–114.

Tondl, G. (1998): 'Regional Policy in the Southern Periphery', *South European Society and*

*Politics* 3/1, pp.93–129.

von Beyme, K. (1994): *Systemwechsel in Osteuropa* [System change in Eastern Europe], Frankfurt a.M.: Suhrkamp.

Weiler, J.H.H. (1997): 'To be a European citizen-Eros and civilization', *Journal of European Public Policy* 4/4, pp.495–479.

Whitehead, L. (1991): 'Democracy by Convergence and Southern Europe: A Comparative Politics Perspective', in G. Pridham (ed.), *Encouraging Democracy: The International Context of Regime Transition in Southern Europe*, London: Leicester University Press pp. 45–61.

## OTHER SOURCES

Alvarez-Miranda, B. (1996): *El sur de Europa y la adhesión a la Comunidad. Los debates politicos* [Southern Europe and Accession to the Community. The Political Debates], Madrid: Centro de Investigaciones Sociologicas.

Cerny, P. (1990): *The Changing Architecture of Politics, Structure, Agency and the Future of the State*, London: Sage.

European Commission (1994): *Competitiveness and Cohesion: Trends in the Regions. Fifth Periodic Report on the Social and Economic Situation and Development in the Community*, Luxembourg: Office of the Official Publications of the European Communities.

—— (1994): *Portugal – Common Support Framework, 1994–99*, Luxembourg: Office of the Publications of the European Communities.

Ferrera, M. (1996): 'The "Southern Model" of Welfare in Social Europe', *Journal of European Social Policy* 6/1, pp.17–37.

Graham, L.S. (1975): *Portugal: The Decline and Collapse of an Authoritarian Order*, London and Beverly Hills: Sage.

Lucena, M. (1976): *Evolucão do Sistema Corporativo Português* [The Evolution of the Portuguese Corporatist System] (2 vols.), Lisboa: Perspectivas e Realidades.

Magone, J.M. (1996): *The Changing Architecture of Iberian Politics. An Investigation on the Structuring of Democratic Political Systemic Culture in Semiperipheral Southern European Societies*, Lewiston NY: Mellen University Press.

Ministério do Planeamento e Ordenamento do Território (MPOT) (1994): *Preparar Portugal Para o Século XXI. Plano de Desenvolvimento Regional 1994–99* [Prepare Portugal for the 21st century: Plan of Regional Development 1994–99], Lisboa: MPOT.

Passos, M. (1987): *Der Niedergang des Faschismus in Portugal: Zum Verhältnis von Ökonomie, Gesellschaft und Staat/Politik in einem europäischen Schwellenland* [The Demise of Fascism in Portugal: On the relationship of Economy, Society and State/Politics in a European peripheral country], Marburg: Verlag für Arbeiterbewegung und Gesellschaftswissenschaft.

Rhodes, M. (1996): 'Southern European Welfare States: Identity, Problems and Prospects for Reform', *South European Society and Politics* 1/3 (Winter), pp.1–22.

Schmitter, P.C. (1975): *Corporatism and Public Policy in Authoritarian Portugal*, London and Beverly Hills: Sage.

Soares, M.C. (1993): 'Os Acordos de Concertacao Social e Emprego' [The Agreements of Social Concertation and Employment], in Conselho Económico e Social, *Os Acordos de Concertacao Social em Portugal, (I-Estudos)* [The Agreements of the Social Concertation in Portugal (I Studies)], Lisboa: CES.

Wiarda, H.J. (1979): 'The Corporatist Tradition and Corporative System in Portugal: Structured, Evolving, Transcended, Persistent', in L.S. Graham and H.M. Makler (eds.), *Contemporary Portugal. The Revolution and its Antecedents*, Austin/London: University of Texas Press.

# Cyprus and the Onset of Europeanization: Strategic Usage, Structural Transformation and Institutional Adaptation

KEVIN FEATHERSTONE

## INTRODUCTION

A glance at the literature available on Cyprus might suggest that this was an island of interest only for its past and for its complex security position. Yet as a small state in the throes of negotiating its accession to the EU, Cyprus presents an intriguing focus for a study of the process of Europeanization, the subject of this volume. As a small state, the accession negotiations emphasize the huge disparity in structural power between the applicant and the EU, highlighting the force of the external pressure on domestic adjustment processes. Indeed, it has often seemed that the EU's stance towards Cyprus (and the other current applicants) has been one of 'take it or leave it', stressing that the economic and social adjustment process will be on terms firmly set by Brussels. The Cyprus case has the additional aspect of a unique security conundrum, consequent on the Turkish occupation of more than a third of the island. Nicosia is the last divided capital in Europe and overcoming the division of the entire island, while appeasing Turkey, poses a major test of the EU's ability to engineer reconciliation on its doorstep. The EU's relations with Cyprus thus cannot be disentangled from this multidimensional chess game, and on all sides there are careful calculations of the strategic implications of engaging the EU in the island's fate. Moreover, the 'low politics' of the Cyprus application also have distinctive features. As a small state seeking to accede to an organization with an extensive and highly developed system of regulation, the process of institutional adaptation can appear mammoth. The obligations of the *acquis communautaire* require a major revision of the operation and competencies of the state administration.

Against this background, Europeanization is applied here to the domestic impact of the EU in three major areas:

(1) the pattern of discourse (specifically, the EU's role in the strategic calculations of potential gains by key actors);
(2) the structure of state–economy relations (highlighting the transformative effects of EU obligations and their significance, e.g. in relation to financial markets and EMU); and
(3) the operation of the state administration (gauging the adaptation of institutional processes to new demands such as coordination, and the effects on institutional competencies).

The following sections consider each of these aspects in turn, addressing the themes noted. In each of these areas, important processes of domestic adjustment are occurring, with manifold implications for Cypriot society.[1] Overall, the Cyprus case suggests that the significance of the Europeanization process may be more starkly illustrated by reference to the pressures evident on states outside the EU than on states at the very centre of the EU.

The background to the Cyprus application is one of a slow, conditional path to the EU. With Cyprus' largest market, Britain, joining the then EC in 1973, an Association Agreement was established between Cyprus and the Community in the same year. This provided for a customs union in two stages and within a period of ten years. The second stage did not commence, however, until 1988, largely because of the consequences of the island's division in 1974. This second stage was itself divided into two phases, with the process due to be completed in 2002–03. In the meantime, the Cyprus Government submitted an application on 4 July 1990 to enter the EU as a full member.[2] A key turning point came in March 1995 when the EU's Council of Ministers agreed, following a carefully crafted deal with Greece, that entry negotiations with Cyprus could begin six months after the conclusion of the Inter-Governmental Conference of 1996. A 'pre-accession strategy' was then established between the EU and Cyprus to prepare the latter for membership. In December 1997, the European Council confirmed that enlargement negotiations with Cyprus and five eastern European states would begin early the following year. The EU held a European Conference in London in March 1998 formally to open the process and detailed negotiations began on 3 April.

The Cyprus application was inevitably linked to the relations between the Greek and Turkish communities on the island (Joseph 1997). The Turkish invasion of the island in 1974 – following an abortive coup attempt in Cyprus by the Greek Colonels – created a long-term instability. In 1983, the Turkish Cypriots proclaimed a 'Turkish Republic of Northern Cyprus' (TRNC) for their zone, which became immediately an international pariah state, recognised only by Turkey. Successive UN and European declarations have condemned the Turkish actions (Republic of Cyprus 1998). The long-term role of the Western powers (notably Britain and the US) in this situation can be seen as either one of culpability or of genuine attempts at peacemaking. In any event, the progress of reconciliation has been painfully slow. Attempts at rapprochement have formed a continuing parallel drama to that of Cyprus' EU bid. The most recent phase followed the failure of UN-sponsored intercommunal talks held in August 1997 at Troutbeck (New York) and Glion (Switzerland). This led to a new UN initiative in September of the following year. The G-8 summit in June 1999 urged that fresh negotiations should begin in the autumn, with no preconditions, all issues on the table, and full consideration being given to all UN resolutions and treaties. The UN Security Council endorsed this plan a few days later. Proximity talks were held with the UN Secretary-General, Kofi Annan, in New York in December 1999 and were set to continue for at least two further sessions in the first part of 2000. Leaders of the two communities were still far apart as this sequence of talks got underway, however. Rauf Denktash, the leader of the TRNC, insisted on a confederal structure for Cyprus, with recognition of a separate status for the Turkish community. The Greek Cypriots – heading the only internationally recognized government on the island – called for a state with a single sovereignty, as supported by the UN Security Council. The course of these attempts at solving the island dispute looked very uncertain.

With the EU's progress to enlargement, the bargaining game over Cyprus' accession became nested in that over security (on 'nested games', see Tsebelis 1990). The strategic calculations for the two agendas became inextricably linked and this was evident in the Cypriot discourse on the EU (Theophanous 1999).

## A EUROPEAN DISCOURSE: THE STRATEGIC USES OF EU MEMBERSHIP

In the domestic debate on EU entry, the discourse has emphasized that the Cyprus application was, from the outset, primarily political in nature. This meant that EU membership was seen in a rational choice frame:

specifically, in terms of the relative gains that would accrue to Cyprus. The strongest and clearest strategic dimension inevitably involved the position of Turkey, the foreign power that looms largest over the island's fate. EU entry was seen as a foreign policy lever *vis-à-vis* Turkey, a means by which a settlement of the island's division, favourable to the Cyprus Government's stance, could be engineered. EU entry also came to serve an additional strategic use, of lesser but gradually increasing importance. This was to see membership as a tool of *economic modernization*, supported by reformists, overcoming domestic resistance to change. This second strategic usage incorporates the scope for 'blameshift' to the EU: that is, increasing support for unpopular reforms by defining them as necessary if membership is to be achieved.

The two strategic uses overlap. The strategy to gain EU entry rests on a broad political consensus within Cyprus. The majority of political leaders believe that Cyprus should accept that no derogation be sought from EU obligations. Strategically, this avoids giving the EU an excuse to block Cyprus' entry in the event of no settlement being reached with Turkey about the island's future. In accepting this strategy, the effect of the delay in resolving the island's problems is to strengthen the potency of EU membership on the domestic reform process.

The peculiar condition of Turkey's entanglement with the island meant that the security dimension overlay Cyprus' debate on EU participation from the beginning. The impact of the security dimension has been exceptional: its importance was, perhaps, matched only in the earlier cases of West German and Greek entry into the EC. Yet these latter cases were different in nature. Adenauer saw European integration, in part, as a defence against Stalin's encroachment, but it was not seen as a short- or even medium-term tool to end the division of Germany. A closer parallel is that of Karamanlis pushing Greece towards membership as, *inter alia*, it would advantage the country in its disputes with Turkey. But only in the Cyprus case is EU membership seen as a force to unblock a security entanglement. Moreover, none of the other applicants for EU membership have a similar security imperative.

The Cyprus Government's rationale in this context is to calculate that the imminent prospect of EU entry, for that part of the island over which it has actual jurisdiction, would:

(a) weaken Turkey's hold over its TRNC protectorate, as leaders of the latter become more conscious of the relative economic gains to be made by the official Cyprus state;

(b) weaken Turkey's potential to block Cyprus' entry, as Turkey itself seeks early EU membership; and
(c) reinforce the status of the Cyprus state as the only such internationally recognized authority on the island.

Any signal that the EU might retreat from, or delay, the commitment to Cyprus' entry is viewed by Greek Cypriot politicians as a diminution of the EU's historic mission and an emasculation of its foreign policy potential in post-Cold War Europe. The contrary is also relevant: a proactive EU role on Cyprus might produce a rare, distinctive foreign policy success for Brussels and increase its international prestige. A similar logic is evident in the backing given to Greek Cypriots seeking redress against the Turkish authorities via the European Court of Human Rights (ECHR).

The problem for the Cyprus Government is that this strategic usage of EU entry is constrained – potentially countermanded – by the attitudes and interests of the other relevant actors. This constraint produces an exceptional uncertainty over the course that Cyprus might follow, characterizing Cyprus as a more 'difficult' case than that of the other current applicants and creating a highly charged political atmosphere that is itself an impediment to a solution.

The greatest risk for Cyprus is that the major West European governments view it as abusing the EU framework and that they believe the Cypriot problem is too 'hot' to touch. The inclusion of Greco-Turkish disputes over Cyprus poses risks for the EU's gradually developing role in foreign and security policy (CFSP). Further, the initiative at Helsinki in December 1999 to establish an EU rapid reaction force – intended to be a crisis management capability – leaves the EU liable to intervene directly in any future conflict over Cyprus. Moreover, unlike other EU applicants, the question of Cyprus joining NATO is not even on the agenda. No advantage is identified in allowing Cyprus to join the Alliance. Turkey blocked the participation of Cyprus in the 'Partnership for Peace' process, and also its inclusion in the WEU Ministerial Council. In short, the security dimension of the Cyprus application creates major anxieties among EU governments. Seasoned European (and US) diplomats already decry the lack of change in the prevailing structure of intercommunal relations on the island. In this vein, some regard the Greek Cypriots as endeavouring to use the EU to pour new wine in an old bottle. The definition of the game remains the same, but any new opportunity like the EU is latched on to as a matter of attrition, in order to gain relative advantage. All immediate parties to the Cyprus dispute are seen as having an unrealistic expectation of an external 'saviour' coming to rescue them. Recent history suggests that neither the governments of Western Europe nor the US accept such a role. Indeed, Cypriots on all sides are seen as exaggerating the international significance of their local dispute. To some foreign observers, the status quo is less threatening than the risks involved in a bold new intervention. Greek Cypriot attempts to involve the ECHR in the intercommunal disputes are viewed warily in some quarters, as upsetting the existing balance in unpredictable ways. Turkey, it is argued, cannot be held responsible for all that happens in the TRNC territory. Recognition by the ECHR that the TRNC is an established legal order is seen in some quarters as a helpful clarification of existing conditions.

Greek Cypriot arguments about the precedents for divided states entering the EU (Germany, Greenland, Aland) are widely viewed with caution, even scepticism. The major EU governments have typically appeared loath to countenance only the Greek Cypriot community being a *de facto* member. Thus, the strategy has been one of 'constructive ambiguity', keeping all parties to the Cyprus dispute uncertain of the EU's intentions and the likely outcome. It involves two conflicting tasks: convincing Turkey that Cyprus will join the EU, with or without an intercommunal settlement, and at the same time persuading the Greek Cypriots that their entry prospects depend on them displaying a real will to compromise with the TRNC leaders. This dual strategy is seen as increasing the pressure on all sides to shift position and reach a settlement.

Inevitably, the fate of the Cyprus application for EU entry (submitted in July 1990) is tied to that made by Turkey (first submitted in April 1987). The EU is faced with a multidimensional game of chess in which it wishes to avoid a public 'defeat' for any of the players. The linkage between the applications is evident in the developments that have occurred in recent years:

(1) In August 1997, Turkey and the TRNC leaders signed an agreement that signalled the full integration of the TRNC area into the Turkish State *if* the EU proceeded with accession negotiations with Cyprus. The TRNC leader, Rauf Denktash, also threatened not to participate in any intercommunal talks if the EU proceeded with Cyprus' application. While the European Council in December 1997 agreed to move ahead with the Cypriot application and that of five central and

eastern European states, it did not do so with that of Turkey.

(2) In March 1998, Glafcos Clerides, the President of the Cyprus Republic, offered to include Turkish Cypriot representatives as full members of the official Cyprus negotiating team with the EU. However, the Turkish Cypriots refused to accept any form of participation.

(3) Since 1997, the Turkish government had been aggrieved that the EU was not proceeding faster with its own EU entry bid. The European Council, at its meeting in Helsinki in December 1999, finally upgraded Turkey's status as an applicant state. This act had required very delicate handling, to assuage the sensitivities of Turkey and Greece. Javier Solana, the EU's chief CFSP representative, had been dispatched to Ankara during the summit to reassure the government of Bulent Ecevit. Turkey had been accepted as a candidate on the same conditions as the other countries, though the expectation must be that its accession will be much later than that of the states put on the 'fast-track' in December 1997.

Despite the constraints stemming from this Cyprus–Turkey entanglement, there is evidence that the pressure emanating from the EU (collectively and from individual governments), as well as from the US, has helped to improve the climate of intercommunal relations. The decision of the Clerides Government in December 1998 not to deploy the SS-300 ground-to-air missile system, purchased from Russia, is a case in point. Turkey's foreign minister, Tansu Ciller, warned (on 10 January 1997) that her government would take direct military action against Cyprus if the missiles were deployed. EU governments and the US urged that they not be deployed, in order not to heighten tension in the region. Clerides' decision was linked crucially to his EU ambitions. Other shifts of attitude can be detected, away from tense considerations of security. The EU welcomed, for example, the decision of the Greek Cypriot leaders of the AKEL, DIKO and United Democrat parties in 1999 to accept the invitation of the Republican Turkish Party to attend its party conference.

The rigidity of attitude is also very stark. Both Turkey and the TRNC leaders have maintained an intransigent assertion of their rights against international appeals (from both the UN and the EU) for compromise over the island dispute (specifically, the terms of negotiations), thus making a settlement less likely. The risk is of an increasing 'laager' mentality, rejecting international opprobrium, and blocking entry by maintaining the island's division. For Cyprus' entry does threaten traditional Turkish interests. It undermines Turkey's influence over the island, by making its role as a guarantor power (as agreed when Cyprus became independent) less relevant for the Turkish Cypriots.

The interests of Turkey and of the TRNC may be in the process of shifting, however, following the upgrading of Turkey's own EU entry application. The prospect of two Hellenic states – Greece and a Greek Cypriot-led Cyprus – being full members of the EU while Turkey remained outside disadvantages both Turkey's security and economic interests in the region. Moreover, while it is just conceivable that a divided Cyprus might join the EU alone, it is not realistic to expect Turkey to be a full EU member without Cyprus being allowed in. Certainly, there is scope for Turkey to decide its strategy on Cyprus in relation to its view of how the EU is treating its own application, and thereby affect all progress on the island. The hesitant response of Turkey to the EU's Helsinki initiative in December 1999 might be related to the lack of progress in the UN-sponsored intercommunal talks, for example.

As for the TRNC, there have been contradictory signals of how the community might view EU entry. At least one opinion poll has suggested that Turkish Cypriots would welcome Cyprus in the EU, even without Turkish entry.[3] Yet TRNC leaders have been implacably opposed, at least prior to any settlement of the intercommunal dispute. They have also expressed fears of an opening-up of their community's economy to the superior financial power of the Greek Cypriots. There has been a growing economic disparity between the two communities, given the Turkish side's pariah international status. The EU Commission has noted the trend: in 1960, the Turkish Cypriots had an income level equal to 86 per cent of that enjoyed by their Greek Cypriot counterparts; by 1998, however, this figure had fallen to 30 per cent (EU Commission 1998: 29). In an attempt to persuade the Turkish Cypriots to support EU entry, both the EU and the Cyprus government have emphasized the substantial economic aid that would flow to them after membership. The most significant role for the EU in relation to Cyprus could thus come after, rather than before, entry, by allocating large sums of economic aid to the Turkish Cypriots. For its part, the Clerides government has argued that the Cyprus government could use a 'peace dividend' to invest in the current TRNC area, developing infrastructure and raising incomes. The TRNC leaders are faced with stark economic choices: maintaining their *de facto* separation makes them dependent on Turkey, a relatively poor state; accepting EU entry involves reintegration with the Greek Cypriot community. Moreover, the greater the priority given by Turkey to its own EU entry, the more difficult it will be for the TRNC to resist Cypriot accession. Again, EU entry is linked to the desire for domestic reform and 'modernization' in both Turkey and the TRNC, as it has often been elsewhere.

In advance of a settlement of the intercommunal dispute, the prospect of EU entry is already being used as a lever for domestic economic reform among the Greek Cypriots. The use of EU obligations in this fashion is by no means exceptional. Dyson and Featherstone (1996,1999) noted how technocrats in Italy viewed EMU membership as an external constraint (a *vincolo esterno*) by which to impose fiscal and monetary discipline on the often-errant instincts of politicians in the old *partitocrazia*. Grande (1995) also identified a willingness of member governments to be bound by EU commitments. The exceptional feature of Cyprus is, instead, its small size and the limitations this places on the emergence of a stable and deep modernizing cleavage. Within this limitation, it can be noted that the mode of development has omitted full-blown industrialization, but has secured much economic success in recent decades as an increasingly service economy. There is, in consequence, a juxtaposition of both 'modern' and 'traditional' elements in Cypriot society. However, the political system does not provide a ready expression of this cleavage: it may have starker effects in the future. The party system has remained somewhat fragmented around the charismatic personalities of the leaders in a political culture of some paternalism. Indeed, some parties may not outlive their current aged leaders.

Nevertheless, significant differences of interpretation can be identified in strategic thinking about EU obligations. The dominant mode of discourse displays an instrumentalist motivation predominantly – reform as a condition of EU entry – rather than one of the absorption of EU norms and values into a process of domestic social learning (Checkel 1997: 476–7). The Left and the trade unions have sought delays in adaptation to EU rules until the last possible moment, including post-entry, given the costs of adjustment and the uncertainty over when and whether Cyprus will become a full member. By contrast, the government has sought to press ahead with reform in order to secure EU entry.

The use made of EU constraints has changed with the progress of the negotiations. The onset of reform implementation is felt more acutely in domestic society and it is more likely to provoke a clash of values and orientation. Given the large number of Cypriots dependent on the state for employment, the EU encouragement to deregulate the market creates a natural coalition of interest in opposition. By contrast, the EMU obligation for central bank independence allows monetary policy officials to have formal confirmation of the liberal, European status with which they identify. The structural reforms demanded by the EU in the financial services sector also create their own cleavages of domestic interest, as with the liberalization of interest rates freeing access to capital and the regulation of cooperative institutions imposing new obligations upon them (see below). Moreover, the negotiation of entry is a stimulus to a more open process of domestic policy formation, with the government needing inputs from a wider range of domestic actors and interests. The use made of the EU by the government as an excuse for unpopular reforms (e.g. on taxation) blur the motivation behind the policy shifts (i.e. whether they are desired for their own value or merely advanced to satisfy EU entry). EU officials have themselves, reportedly, encouraged Cypriot leaders to defray the responsibility for such reforms by blaming them on Brussels. The electoral advantages of using the EU as such a shroud are obvious, and may become more important in domestic coalition politics as Cyprus approaches the parliamentary elections due in 2001.

Ultimately, the strategic use of the EU as a force for domestic modernization rests on the fact that often the adjustments are very substantial and that the clash of interests among domestic actors suggests that the reform would have been much less likely to happen – then or later – without the existence of the EU constraint. The next section provides evidence of these propositions from the case of state–economy relations.

## EUROPEANIZATION AND STATE–ECONOMY RELATIONS

The pre-accession process has emphasized the powerful and directive nature of the EU's demands on Cyprus with respect to the structure of domestic state–economy relations. The demands made of Cyprus in the entry negotiations, outlined in the Commission's '*Regular Reports*' on Cyprus' progress towards accession, are extensive and typically specific. They envisage the most far-reaching transformation of state–economy relations since Cyprus became independent in 1960. The overall effect of the EU's demands is to liberalize the role of the state in the domestic market, restructuring the power of state institutions, giving more autonomy to market forces and more openness to intervention by foreign capital.

Cyprus is a small state with a service economy dominated by tourism.

In 1999, revenue from tourism was about $2bn, representing 20 per cent of GDP; 14 per cent of the working population is employed in this sector. Spending by foreign tourists – there were 2.43m of them in 1999 – is of a much higher value than that of the goods Cyprus exports (European Commission 1999: 21; Ministry of Trade, Industry and Tourism cited in *The Cyprus Weekly*, 28 January 2000). State ownership of Cyprus Airways and of the Cyprus Tourist Development Agency represents a major public stake in the tourist industry and makes it possible for the visitor to travel to and stay in Cyprus entirely at the service of the state. Indeed, the home market is characterized by extensive state involvement, as evidenced in monopoly public enterprises, restrictions on competition, state aids, and a highly protected financial services sector. As already noted, paternalism in state economic policy also has effects in the wider political system.

Yet the obligations associated with EU accession, and the less direct pressures of globalization, have created a momentum of significant change in the private sector, transforming the domestic climate. Recent changes in the Cyprus stock exchange represent an extreme example of this dynamism, in that they have introduced a new 'casino' capitalism into the domestic economy. The exchange witnessed a 220 per cent rise in prices in 1998, and spectacular increases continued the following year with some stocks rising by over 400 per cent. The effect has been to 'popularize' the ownership of stocks and shares on the island, with close public attention being paid to the fluctuations in prices. At the same time, public attitudes towards market deregulation and privatization have shifted significantly.

The 'economic fundamentals' show considerable long-term strength and potential. Between 1994 and 1998, real average economic growth was 4.3 per cent, having dipped in 1996–97, while in earlier periods it was even higher: 5.5 per cent between 1989 and 1993, and over 7.5 per cent in 1987–88. Inflation was 3.2 per cent between 1994 and 1998 and unemployment 3 per cent. GDP growth in 1998 was back up to 5 per cent, inflation down to 2.2 per cent, and unemployment at 3.3 per cent still represented full employment. With Cyprus' GDP per capita income at $13,453 in 1999 (provisional figure from Ministry of Finance, October 1999), it stood well ahead of each of the other applicant states. Indeed, its GDP per capita (in PPS4) was 79 per cent of the average for the 15 EU states, more than ten percentage points higher than the next applicant state, Slovenia (Eurostat 3/2000), and ahead of EU states like Greece and Portugal.

The Commission has accepted that Cyprus is 'a functioning market economy' and that it 'should be able to cope with the competitive pressures and market forces within the Union' (European Commission 1999: 61). Nevertheless, in its 1999 *Regular Report*, the Commission went out of its way to stress the need for renewed efforts at structural reform and deregulation. The Report was explicit in its reform demands in this general area, for example:

- Progress on privatization has been slow and 'needs to be accelerated'
- The Government has 'an anachronistic stake in business'
- EU competition rules needed to be extended to public undertakings and 'all enterprises need to invest to improve their efficiency'
- There was 'no systematic control' of state aids and a monitoring authority needed to be set up
- There was 'very little progress' on the *acquis communautaire* of the internal market.

It was evident that EU demands in these areas were clashing with deeply embedded policy beliefs and cultural traditions. Thus far, Cypriot political forces had resisted the importation of the neo-liberal norms of contemporary globalization. Instead, it was the prospect of EU membership that was instigating the process of domestic adaptation and this represented an historic change. Pursued for such instrumentalist reasons, there was little to suggest that similar reforms would have been made within anything like the same schedule without the pressure of the EU.

### *The financial market*

Nowhere was the clash of accumulated EU norms and domestic policy traditions more sharply set than in the banking and financial services sector. The Commission has noted repeatedly the need to overhaul statism and protectionism in this sector, and in its 1999 *Regular Report* it highlighted that:

- A comprehensive system of restrictions exists on the free movement of capital, with many such movements being subject to authorization procedures.
- The law on the Central Bank of Cyprus (CBC) must be amended, along with the relevant provisions of the Constitution, to enhance the CBC's statutory independence.
- The legal ceiling on interest rates (of 9 per cent) 'should be removed at the earliest opportunity'.

- In 1998, the obligation of insurance companies to invest at least 20 per cent of their funds in domestic government securities – which gave the public sector privileged access to finance – was abolished.
- The law governing the CBC still provides for the direct financing of the public sector within certain borrowing limits, although the gradual reduction of these limits has been pursued by the government since 1994, and the conversion of the public debt is necessary.
- The heavily protected insurance services sector needs to be opened up to allow EU firms access to the Cypriot market on the basis of a 'single passport' and home country control.
- The CBC does not exercise supervisory control over the cooperative credit and savings societies, which play a prominent role in the domestic economy, but are subject to less stringent prudential standards than banks and their position needs careful review.

This list of demanded reforms represents a major external 'shock' to the ingrained domestic system. The structural impact in Cyprus is to:

(1) Gradually disperse power among financial institutions and to open up the market to foreign competition.
(2) Give commercial freedom to banks in their lending policies and so revise the calculation of risk attached to private borrowing (the 9 per cent ceiling has favoured the allocation of credit to low-risk activities).
(3) Increase the fiscal discipline on the government, by ending its ability to rely on the CBC and other financial institutions to cover its public deficits.[5]
(4) Secure the independence from government of the CBC as an institution.
(5) Enhance the CBC's supervisory function over a more open and competitive domestic financial market.
(6) Revise the status and role of the cooperative societies, creating a pressure for them to transform themselves into banks. Liberalization is expected to leave the cooperatives in a vulnerable position. Their assets represent about 50 per cent of GDP and they carry relatively large non-performing loans (European Commission 1998: 18).

The combined impact of these changes is to revise the structural power of state institutions in the domestic market: giving more autonomy to market forces, further separating the government and the CBC, restricting the monetary and fiscal options available to government, and reforming the regulatory function of state bodies. The transformation of such structural power is thus more complex than a narrow thesis of the domestic strengthening of the state would seem to allow. Moravcsik (1994: 3), most notably, argues that the impact of EU membership is to 'centralize' executive power and 'strengthen' the state (also Moravcsik 1998). While this may be true for when governments participate in EU negotiations, the domestic consequences of EU commitments are much more diffuse, re-ordering state–economy relations and, indeed, civil society. Moreover, it is the existence of pressure from the EU level that affects the speed and destination of reform, creating a momentum beyond the control of any single group of executive or other actors.

### *Cyprus and EMU*

The impact of the EU *acquis communautaire* has increased with the conditions for entry into Stage 3 of EMU. One such instance is the obligation for states to have independent central banks. In practice, the CBC has long enjoyed considerable operational autonomy. The Bank currently enjoys a relatively high public profile and has often been critical of public policy (CBC 1998). Its legal status, however, has sustained the scope for it being subservient to government. Under the 1960 Constitution, the CBC is referred to in the chapters dealing with independent state organizations. Chapter 6, for example, provides for the 'independence' of the bank's Governor, yet the President of the Republic can dismiss the latter at any time (art. 118iv). Moreover, article 119(iv) states that the Governor shall carry out the relevant decisions of the Council of Ministers (Cabinet). The bank receives the advice of the ministries of Coordination and of Finance and it is to comply with this advice, though a two-thirds vote in Parliament may change it. In addition, the Minister of Finance has his own representative on the bank's Board and s/he can exercise a veto right over the Board's decisions. If confirmed by the Minister of Finance, the relevant action of the Board would be suspended, pending an appeal by the Board to the full Council of Ministers. This veto right has never been used, however. There has been no occasion on which the Minister of Finance has objected to the intentions of the CBC's Board. The 1963 law on the CBC also falls short of the new EMU obligations by stating that the Governor's term of office can be *up to* five years, while it is required to be *at least* as long as this. In addition, the 1963 law qualified the Bank's primary objective: it is to foster 'monetary stability' but insofar as it is conducive to the orderly development of the Republic. The latter qualification has to be removed if the EMU obligations are to be met (Treaty of Rome, Art. 105i, and art. 2 of the ESCB Statute).

The Clerides government has set June 2002 as the target date by which the CBC's legal independence would be secured. The issue has raised domestic concerns about accountability among opposition parties. Such political sensitivity suggests that, again, even with the international trend of similar reforms, without the specific obligations of the EU accession process, the reform of the CBC would have been much more problematic.

Similarly, the ending of the remaining possibilities for the monetization of the government deficit – while completing a domestic shift made in 1994 – represents a major structural change in public financing and one owing much to EU obligations under EMU. The amendment of the CBC Law will prohibit such financing by 1 January 2003 (the envisaged accession date) and the CBC's outstanding claims on the government will be converted to long-term debt under market conditions. The transition is not a smooth one: in 1998, the Government actually increased its financial dependence on the CBC (CBC 1998: 41).

Perhaps the most controversial clash between EU obligations and domestic practice in this area has been that concerning the maintenance in Cyprus of a legal ceiling on bank lending rates of 9 per cent. The legal restriction is a colonial legacy, introduced by the British in the early 1940s, but sustained by modern fears of the social consequences of fluctuating rates on the weaker sections of society. As a small state, Cyprus has little scope for domestic competition over rates, and oligopolistic power by large banks (there are just two or three of them at present) could threaten the interests of small borrowers. Previous target dates for abolishing the ceiling were not met, but a bill tabled in January 1999 was finally approved at the very end of the year, with the provision that the ceiling be abolished with effect from 1 January 2001. Clerides' own centre-right Democratic Rally party had previously opposed such reform in the early 1980s, but it now had the responsibility to see it through. The Communists (AKEL) opposed abolition, while the Socialists (EDEK) were prepared to offer conditional support. In the absence of the EU obligation, there is little support for the reform: indeed, many had urged that it be implemented at the last possible stage. The status quo position is popular, but the implementation is indisputably EU linked.

Upon accession, Cyprus, like the other candidate countries, will have derogation from EMU. Nevertheless, the Cypriot government is keen to participate in a successor to the ERM arrangement as soon as possible. Cyprus has sustained a strong currency policy – as required by EMU –

though this has been helped by the protection of the home capital market. The Cypriot pound was linked to the ECU in June 1992, but it always stayed well within the 2.25 per cent margin, and it was pegged to the euro at the same central rate at the start of 1999. Other performance indicators of the Cypriot economy are patchier. The forecasts for 1999 were that inflation would be 1.5 per cent (well within 2.7 per cent EMU ceiling) and long-term interest rates 7.4 per cent (ceiling of 7.7 per cent). By contrast, the deterioration of public finances has become a medium-term problem: the budget deficit was forecast to be 5.6 per cent in 1999, rising to 6.9 per cent in 2000 (ceiling of 2.7 per cent) and government debt 62 per cent of GDP in 1999, rising to 67 per cent in 2000 (ceiling of 60 per cent). Yet there is much confidence that these figures will be well within their EMU limits by the time that Cyprus is expected to enter the EU at the start of 2003. The budget deficit target for 2002 is two per cent, for example.

A more specific focus for Europeanization is the adaptations required by the state administration itself: these are examined in the next section.

## INSTITUTIONAL ADAPTATION

The pre-accession relationship between Cyprus and the EU has entailed several forms of institutional adaptation. Firstly, the negotiations with the EU have prompted an *ad hoc* adaptation of institutional procedures at home in order to coordinate policy and strategy on them (for international comparisons, see Rometsch and Wessels 1996). Secondly, the negotiating stance adopted by the EU Commission involves explicit pressure on the Cyprus Government to invest greater resources in certain administrative areas, in order to comply with the expectations placed upon member governments. Thirdly, assimilating the *acquis communautaire* has expanded the scope of legislation and with it the scope of state activity. Not since independence has the Cyprus state administration been so exposed to (non-military) external pressure and it has forced a fulsome response.

Initially, the prospect of entry negotiations with the EU provoked a bout of 'turf-fighting' between different parts of the government machine and this sustained some instability. The Ministry of Foreign Affairs (MFA) in particular had sought to assert its leadership over the process. A proposal made in 1991 for the Ministry to be the chief negotiator, supported by a Minister for EU Affairs and a Permanent Secretary, never materialized. It faced important constraints. The Constitution of 1960 limits the total number of ministries to ten, thus limiting the scope for innovation. As the proposal implied a shift of specialist staff from the Planning Bureau (under the Ministry of Finance) to the MFA, staff facing such a move were wary of the impact on staff promotion prospects, etc.[6] In 1997, it was proposed that the Planning Bureau should become the chief negotiator, with the Permanent Secretary of the MFA shifting to the Bureau. Yet this arrangement needed the approval of the House of Representatives and this was not sanctioned. Instead, a more *ad hoc* arrangement was made. President Clerides appointed one of his predecessors, Georgios Vassiliou, to the post of Chief Negotiator, with effect from February 1998. Vassiliou brought to the job his personal political prestige, but he was unable to assume ministerial status given the constitutional limitation. Thus, Vassiliou was prohibited from giving direct instructions to the various ministries; instead, he had to route them via the ministers of foreign affairs and of finance. This arrangement barely concealed personal and bureaucratic tensions. Vassiliou was not granted an independent budget, but given a subvention from that allocated to the President and the negotiating team is funded by the various ministries from which they came. The Ministerial Committee on the EU was previously under the auspices of the MFA, but it was placed directly under the President in order not to offend Vassiliou's sensitivity as a former President being asked to operate under the Foreign Minister. Vassiliou attends the relevant Cabinet meetings, and normally the regular Monday meetings of the Parliament's own EU committee. An additional complication was that Vassiliou remained a partisan political figure: leader of his own political party (United Democrats) and, until mid-1999, a member of the House of Representatives.

The coordination process thus settled on a unique arrangement. The Minister of Foreign Affairs (Ioannis Kasoulides) led for Cyprus in the ministerial level meetings with the EU and the other applicant states. Vassiliou led the Cypriot delegation at the level of officials and he also headed the coordination process at home. In specific policy sectors, there was a division of expertise: the MFA assumed the main technocratic responsibility on Pillar Two (CFSP); the Planning Bureau did the same for Pillar One (the EC); and both coordinated with the ministries of the Interior and of Justice for Pillar Three (JHA). The Planning Bureau did the bulk of the domestic monitoring work: specialist staff scrutinize the *acquis*; follow the preparation of the appropriate domestic legislation; and seek to uphold the agreed schedule. The MFA had responsibility for directing the flow of information with Brussels (via the Permanent

Representation of Cyprus) and between institutions at home. Vassiliou's negotiating team comprised less than ten officials, drawn from the MFA, the Planning Bureau, and the Law Office of the Republic, together with the Permanent Secretary of the Planning Bureau, the Permanent Secretary of the Ministry of Agriculture (because of his personal expertise) and Vassiliou's own advisor. The European Commission's own *Regular Report* of 1999 recognized the delicate nature of these arrangements. 'All major political decisions,' it said, were taken 'by the Council of Ministers (Cabinet) after the consultations of the Chief Negotiator with the President of the Republic' (1999: 46). The complexity of the arrangements sustained a workable compromise.

The assimilation of EU obligations into domestic legislation encountered difficulties that were also overcome by an *ad hoc* arrangement. The Commission has monitored closely the speed of legislative adoption (European Commission 1998, 1999). In response, Vassiliou initiated a new fast-track procedure by which to adopt the *acquis*. Under this scheme, an appropriate bill is sent to the new 'Grand Committee for EU and External Affairs' in the House of Representatives and, if approved, it then goes directly to the plenary session for adoption, removing the need for further discussion by other committees. The procedure was first followed in June 1999, when a package of bills was approved within a week. The Commission welcomed this innovation and also the greater use of framework laws, by which technical details can be settled by administrative regulations (European Commission 1999: 8). By the end of 1999, the progress of legislation was consistent with the target dates set.

The negotiating position pursued by the Commission also involved requests for a revision of domestic institutional structures and resources. The Commission was very directive in detailing the reforms that should be adopted prior to accession. Its 1999 *Regular Report* included a series of such reforms, for example:

- A central national intelligence agency 'could be created' to help the Cyprus Police, and a 'National Drugs Monitoring Centre'.
- The Cyprus Government should 'allocate sufficient administrative and budgetary resources' to the environment sector to ensure implementation of EU policies.
- The 'little progress' on immigration, asylum and visa control issues should be overcome by strengthening its visa regime, adopting new asylum legislation, ratifying the Council of Europe convention on

data protection, and adopting international instruments for judicial cooperation.

- 'The existing administrative structure is not sufficient in terms of human, technical and financial resources to be able to implement the *acquis* effectively'.
- The staffing of the Law Office of the Republic should be increased, European training for judges introduced, and the courts' administrative infrastructure strengthened.
- Veterinary and phytosanitary standards needed to be aligned.
- 'Substantial legislative work' was necessary on transport, and maritime safety in particular.

Such cases testify to the specificity and depth of the EU's demands on its prospective members. EU membership is seemingly dependent on the adoption of a whole series of measures, from a new forgery-proof visa to better laboratory testing of silencers and oil filters on motor vehicles. While the effect is to boost the capacity and efficiency of the state administration – via convergence with EU norms – it is clear that both the timing and the content of such reforms was crucially dependent on the bid to seek EU entry.

Moreover, the adoption of the *acquis communautaire* expands the scope of the current body of legislation in Cyprus, and thereby enlarges the activity of the state. In certain areas of technical regulation, Cyprus has had little legislation on the statute book. In some cases this is because the absence of the appropriate domestic conditions make legislation largely irrelevant, as in parts of environmental legislation (e.g. nuclear safety and radiation protection; unleaded petrol; shellfish waters). More broadly across the environmental field, it is a matter of up-grading and specifying new standards. In 1998, the Commission noted that 'the vast majority of the *acquis* (on environmental matters) remains to be transposed' (European Commission 1998: 33). Similarly, though Cyprus' ship register ranks sixth in the world, the regulation of maritime transport has been limited and criticized for being applied with a light touch. EU demands have led Cyprus to enhance its inspection of merchant vessels, with a view to reducing the exceptionally high detention rate of its shipping overseas. More generally, trading and product standards are being revised and expanded in line with the *acquis*: but as late as 1999, just 15 per cent of existing European standards had been adopted (European Commission 1999: 25).

The overall effect of the adoption of the *acquis* in these areas is again to increase the convergence of the state administration in Cyprus – its capacity and scope – to that of West European norms. It is not a matter here of strengthening the state *vis-à-vis* other domestic actors so much, as an act of administrative 'modernization', brought about by increased exposure to EU-regulated transactions.

## CONCLUSIONS

Analyzing the processes of Europeanization evident in Cyprus clarifies a number of important features. As a small state, the imbalance in structural power with the EU is huge and the process of adaptation is overwhelmingly 'top–down' from Brussels. The EU's demands constitute a powerful and directive pressure for adjustment in domestic state–economy relations and for the operation of the state administration. Indeed, with the exception of the special circumstances of the 1974 invasion, the stimulus from the EU represents the most important transformation of Cypriot society in four decades of independence. Internally, the EU imposes a managed system of policy convergence among its members, while mediating the pressures of globalization (Brinar and Svetlicic 1999). Across a range of major reforms – such as the cases of financial market liberalization, banking reform and CBC independence that have been highlighted here – EU pressure has been crucial to the pace of reform, if not also its content and direction.

Not only is the magnitude of adaptation in this Europeanization process broad and deep; it is also producing other qualitative changes. Domestically, it is not a simple matter of government empowerment from the EU, but rather a restructuring of institutional power and resources. Internally, the state administration faces a cold shower of EU-defined modernization. In relation to wider society, the state has, in many respects, less power over market forces and the new market openness strengthens the position of a range of private sector interests, domestic and foreign. Domestically, 'empowerment' is thus differential and diffuse in this process of transformation.

Identifying Europeanization with economic modernization is not exceptional (e.g. Featherstone 1998). A more distinctive feature of the Cyprus case is the strategic discourse that sees the EU as a vital foreign policy lever. Such a conception originated with the Greek Cypriots and has been extended to Turkey and the EU itself. High expectations are being placed on the strength of the EU to restructure the hitherto intractable problems of solving the Cyprus 'problem'. This conception of the utility of

'Europeanizing' the problem is also hazardous, should little benefit accrue. It focuses attention, however, on the essential tragedy of Cyprus – that of its vulnerable security position – alongside which other dramas can sometimes appear as fanciful diversions. The EU entry bid of Cyprus forces the organization and its member governments to make strategic choices between the agendas of Europeanization and of more traditional regional security balances. Therein lies the immediate fate of Cyprus.

## NOTES

1. The fieldwork for this article included a series of personal interviews conducted in Cyprus in October 1999. I would like to record my gratitude to those that gave of their time so freely and were so helpful. I am also grateful to those colleagues who commented on a draft of this article, in particular George Kazamias (Bradford) and Joseph Joseph (Cyprus). Any errors remain, of course, mine alone.
2. The EC Commission issued its Opinion on the application on 30 June 1993 and the Council of Ministers endorsed this on 4 October 1993. Technical discussions ensued between the Commission and Cyprus from November 1993 to February 1995.
3. A poll in January 2000 showed that 74.6 per cent of Turkish Cypriots favoured accession to the EU even if Turkey did not become a member. Reported in *Cyprus News*, London, 1–31 January 2000.
4. PPS: Purchasing Power Parities.
5. EU obligations have also led to a restructuring of indirect taxation to accommodate value added tax (VAT).
6. While the Planning Bureau is placed under the Ministry of Finance, it is an independent agency, not a directorate. Its chief domestic responsibilities are the Development Plan and Budget of the Government. Its functions are similar to ministries of national coordination or of economics in other European states. In 1999, the Bureau had a total staff of approximately 40, with about 12 engaged in EU work.

## REFERENCES

Brinar, I., and M. Svetlicic (1999): 'Enlargement of the European Union: the case of Slovenia', *Journal of European Public Policy* 6, p.5.

Central Bank of Cyprus (1998): *Annual Report*, Nicosia: Central Bank of Cyprus.

Checkel, J. (1997): 'International Norms and Domestic Politics: Bridging the Rationalist–Constructive Divide', *European Journal of International Relations* 3, pp.473–25.

Commission of the European Communities (1998): *Regular Report from the Commission on Cyprus' Progress Towards Accession*, Luxembourg: Office for Official Publications of the European Communities.

—— (1999): *1999 Regular Report from the Commission on Cyprus' Progress Towards Accession*, Luxembourg: Office for Official Publications of the European Communities. COM (1999) 502 final.

Dyson, K., and K Featherstone (1996): 'Italy and EMU as a "*Vincolo Esterno*": Empowering the Technocrats, Transforming the State', *South European Society and Politics* 1 (Autumn), p.2.

—— (1999): *The Road to Maastricht: Negotiating Economic and Monetary Union*, Oxford: Oxford University Press.

*Eurostat* (2000): 'Statistics in focus', Theme 2, 3/2000, Luxembourg: Office for the Official Publications of the European Communities.

Featherstone, K. (1998): '"Europeanization" and the Centre Periphery: The Case of Greece in the 1990s', *South European Society and Politics* 31 (Summer), p.1.

Grande, E. (1995): 'Das Paradox der Schwache. Forschungspolitik und die Einflusslogik europaischer Politkverflechtung', in M. Jachtenfuchs and B. Kohler-Koch (eds.), *Europaische Integration*, Opladen: Leske and Budrich.

Joseph, J.S. (1997): *Cyprus: Ethnic Conflict and International Politics – From Independence to the Threshold of the European Union*, London: Macmillan.

Moravcsik, A. (1994): 'Why the European Community Strengthens the State: Domestic Politics and International Cooperation', *Working Paper 52*, Harvard University: Center for European Studies.

—— (1998): *The Choice for Europe: Social Purpose and State Power from Messina to Maastricht*, London: UCL Press.

Republic of Cyprus (1998): *European Stand on the Cyprus Problem*, Nicosia: Press and Information Office.

Rometsch, D., and W. Wessels (eds.) (1996): *The European Union and member states: Towards institutional fusion?* Manchester: Manchester University Press.

Theophanous, A. (1999): *Greece, Cyprus, Turkey and the European Union*, Nicosia: Research and Development Center, Intercollege.

Tsebelis, G. (1990): *Nested Games: Rational Choice in Comparative Politics*, Berkeley: University of California Press.

# Europeanization and Domestic Macro-Economic Policy Regimes

# Managing the Spanish Economy within Europe

CARLES BOIX

How does the internationalization of national economies affect their governance? How does the creation of a single European market and a quasi-unified economic authority affect the ability of national governments to deliver growth and ensure fair economic results? Do the Left and the Right have, under these conditions, any distinct economic programme to manage the economy?

Spain's experience of the 1980s and 1990s provides an excellent case study to explore these questions. Following a gradual process of trade liberalization and overall economic internationalization that started in 1959, Spain has unconditionally embraced the EC/EU in the last decade and thus accelerated its gradual loss of sovereignty over fiscal and monetary policies. At the same time, and except for Greece, it has been the country that has experienced the longest (and more solid) socialist government in the last decade and a half in Europe: the Spanish Socialist Party (*Partido Socialista Obrero Español* (PSOE)) governed alone from 1982 to 1993 and as a minority government until 1996.

To examine the relationship between economic internationalization, European integration and Leftist economic policies, this article is organized as follows.[1] First, it examines briefly Spain's integration in the EU. It then describes the set of macroeconomic policies developed by the socialist government, both as a response to the process of European integration and in reaction to the government's incapacity to build a corporatist model. It moves on to examine how the government implemented an active industrial policy to restructure the publicly owned enterprises sector and to expand the Spanish public stock of human and physical capital in response to the process of internationalization. Finally, it explores how social spending was expanded to compensate the unemployed and the losers of the transformation of the Spanish economy.

## INTERNATIONAL CONDITIONS: THE PROCESS OF EUROPEAN INTEGRATION

After several years of protracted negotiations, Spain fully joined the EC in 1986. Support for its membership had been intense among all the political parties since the very beginning of the transition to democracy. The centre-right coalition, Unión de Centro Democrático, which governed until 1982, had applied for admission into the EC in 1977 and managed the first period of negotiations with Brussels. The PSOE had proclaimed the need to join the European Common Market as early as 1964. After stating its opposition to the Common Market in the 1960s, the Spanish Communist Party eventually declared itself in favour of joining the EC by 1974-75.[2]

The attitudes of the Spanish political parties merely reflected the overwhelming public support for the process of European integration. As shown in Table 1, about two thirds of all Spaniards consistently endorsed the European project throughout the 1980s. Those levels of support made Spain second only to Italy in its levels of allegiance to the Community. Moreover, the political and business elites converged in stressing the important economic benefits that entering the EC would yield to the Spanish economy: a vast market and a place to look for readily available capital.

Spain's unanimous support for the EC derived, generally speaking, from a general belief linking integration with Europe to the culmination of the country's modernization process. More particularly, from a political dimension, the EC was seen as a particularly useful mechanism to strengthen democracy. From an economic point of view, EC

TABLE 1
SPANIARDS' ATTITUDES TOWARDS INTEGRATION IN THE EUROPEAN COMMUNITY

Generally speaking, do you think that belonging to the EC is either good, bad, or neither good nor bad for your country?

| Year | 1980 | 1981 | 1982 | 1983 | 1984 | 1985 | 1986 | 1987 | 1988 | 1989 | 1990 |
|---|---|---|---|---|---|---|---|---|---|---|---|
| Good | 55 | 52 | 50 | 48 | 54 | 60 | 64 | 61 | 66 | 66 | 67 |
| Bad | 7 | 5 | 6 | 6 | 5 | 7 | 7 | 4 | 7 | 5 | 5 |
| Neither good nor bad | 15 | 16 | 21 | 17 | 18 | 20 | 15 | 18 | 18 | 15 | 20 |
| Doesn't know/ doesn't answer | 25 | 26 | 23 | 30 | 21 | 13 | 17 | 14 | 11 | 14 | 6 |

*Source*: Alvarez-Miranda (1996), taken from Eurobarometer surveys.

membership was also judged to be highly beneficial. In the first place, the failure of the autarkic policies of the 1940s and 1950s contrasted with the economic expansion that had followed the liberalization of trade approved in 1959–60 and made advisable a further commitment to free trade. In the second place, the European market offered substantial net gains to important parts of the Spanish economy: agricultural producers; mass-production companies (e.g. the car industry); small firms in industrial districts (e.g. shoe-makers, furniture makers) that still competed on price; and an abundant mass of unskilled and semi-skilled labour, similar to today's eastern European workers in wages and qualifications. Finally, any opposition to the EC was defused by laying out generous compensation schemes for those firms and sectors that were expected to suffer heavier economic losses.

The strength of Spain's commitment to the European project hardly declined over time. After joining the EC in 1986, the Spanish government announced the integration of the peseta into the European exchange rate system (ERM) in June 1989. Similarly, Spain warmly embraced the creation of the EU. Monetary policy was fully devolved to the Bank of Spain in 1994. Both the 1993–96 socialist government and the present conservative government pursued restrictive policies to tame inflation and cut the public deficit. Unions and businesses agreed, in turn, to (moderate) labour market reforms and to contain wage increases to ease the transition into EMU. It is true that integration into the EU has eventually broken down the traditional political consensus that once prevailed on European issues. *Izquierda Unida* (a radical left coalition led by the PCE) has opposed both the stability pact and the launching of the euro. However, its positions remain marginal and have been contested even within the coalition.

## MACROECONOMIC DISCIPLINE AND EUROPEAN INTEGRATION

Because of the fiasco of the French socialist experience of 1981–82, as well as the constraints imposed by the fiscal and external balances of the Spanish economy, the Socialist party avoided any expansionary policies in the wake of its landslide victory of October 1982. During the first two years in office, González first relied both on a partial tightening of monetary policy accompanied by some wage moderation, secured through an intermittent incomes policy, and on a mild reduction of the public deficit. Yet, with domestic demand down one per cent in 1984, and unemployment close to 2.9m people or 21.7 per cent of the active population by the end of the year, the government signed a broad social pact with the UGT (General Workers' Union), the socialist trade union, to both further its anti-inflationary goal and rekindle the economy.[3]

Economic conditions in Spain eventually turned around by mid-1985. After several years in which domestic demand and overall growth had been almost flat, private consumption grew by around two per cent in 1985 – the strongest increase since 1977 – and then by 3.6 per cent in 1986. Partly because of the national wage agreement of 1984, inflation fell to 8.3 per cent by the end of 1986 and then to less than five per cent by the summer of 1987. Above all, by the summer of 1985 Spain entered an expansionary cycle that, after peaking at the end of 1988 (with GDP growing at an annual rate of 5.5 per cent in real terms), lasted through the beginning of 1992. Total employment started to expand by mid-1985 and unemployment to decline in relative terms in the first semester of 1986.

After securing the integration of Spain in the EC, the socialist government won a narrow victory in the referendum on the Spanish membership in NATO held in March 1986. Three months later, González was returned to office with 43.5 per cent of votes.

As soon as the economy started to grow, the Ministry of the Economy, now in the hands of Carlos Solchaga, abandoned the temporary fiscal impulse engineered in 1985 and emphasized again its commitment to achieve a general macroeconomic framework that, based on the containment of wages and prices, a reduced public deficit and a balanced current account, could deliver long-term, non-inflationary growth. Although the cabinet's determination to sustain stable macroeconomic policies partly resulted from the lessons of the 1960s, the failed experiment of the French socialist government and the macroeconomic imbalances inherited in 1982, it was bolstered, throughout the decade, by the growing concern shared by top government officials about the overall competitiveness of the Spanish economy in increasingly liberalized international markets for capital, goods and services.

Until the late 1970s substantial legal restrictions on capital controls had been in place across all OECD nations. This circumstance, in combination with the regime of floating exchange rates (or rather flexible currency agreements, such as the European snake) that followed the collapse of the Bretton Woods system, had given policy-makers (including Spain's UCD government) considerable autonomy for about a decade. By the mid-1980s, however, a strong process of financial liberalization across the advanced world had led to a system of complete capital mobility which would, in turn, make an autonomous monetary policy impossible to follow.

This process of financial liberalization partly originated in the rapid growth of capital flows that started in the 1960s. Both the expansion of the pool of international capital and the parallel technological innovations in financial markets that reduced transaction costs, imposed (or were perceived to impose) considerable opportunity costs on those countries that persisted in maintaining capital controls (Goodman and Pauly 1993; Eichengreen 1996). Still, the growth of capital flows did not result mechanically in the deregulation of financial markets across the OECD area. It rather combined with a process of competitive liberalization that led, in due time, to complete capital mobility. In a process resembling a tipping model, the relaxation of controls in, at first, a small set of countries triggered accelerating pressures to deregulate elsewhere over time. In the early 1970s the US moved close to abolishing its remaining regulatory mechanisms. Several small countries in Europe, such as Austria, Denmark, Finland, Ireland and The Netherlands, and Japan approved substantial reductions in their systems of capital controls throughout the 1970s. Above all, the United Kingdom abolished its full set of financial restrictions in one dramatic move in 1979 (Simmons 1999). As the number of countries that had embraced a liberal regime in the financial arena grew, the opportunity costs of maintaining a system of capital controls escalated for those that had not yet deregulated. There was a generalized expectation that those countries that had chosen to exclude themselves from the (expanding) 'zone of full capital mobility' would find themselves at an increasing disadvantage in the economic arena in two ways: first, they would fail to attract foreign investment; and secondly, they would be perceived as unreliable in their fight against inflation. The European Single Market project, mainly built around the idea of free factor mobility, would intensify the race toward financial deregulation. To avoid being left out of the advantages of capital mobility and a single market, both the southern European and Scandinavian countries embraced the liberalization strategy in the late 1980s and early 1990s – even Norway, a country that was not an EU member.[4]

As a result of this generalized process of economic liberalization, compounded by the expected benefits from the integration process into the EC since 1986, Spain and the socialist government became, so to speak, strict 'price-takers' in the area of economic policy-making. The Spanish cabinet was pushed, by the external environment, to fully commit to a policy paradigm in which competitiveness was the fundamental objective to be achieved through low inflation and balanced macroeconomic aggregates.[5] Accordingly, Spain dismantled its panoply of capital controls in the second half of the 1980s.

Naturally, as complete capital mobility was established, monetary authorities could only engage in expansionary policies if they accepted corresponding currency depreciations. But a devaluation clashed directly with the European economic and political project, threatened the credibility of the governmental commitment to balanced long-term growth and jeopardized those capital inflows still essential to sustain Spain's growth rates (Zabalza 1990). Thus, the achievement of real competitiveness in the framework of a common market required thorough governmental efforts to fight inflation (Solchaga 1986: 31ff.). In the context of deregulated international markets and of Spain's membership in an optimal or quasi-optimal currency area such as the European one, adherence to a multilateral currency area or even to a monetary union would then become a rational response. With interest rate differentials washed out by the threat of capital flows, exchange rate stability had become a strictly Pareto-improving decision.[6] In other words, joining the EMS (in 1989) and later embracing the creation of the euro seemed the 'natural' steps to be taken in response to powerful international financial markets, the decline of capital controls and the demise of one-country Keynesian policies.

## THE BREAKDOWN OF A CORPORATIST SOLUTION (WITHIN THE EUROPEAN FRAMEWORK)

### *The failure of government–union negotiations*

Once the Spanish cabinet had chosen to both embrace the process of European integration fully and combat inflation in order to enhance national competitiveness, it was clear to top government officials that they were left with only two possible policy alternatives to achieve those goals. On the one hand, the government could attract unions into a social compact to ensure moderate wage increases and therefore lower inflation. On the other hand, were social concertation not available, the cabinet would be forced to quell inflation 'through either a more restrictive monetary policy, the exchange rate, appreciating the peseta, or a blunt reduction of public expenditure' (Solchaga 1988: 29).[7]

The first alternative was clearly the preferred course of action for the socialist cabinet. It responded to the traditional social democratic project that included the union movement in the policy-making process in order to build strong welfare policies. It avoided harsh monetary policies that could alienate an essential part of the socialist electorate. It had worked well during 1985–86 in reducing inflation and sustaining the economic recovery. And, finally, given the governmental conviction, espoused publicly and supported by official reports, that wages were the main causal component of the inflationary process, a social compact to moderate them appeared to be the most direct and less costly way to reduce inflation (Solchaga 1988, 1991a; Zabalza 1989, 1991).

For that purpose, the government made several attempts at social concertation during the decade. In order to control inflation, the government repeatedly asked the economic agents to abide by the wage bargaining pattern that had been employed since the first national accords were struck in 1978. According to that model, wage increases should be limited to the level of expected inflation, a target that was based, in turn, on government forecasts. In exchange for wage moderation, the government promised to negotiate a 'social wage' around the 'differences in taxation endured by wages and low incomes and by higher incomes; as well as the structure and volume of social expenditure' (Solchaga 1988: 30).

In the negotiating rounds for 1987, however, UGT, the socialist trade union, which had been instrumental in securing the social agreement of 1985–86, disassociated itself from the government programme for a social pact.[8] As unionists tirelessly stressed, the social concertation of 1985–86 had resulted in a fall in real wages of almost one point, but unemployment had barely decreased. Thus, rejecting the traditional model of wage settlement that linked wages to expected inflation, the UGT leaders asked for a wage increase two points above the official inflation target of five per cent for 1987 in order to restore real wages. Underlying their specific demands on wage bargaining, unions were proposing a macroeconomic strategy essentially at odds with the government understanding of the Spanish economy. Claiming that wage pressure had no substantial impact on inflation, they urged González to expand demand strongly to absorb unemployment. The clash over macroeconomic policies was compounded by growing disagreements on social policies and on the state's role in the economy. The unions urged the government to comply with the promises entered into in the 1984 national agreement (AES) so that unemployment benefits reached at least 48 per cent of all the unemployed (20 points over the actual level of coverage), and to accept the pension system they had drafted. Finally, the

UGT started to sketch a plan that called for an increasing public control of all investment through so-called 'investment funds' to be determined by law.

The government appeared uncompromising. Breaking the established wage-setting system threatened its anti-inflationary policy. Furthermore, in the wake of a recovery in fiscal revenues, the reduction of the public deficit to increase the level of national savings and investment had priority over a boost of public consumption and social transfers. Similarly, the proposal to control private investment was flatly rejected by the government (Solchaga 1988). Negotiations quickly became sour and a national collective agreement for 1987 turned out to be impossible (Redondo 1988; Espina 1991).

The wage agreements for 1987 between unions and business organizations averaged an increase of 6.5 per cent, therefore close to the UGT demands. Inflation, however, fell 3.5 percentage points to an average 5.3 per cent in 1987 – and by the end of 1987 it had dropped to 4.6 per cent. To government and unions alike, the outcome confirmed their corresponding policy positions. On the one hand, Solchaga, invigorated by the almost perfect match between the planned goal and the actual result, announced an inflation target of three per cent for 1988. On the other hand, for the trade unions the wide gap between wage and price increases definitely upheld their claim that both were only weakly linked. Consequently, the UGT responded to the ambitious government target by asking for pay increases ranging from four to six per cent in 1988 and by insisting that social expenditures should be strongly expanded. Given the optimal combination of accelerating growth and falling inflation enjoyed at that time by the Spanish economy, the incentives for a social pact grew dimmer and eventually the prospects for a national agreement waned again.

With demand growing heartily, however, the deflation process became stalled by the summer of 1988. After reaching an all-out low of 4.4 per cent in the second quarter of 1988, inflation bounced back to 5.7 per cent at the end of the third quarter, therefore threatening to broaden the inflation differential with the EC and to upset González's macroeconomic strategy. The socialist cabinet had to face again, even more intensely, the dilemma of either attracting trade unions back into a social compact or using stabilizing fiscal and monetary policies alone. But concertation could not come about easily. With actual inflation two points higher than the official target, the cabinet's credibility had been seriously damaged among the social partners. Moreover, encouraged by the expectations generated by the economic boom, over time the unions had radicalized. The negotiations between the cabinet and the unions during the summer of 1988 stumbled upon the same obstacles of previous years. Furthermore, a youth employment and training scheme (*Plan de Empleo Juvenil* (PEJ)), designed by the cabinet to subsidize employers to take on school leavers on short-term contracts and at the minimum wage, was adamantly opposed by the unions. In order merely to open negotiation rounds in the autumn, the UGT demanded the immediate withdrawal of the PEJ, the extension of unemployment coverage according to the 1984 agreement and increases in pensions and public sector wages to compensate for higher than expected inflation. With negotiations in a stalemate, the UGT and the communist union, CCOO, joined in a one-day general strike in December 1988 to bring the government to its knees and to extract from it a set of social concessions the cost of which was put at least at Pta.450bn ($3.9bn or more than one per cent of the 1988 GDP) (Juliá 1988).

Given the extraordinary success of the strike, González promptly conceded the cabinet's defeat in parliament, and agreed both to shelve the youth employment plan and to adjust pensions and public sector wages to inflation, but rejected the expansion of unemployment coverage levels. After long and tense negotiations at the beginning of 1989, the government decided to stick to the initial offer made by González in December, the cost of which was put at Pta.190bn ($1.6bn). At that point, the stable pattern of social pacts established in the mid-1970s could be declared irreversibly lost.

The government attempted repeatedly, however, to set up a new social pact to cool down the economy and to reduce inflation. Explicit calls made by the Minister of the Economy in July 1989 and by González himself in August 1989 were rejected by the UGT. In response to the entry into the EC exchange rate system, UGT and CCOO launched a joint platform (*Propuesta Sindical Prioritaria*) demanding more extensive social expenditure (including the recognition of the so-called 'social debt' or all the promises on social expenditure made by the government in 1984, and still to be implemented), greater government planning of the economy, an extensive housing policy and a fairer tax system.

A slight setback in the general parliamentary elections of October 1989, mostly to the benefit of a loose coalition to the left of the PSOE, which put the socialist party one seat below the absolute majority, pressed González to renew his effort at achieving a social pact. Shortly after formal talks were revived at the beginning of 1990, the government made strong concessions on social issues. Minimum pensions were to be raised up to the minimum wage level in 1990 (in 1983 the minimum pension was only 77.9 per cent of the minimum wage) and the same would be implemented for widows' pensions in 1992. Increases on pensions were scaled to favour the lowest income levels. The government established non-contributory pensions (i.e. pensions for people that had never paid social security contributions), paying Pta.26,000 monthly in 1991, about half the legal minimum wage. In addition, the ratio of unemployed people covered by several kinds of unemployment benefits – including the scheme for temporary rural workers – was expanded. While in 1988 only 28.8 per cent of all those that had registered as unemployed were covered (2.5 points above the 1983 level), in 1991 the ratio had gone up to 51.9 per cent (i.e. around 1.4m recipients). Accordingly, unemployment benefits would jump from 2.7 to 3.8 per cent of GDP in three years – at a time in which unemployment fell more than three percentage points.[9] In spite of those unconditional social concessions, all governmental expectations for wage moderation proved illusory. At the beginning of the year the Minister of the Economy warned that were wages to rise above 7.3 per cent, harsh fiscal and monetary measures must ensue. The first major collective agreement of 1990, in the construction sector, called for a wage rise of 8.5 per cent, and all wage settlements during the first quarter of the year averaged 8.3 per cent. Meanwhile, at the UGT's national congress in April 1990, its leader, Nicolás Redondo, assured union representatives that he would keep on with 'the trade union strategy begun in 1987: definitive rupture with the PSOE and the maintenance of joint action on wage claims with CCOO' (EIU 1990, 3rd trimester).

Government plans to unveil a global 'competitiveness pact', aimed at stimulating Spanish productivity in the immediate future, were announced by the summer of 1990. Unions immediately interpreted the proposal as yet another incomes policy to ensure that real wage increases were offset by productivity growth, and, while presenting the budget for 1991, Solchaga had to announce a delay on the negotiations on the pact. Even with economic growth beginning to slow down, the negotiation rounds for 1991 yielded an average wage increase of 8.1 per cent. Pressed by the stringent conditions laid down in Maastricht for the EMU, yet willing to avoid restrictive fiscal and monetary policies, the government eventually presented a competitiveness pact, under the name 'Social Pact for Progress', in June 1991. The pact insisted on approximating wage increases to the rates prevalent in low inflationary European countries and asked for wage increases to be linked to productivity gains. Yet it asked for salary reviews to be subject to a common clause in order to guarantee that wage earners would see some increase in real incomes. In a departure from a previous position within the government, it called for a set of controls on distributed profits, which could not grow at a pace higher than wages, and designed favourable tax incentives for those profits reinvested in the company. Although further away from a traditional incomes pact to control wages, the Social Pact of Progress failed again to attract the trade unions. Wage settlements for 1992 fluctuated around an increase of 7.2 per cent and, after a renewed period of confrontations, the unions staged a second one-day general strike in the spring of 1992, which was, however, mostly a failure.[10] As a matter of fact, new legislation passed in the early 1990s enhanced union power and labour market rigidities in the labour market. The legislation on labour procedures approved in 1990 increased the compensation to be paid to workers who had been laid off unfairly. A 1991 law on new employment contract monitoring extended the right of workers' representatives and unions to screen the legality of most new hiring contracts. Ongoing negotiations (since 1991) on the regulation of the right to strike showed the capacity of unions and the left wing of the PSOE to sustain a legal environment favourable to the former. And after the cabinet had drafted a moderate proposal that excluded all main demands from unions, the latter outmanoeuvred the government through direct negotiations with the socialist parliamentary group (Fernández-Castro 1993).

### *Consequences of the failure: fiscal strains and restrictive monetary policies*

From 1985–86 to 1989, the government was able to pursue its programme of fiscal consolidation with little political cost. The general government deficit fell from 6.9 to 2.8 per cent of GDP in four years. The decline in overall net lending was driven more by the spectacular improvement experienced by the Spanish economy in the mid-1980s than by a disciplined fiscal policy. Adjusting for the economic cycle, it is clear that the government only designed a restrictive fiscal policy in 1986 and 1987. Fiscal restraint waned, however, from 1988 on. Even in the presence of a booming economy, the size of the 'fiscal impulse' (i.e. the change in the budget balance adjusting for the business cycle) oscillated around one point of GDP during four years in a row.

Up until 1988, unexpected high revenues comfortably absorbed all expenditure overruns. However, from 1989 the governmental fiscal strategy was subjected to considerable strain. The intensifying pressure from unions to increase social spending could have been warded off had the PSOE kept its majority in Parliament. But the electoral losses suffered in 1989 – which deprived the PSOE of an outright majority – persuaded the cabinet to increase social transfers to avoid losing more popular support. The expansion of social spending severely jeopardized the governmental budgetary plans. Reversing its slightly downward trend since 1985, total public expenditure rose from 41.1 per cent of GDP in 1988 to 43.3 per cent of GDP in 1990. Subsequently, partly because of a sharp economic downturn, public spending increased quickly at an annual average of two percentage points of GDP during the following three years. By 1993, it amounted to 49.6 per cent of GDP.

Since the expansion of social expenditure was done without reducing capital spending – which still constituted the core of the PSOE's economic strategy – higher taxes would have been necessary to avoid a fiscal deficit. Taxes were raised, however, in a limited way. The socialist party reckoned that an increase in taxes could endanger its grip on key centrist voters. As a result, the general government deficit rose from 2.8 per cent of GDP in 1989 to 4.9 per cent of GDP in 1991 and then to 7.5 per cent in 1993. Public debt jumped from 45 per cent of GDP in 1991 to 64 per cent of GDP in 1994.

The government's incapacity to either restrain social transfers or increase taxes forced González, in turn, to rely on a tight monetary policy to achieve its goals. Until well into the economic recovery in the mid-1980s, monetary policy had played a variable role in the González government's overall economic policy – tightly set through 1984 and accommodating in 1985–86 under the 'Acuerdo Económico y Social' with UGT and CEOE. After the summer of 1988, monetary policy came to play a stronger and more distinctive role. Economic and political conditions clearly had changed at that time. While inflation was experiencing an upturn, the renewal of the social compact to combat it looked less and less promising. Public authorities eventually decided to raise intervention rates in early September. Further measures adopted in February 1989 to curb private credit and foreign capital inflows sent nominal short-term interest rates up to 15 per cent. In real terms the latter were among the highest in Europe: about five percentage points above German interest rates.

Still, the measures taken in February were soon perceived to be insufficient. Because of accelerating financial innovations that had boosted liquidity in the Spanish financial market, the traditional system of targeting monetary aggregates had become increasingly uncertain as a means to conduct monetary policy. In addition, the increasing mobility of capital within the EC was making impossible the conciliation of both a monetary policy directed to reducing inflation and the maintenance of an exchange rate favourable enough to Spanish exports. Cutting through all these dilemmas, the Spanish government decided to integrate the peseta in the ERM in June 1989.

To sustain the commitment to an implicitly coordinated monetary policy (with the EC) and to decelerate the rhythm of domestic activity, the integration into the ERM was followed by a package of fiscal measures to reduce the deficit and a temporary set of credit controls. As pointed out above, in spite of successive calls for fiscal discipline both from within the government and from the Bank of Spain (Banco de España 1989: 98ff., 1991: 99ff.) to sustain the anti-inflationary strategy and to avoid overburdening monetary policy, the public deficit could not be tamed. Fiscal policy turned out to add fuel to the expansion of domestic demand. Accordingly, monetary policy was left alone to sustain the deflationary macroeconomic strategy of the socialist government. High interest rates proved to be at the crossroads of a southern European social democratic strategy of macroeconomic stability (to be implemented without the unions) and state interventionism (to be achieved through a medium-term aggressive fiscal policy).

Even in the face of a sharp downturn in economic activity, interest rates would remain extremely high until 1993. Nominal short-term interest rates reached 16 per cent at the end of 1989 and then fell to 15 per cent throughout 1990. In real terms, that implied rates of eight per cent until the end of 1990. The oil shock of 1990 slowed the growth rate down even more and, as inflation went down by the first quarter of 1991, monetary policy was slightly loosened. Nominal short-term interest rates fell by two points and stabilized around 12.5 per cent. In real terms, interest rates declined by one point to seven per cent. That modest downward trend was reversed in 1992. Although total domestic demand had slowed, wage increases and inflation remained high. Then, as the year progressed, a mounting climate of uncertainty over the Maastricht project turned against the ERM. In September 1992 the generalized financial turmoil of European markets put pressure on the peseta. The government, however, for whom the European programme of convergence had strong political value, decided to sustain a tight monetary policy. The Bank of Spain intervened massively, temporary foreign exchange controls were again introduced (from mid-September to late November) and the intervention rate was pushed upwards. By the end of 1992, nominal short-term interest rates were over 15 per cent – almost ten per cent in real terms. As the EMS crisis continued and the worldwide economic downturn effectively hit Spain, it was now apparent that the government was increasingly trapped into implementing a very costly economic strategy. Only a prolonged round of devaluations forced by the behaviour of the international financial markets and the clear loss of the socialist majority in 1993 would finally compromise monetary discipline, and therefore break up the strained equilibrium of political pressures and competing policies that had characterized the González government since the mid-1980s.

## SEARCHING FOR COMPETITIVENESS

### *The role of industrial policy*

The PSOE's industrial policy was characterized, in turn, by the combination of very selective privatizations, the consolidation of firms in several sectors to generate economies of scale, and the (late) introduction of competitive markets in several instances. Those changes derived from the interaction of technological shocks, the process of European integration and the socialist government's commitment to the public enterprise sector as a means of pursuing an active industrial policy.

FIGURE 1

THE SPANISH ENERGY SECTOR, 1980–95

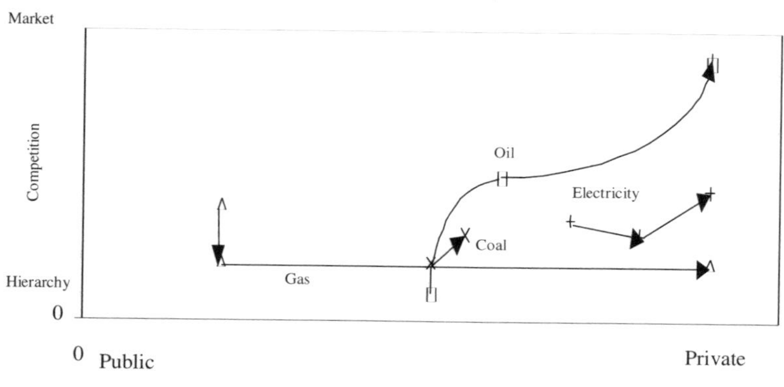

FIGURE 2

SPANISH TRANSPORTATION AND COMMUNICATION SECTORS, 1980–95

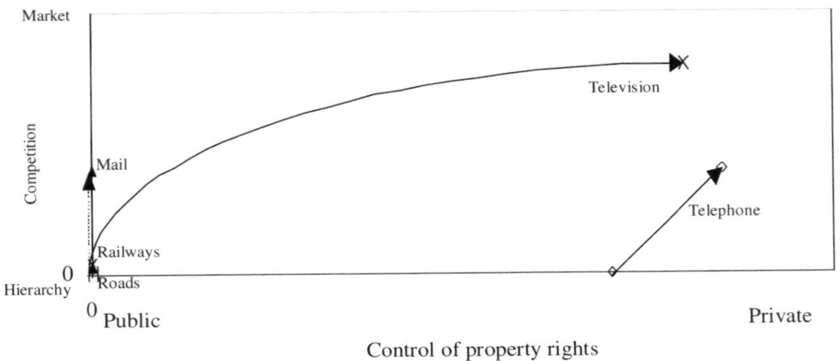


FIGURE 3

THE SPANISH INDUSTRIAL AND FINANCIAL SECTORS, 1980–1995

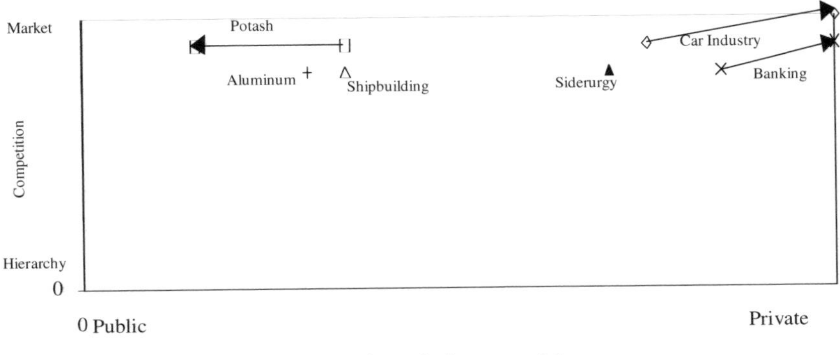

Figures 1–3 summarize the evolution of those Spanish production sectors where public firms had a substantial role from 1980 to 1995. All figures examine their evolution along two dimensions: the extent of public ownership (the horizontal axis) and the degree of competition (the vertical axis). The degree of competition includes the changes that take place both as a result of the introduction of new firms and deregulation measures (and which result in an expansion of the extent of competition) and as a result of mergers and consolidation strategies (which shifted the sector in the opposite direction). Figure 1 describes the energy sector; Figure 2 includes the transportation and communication sectors; and Figure 3 represents the remaining sectors (manufacturing and finance).

Nationalistic policies led in the 1940s and the 1950s to the state playing a major role in promoting the country's industrialization. By the early 1980s, Spanish state-owned companies accounted for nearly ten per cent of both national value added and total compensation to employees, and for almost 15 per cent of all gross fixed capital formation. The level of investment supplied by all public companies was only significantly higher in Austria, Greece, Norway and Portugal and similar to that in Italy and the UK. Although overall rather diversified, the Spanish public enterprise sector played a key role in mining, heavy industry (e.g. steel, ship-building and aluminium), oil, electricity, telecommunications, railways, and maritime and air transport.

The level of public ownership experienced relatively minor changes under the PSOE government. Privatizations were limited to the car industry in the early 1980s and in the oil, communications and banking sectors at the end of the decade (the latter mainly resulting from a set of European Commission regulations). Overall, between 1982 and 1993, the sale of public assets led to revenues equal to 0.9 per cent of the Spanish yearly GDP (in Great Britain and for the same period, privatization revenues amounted to 12 per cent of the British annual GDP). From 1993 to 1996, that is, under a minority socialist government supported by centre-right regionalist parties, the sale of state assets rose to 1.4 per cent of GDP.

Spain's policy of maintaining the publicly owned enterprises sector remained almost unaltered until the mid-1990s and fits the strategy followed by other social democratic European governments (Boix 1998, ch.4). The González government decided to employ the publicly owned enterprises sector to speed up its strategy of human and physical capital formation and to increase the international competitiveness of the Spanish economy. Accordingly, capital formation by public firms grew around 15 per cent every year in the mid- and late 1980s, a rate higher than that in the private sector and in the general government. Moreover, capital formation was directed toward the telecommunications sector (Telefónica tripled its investment in real terms from 1986 to 1990), railway transport (RENFE, the state-owned rail company also tripled its investment during the same period), oil and gas (the *Instituto Nacional de Hidrocarburos*' investment in 1990 was 2.5 times bigger than in 1986 in real terms) and air and sea transport (investment grew eight times from 1986 to 1990 in real terms). All other sectors, which included more traditional industries such as steel, mining, aluminium and ship-building, had their rates of investment unchanged or even curtailed (in real terms). Besides increasing fixed investment, public companies made an important effort in human capital formation. The *Instituto Nacional de Industria* (INI) doubled its expenditure on R&D to two per cent of its total sales in those years, putting it above the European average and at levels similar to other big European industrial concerns.

Changes in the extent of competition varied substantially across sectors. The creation of several regional and private TV networks, the progressive dismantling of the telephone monopoly, and the emergence of several *de facto* competitors to the public mail system led to a considerable increase in competition in the telecommunications sector. In the energy sector, the distribution of oil was thoroughly liberalized. Yet deregulation remained almost absent in other areas. As a matter of fact, the Spanish government actively promoted the consolidation of entire manufacturing sectors, resulting in a severe reduction of competition, solely counterbalanced by Spain's integration in the EU. After buying shares in several private companies (*Viesgo*, *Fecsa*, *Sevillana*, *Saltos del Nansa*), the electricity subholding company *Endesa* reinforced its predominant position in the domestic market and became one of the six largest electricity groups in Europe. In the gas sector, the government favoured the consolidation of several companies in *Gas Nacional* which, after 1995, controlled close to nine tenths of the industrial and domestic markets. The electronics sector was organized around Inisel, which through several mergers and shares' exchanges became one of the biggest European subholding companies (Espina 1992). In the area of potash production, INI bought *Potasas del Llobregat* and ended up controlling 88 per cent of total national output in this sector (against 67 per cent in 1984). In oil and gas production and distribution, the Spanish government successfully maintained INH in a solid position after the process of European integration injected competition in the sector.

Similarly, in 1991 all state banks were merged into CBE (*Corporación Bancaria de España*, later *Argentaria CBE*) to form the third largest banking group in the Spanish financial sector.

It is easily seen that competition only increased in those sectors in which technological breakthroughs (such as cable TV or the mobile phone) altered the production and distribution of goods and broke up previous natural monopolies. Pressed by the European Commission and emerging domestic firms, the state eventually accepted the need to free up markets and regulate competition. By contrast, in those sectors where there were no technological changes (i.e. where the existing natural monopolies or fully competitive markets have remained unchanged), the Spanish government pushed for their consolidation and vertical integration to respond, through the creation of substantial economies of scale, to the internationalization of the Spanish economy. As a matter of fact, in spite of considerable pressure from Brussels, several industries (such as coal, steel, and ship-building) continued to receive substantial public subsidies.

### *The role of public capital formation*

With macroeconomic policy constrained by the need to achieve low inflation and join the EMU, the González government was left with only one possible (social democratic) strategy to reduce unemployment and catch up with Europe: promoting the transformation of the supply conditions of the Spanish economy through massive public spending in human and physical capital. Accordingly, the González government raised revenues systematically – 7.7 percentage points of GDP. Containing social expenditure – which hardly increased prior to 1990 – and cutting subsidies and capital transfers substantially, most revenues were used initially to lower the public deficit and increase the level of public (and hence total) savings. By 1989 the public deficit was standing at 2.8 per cent of GDP or 3.2 percentage points less than in 1986, although a sudden increase in social spending in 1990–91 pushed the public deficit up to around five per cent of GDP.

The containment of the public deficit to boost the pool of savings was immediately followed by a systematic public capital formation strategy. Fixed capital formation (i.e. spending on basic infrastructures and on transportation) was steadily increased by 2.1 points of GDP up to 5.2 per cent of GDP in 1991. Another two percentage points of GDP were allocated to both general education expenditure and new manpower programmes. A similar and complementary strategy was developed regarding the public enterprise sector. After approving painful restructuring plans and minimal privatizations, in the mid- and late 1980s the government engaged several key public firms in strong investment plans and in opening up new markets abroad.

## COMPENSATORY POLICIES

To compensate for the introduction of a stable macroeconomic framework (and, more generally, to fulfil the party's social democratic platform), the PSOE's economic and social policies took on a clear redistributive character. Social policies were expanded notoriously after 1988. As a result, social expenditure went up from 25.3 per cent of the disposable household income in 1980 to 33.7 per cent ten years later. Contributory pensions were upgraded and to some extent equalized, and new categories, such as non-contributory pensions, were created. Unemployment benefits were extended to cover more than half the registered unemployed by 1991. Health coverage was improved and expenditure on public education increased more than any other item, excluding fixed capital formation (Bandrés 1993). The allocation of new expenditure was extremely progressive. Public expenditure as a proportion of the average consumption of the lowest income decile went from 119.2 per cent in 1980 to 204.3 per cent in 1990. For the fifth income decile, it went up from 48.4 to 75.1 per cent. For the top income decile it hardly changed: public expenditure represented 31.0 per cent of the average consumption in that income fraction in 1980 and 36.6 per cent ten years later (Gimeno 1993).

The aggressive build-up of fixed capital stock, mostly in the form of ambitious infrastructure projects, was distributed unequally across regions, to a large extent in accordance with purely redistributive concerns in favour of the least developed areas.

Finally, the expansion in the state's role was accompanied by a significant increase in tax collection, mostly implemented through a very progressive personal income tax. This had significant redistributive effects. In 1982 the Gini index of the Spanish income distribution was 0.331 before and 0.304 after taxes. In 1990, it was 0.416 before and 0.367 after taxes. That is, even though the initial distribution of declared income had become more unequal, the redistributive effect of the income tax system increased. The difference in the Gini index before and after taxes had risen from 0.027 in 1982 to 0.049 in 1990 (Lasheras *et al.* 1993).

The redistributive nature of the PSOE's social policies can be also gauged by looking at how Spanish citizens judged the government's tax and expenditure policies. In July 1991, 56 per cent of all surveyed thought they were paying more in taxes than what they were receiving in public services. That proportion reached 92 per cent among businessmen and top managers and 69 per cent among mid-managerial positions. Among industrial workers it was 56 per cent: that is, the national average. Instead, only 40 per cent of retired people and 33 per cent of agricultural workers said that they were receiving less than what they had paid. A similar gap appeared in relation to income levels. Whereas 72 per cent of those earning more than Pta.200,000 every month said they were receiving less than they were paying, among those earning less than Pta.50,000, the percentage was only 36 per cent.[11]

It is clear that the development of generous social policies contributed to a strengthening of the core of the electoral coalition that supported the PSOE – the industrial working class, agricultural labourers, the retired population, the unemployed – in spite of the sharp economic crisis that hit Spain in the early 1990s (Boix 1998, ch.6; Maravall and Fraile 1998).

## CONCLUDING REMARKS

In exploring the ways in which the integration of the Spanish economy in the EC affected the socialist government's economic policies, this article sheds light on the set of economic strategies left to social democratic governments in an increasingly interdependent world economy.

As the process of economic integration unfolded, the capacity of the Spanish governments to manipulate the economic business cycle to sustain full employment declined dramatically. With increasing trade openness, a higher portion of domestic demand became satisfied abroad and, as a result, internally engineered expansionary policies simply risked propelling imports up, increasing trade deficits and eroding economic competitiveness. Similarly, as capital mobility progressed, the policy-makers' autonomy to shape fiscal and monetary policies evaporated dramatically as well. While the Spanish government maintained a floating exchange rate, domestic monetary expansions could have been possible in the short run through currency depreciations. But its effects were likely to be quickly outweighed by both the increasing cost of imports and a wage push that would neutralize the gains of the depreciation. As a matter of fact, currency depreciations clashed directly with the growing emphasis that the European core countries put on monetary and exchange stability over the 1980s. After the devaluation of 1982, the Spanish cabinet resisted any move to absorb the systematic inflation differential with Europe through depreciation. Once a fixed exchange regime was established, first unilaterally, then through EMU, monetary policy was effectively surrendered to Europe.

The constraints that the process of European integration imposed on the Spanish socialist cabinet were aggravated by the structure of the Spanish unions. As stressed by the literature on social democratic corporatism, unless they can count upon a highly organized labour movement, left-wing governments progressively abandon expansionary policies to fight unemployment. In Spain, the González government never discarded the possibility of striking a deal with the union movement to reduce inflation without having to resort to an excessively tight monetary policy. But the incentive structure of the small and radicalized Spanish trade unions was seldom aligned with the goals of the PSOE government. A corporatist pact was only possible in 1985–86 in response to a critical economic downturn. As the economy overheated and the labour market tightened up in the late 1980s, any chances of a social pact waned and the socialist government could only use interest rates to choke inflation and sustain the peseta.

As the economy becomes increasingly open and the old corporatist system is unavailable (a scenario that has become more common over time: see Pontusson 1991; Lange *et al.* 1995) social democrats are left with two fundamental tools. On the one hand, they must focus on building up a public stock of human and physical capital (to ensure the competitiveness of the domestic economy while equalizing conditions). On the other, they develop a set of policies geared toward domestic compensation. These two responses were present under the González government in Spain. Public expenditure rose by a fourth under the PSOE government. Two thirds of the increase were allocated to raise public savings as well as fixed and human capital formation. Key public firms were asked to join in the effort to revamp the supply side of the Spanish economy. Moreover, unemployment benefits were expanded, pensions were upgraded and a universal health care system was established.

The process of internationalization and the failure of the social democratic corporatist model generated important electoral tensions that eventually weakened the PSOE programme. Governing in a country with a relatively unskilled workforce – the levels of educational attainment in Spain are low relative to other European countries – it made economic sense to intensify all capital formation efforts to avoid the trap of an excessively high social wage. Yet the almost exclusive focus on public investment until 1989 (to the detriment of public transfers) had important political costs. A severe general strike in 1988 demanding more social spending threatened to ruin the macroeconomic strategy pursued by the government and to alienate important parts of the industrial working class from the government. In the 1989 parliamentary elections, PSOE's share of the vote dropped from 43.4 to 40.3 per cent. The radical Left more than doubled its vote from 4.6 to 9.2 per cent. González responded by increasing social spending along with public capital formation. Since taxes could not be increased substantially without losing centrist voters, the public deficit began to rise rapidly. The resulting expansionary fiscal policy only reinforced the need to tighten monetary policy. Still, the economic strategy of high taxes and public investment (and generous social transfers) maintained González in power for 16 years (the last three with the external support of centrist regionalist parties). Although PSOE lost part of its massive support of 1982, it consistently polled close to two fifths of the vote through the mid-1990s. Among blue-collar workers and the rural 'proletariat' of temporary workers, PSOE received 60 per cent of the votes cast (or over 40 per cent of the total electorate). Support was almost as high among pensioners and the unemployed receiving state benefits. In 1993, PSOE continued to lead the Conservative party among the lower-middle classes with a small advantage.

## NOTES

1. I would like to thank the following for their comments: Alícia Adserà, James E. Alt, Kevin Featherstone, Peter E. Hall, José María Maravall and Ton Notermans, as well as the participants at the ARENA Meeting on 'Social Democrats and EMU', Oslo, 28–31 May 1998.
2. For an analysis of the attitudes of the Spanish political parties toward the EC, see Álvarez-Miranda (1996).
3. For a detailed analysis of the first legislature of the socialist government, see Boix (1997, 1998, 2000).
4. This interpretation borrows heavily from Gruber's (1999a, 1999b) concept of 'go-it-alone power' to explain the formation of international institutions. In Gruber's account, international institutions need not be the result of straightforward Pareto-improving cooperative agreements among equal partners. Instead, they may emerge as a set of core countries which establish agreements or embark on strategies that, by modifying the status quo, force the remaining countries to join the same institution or pattern of behaviour to minimize the losses that may occur from not doing so. The

process of capital deregulation (and, in particular, its institutionalization in continental Europe through the EU project) fits this explanation particularly well. Notice then that this account differs in equal proportions from two rather extended interpretations: those that directly link the process of deregulation to changes in international financial markets (McKenzie and Lee 1991; O'Brien 1992; to some extent, Goodman and Pauly 1993), as well as those that attribute the decision to liberalize to purely domestic conditions, such as the hegemony of centre-right governments (Notermans 1993), or the internal balance of power among sectoral interests (Frieden 1991).

5. For the position of the cabinet, see de la Dehesa (1988) and Solchaga (1990). For the party, see Programa 2000 (1988).
6. See Solchaga (1990). Any depreciation policy through the exchange rate was to be foregone as well for the sake of price stability since, according to the view of the public authorities, 'the costs of joining the EMS would be nominal rather than real because, in an economy like the Spanish one, with a high level of wage indexation, any variation in the nominal exchange rate would quickly be transmitted into prices and the capacity to affect the level of competitiveness and real growth would be transitory' (Banco de España 1989: 39). A good analysis of the policy reasoning that led to the integration of Spain in the ERM can be seen in Malo de Molina and Pérez (1990). See also the Bank of Spain's *Informe Anual* for 1989 (Banco de España 1989), especially pp.37ff.
7. A straightforward exposition of these two alternatives and their costs and benefits by the Minister of the Economy himself can be found in the presentation of the Budget for 1989 (Solchaga 1988: 29ff.), the Budget for 1990 (Solchaga 1990: 33ff.) and the Budget for 1992 (Solchaga 1991b: 12ff.).
8. Espina (*La Vanguardia*, 12 February 1989, reproduced in Espina 1991) locates this shift in the aftermath of the 1986 elections for union representatives in which UGT's expectations of winning a strong mandate were not fulfilled. Blaming these results on its participation in the 1985–86 social compact, UGT would have decided to adopt a more critical stance towards the government in order to regain votes to its left.
9. All data are taken from Godé (1990), Jiménez Fernández (1990, 1991), Ruiz Alvarez (1992) and García Perea and Gómez (1993).
10. Besides the strategies of social concertation or restrictive macroeconomic policies, the government could have followed a third scenario: it could have curtailed union power and, above all, reformed the labour market to make it flexible, highly responsive to the economic cycle and less prone to inflationary pressures. The government was either unable or unwilling to follow that alternative. After the government legalized some forms of temporary contracts in 1984 with the acquiescence of unions, further attempts to reform a highly regulated labour market were staved off regularly.
11. The data is from *Revista Española de Investigaciones Sociológicas*, 'Datos de opinión. Los españoles ante el pago de impuestos' (July–Sept. 1991, vol.55), p.240.

## REFERENCES

Alvarez-Miranda, B. (1996): *El sur de Europa y la adhesión a la Comunidad: los debates políticos* [Southern Europe and adhesion to the Community: the political debates], Madrid: Centro de Investigaciones Sociológicas – Siglo Veintiuno de España Editores.

Banco de España (1989): *Informe Anual* [Annual Report], Madrid: Banco de España.

—— (1991): *Informe Anual* [Annual Report], Madrid: Banco de España.

Bandrés, E. (1993): 'La eficacia redistributiva de los gastos sociales. Una aplicación al caso español (1980–1990)' [The redistributive efficacy of the social expenditure. An application to the Spanish case (1980–1990)], in *I Simposio sobre Igualdad y*

*Distribución de la Renta y la Riqueza* [Symposium on Equality and Distribution of income and wealth], Madrid: Fundación Argentaria, vol.VII, pp.123–71.

Boix, C. (1997): 'Searching for Competitiveness: The Spanish Public Sector in the 1980s and 1990s', in J.E. Lane (ed.), *Reforming the Public Sector*, Sage, ch.11.

—— (1998): *Political Parties, Growth, and Equality. Conservative and Social Democratic Strategies in the World Economy*. New York: Cambridge University Press.

—— (2000): 'Partisan Governments and Macroeconomic Policies in OECD countries, 1961–93', *World Politics* 53 (fall 2000), pp.38–73.

de la Dehesa, G. (1988): 'Los límites de la política económica española' [The Limits of Spanish Economic Policy], *Leviatán* 32, pp.27–37.

Eichengreen, B. (1996): *Globalizing Capital: A History of the International Monetary System*, Princeton NJ: Princeton University Press.

EIU (1986–93): *Country Report. Spain*, London: Economist Intelligence Unit.

Espina, A. (1991): *Empleo, democracia y relaciones industriales* [Employment, Democracy and Industrial Relations], Madrid: Ministerio de Trabajo y Seguridad Social.

—— (1992): *Recursos humanos y política industrial: España ante la Unión Europea* [Human resources and industrial policy: Spain before the EU], Madrid: Fundesco.

Fernández-Castro, J. (1993): 'The Creation of a New Industrial Relations System and Political Change: The Case of Spain', unpublished paper, Massachusetts Institute of Technology: Sept. 1993.

Frieden, J.A. (1991): 'Invested Interests: The Politics of National Economic Policies in a World of Global Finance', *International Organization* 45, pp.425–51.

García Perea, P., and R. Gómez (1993): 'Aspectos institucionales del mercado de trabajo español, en comparación con otros Países comunitarios' [Institutional aspects of the Spanish labour market in comparison with other community countries], *Banco de España. Bolet'n Económico* [Bank of Spain, Economic Bulletin] (Sept.), pp.29–47.

Gimeno, A. (1993): 'Incidencia del gasto público por niveles de renta (España 1990 vs. 1980)' [Incidence of public expenditure for the levels of income (Spain 1990 vs 1980)], *I Simposio sobre Igualdad y Distribución de la Renta y la Riqueza* [Symposium on Equality and Distribution of income and wealth], Madrid: Fundación Argentaria, vol.VII.

Godé Sánchez, J.A. (1990): 'Los gastos sociales en el Presupuesto de 1990' [Social expenditure in the 1990 Budget], *Presupuesto y Gasto Público* [Budget and Public Expenditure] 2.

Goodman, J.B., and L.W. Pauly (1993): 'The Obsolescence of Capital Controls? Economic Management in an Age of Global Markets', *World Politics* 46.

Gruber, Lloyd (1999a): 'Rationalist Approaches to International Cooperation: A Call for Theoretical Reorientation', *The Irving B. Harris Graduate School of Public Policy Studies. Working Paper Series* 99.14.

—— (1999b): 'Interstate Cooperation and the Hidden Face of Power: The Case of European Money', *The Irving B. Harris Graduate School of Public Policy Studies. Working Paper Series* 99.16.

Jiménez Fernández, A. (1990): 'La Seguridad Social en 1990: El presupuesto del consenso social' [Social Security in 1990: the budget of the social consensus], *Presupuesto y Gasto Público* [Budget and Public Expenditure] 2.

—— (1991): 'La política de prestaciones que informa el contenido del presupuesto de la Seguridad Social para 1991 y breve descripción de este último' [Transfer policies in the 1991 Social Security Budget and a short description of the latter], *Presupuesto y Gasto Público* [Budget and Public Expenditure] 4.

Juliá Díaz, S. (ed.) (1988): *La desavenencia: partido, sindicato y huelga general* [The discord: party, trade union and general strike], Madrid: El País/Aguilar.

Lange, P., M. Wallerstein and M. Golden (1995): 'The End of Corporatism? Wage Setting in the Nordic and Germanic Countries', in S.M. Jacoby (ed.), *The Workers of Nations.*

*Industrial Relations in a Global Economy*. Oxford: Oxford University Press.
Lasheras, M.A., I. Rabadán and R. Salas (1993): 'Política redistributiva en el IRPF entre 1982 y 1990' [Redistributive policy in personal income tax between 1982 and 1990], *Cuadernos de Actualidad de Hacienda Pública Española* [Current Affairs Notebooks on the Spanish Exchequer] 7.
Malo de Molina, J.L., and J.P. Fernández (1990): 'La Política monetaria española en la transición hacia la unión monetaria europea' [Spanish monetary policy in the transition to the European Monetary Union], *Papeles de Economía Española* [Papers on the Spanish Economy] 43.
Maravall, J.M., and M. Fraile (1998): 'The Politics of Unemployment. The Spanish Experience in Comparative Perspective', *Centro de Estudios Sociales Avanzados Fundación Juan March Working Paper Series* [Centre for Advanced Social Studies, Juan March Foundation Working Paper Series] 124, June.
McKenzie, R.B., and D.R. Lee (1991): *Quicksilver Capital: How the Rapid Movement of Wealth Has Changed the World*, New York: Free Press.
Notermans, Ton. (1993): 'The Abdication from National Policy Autonomy: Why the Macroeconomic Policy Regime Has Become So Unfavorable to Labor', *Politics and Society* 21, pp.133–68.
O'Brien, R. (1992): *Global Financial Integration: The End of Geography*, London: Pinter.
Pontusson, J. (1991): 'The Crisis of Swedish Social Democracy', unpublished paper, Cornell University: March 1991.
Programa 2000 (1988): *La economía española a debate* [Debating the Spanish economy], Madrid: Siglo XXI.
PSOE (1982): *Programa Electoral* [Electoral Programme], Madrid: Partido Socialista Obrero Español.
Redondo, N. (1988): 'Los objetivos del sindicalismo' [The objectives of trade unionism], *Anuario El País 1988*, Madrid: PRISA, p.357.
Revista Española de Investigaciones Sociológicas, 'Datos de opinión. Los españoles ante el pago de impuestos' [Survey data. The Spaniards and taxes] July–September 1991, vol.55.
Ruiz Alvarez, J.L. (1992): 'Un análisis económico de las recientes Políticas presupuestarias del mercado de trabajo' [An economic analysis of recent budgetary policies toward the labour market], *Presupuesto y Gasto Público* [Budget and Public Expenditure] 7.
Simmons, B. (1999): 'The Internationalization of Capital', in H. Kitschelt, P. Lange, G. Marks and J. Stephens (eds.), *Continuity and Change in Contemporary Capitalism*, New York: Cambridge University Press.
Solchaga, C. (1986): 'Discurso en la presentación de la Ley de Presupuestos Generales del Estado para 1987 ante el Congreso de Diputados' [Opening speech in the presentation of the Law of the general budget of the state for 1987 before the Congress of Deputies], *Hacienda Pública Española* [Spanish Public Finance] pp.102–3.
—— (1988): 'Presentación del proyecto de Ley de Presupuestos Generales del Estado para 1989' ['Presentation of the draft law of the general budget of the state for 1989'], *Hacienda Pública Española* [Spanish Public Finance] 112.
—— (1990): 'Presentación del proyecto de Ley de Presupuestos Generales del Estado para 1990' [Presentation of the draft law of the general budget of the state for 1989] *Presupuesto y Gasto Público* [Budget and public expenditure] 2.
—— (1991a): 'Presentación del proyecto de Ley de Presupuestos Generales del Estado para 1991' [Presentation of the draft law of the general budget of the state for 1991] *Presupuesto y Gasto Público* [Budget and public expenditure] 4.
—— (1991b): 'Presentación del proyecto de Ley de Presupuestos Generales del Estado para 1992' [Presentation of the draft law of the general budget of the state for 1991] *Presupuesto y Gasto Público* [Budget and public expenditure] 6.
Zabalza, A. (1989): 'Crecimiento, empleo y Política fiscal en la CEE y en España' [Growth,

employment and fiscal policy in EEC and Spain], *Papeles de Economía Española* [Papers on the Spanish Economy] 41.
—— (1990): 'El Presupuesto y su contexto económico' [The budget and its economic context], *Presupuesto y Gasto Público* [Budget and public expenditure] 2.
—— (1991): 'El sector público español ante el mercado único' [The spanish public sector before the single market], *Papeles de Economía Española* [Papers of the Spanish Economy] 48.

# Economic Adjustment and Financial Reform: Greece's Europeanization and the Emergence of a Stabilization State

GEORGE PAGOULATOS

In 1990, when Greece's arduous course to economic convergence with the rest of the EC can be claimed to have begun, Greece registered its own misery index in the form of the most depressing combination of macroeconomic indicators in the Community. It had the highest inflation rate (20.4 per cent) and the highest public sector borrowing requirement (21 per cent in GDP terms), combined with the lowest GDP per head (47.2 per cent of the EC average) and the lowest GDP growth rate (–0.1 per cent) in the entire EC (European Commission 1994). Since her 1981 accession to the EC, with the exception of a stabilization parenthesis in 1985–87, Greece consistently increased her distance from the Community (Kazakos 1992).

For a country with the most pronounced overall economic and structural divergence from the EU standard, Europeanization can be taken to comprise a minimum notion of 'normalization' (Giuliani 1999: 6). Indeed, convergence to the EU standard implies overcoming the set of circumstances that define a peripheral country's standing as divergent, 'laggard' or 'exceptional'. True, nearly every EU country can lay claim to some form of 'exceptionalism' in the institutional, sociopolitical or cultural sphere. However, the consistent and cumulative occurrence through the early 1990s of serious indicators of relative economic delay in the case of Greece unambiguously testifies to divergence.

Admittedly, convergence in this case is a euphemistic misnomer, as it is literally meant to signify two or more parties heading towards each other, aimed to meet midway or at a more advanced point. Here, Europeanization can be understood mostly as 'catch-up', that is a unidirectional progress of peripheral and lagging countries towards a certain set of advanced economic and institutional features identified with the EU core (cf. Gibson 2001). Though the notion involves mostly structural transformations (a well functioning executive and bureaucracy, a state that is 'as small as possible and as large as necessary', an efficient market, an autonomous and vigorous civil society), the achievement of these objectives, among others, is crucially predicated on a stable macroeconomic environment. That is why, for Greece, the objective of economic Europeanization over the 1990s has been almost fully identified with obtaining the nominal Maastricht criteria and achieving EMU entry.

Several dynamics underlie the process of Europeanization as convergence or 'catch-up'. Colin Bennett (1991) has singled out:

- emulation, where state actors copy action taken elsewhere;
- elite networking, where convergence is brought about by transnational policy communities;
- harmonization through the international regimes and the recognition of interdependence resulting from the transnationalization of economies; and
- penetration by external actors and interests, where states are forced to conform to actions taken elsewhere by external actors.

Taking account of the dynamics underlying Europeanization helps recall its fundamentally political character. That is underlined, among others, by Ladrech (1994: 69) in his definition of 'Europeanization' as 'a process reorienting the direction and shape of politics to the degree that EC political and economic dynamics become part of the organizational logic of national politics and policy-making'. Under the above framework, Europeanization is commensurate to the degree of internalization of the EU economic and institutional objectives by domestic political and policy elites (cf. Ioakimidis 1996).

This article focuses on the economic and financial policy objectives and transformations underpinning Greece's course towards economic integration and the monetary union.[1] The argument developed here is that Greece's economic Europeanization followed an orthodox path of subjecting the economy to external constraint mechanisms (the EC balance of payments support loans, capital liberalization, entry into the EMS with particular strings attached, alignment behind the Maastricht convergence targets) that enabled governments to ease sociopolitical resistances and to conform to the dictates of economic policy pragmatism. And it is also argued that Europeanization was achieved through the transition from a growth state (which by that time – having failed its growth mission – had been reduced merely to an interventionist or a distributive state) to a stabilization state.

## THE 1980S: THE POLITICS OF ABORTED ADJUSTMENT

Greece's 1981 entry to the EC coincided with the rise to power that same year of the socialist party (PASOK) under Andreas Papandreou, carrying an anti-EC agenda promising socializations and extensive social spending. As PASOK sought to stabilize its political grip by targeting left-wing voters and appealing to socioeconomically marginalized strata, redistribution or plain electoral distribution constituted a main pillar of its political strategy. Consequently, in the 1980s Greece further diverged from the EC (Verney 1996). Between 1975 and 1990, the Greek public sector as a percentage of the total economy expanded from about 35 per cent in 1975 to 60 per cent in 1990. One fifth of this 25 per cent increase took place between 1975 and 1980, and the remaining four fifths occurred in the 1980s (Balfoussias 1993: 135–7).[2] This public sector expansion was the exact opposite of parallel OECD and EC trends. In 1975, public spending in Greece, at 32.4 per cent of GDP, was by 5.5 per cent lower than the OECD average and 12.3 per cent lower than the EC average; however, by the end of the 1980s Greek public spending had climbed to 55.7 per cent of GDP (i.e. 16 per cent higher than the OECD average and 8 per cent higher than the EC average; Balfoussias 1993: 140–41).

Thus PASOK policy-makers postponed the liberalization reforms encouraged by the EC, and demanded – through the 1982 Memorandum – special assistance from the EC tantamount to renegotiation of Greece's terms of entry. PASOK also attempted (during the first government term, 1981–85) to pursue its own supply-side 'structuralist' strategy of state interventionism emphasizing institutional reforms such as democratic planning and socialization, under the theoretical premise of subordinating monetary stability to the goal of industrial and agricultural protection, restructuring and development (Tsakalotos 1991; Lavdas 1997: 148ff.). What eventually prevailed was a politically expedient strategy of extensive social spending (far exceeding government revenues), much of which admittedly brought Greece closer to the EC standards of social expenditure. However, most of that fiscal and credit expansionism was distributively minded, targeting selected voter categories. The demand boost did not lead to more growth but ended up increasing consumption and budget deficits. Thus, independent economic policy led to policy outcomes clearly divergent from the EC standard.

The 1981–85 period was characterized by a very slow progress in liberalization and the removal of trade barriers, conforming to the hard core of Greece's obligations to the EC. Though tariffs and quotas were dismantled, in accordance with the interventionist strategy of the first half of the 1980s, they were replaced by protectionist selective policies relying on non-tariff barriers such as a regulatory tax on imports (established in 1984 and abolished only as late as 1989) and export subsidies (Katseli 1990: 236). In addition, a wide number of ailing and overindebted industrial firms were brought under the Industrial Reconstruction Organization (IRO), established in 1983, which was given the objective of overhauling the companies and returning them to the market. In effect, these firms remained under the IRO until well into the 1990s, kept alive by constant financial transfusions that burdened the public debt while often constituting a form of illicit subsidy.

### *The 1985 Stabilization Programme and reversion to economic expansionism*

Economic adjustment in the 1985–87 period was spearheaded by a serious macroeconomic crisis. Directly upon its June 1985 re-election to power, PASOK was faced with the immediate spectrum of an urgent balance of payments crisis, on top of inflation galloping in the area of 20 per cent, fuelled by the monetization of rising public deficits. A stabilization programme was thus launched in the autumn of 1985. Of neo-Keynesian inspiration, the programme was designed sharply to curtail domestic demand, reduce the public sector borrowing requirement (a reduction of public expenditure was decided) and enhance competitiveness (a 15 per cent drachma devaluation was implemented followed by a tight incomes policy). The programme was backed by an EC balance-of-payments support loan, which accelerated the implementation of certain adjustment measures such as the gradual abolition of several subsidies provided through the credit system, the liberalization of some state monopolies (salt, petroleum, matches, etc.) and other state interventions in the economy. Supported by a favourable international economic conjuncture of falling oil prices, the stabilization programme succeeded in curtailing inflation and stimulating growth. However, almost no structural reforms were systematically advanced in the second half of the 1980s. No privatization measures were implemented (despite the rise of the IRO enterprises into a major financial burden for the budget), and no market liberalization programme was pushed through, with a single notable exception: the gradual liberalization of the financial system.

The way for financial liberalization had been paved through the gradual rationalization and upward unification of interest rates after 1984. However, the rationale for financial reform was perhaps predominantly of a macroeconomic rather than a microeconomic type, and it had much to do with the prospect of European financial liberalization and integration (the so-called 'external' or 'capital constraint'). Financial liberalization in the second half of the 1980s was necessitated by the urgent need for macroeconomic stabilization. The regime of administered credit at low or even negative real interest rates exercised a constant inflationary impact; at the same time, fixed interest rates and the lack of a money market prevented the Bank of Greece from exercising effective monetary policy towards disinflation. Thus, credit rationalization and liberalization, and the gradual upward adjustment of interest rates, was necessitated by the objective of macroeconomic adjustment, and that despite the aggravating impact liberalization was bound to exercise on the cost of financing the government's borrowing requirement.

Moreover, by 1985–86 the prospect of the single financial market and capital liberalization in the EC had become clearly visible, intensifying the need to render the domestic financial system more efficient and competitive. Financial and capital liberalization posed an external constraint and had to be preceded by the abolition of administered credit and interest rate controls at the national level. To summarize the rationale crudely: if real interest rates remained negative or at lower than market levels, and the national financial system was not competitive and efficient enough, then (when capital controls were lifted) savings would flow out of the country and the payments balance would collapse. As capital is internationally attracted by less regulated markets, the process of financial internationalization in Europe rendered the domestic allocation of resources through direct monetary instruments (credit controls and regulations, interest rate ceilings and directed credits) undesirable and ineffective.

The Economic and Monetary Union (EMU) programme came as a subsequent wave of institutional reform, the entry into which was contingent on the participation of national currencies in the European Monetary System (EMS). The combination of liberalized capital movements and exchange rate stability necessitated the full alignment of national monetary policies behind the EMS even for those EC/EU member states that had not yet entered the EMS (Branson 1990; Eichengreen and Frieden 1994). Through the 1990s, and until the 1998 entry in the EMS, the Bank of Greece pursued an orthodox policy of real appreciation of the drachma *vis-à-vis* the basket of EMS currencies. The effort to restore anti-inflationary credibility – given Greece's standing as the country with the worst inflation record in the EU – led to the entrenchment of real interest rates at exorbitantly high levels, until the beginning of their gradual convergence in 1998 towards the average interest rates of the EU zone in order to meet the EMU entry requirement.

While financial liberalization continued, bolstered by the pressure of the single financial market programme, and then later aimed toward the definite deadlines of the EMU programme, other structural reform policies stalled for the rest of the 1980s. Credit liberalization entailed dynamic implications not only for the banking and financial market (which was opened to the pressures of domestic and cross-border competition and, prospectively, in the 1990s to the trend towards economies of scale through mergers and acquisitions); its implications also involved a number of economic sectors and categories that were being subsidized through discretionary cheap credit. These included the manufacturing sector and especially small and medium-sized enterprises, exporters, agriculture, as well as particularly targeted subcategories such as agro-industry and others. Over the period between 1987 and 1992, credit to these categories was deregulated, left to be determined by the market.

Aside from that gradual programme of financial liberalization, which was supplemented by significant measures of stock exchange modernization in 1988, no other notable policies of structural liberalization were advanced in the 1980s. The stabilization programme was abandoned in the spring of 1987 as the economy was picking up. Premier Papandreou was probably intent on taking advantage of the visible improvement to call an early general election in 1988. An unexpected deterioration in his health, however, prevented the alleged plan from materializing. Greece was dragged into a prolonged period of pre-electoral economic expansion, three national elections and consecutive caretaker coalition governments before a majority government of the centre-right party, New Democracy (ND), was able to emerge in April 1990. By that time the economy had deteriorated severely, with inflation galloping over the levels of 20 per cent, and the government deficit at unprecedented heights. The coexistence of two or three parties in coalition governments, instead of mutually counterbalancing clientelistic demands and public spending, ended up actually multiplying them.

## THE TURN OF THE 1990S: ECONOMIC ADJUSTMENT AS PRINCIPAL POLICY PRIORITY

The April 1990 election brought to power a neoliberal-leaning conservative ND government whose official ideological and political proclamations contained unambiguous commitment to the economy's liberalization, marketization and privatization. So the European pressure – which by that time had intensified following the late 1980s experience of ungovernability – found fertile ground. When the ND government turned to the EC for another balance of payments support loan in 1991, the Commission was keen to include austere adjustment policies among its conditions, as well as a stricter surveillance mechanism. The structural reform agenda included the beginning of a timid liberalization process in the labour and insurance markets, the opening of competition through a range of market liberalization measures, the aim of a reduction of public sector employment by ten per cent in three years (which was not achieved), and privatization. The latter was hailed as a strategy for rendering the public sector leaner and the market more competitive and efficient, but in reality was pursued mostly for the purpose of raising revenue for the state budget. Again in the early 1990s, macroeconomic stabilization, the reduction of an alarming public deficit and the suppression of inflation took precedence over microeconomic reforms.

The 1991 stabilization programme failed to achieve its goals. Progress in privatization was very slow especially until 1992, because of intense politicization and opposition, combined with the government's frail one-seat majority in Parliament (Pagoulatos, forthcoming 2001a). From 1992 the privatization effort was stepped up, its scope of ambition expanding to include public utilities. That only managed to further intensify political and special interest opposition to the government, culminating with its premature fall from power in the autumn of 1993. By that time the government's main achievements contained only a few privatizations of mostly lame duck enterprises, several failed attempts (including smaller banks, shipyards, and notably OTE, the Greek Telecommunications Organization), and a considerable range of market liberalization measures (including the liberalization of the collective wage agreement framework) which had been accelerated under the explicit pressure of the single European market deadlines. Some of the attempted reforms (such as the liberalization of public procurement and the privatization of OTE) had met with the fierce resistance of organized interests and were left incomplete. In addition, the government's effort to combine disinflation with the reduction of the public deficit proved extremely difficult. Financial liberalization and the dramatic rise in interest rates to support disinflation added a serious burden to the cost of public borrowing (the compulsory investment of commercial bank deposits in government paper was gradually phased out between 1991 and 1993). As any significant improvement in public revenue collection failed to be recorded, and as privatization was not delivering the anticipated receipts, the government toward the final year of its term raised the oil tax, which cancelled much of the gains in fighting inflation. On top of all that, the spectrum of an early general election nearing, the government's macroeconomic policies exhibited the familiar (from the 1980s) electoral cycle. As a cumulative effect of all the above, the ND's government term managed to exhibit poor results in economic adjustment.

Perhaps the ND government's most significant economic legacy was that, despite its poor tangible outcomes, it managed to begin the reversal of the vicious circle of the 1980s, and to bring Greece in full and solid conformity with the EC/EU policy trend. While the adopted (or attempted) reforms were part and parcel of the ND party's political and ideological programme, they were mostly presented as 'imposed' by the EU. Obligation to the EU and Commission pressure rather than original political preference was invoked as perhaps the principal line of legitimizing discourse for justifying macroeconomic stabilization, privatization and market liberalization (cf. Ioakimidis 1996). This utilization of the EU as a scapegoat for necessary reforms is easy to explain if one considers the severe political cost of the policies (which finally materialized by the loss of ND's parliamentary majority), combined with the pervasive though gradually declining politicization of Greek society, the polarizing practice followed by the PASOK-led opposition and the particular interests affected by the reforms (public sector trade unions, economic interests losing from privatization, etc.), as well as the significant intragovernmental dissent over ND's 'neoliberal' policies. This intragovernmental opposition, led by status quo interests and clientelistically operating party barons, is also understandable given the conservative party's traditional attachment to state *dirigisme* (officially challenged only in the second half of the 1980s), and most importantly the embedded clientelistic reflexes of the party machine (Kalyvas 1998; Pappas 1999). To counter all these concerted resistances to reform, and given the relative ineffectiveness of their official ideological proclamations or technocratic arguments, ND government reformers resorted to a 'scapegoat' political discourse.

After the October 1993 general election, ND was replaced in power by PASOK. The new Papandreou government officially abandoned ND's privatization programme and sought to rhetorically distance itself from its predecessor's 'neoliberal' record, which by now had turned widely unpopular. In reality, however, the 1993 PASOK government offered a continuation of ND's policies packaged in a social democratic (or, at times, even old-fashioned socialist) rhetoric (cf. Tsakalotos 1998). The non-accommodative monetary policy that had been inaugurated in 1990 (hard drachma and high real interest rates) continued with new vigour, carrying the brunt of disinflation and macroeconomic stabilization, given the difficulty in curbing drastically public spending. Moreover, and despite the renationalization of one company (the Athens Bus Company), privatization continued, though scaled down in ambition (Pagoulatos and Wright 1999). Again the EU constraint was invoked, the scapegoat rhetoric stronger than during the ND government term.

If the 1980s was the decade of policy experimentation, erratic and inefficient economic management and discontinued measures, the 1990s was a decade of stability, consistency and continuity in policy direction, and a gradual build-up of economic policy success. The definitive influence for that transformation certainly had much to do with the EU factor, which imparted Greek economic policy-makers a clear, tangible and positive set of policy directions. Throughout the 1980s, the two main parties were divided and highly polarized over economic and structural policies; by late 1993, however, when the socialists had reascended to power, the same economic strategy of Europeanization (unambiguously translated into obtaining the Maastricht convergence targets) was officially shared by both PASOK and its conservative opposition. Arguably, this had as much to do with the PASOK government's policy agenda as it did with ND's political agenda. The latter resorted to tactical opposition and the typical charges of inefficacy without really challenging the socialist incumbents' strategic policy objectives. After Premier Papandreou's death, his succession by Costas Simitis, and PASOK's re-election to power in 1996 under Simitis, economic adjustment was pursued with renewed commitment and vigour.

The impact of the EU factor became as salient as ever in the post-1996 period. By that time, the sociopolitical consensus for adjustment had spread and matured. There was a wider understanding and acceptance not only of the EU in general, but of the socioeconomic reforms necessary as the price to be paid for joining the EMU. Moreover, the 1996 rise of Simitis brought to power the most Europeanist faction of

PASOK, rallying behind the vision of 'modernization' and Europeanization of Greek society (cf. Featherstone 1998: 24). Along with these important developments at the politico-ideological level came the structural change of a financially liberalized environment, as capital movements had been freed since 1994. Moreover, by 1998–99 there was a growing proximity and visibility of the EMU nominal convergence targets, and EMU entry was regarded optimistically as finally achievable. Thus, increasingly after 1996, not only the EU impact was enhanced, but the government's handling of the EU factor shifted from a scapegoat strategy to a positive, fully-fledged endorsement of the European and EMU vision, as a national objective imposed not only by its necessity but by its desirability and growing feasibility, too. At the same time, the external constraint derived from capital liberalization bestowed adjustment policies with a quality of irreversibility, as discussed below.

The declared target of the 1996 Simitis government was to meet fully the Maastricht criteria by early 2000 in order to join EMU at the start of 2001. Convergence excludes the debt to GDP ratio criterion, the current rate of which is over 100 per cent. It is estimated that a period of 14 years would be required to bring the debt down to 60 per cent of GDP if the government's net primary borrowing requirement were to be sustained at a five per cent level, real long-term interest rates were five per cent, and real annual output growth remained at four per cent (OECD 1998a: 63). Under less propitious conditions, public debt convergence could require several decades. Achieving the public debt convergence target would presuppose significant progress in overhauling the public health care and pension systems; the latter's financial needs are expected to grow exponentially if the system is not reformed. Though both the ND and the PASOK governments of the 1990s have converged over the reforms deemed necessary in that domain (introducing competition in health provision, releasing long-suppressed daily hospital charges, introducing independent and efficient third-party payers, separating health funds from pension funds and unifying health funds), implementation of most of these reforms has been delayed in fear of the sizeable political cost.

Considerable effectiveness has been exhibited by the Simitis administration in curbing public expenditure and improving revenue collection, two areas largely responsible for previous governments' poor fiscal results (OECD 1998a: 53). On the contrary, very little has been done in overhauling the ties between the government sector and a few protected, monopolistically operating private companies. Such private companies (large, privileged state suppliers, and enterprises operating in oligopoly or monopoly sectors such as telecommunications) remained entrenched, their sphere of operation protected as ever from external competition. Because of the consolidated political power of such groups – control over a significant portion of the media, networking across the political spectrum – it was deemed that a strategy of confrontation would involve sizeable political losses for the sake of questionable (in their short-term use) gains. The rationale against a bolder pace in privatization had a similar quality. Though equity stakes of public enterprises have been floated on the stock market repeatedly, there has been a consistent effort to refrain from an actual transfer of majority control to private hands; such ownership transfer has been confined mostly to ailing industrial subsidiaries controlled by IRO and by state banks. Aside from Olympic Airways (whose management was finally assigned to British Airways after a chain of hapless Commission-sponsored efforts to overhaul the company), the most notable exception has been a string of bank privatizations. However, this is only indicative of the new power balances being formed in the rapidly growing financial sector. The need to allow the three major (and now mutually competing) privately owned banking groups to acquire an efficient scope has forced the socialist government to defy fierce reaction on the part of banking sector trade unions.

To be sure, alongside the state-protected and collusive sectors of the economy there exist sectors and industries that underwent significant restructuring over the late 1980s and especially over the 1990s and are developing along competitive and extrovert lines, many of them expanding dynamically into the Balkans. These have included profit-making champions of the industrialization wave of the 1960s (such as firms in the cement and plastics industry), as well as firms that took advantage of market opportunities and the effective barriers obstructing transnational corporations to cover demand for new products (e.g. firms in the food sector and dairy products; Lyberaki 1996: 223). They have also included a number of new generation medium-sized engineering and software firms employing new technologies (Lyberaki: 1996). Such sectors and companies form the winners and champions of economic modernization. In addition, parallel modernization-related developments have triggered sector-specific growth. First, financial liberalization and the improvement of Greece's chances for joining the EMU were followed by a dramatic boom of the capital market, a wave of privatizations, mergers and acquisitions in the banking sector and the establishment of a large number of financial sector firms. Secondly, the inflow of structural funds (Community Support Frameworks I–III) for public infrastructure projects and the building spree associated with the preparation of the 2004 Olympic Games have given a drastic push to the construction sector. Though this latter development is rather conjunctural, it has created solid conditions for dynamic sectoral development and restructuring. An additional positive pressure for business reorganization has resulted from the 1990s' macroeconomic policies. The abandonment of monetary accommodation for an anti-inflationary, non-accommodating stance over the 1990s forced businesses actively to pursue competitiveness through productive restructuring instead of comfortably relying on exchange rate depreciation. The achievement of monetary stability at the end of the 1990s finally created a highly propitious environment for long-term business planning and investment.

## THE EXTERNAL CONSTRAINT OF FINANCIAL LIBERALIZATION

The importance of the external constraint factor cannot be exaggerated easily. Structural reforms such as privatization, and labour and social insurance reforms became a principal part of the government's actual agenda in earnest only after the March 1998 drachma devaluation and EMS entry. It was only then that the PASOK government for the first time appeared relatively determined to implement directly these policies in defiance of their political cost. Very much like other EU countries had done by binding themselves to the Maastricht criteria, the Greek government chose to enter an externally imposed discipline mechanism that forced adjustment by rendering the cost of non-compliance insufferable (cf. Dyson and Featherstone's (1996) *vincolo esterno*). It was not only that structural reforms such as privatization and liberalization in the labour and health and insurance sectors were among the terms under which Greece had been admitted to the EMS in March 1998. It was not even that Greece's ambition of meeting the convergence targets in order to qualify for the second EMU wave of 1 January 2001 rendered policies such as privatization inevitable, if only as a revenue raiser for the state budget. It was also that financial liberalization multiplied the costs of any substantial derogation from the pursuit of healthy economic 'fundamentals' and of any serious stain on the government's policy 'credibility'. The entry of the drachma to the ERM in an environment of free capital movement (capital fully liberalized after the spring of 1994) and high interest rate differentials led to a massive inflow of mainly short-term capital; this posed a constant threat of a tantamount outflow (with perilous effects on the external account and the economy at large) if the first signals of government retreat from its announced policy targets were to be emitted. The imminence and salience of this external constraint, combined with all the factors mentioned earlier, exercised probably the most potent external suasion for Greek economic adjustment exerted since the 1980s.[3]

Moreover, financial liberalization has helped the government overcome political resistance to economic adjustment associated with the latter's redistributive implications. According to a mainstream political science approach echoing Olson (1965), most economic reform programmes are bound to generate losers whose accumulated political power probably exceeds that of the winners of the reforms, given the collective action problem. The higher 'reform dividend' gained through a more efficient allocation of resources is distributed among the broader public, cumulating over the medium and longer term. It thus cannot offset the distributive losses of particular interest groups deprived of their 'acquired rights', as those special interest groups are better organized and vocal whereas the general public is by definition dispersed and less well –if at all – organized.

The rapid development of the capital market, especially over the 1998–99 period, offered an unprecedented opportunity for overcoming the political and redistributive cost of orthodox policies by offsetting them with the newly acquired 'stake' of a broad coalition of stock-owners in macroeconomic stability.[4] With the estimated total of investors in the Athens Stock Exchange well exceeding one million (one tenth of the Greek population), the government acquired a crucial ally in the application of orthodox adjustment policies (i.e. policies guaranteeing the steady inflow of international capital and stock market growth). The model of 'popular capitalism' that emerged through the diffusion of equity stakes to the wider public enhanced public support for the government's privatization plans and allowed several public enterprises to raise capital in the stock market. Apart from engendering an ideological shift towards pro-market economic policies and facilitating sustained support of economic reforms, the rapid development of the capital market even provided direct funding for redistributive policies, thus circumventing the straitjacket imposed by the EMU fiscal convergence targets. Indeed, in September 1999 the Simitis government announced a significant, electorally driven Drs 475bn (1.4bn euro) package of social benefits and tax breaks to lower income groups, to be funded mainly through doubling the state tax on stock market transactions from 0.3 to 0.6 per cent.

Clearly, the government's dependence on capital market growth and its ability to transform it into political advantage has a reverse implication as well: if the financial boom is replaced by a bust then public confidence and support will give place to public disaffection. However, the still relatively high concentration of stock in the hands of government-controlled or family-run companies[5] allowed government a certain degree of manipulation of stock market growth and the ability to prolong the resulting euphoria. Though not for long: the year 2000 was one of the worst for the Athens Stock Exchange, with its general index plummeting by some 40 per cent.

## THE SHIFT TO A STABILIZATION STATE

Financial liberalization at the domestic level denotes a deeper transformation in the state's financial role. In Greece (and southern Europe in general), over the post-war decades the state pursued growth through a far-reaching regime of institutional interventions and policies that instrumentalized the financial sector. In the decades from the 1950s through the early 1970s, the state could be classified as a 'growth state' with regard to its financial role. Though the transformation of the international economic regime over the 1970s (the collapse of Bretton Woods, the international rise of monetary instability and inflation, expanding capital liberalization and globalization) belied that post-war mission leading to stagflation instead of growth, and the rampant distributionism of the 1980s aggravated the picture, the institutional configuration of the state–finance relationship remained mostly intact. It was based on the twin pillar of state-administered and restricted finance and widespread ownership control over the banking system. The process of financial liberalization that began slowly after 1987 and picked up pace in the 1990s signified the abandonment of the entire post-war, growth-oriented, state–finance configuration. It was thus in Greece, and the 'financially repressed' southern European systems in general (Gibson and Tsakalotos 1992), that economic adjustment was pursued principally through a shift from the growth state to a stabilization state.[6]

The change of international and European economic regime over the 1970s and early 1980s and its attendant institutional and ideological transformations denote a change in the quality and configuration of the factors circumscribing the state's role over finance. Consequently, these constraining factors point to state capacities in the sense of the economic and political feasibility of the state's policy options, and in that sense they also denote a change in the state's policy preferences and priorities.

The need to abandon the particular model of the state's role in finance became stronger in Greece and southern Europe because it was there that growth had been pursued through the principal reliance on specialized state banking institutions, financial restriction and administered credit (Pagoulatos 1999b). Thus, the transformation of a growth state into a stabilization state is not a mere reflection of the shift from a growth regime to a disinflationary regime in western Europe (Forsyth and Notermans 1997; cf. McNamara 1998). While developed west European economies in the post-war era were subject to a growth regime (enabling monetary stability but prioritizing employment), the mechanisms of growth did not pertain to the state's role over the financial system but involved mainly the exercise of other macro- and microeconomic instruments of a usually Keynesian hue (Forsyth and Notermans 1997).

What defines a growth state and what distinguishes it from a stabilization state? A growth state seeks to enlist a mechanism of controlling and allocating financial resources to the primacy of economic growth. An institutional framework is thus devised so as to substitute for the market's perceived failure to promote long-term development. Through various institutional instruments (political subordination of the central bank, bank nationalizations, credit and capital controls, financial regulations, selective credit policies and indicative planning, specialized banking institutions), domestic production is protected, and finance is directed to economic activities considered as pivotal for economic development (see Zolotas 1962, 1965). The principal attachment of the state to the growth objective does not mean that macroeconomic stability is ignored. The mostly neoclassical economic record of Greek post-war governments (as well as that of authoritarian Portugal and to a lesser extent Spain) until 1973 unambiguously testifies to the fact that price stability and payments equilibrium were consistently at the forefront of government objectives (Zolotas 1965; cf. Halikias 1978). But these were not viewed as objectives in themselves, but as the necessary preconditions for allowing sustained economic growth. Growth was the paramount objective, and macroeconomic stability was the necessary precondition for achieving it (cf. Psalidopoulos 1990). The growth objective over the post-war decades was even more explicit in the countries of Europe's southern periphery (Spain, Portugal and Greece): the keyword there was not just growth but development, signifying a more far-reaching process than growth, not just more output but a different composition of output than previously produced, derived from technical and institutional transformations.

The transition from the growth state to a stabilization state with regard to the state–finance connection is anteceded by two major events or processes. One is the acquisition of a satisfactory state of development, which has placed Greece amidst the broader group of developed countries, even if at the rear of that group. That is obtained by EU membership, through which Greece partakes in the collective dividend of European advancement, be it in the form of institutional modernization, international political upgrade, structural adjustments in various fields, or plain increased financial inflows. This also implies that the pace of Greece's economic policies in the 1980s and especially in the 1990s is set by the EU's developed economies. The primacy of the EU's disinflationary objective is far from difficult to demonstrate, evident as it is in the unprecedented power granted to the European Central Bank (ECB) combined with an average inflation now in the area of two per cent. The second major event is, of course, the institutional and ideological decline of the post-war development model that had underpinned the strategies and policies of the growth state. The descent of *dirigisme* is the most definitive trait of that event. To these should be added a third factor, closely associated with the above, as summarized by Haggard and Maxfield (1993: 308): '[W]hen macroeconomic instability has proven a political liability, political leaders will be more willing to delegate authority to conservative agencies [such as central banks.] [On the contrary,] when the greater political challenge is growth, governments are more likely to intervene.'

A stabilization state is not a Keynesian state pursuing stabilization through countercyclical or interventionist policy means (such as the incomes policies, price and credit controls extensively relied upon by Greek governments through the 1980s), which under the new liberalized environment have been rendered obsolete or ineffective.[7] Macroeconomic stability is not just a temporary policy objective but the long-term government aim and a constitutive pillar of government policy. Consequently, while the growth state pursues economic stabilization through its available interventionist institutions and policy instruments, the stabilization state devises the appropriate institutions and instruments for long-term stabilization: a liberalized, globalized, 'deep' capital and money market acting as a deterrent to expansionist policies; most importantly, an independent central bank, institutionally prohibited from participating in the primary market for public debt, and officially endowed with statutory commitment to price stability.[8] Or a stabilization state enters a self-binding process of subscribing to international institutions such as the EMU nominal convergence criteria or surveillance mechanisms. A stabilization state will seek to rely on market allocation and to diminish state interventions under the premise that interventions would create longer-term disequilibria by distorting market signals and resource allocation.

A growth state would seek to stimulate the economy by relaxing fiscal and monetary policy, as indeed was the case in Greece in periods such as 1963–65, 1974–77 and 1981–82, not to mention the purely electorally driven expansions. It would implement selective interventions aimed at supporting economic sectors deemed as 'productive', as with the entire system of Greek protectionist policies of the post-war decades. On the contrary, a stabilization state would allow for growth through enhancing private profit opportunities, enlarging the scope of the private economy, and seeking to maximize the expected efficiency advantages of market allocation.

For the stabilization state, growth is no more the principal objective. The stabilization state treats macroeconomic stabilization (and price stability more specifically) as the principal objective for the sake of which economic growth and employment can be deferred. No doubt, this is predicated upon the re-ascendancy of neoclassical economic ideas in Europe in the second half of the 1970s, in the same way that the growth state was ideologically premised upon the pro-industrialization, developmentalist bias of the post-war decades combined with the contextual influence of Keynesian ideas placing employment and growth at the forefront of government objectives. The influence of Keynesianism in the post-war development process in southern Europe and Greece was thus indirect and residual: it reinforced belief in the objective of growth, and it asserted a strong state role in bringing it about.

The characterization of the Greek state of the 1990s as 'stabilization state' does not imply that state policies remain unflinchingly committed to stabilization throughout that period, nor – even more – that other principal objectives (redistribution or electorally minded expansionism) leave the picture. What this distinction signifies is that the constitutive factors of the environment within which the state's role is defined have changed fundamentally. The broader state strategy and policies that under the post-war or post-authoritarian conventional wisdom used to appear as necessary, desirable or feasible are now (under the new EU configuration) treated as politically precarious, economically hazardous or fundamentally flawed.

The state enrolment from a 'growth' to a 'stabilization' mission is not simply a mirror image of its external environment. External pressures and constraints do not amount to one-way options; they simply increase, often unbearably so, the cost of non-compliance. The decision whether to conform continues to rest in the hands of national policy-makers, as several examples of non-conformist government policies have demonstrated. More importantly, what is of interest here is not just the extent to which external pressures are internalized by the domestic policy system, but the deeper transformations these pressures help to bring about in state ideology, preferences, strategy and ultimate policy behaviour. The state's role in the economic process is defined under the conceptual framework of a new paradigm that determines the meaning state actors impart to their policies as well as the direction these policies take (cf. Hall 1992). It is in that sense opportune to refer to a substantive transformation of the state's role in the economy.

The transformation into a stabilization state is not just a simple transition stage to the EMU, a transitory occurrence bound to fade away as soon as national currencies enter the euro and monetary policy is ceded to the ECB. For one thing, the integration of Greece in the European economy does not release but even further binds her to the objective of sustained macroeconomic stability. As an OECD country report noted recently, with the prospective loss of a central bank able to tailor policy towards the requirements of the national economy, 'the onus of macroeconomic policy adjustment falls on fiscal policy in the short term and structural policies over the longer run' (OECD 1998b: 46). This time, fiscal discipline is vested with the powerful institutional guarantees of the Stability Pact (prescribing a maximum budget deficit of three per cent of GDP). Even if euro member states were to defy the Stability Pact rules (a fading possibility since the resignation of Oscar Lafontaine from Germany's Finance Ministry), the Pact's disciplinary role would be taken over by public debt markets (demanding prohibitive interest rates on new debt), the Maastricht Treaty no-bail-out clause (prohibiting EU governments from helping each other), and potentially financial regulators as well (prohibiting large exposures of banks to government bond holdings) (Lemmen 1999). Thus, under the EMU disinflationary economic regime, economic growth can only be pursued to the extent that it does not compromise macroeconomic stability in a rather austere definition of the term. True, the EMU's ultimate promise is not just stability but, quite importantly, growth through the conducive circumstances of long-term monetary stability, liberalized markets and low interest rates (cf. Tsoukalis 1997: 179ff.; European Commission 1998). However, the Maastricht legacy and the ECB's considerable power have clearly suggested that if, in the proverbial trade-off between stability and growth, push comes to shove, then it is growth that will be deferred and not the other way round.[9]

Thus, in the post-EMU landscape the state in the broader sense acts as custodian of macroeconomic stability, and growth is expected to result:

(1) from expanding privatized and liberalized banking and financial systems operating upon market efficiency standards that enable them to afford low interest rates;
(2) from increasingly liberalized product and labour markets (which of course are far from devoid of social and redistributive implications);
(3) from any remaining EU structural funds – at least for the European periphery; and
(4) in the transitional period of high interest rate differentials and liberalized capital account, growth has been promoted by the inflow of foreign capital (much of which, however, has been of a short-term speculative as well as inflationary nature).

With regard to (1) above, the Stability Pact is expected to liberate financial resources to be directed to investment and long-term growth. Thus the chosen policy mix seems to be one of tight fiscal policy that will eventually enable lower interest rates (the Clinton–Greenspan policy mix) rather than lax fiscal policy that would call to be counterbalanced by harsh monetary policy (the Reagan–Volker mix).[10]

A combination of some or all of these four factors have produced remarkable growth in Greece as well as Spain and Portugal, especially from the second half of the 1990s. This, however, does not refute but rather substantiates the argument, demonstrating perhaps a tentative success of the stabilization strategy.

Compare the above with the growth instruments available in the hands of the state in the growth state era: monetary and fiscal policies to stimulate demand, industrial and sectoral policies, protectionist measures, and a large array of government-controlled financial instruments; all have been severely diminished or rendered obsolete. Thus the growth functions of the stabilization state emerge as residual and minimalistic: they are what remains after the state's macroeconomic stabilization objective has been served. Most importantly, the growth functions are not to be carried out by the state but by the market.

The above notwithstanding, a stabilization state is not exactly tantamount to a neoliberal state. The latter, if true to its ideological proclamations, would enhance those exact types of institutional arrangement that would promote market competition in the allocation of financial resources. On the contrary, competition was not a directly pursued effect, and financial liberalization across southern Europe (at least in the short term) gave way to strong instances of banking cartelization (Pérez 1997; Pagoulatos forthcoming). Wherever competition followed, it was mostly limited to banking services rather than interest rates – the spread between lending and deposit rates remained high – all this meaning that the competitive effects of liberalization in the financing of business borrowers were not as pronounced as the neoliberal project would anticipate.

However, the stabilization state that replaced the growth state was not in the full sense tantamount to a 'monetarist' state either. True, Greece began setting monetary targets in 1979, two years after Spain and Portugal. While the influences of monetarism were clearly discernible in a number of factors (the primacy of disinflation, the extensive reliance on protracted monetary austerity), the differences were equally significant. To begin with, the endorsement of fixed exchange rates (the EMS project) is a departure from the monetarist doctrine (McNamara 1998: 173). Moreover, monetarism in the strict sense (of a practical lack of monetary activism for the sake of a stable and predictable monetary growth) was applied rarely. Monetary targets were set but usually grossly overshot until eventually – toward the mid-1990s – abandoned for the sake of inflation targeting. And in some cases, as in Greece, the transformation into a stabilization state was not launched with monetarist or neoliberal policies but with a typical neo-Keynesian stabilization programme in 1985–87, designed and implemented by government policy-makers whose anti-monetarist views were never disguised. It does appear then that the most consistent, definitive feature of that transformed economic role of the state was not the attachment to ideological doctrine of a neoliberal or monetarist character, but a more or less pragmatic (depending on the particular government in power) pursuit of stabilization, as encompassed in the Maastricht Treaty, though framed under the conceptual impact of the neoclassical economic reascendance in Europe.

## CONCLUSION

Three principal arguments have been advanced in this article. First, Europeanization catch-up – more in the nominal-macroeconomic than in the structural sense – has been the most pronounced economic objective of Greek governments during the brief 1985–87 parenthesis and especially throughout the 1990s. Secondly, in a traditionally state-driven economic and financial system such as that of Greece, economic Europeanization has been pursued mainly through extensive reliance on monetary austerity predicated upon financial liberalization, and through the transformation of the growth state into a stabilization state. Governments have used macroeconomic policies to trigger the disciplining mechanisms that would facilitate structural adjustment by eroding domestic sociopolitical resistance. Finally, the main strategy employed for the transformation of a growth state into a stabilization state has been one of surrendering government control over finance to the regulatory authorities of an increasingly autonomous central bank and to the allocative functions of a rapidly internationalizing market (cf. Pagoulatos 1999c).

## NOTES

1. This article is based on the paper 'Adjustment Politics in Greece and the EU Factor: From Scapegoat to Ulyssean Mast', presented at the panel 'The Southern European Periphery and its Liberalization' of the European Community Studies Association (ECSA) Sixth Biennial International Conference, Pittsburgh, 2–5 June 1999 (hence Pagoulatos 1999a). Useful comments on the part of the panel participants and especially Kevin Featherstone are gratefully acknowledged.
2. The public sector is estimated on all three generally utilized criteria: the scope of state control over real productive resources; the degree of expansion of public expenditure compared to total economy growth; and the financing effects of public spending.
3. However, Greece's entry into the EMS after a drachma devaluation, combined with the newly acquired central bank independence and the replacement of monetary targeting with inflation targeting, comprised a new monetary policy framework of increased credibility that made it easier for the Bank of Greece to tighten monetary policy without the undesired effect of attracting large capital inflows (OECD 1998a 41).
4. By the end of July 1999, total market capitalization of the Athens Stock Exchange (ASE) was at 134bn euro (i.e. a rough equivalent of over 130 per cent of the country's GDP). In absolute terms this was lower than total market capitalization in major European stock markets such as that of Frankfurt (1,090bn euro), Paris (988bn euro) or Milan (483bn euro), but higher than that of Copenhagen (89bn euro), Dublin (67bn euro), Lisbon (51bn euro) or Vienna (31bn euro) (*Kathimerini*, 21 September 1999). Under the exuberance of shrinking inflation, predicted entry in the EMU and a prospective fall

in interest rates, total market capitalization of the ASE grew by 133 per cent in 1998 and by 68 per cent in the first semester of 1999 alone (*To Vima*, 5 September 1999).

5. Average dispersion or free float of stock at the ASE has been estimated to be among the lowest in the EU, at 34 per cent compared to a 67 per cent average for the Euro-zone countries (report by Morgan Stanley, cited in *Kathimerini*, 14 September 1999).
6. This section draws on Pagoulatos 1999b.
7. The liberalization of collective bargaining in Southern Europe over the late 1980s and early 1990s has eroded the governments' ability to exercise incomes policies, limiting their impact to public sector salaries. As for price and credit controls, they were deemed incompatible with the European single market programme and were gradually abolished throughout the EU.
8. In 1997, in compliance with the Maastricht Treaty, the Bank of Greece was granted legal independence through the institution of price stability as its principal statutory objective, independence from any government instructions or advice, exclusive central bank authority in the exercise of monetary policy, a six-year renewable term for the governor and deputy governors, and a Monetary Policy Council to assist the governor.
9. Eichengreen and Wyplosz (1998) estimate that if the Stability Pact had been in force over the period 1974–95, the cumulated output losses for France, Italy and the UK would range between 5 and 9 per cent of GDP – an estimate disputed by Bean, who holds that the output losses are at least half as much as Eichengreen and Wyplosz suggest (Eichengreen and Wyplosz, 1998: 106).
10. Point owed to Pier Carlo Padoan.

## REFERENCES


Balfoussias, A. (1993): *Δημοσιονομικές εζελίζεις στη Δεκαετία τον* [Fiscal Developments in the 1980s], Athens: KEPE.

Bennett, C.J. (1991): 'Review article: what is policy convergence and what causes it?', *British Journal of Political Science* 21, pp.215–33.

Branson, W.H. (1990): 'Financial market integration, macroeconomic policy and the EMS', in C. Bliss and J. Braga de Macedo (eds.), *Unity with Diversity in the European Economy: The Community's Southern Frontier*, Cambridge: Cambridge University Press.

Dyson, K., and K. Featherstone (1996): 'Italy and EMU as a "Vincolo Esterno": Empowering the Technocrats, Transforming the State', *South European Society and Politics* 1/2, pp.272–99.

Eichengreen, B., and J.A. Frieden (1994): 'The Political Economy of European Monetary Unification: An Analytical Introduction', in B. Eichengreen and J. Frieden (eds.), *The Political Economy of European Monetary Unification*, Boulder: Westview.

Eichengreen, B., and C. Wyplosz (1998): 'Stability Pact: More than a minor nuisance?' *Economic Policy* (April), pp.65–113.

European Commission (1994): 'Annual Economic Report for 1994', *European Economy* 56.

—— (1998): 'Growth and employment in the stability-oriented framework of EMU', Commission communication to the Council, *European Economy* 65, pp.163–210.

Featherstone, K. (1998): ''Europeanization' and the Centre Periphery: The Case of Greece in the 1990s', *South European Society and Politics* 3/1, pp.23–39.

Forsyth, D.J., and T. Notermans (1997): 'Macroeconomic Policy Regimes and Financial Regulation in Europe, 1931–1994', in ibid. (eds.), *Regime Changes*, Providence: Berghahn Books.

Gibson, H. (forthcoming 2001): 'Economic Change in Southern Europe: Prospects for convergence', in ibid. (ed.), *Economic Change in Southern Europe*, London: Macmillan.

Gibson, H., and E. Tsakalotos (1992): 'The Removal of Capital Controls, 1992 and the Financial Sector', in H. Gibson and E. Tsakalotos (eds.), *Economic Integration and Financial Liberalization: Prospects for Southern Europe*, London: Macmillan.

Giuliani, M. (1999): 'Europeanization and Italy', paper presented at the European Community Studies Association (ECSA) Sixth Biennial International Conference, Pittsburgh, 2–5 June.

Haggard, S., and S. Maxfield (1993): 'Political Explanations of Financial Policy in Developing Countries', in S. Haggard, A. Lee and S. Maxfield (eds.), *The Politics of Finance in Developing Countries*, Ithaca, NY: Cornell University Press.

Halikias, D.J. (1978): *Money and Credit in a Developing Economy. The Greek Case*, New York: New York University Press.

Hall, P. (1992): 'The movement from Keynesianism to monetarism: Institutional analysis and British economic policy in the 1970s', in S. Steinmo, K. Thelen and F. Longstreth (eds.), *Structuring Politics*, Cambridge: Cambridge University Press.

Ioakimidis, P.C. (1996): 'Contradictions between policy and performance', in K. Featherstone and K. Ifantis (eds.), *Greece in a Changing Europe*, Manchester: Manchester University Press.

Kalyvas, S. (1998): 'The Greek Right: Between Transition and Reform', in F. Wilson (ed.), *The European Center-Right at the End of the Twentieth Century*, New York: St Martin's Press.

Katseli, L. (1990): 'Economic Integration in the Enlarged European Community: Structural Adjustment of the Greek Economy', in C. Bliss and J. Braga de Macedo (eds.), *Unity with Diversity in the European Economy*, Cambridge: Cambridge University Press.

Kazakos, P. (1992): 'Socialist attitudes towards European integration in the 1980s', in T.C. Kariotis (ed.), *The Greek Socialist Experiment*, New York: Pella.

Ladrech, R. (1994): 'Europeanization of domestic politics and institutions: the case of France', *Journal of Common Market Studies* 32, pp.69–98.

Lavdas, K. (1997): *The Europeanization of Greece. Interest Politics and the Crises of Integration*, London: Macmillan.

Lemmen, J. (1999): 'Life Without the Stability Pact', Special Paper No.109, LSE Financial Markets Group, Jan.

Lyberaki, A. (1996): 'Adjustment and Resistance to Change: Virtues and Vices of the Greek Economy over the Last Decade', *Journal of Modern Hellenism* 12–13, pp.219–37.

McNamara, K.R. (1998): *The Currency of Ideas. Monetary Politics in the European Union*, Ithaca NY: Cornell University Press.

OECD (1998a): *OECD Economic Surveys: Greece*, Paris: OECD.

—— (1998b): *OECD Economic Surveys: Spain*, Paris: OECD.

Olson, M. (1965): *The Logic of Collective Action*, Cambridge MA: Harvard University Press.

Pagoulatos, G. (1999a): 'Adjustment Politics in Greece and the EU Factor: From Scapegoat to Ulyssean Mast', paper presented at the panel 'The Southern European Periphery and its Liberalization', European Community Studies Association (ECSA) Sixth Biennial International Conference, Pittsburgh, 2–5 June.

—— (1999b): 'Financial Repression and Liberalization in Europe's Southern Periphery: From "Growth State" to "Stabilization State"', paper presented at the panel 'Markets and Ideas', European Community Studies Association (ECSA) Sixth Biennial International Conference, Pittsburgh, 2–5 June.

—— (1999c): 'European Banking: Five Modes of Governance', *West European Politics* 22/1, pp.68–94.

—— (forthcoming 2001a): 'The Enemy Within: Intergovernmental Politics and Organizational Failure in Greek Privatization', *Public Administration*.

—— (forthcoming 2001b): 'The Liberalization of Southern European Financial Systems', in K. Lavdas (ed.), *Junctures of Stateness: Political Boundaries and Policy Change in Southern Europe*, Aldershot: Ashgate.

Pagoulatos, G., and V. Wright (1999): 'The Politics of Industrial Privatization: Spain, Portugal and Greece in a European Perspective', *Rivista Trimestrale di Diritto Pubblico* 3 (Oct.), pp.613–62.

Pappas, T.S. (1999): *Making Party Democracy in Greece*, London: Macmillan.

Pérez, S.A. (1997): *Banking on Privilege. The Politics of Spanish Financial Reform*, Ithaca NY: Cornell University Press.

Psalidopoulos, M. (1990): *Κεϋνσιανή Θεωρία και Ελληνκή Οικονομική Πολιτική: Μυθος και Πραγματικότητα* [Keynesian Theory and Greek Economic Policy: Myth and Reality], Athens: Kritiki.

Tsakalotos, E. (1991): *Alternative Economic Strategies: The Case of Greece*, Aldershot: Avebury.

—— (1998): 'The political economy of social democratic economic policies: the PASOK experiment in Greece', *Oxford Review of Economic Policy* 14/1, pp.114–38.

Tsoukalis, L. (1997): *The New European Economy Revisited*, Oxford: Oxford University Press.

Verney, S. (1996): 'The Greek Socialists', in J. Gaffney (ed.), *Political Parties and the European Union*, London: Routledge.

Zolotas, X. (1962): *The Role of the Banks in a Developing Country*, Athens: Bank of Greece.

—— (1965): *Monetary Equilibrium and Economic Development*, Princeton NJ: Princeton University Press.

# Europeanization and National Identity

# Europeanization and Convergence via Incomplete Contracts? The Case of Turkey

MEHMET UGUR

## INTRODUCTION

Turkey's association with the EU has always been presented as a signal of the country's European orientation and an anchor ensuring the irrevocability of the Europeanization process. For example, Turgut Ozal, the Turkish Prime Minister who engineered the membership application in 1987, stated that the application 'will ... eliminate any ambiguity by anchoring once and for all the destiny of the Turkish people with that of Western Europe' (Ozal 1986). Alain Lamassoure, the President of the EU Council in the first half of 1995, echoed this view by stating that 'the EU wants a stable, prosperous and democratic Turkey that is anchored in Europe and is part of the European security architecture' (*Agence Europe*, 7 April 1995: 2). Yet EU–Turkey relations have always been marked with tensions and frequent deviations from declared commitments. As a result, Turkey is currently the most economically integrated yet politically distanced candidate for membership. Ugur (1999) analyzed this anomaly in the light of an anchor/credibility dilemma. Developments leading to the acceptance of Turkey as a candidate country in the Helsinki Summit of 10–11 December 1999 can be interpreted as steps towards addressing this anomaly. However, it is still too early to predict the extent to which the EU and Turkey are likely to resolve the dilemma and ensure the continuity of Turkey's integration with Europe.

This article argues that Turkey's convergence towards EU standards has remained suboptimal and unsystematic because of two factors: the control-reliance and muddling through that characterized Turkish decision-making, and the incomplete nature of the contracts governing EU–Turkey relations. Oscillation between control-reliance and muddling through has been the norm because of the Turkish state's dominant position *vis-à-vis* civil society. This dominance is observable not only in the regulation of the economic environment, but also in the state's distribution of quasi-private goods such as access to business opportunities, employment, cheap inputs and consumer goods, and protection against foreign competition, etc. However, contracts between the EU and Turkey are incomplete because their enforcement depends on voluntary compliance rather than the existence of a supranational authority that could enforce implementation. The only authority created for this purpose is the Association Council, which decides by double unanimity: unanimity between EU member states and unanimity between the EU and Turkey.

To elaborate this argument, the article is organized into three sections. In the first section, it is demonstrated that Turkey's economic convergence towards the EU has remained too little and occurred too late. While macroeconomic policy has been totally divergent from that of the EU, microeconomic policy has converged only in a half-hearted manner. This limited convergence has been because of excessive discretion enjoyed by Turkish policy-makers on the one hand and excessive penetration of the policy-making process by organized interests on the other. Coupled with the incomplete nature of the contracts between the EU and Turkey, these aspects have led to frequent deviations from the convergence commitment. Although the Turkish economy is currently considered by the EU Commission to be a functioning market economy, the convergence that this assessment implies has been largely unsystematic and decoupled from the European orientation.

The second section examines Turkey's political convergence towards EU standards. Evidence of Turkey's democratization, human rights practice and the Cyprus issue also suggests that unsystematic convergence and frequent deviations have been the norm. In fact, Turkey, unlike Spain and Portugal in the 1980s and central and eastern European countries in the 1990s, has never come to the point of accepting European integration as a reference point either for the formulation of the reform agenda or for the legitimation of the limited reforms carried out. On the contrary, Turkish policy-makers have consistently tried to de-link any partial reform from Turkey's European orientation. While the incomplete nature of the contracts between the EU and Turkey has facilitated this choice, the dominance of the Turkish state *vis-à-vis* civil society has made it the most likely outcome.

Finally, the article examines the likely impact of the Helsinki conclusions on EU–Turkey relations in the future. As indicated above, the Helsinki decision, by signalling a membership prospect to Turkey, can be a step towards resolving the anchor/credibility dilemma in EU–Turkey relations. However, the resolution of this dilemma also requires a radical change in the official Turkish policy and in private sector attitudes concerning integration. The change must be in the direction of a consensus about the desirability of Europeanization in terms of economic policy and political culture. The evidence of Turkey's post-Helsinki announcements and the current political party configuration suggests that one can only be cautiously optimistic about the feasibility of such a change. Therefore, a transparent pre-accession partnership is necessary to tighten the existing contracts and make Turkey's future deviations from declared commitments less likely. This can be done by an EU insurance covering some of the risks associated with Turkey's convergence and an explicit conditionality linking EU assistance with concrete steps towards convergence by Turkey.

## ECONOMIC CONVERGENCE: TOO LITTLE, TOO LATE

The Turkish policy-making process reflects the characteristics of what Etzioni (1967, 1968) described as 'control-reliance' and 'muddling through'. One implication of these modes of governance is low policy output and innovation because of heavy investment in 'control technology' in the former and societal penetration of the policy process in the latter. In other words, the state is either too strong or too weak *vis-à-vis* civil society. Its strength is owing to its heavy involvement in the economy and its top–down approach to democratization. Its weakness is a mirror-image of its strength and is implied by the way in which state rule is legitimated. The legitimacy of the political regime in such polities depends on the government's ability to accommodate societal demands for the distribution of quasi-private goods rather than on the efficiency and equity of its regulatory function.

It is easy to see why control-reliance and muddling through work against the implementation of incomplete contracts. On the one hand, these modes of decision-making make the Turkish government's deviations from declared commitments more likely because either the state or organized interests can emerge as veto groups preventing compliance with those commitments. On the other, the absence of an authority that would enforce the contracts reduces the cost of such deviations and increases the probability of their occurrence. This cost/incentive structure unleashes a vicious circle that exacerbates the non-credibility of the declared commitments. In the initial round, the high probability of deviations from a declared commitment induces the organized interest groups to consider the commitment as non-credible. Once this is the case, these actors would refrain from adjusting their future strategies in line with the declared policy choice. On the contrary, they would invest heavily in securing deviations from the declared commitment – leading to more frequent deviations which, in turn, reinforce the organized interest groups' belief that the declared commitment is non-credible.

This analytical perspective captures the most significant aspects of the political economy of the policy-making in Turkey. The Turkish state has been heavily involved in the economy since 1930. It played an active role not only in the traditional sense of undertaking large infrastructure projects and regulating the economic environment, but also in terms of being a major producer and employer in the tradable goods sector. This experience has been described as *Devletçilik* (*étatism*) in the literature and the policy discourse.[1] As a result, by 1960 the public sector was generating 53.2 per cent of total output and 56.2 per cent of the total value added in the light industrial sectors. These shares were higher in the heavy industrial sectors, reaching 55 and 66.2 per cent, respectively (DIE 1973). *Étatism* has continued to shape Turkey's economic development even after the liberalization reforms of the 1980s. The state's share in total fixed capital formation increased from 44.5 per cent between 1972 and 1979 to 62.5 per cent between 1980 and 1988. After 1988, this share declined gradually, but remained high at the level of 45 per cent in 1992 (Central Bank of Turkey 1982–93).

This involvement led to a number of adverse results. First, *étatism* became increasingly inefficient because of the predominance of political motives in the running of the state-owned economic enterprises (SEEs). Secondly, the state's extensive involvement in the economy encouraged rent-seeking behaviour by the private sector (Krueger 1974). Thirdly, *étatism* fostered a free-riding culture whereby the private sector expected the state to take on high risks and pave the way for lower-risk investment opportunities for private investors. This culture was so deep rooted that it proved difficult to overcome even after the introduction of the export-oriented liberalization programme in 1980. Therefore, it was not surprising to observe that the share of private sector investment declined from 55.5 per cent between 1972 and 1979 to 37.5 per cent between 1980 and 1988. Finally, *étatism* placed the government budget under heavy strain and led to macroeconomic instability. As instability increased the risks for private economic actors, it made the policy-making process more receptive to their demands for special treatment.

Most of these consequences have been examined extensively in the academic literature and the reports of international organizations analyzing Turkey's economic performance.[2] Therefore, the analysis below is limited to the impact of *étatism* on the credibility of Turkey's European orientation. When viewed from this perspective, it is clear that *étatism* has reduced the scope for credible commitments to such convergence for two reasons. First, it led to a high level of organized interest pressure on the state as the latter became a centre of gravity for private sector claims and counterclaims concerning the distribution of economic values. Secondly, both the state and organized interest groups were motivated (and in fact enabled) to blur the transparency of the policy issues in EU–Turkey relations by equating their parochial interests with an overarching national interest that must be upheld irrespective of the commitments undertaken in existing contracts.

Under these conditions, even societal groups in favour of integration with the EU were induced to secure deviations from the convergence requirements as and when necessary. Turkish policy-makers could not resist such demands not only because of the non-transparent links between societal groups and the state, but also because of the adverse consequences of the discretionary practice built into the policy process. As discretion reduced the predictability and consistency of the government's economic policy, contracts between economic actors became less binding and the parties involved tended to relate their private losses within the contract to unpredictable government decisions (Saracoglu 1995). Therefore, the Turkish government was forced to internalize these losses as the discretion it enjoyed enabled the economic actors to present their private losses as social losses that the state must internalize.

### *Macroeconomic policy divergence*

Faced with such demands, the Turkish government had to discover ways of internalizing private risks. This internalization could not be realized by shuffling private risks between different interest groups as lobbying for special treatment became generalized. Therefore, the Turkish government had to resort to monetary/fiscal expansion in order to bail out the private sector in periods of depressed economic activity or to expand the capacity of the state as a provider of economic rents. Contracts governing EU–Turkey relations could not function as restraints on such tendencies as their provisions concerning macroeconomic convergence were merely statements of intent. Neither the rules of the coordination game nor the distribution of the costs/benefits resulting from policy coordination were specified. Under these circumstances, the cost of deviations from convergence remained minimal and the benefits of working towards that target were either uncertain or distributed unequally. Therefore, the incomplete nature of the contracts governing EU–Turkey relations has made Turkey's macroeconomic policy divergence either more likely or less costly.

One indication of the macroeconomic policy divergence was the increase in Turkey's budget deficit and the debt/GDP ratio. In the 1980s, when EU governments were preoccupied with fiscal consolidation and public sector downsizing, the Turkish government embarked on fiscal expansion. As can be seen from Table 1, the ratio of public debt to gross domestic product (the debt/GDP ratio) increased from 20.7 per cent in 1980–83 to 46.1 per cent in 1988. Similarly, the budget deficit/GDP ratio also increased from 1.7 to 3.1 per cent over the same period. Although these ratios were not excessively high when compared with European levels, the doubling of the figures in five years was in clear contrast to the fiscal orthodoxy that EU member states were following in the 1980s.

TABLE 1
TURKISH AND EU MACROECONOMIC POLICY INDICATORS

| | Budget deficit/GDP ratio(%) | Public debt/GDP ratio(%) | Treasury Bill rates(%) | Exchange rate (TL per US$) | Consumer price inflation (%) |
|---|---|---|---|---|---|
| 1987 | 3.2 | n.a. | 41.97 | 1,012 | 41.0 |
| 1988 | 3.1 | 46.1 | 54.5 | 61,815 | 74.0 |
| 1989 | 3.4 | 39.5 | 48.01 | 2,314 | 67.0 |
| 1990 | 3.0 | 30.3 | 43.46 | 2,390 | 60.4 |
| 1991 | 5.2 | 31.7 | 67.01 | 5,080 | 65.7 |
| 1992 | 4.1 | 32.9 | 72.17 | 8,654 | 70.6 |
| 1993 | 6.5 | 32.4 | n.a. | 14,473 | 65.6 |
| 1994 | 3.7 | 42.3 | 160.7 | 38,726 | 103.9 |
| 1995 | 3.9 | 40.1 | 125.8 | 59,6509 | 2.4 |
| 1996 | 8.5 | 37.6 | 132.4 | 107,7758 | 0.3 |
| 1997 | 7.5 | 36.3 | 105.2 | 205,6058 | 4.5 |
| 1998 | 7.6 | 35.4 | 108.6 | n.a. | n.a. |
| EU12 averages | | | | | |
| 1981–90 | 4.5* | n.a. | 11.1** | n.a. | 6.4 |
| 1994 | 5.8 | n.a. | 8.1 | n.a. | 4.1 |

* Net borrowing, which may be more or less than budget deficit.
** Market interest rates.
*Source*: IMF (1998a: 868–73; 1998b: 139); Somers (1991: 265); and Kennen (1996: 133).

Turkey's attempt at stabilizing its fiscal expenditures from 1989 onward proved short-lived: the deficit/GDP ratio increased again to 6.5 per cent by 1993 and the debt/GDP ratio climbed to 42.3 per cent in 1994. The cost of this fiscal laxity was reflected in high interest rates that the Turkish government had to pay on its borrowing. From 1991 onward, the treasury bill rates exceeded not only the inflation rates with a margin of two to 50 per cent, but also the deposit rates offered by the banking system.

This fiscal divergence was also accompanied by divergence between Turkish and EU monetary policy. While European monetary policy, especially from 1987 onward, was geared towards controlling inflation and paving the way towards monetary integration, Turkish monetary policy was geared to accommodate the fiscal laxity. Consequently, inflation in Turkey remained excessively high, reaching a level of 103.9 per cent in 1994. Turkey's exchange rate policy was also divergent. Whereas EU member states were preoccupied with exchange rate management through the European Monetary System, Turkey followed a floating exchange rate policy that exacerbated the inflationary pressure and marked Turkey's reluctance to approximate its policy with that of the EU.

Underlying these divergent policy choices was the Turkish government's inability to finance the cost of internalizing the private risks through taxation. Although weak taxation capacity is a problem for most developing countries, the striking aspect of the Turkish case is that the Turkish government's tax policy decisions have actually had an adverse effect of reducing the income elasticity of tax receipts. As can be seen from Table 2, the buoyancy coefficient for tax receipts, which incorporates the impact of taxation decisions, have been consistently lower than the built-in elasticity coefficient, which is purged of the impacts of taxation decisions.

These figures suggest that the Turkish government's tax receipts would have been higher had no tax policy decisions been taken during the period 1975–93. The same can be said of the two subperiods

TABLE 2
BUOYANCY AND BUILT-IN ELASTICITY COEFFICIENTS OF TAX RECEIPTS IN TURKEY

| | Indirect tax receipts | Direct tax receipts | Total tax receipts |
|---|---|---|---|
| 1975–93 | 1.43 (1.05) | 1.40 (1.02) | 1.43 (1.02) |
| 1975–82 | 1.32 (0.91) | 1.56 (1.15) | 1.41 (1.03) |
| 1983–93 | 1.64 (1.25) | 1.37 (1.02) | 1.55 (1.12) |

*Note*: Buoyancy coefficients shown in parenthesis.
*Source*: Ersel and Kumcu (1995: 191).

corresponding to import-substitution (1975–82) and export-oriented liberalization policy (1983–93). In fact, the government's taxation capacity under liberalization was weaker than the period of import-substitution, as can be seen from the wider gap between the built-in elasticity and buoyancy coefficients during the 1983–93 period. This is not surprising because the state's receptiveness to private sector pressure actually increased in the liberalization period. This was so for two reasons: first, increased macroeconomic instability strengthened the hand of the private-sector lobbyists demanding internalization of the private risks; and secondly, the export-oriented strategy was based on large-scale subsidization of exports and investment.

One inevitable consequence of the weak taxation capacity was the resort to fictive resources in the form of central bank credits. A simple calculation shows that, over the 1981–93 period, 61.7 per cent of the general government deficit (excluding the SEE deficits) has been financed by short-term borrowing. Of this, 56.5 per cent has been in the form of central bank credits.[3] In other words, the Turkish government has tried to compensate for its weak taxation capacity by printing money and imposing an inflation tax on society at large. Consequently, societal groups with the capacity to engage in currency substitution have managed to externalize the cost of inflation onto others, mainly wage earners with little or no savings that can be held in foreign currency denominated accounts. In addition, the government itself developed a vested interest in maintaining the discretionary policy and the high levels of inflation associated with it as inflation reduced the real value of the public debt. Therefore, and irrespective of the private sector pressure for deviations from convergence, the government too has become motivated to deviate from the commitment to macroeconomic policy convergence, as reflected in the contracts governing EU–Turkey relations.

### *Microeconomic policy: limited and non-credible convergence*

The contracts governing EU–Turkey relations – the Association Agreement (AA) of 1963 and the Additional Protocol (AP) of 1970 – provided for Turkey's convergence towards EU standards in a number of microeconomic policy areas: trade and trade-related policies, agriculture, competition and indirect taxation. Of these, only trade and trade-related policy convergence was specified in detail. According to the AP provisions, Turkey would eliminate its tariffs on manufactured imports from the EU over a 22-year period, starting in 1973. The alignment with the EU's common external tariff (CET) would also be completed over the same period. In both areas, this period was limited to 12 years for sectors that the Turkish government considered less sensitive. Convergence and policy coordination in other areas was mentioned as a prerequisite for Turkey's closer integration with the EU, but neither deadlines nor road maps were specified.

Given the oscillation of the decision-making between control-reliance and muddling through on the one hand, and the incomplete nature of the contracts governing EU–Turkey relations on the other, it was not surprising to observe that the convergence of Turkey's microeconomic policy towards that of the EU has been limited. Soon after the conclusion of the AP, Turkey demanded revisions of its trade-related provisions in 1972. The main reason was the conflict between the protectionist requirements of Turkey's Third Five-Year Development Plan covering the 1973–77 period and the AP obligations of gradual trade liberalization and adoption of the CET. In other words, import-substitution was invoked by the Turkish government as a reason for deviations from its commitments under the AP.[4] Having failed to secure revision, the Turkish government suspended the gradual tariff reduction and the adoption of

TABLE 3
TURKEY'S COMPLIANCE WITH AP PROVISIONS ON TARIFF DISMANTLING AND ALIGNMENT WITH THE CET

3A: TARIFF REDUCTION

| | 12-year list | | 22-year list | |
|---|---|---|---|---|
| | AP provision (cumulative reduction) | Turkey's compliance (cumulative reduction) | AP provision (cumulative reduction) | Turkey's compliance (cumulative reduction) |
| 1973–85 | 100% | 20% | 30% | 10% |
| 1986–95 | None | 80% | 70% | 90% |

3B: ALIGNMENT WITH CET

| | 12-year list | | 22-year list | |
|---|---|---|---|---|
| | AP provision (cumulative reduction) | Turkey's compliance (cumulative reduction) | AP provision (cumulative reduction) | Turkey's compliance (cumulative reduction) |
| 1973–85 | 100% | None | 50% | None |
| 1986–95 | None | 90% | 50% | 85% |

the CET unilaterally after two reductions in the 1970s. The divergence between envisaged and actual compliance can be seen in Table 3.

It is interesting to note that Turkey's membership application in 1987 took place against a background where Turkey's compliance with the AP's trade policy provisions was only 10–20 per cent with respect to tariff reductions and 0 per cent with respect to adoption of the CET. Following the membership application, Turkey accelerated its compliance in order to strengthen its case. However, this policy change was not credible for three reasons. First, the policy change was accompanied with the introduction of non-tariff barriers in the form of surcharges on imports. The most common instrument used for this purpose was compulsory contributions to funds, which were earmarked for the financing of certain projects such as mass housing. According to the EU Commission's calculations, such compulsory contributions amounted to six per cent of the total import value in 1988 (EU Commission 1989: 187). Therefore, the effective rate of protection enjoyed by Turkish manufacturing industry was 18 per cent in 1994 – with peaks reaching 30–50 per cent in certain sectors such as beverages, clothing, plastics and transport vehicles (Togan and Yilmaz 1995: 155). Secondly, Turkey's trade policy reforms were non-credible because of the high level of subsidies granted to investors and exporters. For example, in the mid-1980s, investment subsidies amounted to 57–104 per cent of the initial investment cost depending on the company's export performance and the region where investment was made. Incentives for exporters, on the other hand, peaked at 12 per cent of total export value in 1984 and gradually declined to four per cent in 1990 (TUSIAD 1992: 107).

The third reason why Turkey's trade policy reform suffered from lack of credibility was the government's excessive use of decrees as substitutes for, or complements to, laws enacted by parliament. These decrees are drafted by civil servants and issued subject to *ex post* parliamentary approval. This type of policy codification creates ample scope for non-transparent connections between organized interests, members of parliament and civil servants. Because a decree remains in force even if parliamentary approval is delayed for a long time, the returns on lobbying civil servants are high. Evidence from the Turkish media clearly suggests that organized interests are highly effective in deploying MPs from the majority party or parties for lobbying civil servants. This type of clientelistic arrangement not only reduces the capacity of the legislative organ to control the executive, but also the predictability of the policy outcomes – thereby exacerbating the credibility problem in Turkish policy-making.

Partly because of this credibility problem and partly because of concerns about foreign competition, the Turkish private sector has always been ambivalent about Turkey's European orientation. For example, in a survey conducted in 1977, only eight per cent of the firms interviewed were in favour of immediate EU membership (TUSIAD 1978: 6–21). The majority (80 per cent) was in favour of membership only in an unspecified future. Also, 63 per cent thought that full membership would have adverse effects on Turkish industry. Asked about what should be done to strengthen EU–Turkey relations, 77 per cent of the firms demanded better protection against EU competition and 54 per cent demanded that tariff reduction for EU imports should be limited. It must be indicated that this ambivalent attitude was not limited to the 1970s when import-substitution policy could have fostered protectionist tendencies.

In another survey conducted at the time when Turkey made its membership application in 1987, about 84–97 per cent of the respondents were in favour of Turkey's membership if the time horizon was not specified. However, when the time horizon was specified as 1995, the level of support dropped by more than half to 32–49 per cent (see Table 4). That this fall was related to concerns about convergence costs could be seen in the response to a question about the adjustment measures the firms were implementing. The proportion of those taking full or partial measures (29–40 per cent) was even lower than that in favour of membership by 1995. In addition, large, compared to small and medium-sized, firms were only marginally more willing to support EU membership or undertake adjustment measures.

The evidence examined above confirms the argument made earlier: Turkey's economic convergence towards the EU has been limited and

TABLE 4
PERCENTAGE OF FIRMS RESPONDING 'YES' TO QUESTIONS ON TURKEY'S EU MEMBERSHIP (1988)

| | Small firms (25–99 employees) | Medium-size firms (100–499 employees) | Large firms (>500 employees) |
|---|---|---|---|
| Do you want Turkey to accede to the EU? | 84.4 | 95.3 | 97.3 |
| Do you want accession by 1995? | 32.0 | 42.2 | 48.7 |
| Are you taking full or partial measures for adjustment? | 28.6 | 37.0 | 40.7 |

*Source*: Kazgan (1989: 21).

unsystematic. This result has been because of the credibility problem faced by Turkish policy-makers and the incomplete nature of the contracts governing EU–Turkey relations. While the credibility problem led to deviations from the declared convergence commitment, the incomplete contracts meant that there was little that the EU could do to reduce the probability of such deviations. Given that these aspects of the EU–Turkey relations were apparent for economic agents, the latter revised their expectations accordingly and tried to secure special treatment rather than undertaking structural adjustment towards integration. Turkish policy-makers proved receptive to such demands because the successive governments themselves also had misgivings about the desirability of irrevocable convergence for two reasons: first, a high scope for discretion in economic policy was essential for the legitimation of the political regime; and secondly, the existence of an extensive public sector, in itself, required deviations from declared micro- and macroeconomic convergence.

It can be argued that the Customs Union (CU) may alter the cost/incentive structure faced by the Turkish government and function as an anchor that locks in economic reforms. This view has been voiced by the IMF and the World Bank with respect to free trade arrangements between developed and developing countries. The post-CU developments in Turkey lend only qualified support to this argument, however. By 1999, Turkey has complied with some of the convergence requirements implied by the CU. Turkey's commercial policy is now aligned with that of the EU with the exception of concluding preferential trade agreements with Mediterranean and some central and eastern European countries. With respect to the protection of intellectual and commercial property rights, Turkey has aligned its laws concerning pharmaceutical processes and products, but similar legislation for sectors listed in Annex 8 of the CU decision has not yet been enacted. There have been some steps taken towards transposing the EU's technical standards into Turkish legislation to remove non-tariff barriers to trade, but a significant number of standards have not yet been transposed for chemicals, textiles, footwear, glass and transport vehicles. As far as competition policy is concerned, a Competition Board has been established and information has been submitted to the EU about Turkey's state aid to industry. However, there is still significant divergence in other areas – including public procurement, agriculture, consumer protection, social policy, health and safety, and excise duties (EU Commission 1999).

What is more important, however, is the extent to which these reforms can be rendered irrevocable by the CU's existence. Despite the optimism expressed about the 'anchoring effect' of free trade arrangements between developed and developing countries (Francois 1997; Galal and Hoekman 1997), it will be argued here that the EU–Turkey CU, unless upgraded with a pre-accession strategy (discussed below), would not be an effective arrangement for ensuring the continuity of Turkey's convergence towards EU standards. One reason is that the static, single-shot benefits of the CU are limited. They range between 0.5 and 1.5 per cent of the benchmark GDP, depending on Turkey's tax policy reforms and the alignment of the commercial policy with that of the EU (Harrison *et al.* 1996: 23–4). Given the factors that underpinned Turkey's past deviations from the commitment to convergence, these benefits may not be large enough to tilt the balance in favour of an irrevocable commitment in the future. Another reason is that political parties or organized interests against the CU will be in a strong position to argue their case as CU membership implies compliance with EU decisions in which Turkey does not take part.

## FURTHER INDICATORS: LIMITED DEMOCRATIZATION AND DIVERGENCE OVER THE CYPRUS ISSUE

The deviations of successive Turkish governments from the commitment to democratization have been so frequent that Turkey is now considered less democratic than the post-1989 regimes in central and eastern Europe. This is confirmed by a report commissioned by TUSIAD (The Turkish Industrialists' and Businessmen's Association representing large business corporations), which stated:

> Countries which are not much better than Turkey in terms of economic conditions are now ahead of Turkey on the path of pluralistic-liberal democracy based on human rights and the supremacy of law … Most of these countries have now speeded up their march towards political modernization or democratization. (TUSIAD 1997: 19).

One contributing factor has already been indicated above: the Turkish state's heavy involvement in the economy meant that regime legitimacy was dependent not on the extent of democratic representation and efficiency, but on the extent to which the government was able to distribute economic rents. This type of policy-making affected societal expectations accordingly, leading to a paternalistic approach to the state whereby the lack of democratization was tolerated in return for access to state-provided economic rents. What is suggested here is not the lack of societal pressure for democratization; it is rather that the context for state–society interaction has increased the returns on lobbying for the attainment of economic rents whereas it decreased the returns on campaigning for democratization. In fact, the latter has always involved very high risks – ranging from detention through torture to very long prison sentences and, sometimes, executions. Consequently, two negative results were obtained: on the one hand, the distribution of economic rents required the creation of fictive resources; on the other, grass-root demands for democratization went through a cycle of ascendance and collapse depending on the cost of expressing democratization demands.

It is necessary to indicate here that powerful interest groups in Turkey are becoming increasingly aware of these consequences. Therefore, we see a tendency to adopt a critical stance against economic instability and lack of democratization. These criticisms, however, conceal more than they reveal. In a skilful manner, they present these deficiencies as outcomes of 'bad government' rather than the result of state–society interaction that has produced bad government. In other words, the criticism levelled at the government ignores the rent-seeking attitudes of the organized interests that have a vested interest in 'bad government'. Thus, such criticism is likely to remain half-hearted and ineffective not only because of the economic actors' strategic behaviour, but also because the government will discount them significantly as it is aware of their preference for rent-seeking.

### *Catching up with contemporary civilization – a checkered record*

The Turkish political elite has always declared a commitment to catch up with 'contemporary civilization' – interpreted since 1923 as the embodiment of Western values in terms of democracy and the respect for human rights. This commitment, however, has been relinquished frequently as a result of either a change in the state's preferences or because of the absence of a bottom–up mechanism of checks and balances. One indicator of this problem has been the overthrow of the civilian government by the military three times since 1960, and the civilian support that the military enjoyed after each coup. These interventions increased not only the probability of further interruptions in the democratization process, but also the military's dominance over the civilian wing of the Turkish state. It is ironic to observe that this dominance has become even more institutionalized as Turkey tried to revive its relations with the EU since the second half of the 1980s. That is why the EU Commission, in its 1998 Report on Turkey, felt it necessary to indicate that one of the anomalies affecting EU–Turkey relations adversely was the lack of civilian control on the military.

Another factor underpinning Turkey's limited democratization has been the blurring of the distinction between political parties and interest groups. The former have increasingly acquired the characteristics of large interest groups by trying to maximize support on the basis of patronage rather than programmatic differences. The state has given added impetus to this tendency by restricting political parties' activities and closing them down when they ventured beyond the programmatic framework drawn by the state itself. These tendencies have strengthened the state's position as the sole authority determining the definition of the 'national interest'. Indicators of these tendencies can be seen clearly in the Law on Political Parties (LPP) of 1983. Article 4 of the LPP stipulates that political parties must operate in loyalty to *Kemalist* principles and reforms. Also, article 78 states that parties may not pursue the goal of changing the principles laid down in the preamble to the 1982 Constitution, which included the provision that thoughts and opinions contrary to Turkish national interests and Turkish historical and moral values shall not enjoy protection under the law. Finally, article 97 provides that a political party 'may not engage in attitude, statement or action' against the military regime of 1980–83 and its acts or decisions.

It is obvious that these provisions severely restrict the scope for party competition on the basis of programmatic differences. On the contrary, they force the political parties to compete on the basis of favours that they can distribute. Given this framework, the scope for military intervention increases as the latter can present itself as the ultimate authority that saves the country from the negative externalities of competition between political parties, which pursue their narrow interests at the expense of society. This was why political parties were dissolved after the military interventions of 1960 and 1980; and were tamed into supporting the military's programme in 1971–74. After 1982, this practice has become more widespread. Since then, the Constitutional Court has made eight decisions of dissolution based on violation of the ideological framework that the parties must conform to. Although constitutional amendments made in 1995 provided for certain relaxations, these amendments are not yet incorporated into the LPP and did not prevent the dissolution of the Kurdish parties or the Islamic Welfare (Refah) Party.

A third factor that underpins the lack of democratization is the protection accorded to members of parliament who toe the state's official line. Article 83 of the Constitution provides that an MP's parliamentary immunity can be restricted if his declarations outside the parliamentary platform constitute a criminal offence. This provision, however, does not apply to other crimes (such as corruption) which may even bar a person from becoming an MP. In other words, article 83 obliges MPs to toe the official ideological line, but provides them with the prospect of 'monopoly profits' on non-transparent deals once they are in parliament. This is not only a blank cheque for corruption and the reduced authority of parliament, but also a practice that runs counter to developments in EU countries. For example, in France and the UK, parliamentary immunity is a right that only protects MPs against civil suits and not against criminal prosecutions. In Turkey, however, the institution of immunity has been transferred into a mechanism of protection against criminal prosecution (TUSIAD 1997: 71). Under these circumstances, a process of adverse selection becomes inevitable: potential candidates in favour of democratization are discouraged, whereas those concerned with personal gains are encouraged to run for election.

Given this set-up, Turkey's democratization and human rights record has become the most often quoted reason for Turkey's exclusion from the current enlargement process. This is not surprising. Nor is it a conspiracy designed to keep Turkey out of the emerging European structures, as Turkish policy-makers would argue. It is made inevitable by the EU's tendency since the late 1980s to incorporate human rights as a significant issue in its relations with third countries. As Fouwels (1997) has demonstrated, the number of EU declarations issued on human rights matters increased from four in the 1981–85 period to 110 in 1991, and remained at an annual average of 75 between 1992–96. The number of interventions made also followed a similar trend: increasing from 20 in 1981–85 to 140 in 1992, and remaining at an annual average of 72 thereafter. In addition, the proportion of UN human rights-related resolutions on which EU member states voted alike increased from 54 per cent in 1986 to 92 per cent in 1996. If one reason for this trend was the EU's attempt at marking its contribution to the emerging world order after the collapse of the Soviet bloc, the other was its concern about minimizing the risks associated with the closer relations sought by central and eastern European countries. In other words, respect for human rights has become an issue that the EU would use as a convergence-fostering and risk-minimizing mechanism.

Just at a time when this EU policy was taking shape, the already high level of human rights violations in Turkey became even higher, mainly because of the escalation of the conflict with the Kurdish Workers' Party (PKK). In addition to the widespread use of torture, the number of extra-judicial executions and 'disappearances' increased significantly from 1992–93 onwards (Amnesty International 1996: 13–19). Also, article 8 of the Anti-Terror Law of 1991 provided for long prison sentences and heavy fines for the expression of 'separatism', leading to a substantial increase in the number of detentions and prosecutions. Political parties with a Kurdish constituency were closed and their MPs were arrested. Inevitably, these developments affected Turkey's relations with the EU negatively and undermined the credibility of the partial reforms introduced as a result of European pressure.

The reforms introduced in the 1990s were clearly related to pressure from the EU, but successive Turkish governments made a tremendous effort to prove that this was not the case. For example, the reform of the penal code in 1991 and the commutation of death sentences to 20 years of imprisonment were clearly related to the negotiations on the so-called 'Matutes Package' that was designed to strengthen EU–Turkey relations after the rejection of the membership application. Also, the 1995 constitutional reform was connected to the negotiations on the CU. In fact, they were designed to secure the European Parliament's approval of the CU decision. Finally, the removal of military judges from State Security Courts in 1998 was closely related to Turkey's attempts at addressing the negative result of the Luxembourg Summit, which kept Turkey outside the forthcoming wave of enlargement.

Nevertheless, the official Turkish policy line was not only to deny any linkage, but also to declare repeatedly that Turkey would not accept any strings attached to its relations with the EU. These signals had a negative impact on the credibility of the reforms on two fronts. On the EU front, member states against Turkey's closer links with the EU (e.g. Greece, Sweden, Denmark) were enabled to strike an alliance with the majority of the European Parliament to keep Turkey's human rights record under the spotlight. On the home front, the emergence of pro-reform expectations was suppressed and the functionality of democratization for integration with Europe was undermined. In other words, non-credible reforms proved to be more costly than otherwise as Turkey had to bow to European pressure without necessarily reaping any substantial benefits in terms of a better prospect for membership or a stronger domestic support for the reform agenda.

*Divergence in foreign policy: the case of Cyprus*

Turkey's military presence in Cyprus and the intransigence of the Turkish-Cypriot leadership in the intercommunal talks were criticized only mildly by the EU until the mid-1980s. However, given that one of the parties to the conflict (Greece) was an EU member and the other two parties (Turkey and the Cypriot government) applied for membership in 1987 and 1990 respectively, this detached EU involvement became unsustainable. A further factor that made detachment unsustainable were developments in eastern Europe, which prompted the EU to make the principles of 'good neighbourly relations' and 'referral of international disputes to relevant international bodies' essential conditions for closer relations. Despite this development, the Turkish policy on Cyprus became more divergent and the integration of northern Cyprus with Turkey was accelerated. This policy was justified on the grounds that EU policy-makers have become increasingly receptive to Greek pressure – the so-called 'Greek factor'.

It is argued here that this rationale is counterproductive and does not hold water for three reasons. First, it is self-defeating because it accords Greece a degree of influence on EU policy-making that is not confirmed by evidence. Secondly, as demonstrated in Ugur (1996), it ignores the fact that the EU has been reluctant to take Turkey as a member both before and after the accession of Greece. Finally, it allows not only Turkey, but also the EU, to conceal their mutual failures in the resolution of the Cyprus problem.

It is clear from the existing evidence that Greece has tried to block the normalization of EU–Turkey relations at various occasions. For example, in the first EU–Turkey Association Council (AC) meeting after the 1980 Turkish military coup, the Greek foreign minister raised the Cyprus issue and stated that Greece would block the implementation of the EU–Turkey association unless Turkish troops were withdrawn (*Financial Times*, 17 September 1986). In 1988, Greece secured the introduction of a statement into the EU's joint communiqué that the Cyprus problem was affecting EU–Turkey relations (*The Guardian*, 25 April 1988; *Financial Times*, 26 April 1988). Greece also succeeded in ensuring that a similar statement was included in the declaration of the Rhodes Summit in 1988. These diplomatic activities of the late 1980s were accompanied by the Greek veto on the release of the Fourth Financial Protocol, which provided for a package of aid and credits totalling ECU 600m.

Nevertheless, the impact of the Greek pressure remained limited only to the suspension of the financial protocol. Greece was unable to block either the revival of the EU–Turkey association or the political dialogue that followed. In fact, Greece had to accept the Commission's 1990 proposal (the Matutes Package) that envisaged:

- completion of the CU by 1995
- financial co-operation
- technological co-operation, and
- re-enforcement of cultural and political links with Turkey.

Although Greece continued to block the release of the financial aid, the Matutes Package was *de facto* implemented and its major component, the CU, became operational in 1996. If a 'Greek factor' ever existed in EU–Turkey relations, it was in the form of both Turkey and the EU presenting Greece as a scapegoat. Turkey, in an attempt to justify its deviations from the EU's approach to the Cyprus problem, criticized the EU for giving in to Greek pressure. Against this, the EU limited its reaction to signalling to Turkey that the Cyprus problem must be resolved before Turkish accession could be possible. This linkage, however, was dictated by the EU's need to avoid the internalization of the Greco-Turkish conflict rather than Greek pressure *per se*.

Ignoring this EU tendency towards risk minimization, Turkey became even less concerned about converging towards the EU's Cyprus policy, which supported the UN's proposal for a bizonal, bicommunal federal state. The first indication in this direction came in 1992, when the EU and Turkey concluded the Matutes Package with the aim of strengthening the association. In that year, the intercommunal talks broke down once again as Mr Denktas, the Turkish-Cypriot leader, rejected the UN proposal for a bizonal, bicommunal federation on the grounds that this solution did not recognize the Turkish Republic of Northern Cyprus (TRNC) as a sovereign state.[5] This policy was followed by a number of steps that intensified the TRNC's integration with Turkey. In September 1994, Turkey signed the 13th joint economic protocol with the TRNC to circumvent the European Court of Justice ruling which required the exports from the North to be certified by the internationally recognized Cypriot government. According to this protocol, the TRNC would use the Turkish Lira as the national currency and apply the Turkish foreign exchange regime. In addition, the TRNC declared that the traffic system would be changed to comply with the right lane driving in Turkey and the incorporation of the TRNC into Turkey's telecommunications code was completed (Economist Intelligence Unit 1994: 24–5).

The integration of the TRNC gathered a new momentum after 1995, following the EU's declaration that negotiations on Cyprus' accession would begin six months after the end of the then Intergovernmental Conference. The joint declaration by Turkey and the TRNC on 28 December 1995 tied the hands of the Turkish-Cypriot leadership by stating that Cyprus should join the EU only when Turkey is accepted. In addition, it announced the establishment of an association council that would take measures to achieve 'partial integration' of the North economically, financially and in terms of security, defence and foreign policy (Kyle 1997: 31). As this process unfolded, two further declarations were made in 1997 with the aim of increasing the TRNC's viability economically and militarily. Then, in early 1998, the Turkish president, Mr Demirel, declared on the Turkish Radio and Television Network that one could no longer speak of a single Cyprus as there were two nations and two states on the island. Encouraged by these developments, Denktas told the Turkish press that he was wrong in the past to uphold the concept of federation and participate in the intercommunal talks. He added that now 'two states' must hold talks to solve the Cyprus problem (*Sabah* [Turkish Daily], 23 February 1998).

Given this evidence, the irrelevance of the 'Greek factor' thesis becomes obvious. What would be a more relevant inference is that Turkish policy-makers have been quite prepared to sacrifice closer links with the EU in return for maintaining Turkey's military presence in Cyprus. This is a clear signal indicating that integration with Europe has been a non-credible commitment because of domestic policy preferences as well as foreign policy priorities. Therefore, Turkey's presentation of the Greek factor as an obstacle to closer links with the EU is nothing but a desperate attempt at concealing its divergent foreign policy agenda. Under these circumstances, the EU's attempts in the 1980s and 1990s at keeping Turkey in its orbit without membership can be interpreted as damage limitation exercises rather than submission to Greek pressure.

## IN LIEU OF CONCLUSIONS: THE PROSPECT AFTER HELSINKI

The Helsinki European Council decision to accept Turkey as a candidate for membership was a significant step in the direction of addressing the anomaly in EU–Turkey relations. First of all, it confirms that membership is a realistic target provided that Turkey fulfils the Copenhagen criteria. Secondly, it signals the EU's willingness to share the burden of convergence through a commitment to set up a pre-accession strategy and allow Turkey to participate in relevant EU programmes. Thirdly, it provides for an 'enhanced political dialogue' that would focus on Turkey's political convergence towards EU standards. Finally, it indicates that the political dialogue will include two issues that Turkey has been adamant to de-link from its relations with the EU: progress on the resolution of the Cyprus problem and compliance with the EU's principles on good neighbourly relations, and referral of disputes to the International Court of Justice (EU Council 1999). These aspects of the Helsinki decision go some way towards dispelling the uncertainty that followed the 1997 Luxembourg Summit. In that sense, they address some of the negative consequences of the incomplete contracts discussed above.

However, there are two further issues to be addressed: the pre-accession strategy that the EU would pursue and the extent to which Turkey would be prepared to tie its hands. As far as the first issue is concerned, the evidence emerging from EU statements indicates that the EU clearly would be in favour of seeing Turkey taking the first step by coming forward with a detailed programme of reforms. It would also like to see a revision in official and societal attitudes towards integration with Europe. The revision is expected to reflect the extent to which (1) Turkey's international economic and foreign policy objectives are compatible with European integration, and (2) a credible societal consensus exists in favour of Europeanization. This expectation can be justified on the grounds that it is up to the Turkish government and society to decide about the desirability of integration with the EU.

However, a pre-accession strategy based mainly on the conditions to be met by Turkey is highly likely to cause a return to the pre-Helsinki stalemate. That is because Turkey will interpret it as an alibi for the EU's failure to substantiate its commitments implied by the Helsinki decision. To reduce the probability of such an interpretation and induce Turkey to embark on the convergence required by membership, the EU must put forward a transparent and binding pre-accession package, irrespective of the current signals coming from Turkey. That is because a detailed and transparent pre-accession package is essentially an indication of the EU's willingness to insure the short-run risks associated with a credible Turkish commitment to Europeanization. Such insurance will strengthen the case for the pro-integration elements in Turkey. More significantly, however, it will constitute a further step in reducing the loopholes and discretion inherent in the incomplete contracts governing EU–Turkey relations. In addition, the need for the EU to take the first step is dictated by the current political party configuration in Turkey, where the nationalist and

Islamic parties are enjoying the highest level of support in their history. Under this condition, expecting a radical change in Turkey's attitudes as a precondition for an EU move is both unrealistic and counterproductive.

As far as the second issue (i.e. Turkey's willingness to tie its hands) is concerned, the evidence is mixed. On the one hand, there are indications of change in Turkey's attitudes towards the EU. In this context, the Turkish Prime Minister's letter to his German counterpart in May 1999 constitutes a turning point. In that letter, Mr Ecevit expressed certain commitments involving the fulfilment of the Copenhagen criteria and a willingness to chart a road map outlining the evolution of the reform process. Therefore, it is not surprising to hear the German Ambassador to Turkey stating that Ecevit's letter to Chancellor Schroeder was a very significant document in the preparations for Helsinki (*Turkish Daily News*, 9 December 1999). Secondly, the Turkish government has agreed to the conditionality implicit in the Helsinki decision with respect to Cyprus and the disputes with Greece. Thirdly, the Helsinki decision was welcomed not only by the nationalist party in the ruling coalition, but also the Islamic party and the supporters of the Kurdish Workers Party. In other words, integration with Europe is currently enjoying widespread support reminiscent of the mid-1980s, when Turkey was preparing for its membership application. Finally, the stand-by agreement concluded with the IMF in late 1999 is linked to a macroeconomic stabilization programme in which fiscal, monetary and exchange rate policy commitments are conducive to the fulfilment of the Copenhagen economic criteria.

Nevertheless, these developments cannot be taken as indicators of an irrevocable European orientation. As an informed observer of EU–Turkey relations, Sami Kohen of the *Milliyet* newspaper, has indicated: the question about Turkey's determination to reassess its domestic and international problems from a new, different angle and to produce new, different strategies is still open. One reason is that the current international economic policy in Turkey is based on the assumption that integration with Europe is important not because the EU is significant as an anchor for structural reforms and corporate restructuring, but because Turkey cannot afford to remain outside the EU when the latter is intensifying its cooperation with the US. In other words, the link with the EU is perceived in terms of its contribution to Turkey's strategic significance for the US rather than from the perspective of convergence towards the EU. This assumption has underlined not only the official policy discourse, but also the strategies of the private sector – as reflected in a report commissioned by TUSIAD (1998).

Even if Turkey embarks on a reform process geared towards fulfilling the Copenhagen criteria, another problem that must be resolved is the societal input into the European orientation. Until now, this input has been very weak for two reasons: the suppression of the civil society organizations within the control-reliant mode of governance and the compliance of the private sector organizations with the official policy line. Even if the recent increase in the number and activities of the non-governmental organizations in Turkey can be assumed to continue as the reforms are carried out, the compliant attitudes of the private sector organizations may not change. The private sector, even the largest companies, has been reluctant to embrace a fully-fledged European strategy. In fact, as late as the autumn of 1998, the Brussels representative of the Economic Development Foundation (*Iktisadi Kalkinma Vakfi*), which has been lobbying in favour of Turkey's EU membership since the 1970s, stated: 'There is differential integration in Europe ... It may be easy to transfer sovereignty in the area of trade policy, but in other areas we may not want to go as far as the Europeans have' (Nuray 1998: 33).

The third reason why Turkey's European orientation may remain non-credible is that Turkey has not spelled out yet its preparedness to defend European values as a common heritage that must be defended jointly rather than merely in terms of their functionality for membership. This may seem an insignificant detail, but it is in fact a reflection of the wider problem as to how Turkey's Islamic values would coexist with a predominantly Christian European culture. This problem may not be as insurmountable as Huntington (1993) would suggest, but it requires innovative thinking that neither the EU nor Turkey seems to have embarked upon. Declarations about tolerance, strong historical ties, the existence of an Islamic community in Europe, etc. cannot substitute for the required innovation. I conclude by stating that, unless these problems are addressed, the Helsinki decision may fall short of ensuring Turkey's integration with Europe. Even if Turkey became a member of the EU without resolving these problems, this would not necessarily mean integration, as Turkey would be preoccupied with securing opt-outs and diluting the integration process.

## NOTES

1. On the role of the state in Turkey's economic development until the 1970s, see Hershlag (1968); Land (1970); Tezel (1986); and Boratav (1982). It is true that the state has started to pull out of the manufacturing sector since 1980, but this withdrawal instigated a new wave of clientelistic relations centred on the distribution of rents associated with granting access to business opportunities.
2. See e.g. OECD (1987, 1988 and 1995); Rodrik (1990); Uctum (1992); Nas (1992); TUSIAD (1995); and Onis and Riedel (1996).
3. This is calculated from Annual Reports of the Turkish Central Bank. For further details, see Ugur (1999: 66).
4. On the incompatibility between the import substitution policy and the AP, see Tekeli and Ilkin (1993: 99–140). On Turkey's request for revision, see Birand (1986: 301–6) and Ugur (1996).
5. The 'Turkish Republic of Northern Cyprus' (TRNC) was declared unilaterally by the Turkish-Cypriot Authorities on 15 November 1983. Following Resolution 541 (S/RES/541) of the UN Security Council on 18 November 1983, no country except Turkey has recognised the 'Turkish Republic of Northern Cyprus'. References to the TRNC here do not necessarily imply recognition on the part of any of the contributors.

## REFERENCES

*Agence Europe*, Agence Internationale d'Information pour la Presse (English Edition): Luxembourg-Bruxelles, various issues.

Amnesty International (1996): *Turkey: No Security without Human Rights*, London: Amnesty International Publications No. EUR/44/84/96.

Birand, M.A. (1986): *Turkiye'nin Ortak Pazar Macerasi* [Turkey's Common Market Adventure], Ankara: Milliyet Yayinlari.

Boratav, K. (1982): *Turkiye'de Devletcilik* [Etatism in Turkey], Ankara: Savas Yayinevi.

Central Bank of Turkey (1982-93): *Annual Reports*, Ankara.

DIE (1973): *Toplumsal ve Ekonomik Gelismenin 50 Yili* [50 Years of Social and Economic Development], Ankara: DIE.

Economist Intelligence Unit (1994): *EIU Country Report on Cyprus*, 4th Quarter, London.

Ersel, H., and E.M. Kumcu (1995): 'Istikrar Programi ve Kamu Dengesi' [The Stability Programme and Public Sector Balance], in TUSIAD, Istanbul.

Etzioni, A. (1967): 'Mixed-Scanning: A Third Approach to Decision-Making', *Public Administration Review* 27/5.

—— (1968): *The Active Society: A Theory of Societal and Political Processes*, New York: Free Press.

European Commission (1989): *The Turkish Economy: Structure and Development*, Brussels: SEC (89) 2290/final.

—— (1999): *1999 Regular Report on Turkey's Progress towards Accession*, http://www.eurep.tr

European Council (1999): *Helsinki European Council Conclusions*, Press Release no.00300/99, 11 December, Brussels.

Fouwels, M. (1997): 'The European Union's Common Foreign and Security Policy and Human Rights', *Netherlands Quarterly Review of Human Rights* 15/3.

Francois, J.F. (1997): 'External Bindings and the Credibility of Reform', in A. Gamal and B. Hoekman (eds.), *Regional Partners in Global Markets: Limits and Possibilities of the Euro-Med Agreements*, London and Cairo: CEPR and ECES.

Galal, A., and B. Hoekman (1997): 'Egypt and the Partnership with the EU: The Road to Maximum Benefits', in ibid. (eds.), *Regional Partners in Global Markets: Limits and Possibilities of the Euro-Med Agreements*, London and Cairo: CEPR and ECES.

Harrison, G.W., *et al.* (1996): *Economic Implications for Turkey of a Customs Union with the European Union*, Washington DC: World Bank.

Hershlag, Z.Y. (1968): *Turkey: The Challenge of Growth*, Leiden: E.J. Brill.

Huntington, S. (1993): 'The Clash of Civilizations', *Foreign Affairs* 72/3.

IMF (1998a): *International Financial Statistics Yearbook*, Washington DC: IMF.

—— (1998b): *IMF Economic Reviews* 2 (May-Aug.), pp.136–40

Kazgan, G. (1989): *Summary Report of the Manufacturing Survey with Special reference to Turkey's Integration with the European Community*, Istanbul: Friedrich Ebert Foundation.

Kennen, P.B. (1996): *Economic and Monetary Union in Europe: Moving beyond Maastricht*, Cambridge: Cambridge University Press.

Krueger, A.O. (1974): *Turkey: Foreign Trade Regimes and Economic Development*, Princeton NJ: Columbia University Press.

Kyle, K. (1997): *Cyprus: In Search of Peace*, London: Minority Rights Groups International.

Land, J.W. (1970): *The Role of Government in the Economic Development of Turkey*, Houston: Rice University Press.

Nas, T.F. (1992): 'The Impact of Turkey's Stabilisation and Structural Adjustment Program: An Introduction', in T.F. Nas and M. Odekon (eds.), *Economics and Politics of Turkish Liberalisation*, Bethlehem: Lehigh University Press.

Nuray, H. (1998): 'AB ile Yeni bir Diyalog Dili Lazim [We Need a New Language for Dialogue with the EU], *Anadolu* 10 (Sept.–Oct.).

OECD (1987, 1988 and 1995): *Economic Survey: Turkey*, Paris: OECD.

Onis, Z., and J. Riedel (1996): *Economic Crisis and Long-Term Growth in Turkey*, Washington DC: World Bank.

Ozal, T. (1986): 'Speech Delivered at the Royal Institute of International Affairs' *Turkish Review* 1/3.

Rodrik, D. (1990): 'Some Policy Dilemmas in Turkey's Macroeconomic Management', in T. Aricanli and D. Rodrik (eds.), *The Political Economy of Turkey: Debt Adjustment and Sustainability*, New York: St Martin's Press.

Saracoglu, R. (1995): 'Istikrar Programi Uzerinde Dusunceler' [Thoughts on Turkey's Stabilization Programme], in TUSIAD, Istanbul.

Somers, F. (ed.) (1991): *European Economies: A Comparative Study*, London: Pitman.

Tekeli, I., and S. Ilkin (1993): *Turkiye ve Avrupa Toplulugu: Ulus Devletini Asma Cabasindaki Avrupa'ya Turkiye'nin Yaklasimi* [Turkey and the European Community: Turkey's Approach to a Europe Attempting to Transcend the Nation State], Ankara: Umit Yayincilik.

Tezel, Y.S. (1986): *Cumhuriyet Doneminin Iktisadi Tarihi* [Economic History of the Republican Era], Ankara: Yurt Yayinlari.

Togan, S., and A. Yilmaz (1995): 'Turkiye ve Avrupa Birligi' [Turkey and the European Union], in TUSIAD, Istanbul: pp.121–67.

TUSIAD (1978): *AET ile Iliskileri Ozel Kesim Nasil Degerlendiriyor* [Private Sector's View of the Relations with the EEC], Istanbul: TUSIAD.

—— (1992): *21. Yuzyila Dogru Turkiye: Gelecege Donuk bir Atilim Stratejisi* [Turkey towards the 21st Century: A Forward-Looking Strategy], Istanbul: TUSIAD.

—— (1995): *Turkiye icin Yeni bir Orta Vadeli Istikrar Programina Dogru* [Towards a Medium-Term Stability Programme for Turkey], Istanbul: TUSIAD Publications.

—— (1997): *Perspectives on Democratization in Turkey*, Istanbul: TUSIAD.

—— (1998): *Turkiye'de Yeni bir Ekonomik ve Ticari Diplomasi Stratejisine Dogru* [Towards an Economic and Commercial Strategy in Turkey], Istanbul: TUSIAD.

Uctum, M. (1992): 'The Effects of Liberalization of Traded and Non-Traded Goods Sectors: The Case of Turkey', in F.N. Tevfik and M. Odekon (eds.), *Economics and Politics of Turkish Liberalization*, Bethlehem: Lehigh University Press.

Ugur, M. (1996): 'Customs Union as a Substitute for Turkey's Membership? An Interpretation of the EU-Turkey Relations', *Cambridge Review of International Affairs* 10/1.

—— (1999): *The European Union and Turkey: An Anchor/Credibility Dilemma*, Aldershot: Ashgate.

# Reluctant Europeans? European Integration and the Transformation of Turkish Politics

SPYROS A. SOFOS

This article provides a brief and, admittedly, cursory outline of domestic responses within Turkey to its long and, at times, volatile relationship with the EC/EU. After an examination of the main parameters within which Turkish politics have developed since the establishment of the Turkish Republic, including the dynamics of the processes of political modernization, the article shifts its focus to the post-1983 political scene and examines its institutional and cultural dimensions. In the last part of the article, the development of the relationship between the EU and Turkey is assessed, as well as the ways in which this has been 'domesticated' in Turkish political life. I show that Turkish political institutions and actors have reacted to the process of closer links with the EU by either attempting to reconcile the principles of Kemalist republicanism with the process of Europeanization or, on some occasions, by opposing change.

## OTTOMAN AND REPUBLICAN MODERNIZATION: DIFFERENT TRAJECTORIES

Encounters between Turkish society and Western modernity and consequent experiments of modernization have a long history, dating back to the Ottoman period. The Ottoman economy became linked to European markets as early as the sixteenth century (Sunar 1987) and they eventually dominated Turkey in the nineteenth century (Kasaba 1988). It is during this latter period that the imperatives of economic and political reform became pressing within the ailing Ottoman empire and were linked with demands for modernization from different sections of the political and economic elites. As a result, Ottoman reformist Sultans, some eagerly, some reluctantly, introduced a series of reforms that culminated in the *Tanzimat* reforms of the late 1830s and – in the next few decades – in a series of legal, political and economic reforms. Although these reforms could be described as attempts at modernization from above and often lacked the broad social foundations that would render them successful, they nevertheless have affected considerably the economic, political and social developments of the last century of the Ottoman empire. Overall, the changes introduced by the reformist Sultans of the nineteenth century could be interpreted as attempts to embrace progressively aspects of Western modernity in response to popular or elite pressure. Clearly, these reforms were not the product of a 'self-generating societal process' (Keyder 1997: 39–40) and were often characterized by a top–down character and by the defensive attempts of the modernizing Sultans to delimit the scope of Ottoman society's transformation. However, these reforms reflected a complex interaction or negotiation between Ottoman tradition and Western modernity and were the product of some degree of genuine societal pressure for their implementation. The modernization project to which they were linked was premised on a conception of modernization that was more in tune with the model of social and political symbiosis of different cultures and traditions characteristic of the Ottoman empire. It both took on board the empire's internal diversity and internalized European and other influences by integrating them in Ottoman society in a variety of ways.[1]

Without neglecting the ultimately authoritarian character of both modernization perspectives, and to underestimate the element of continuity that marks the transition from the Ottoman Empire to Republican Turkey, it could be argued that the modernization project model envisaged by Mustafa Kemal was much more aggressive and *dirigiste* than that exemplified by previous reforms in the nineteenth century. Having to build a modern nation state out of the ruins of the multi-ethnic Ottoman Empire, Kemal embarked on an ambitious programme of modernization of Turkish society, polity and economy, using as a model (albeit with a highly selective interpretation) European modernity. To achieve this, the new Kemalist bureaucratic-military elite had to devise a vigorous reform project, often tantamount to extensive authoritarian social engineering. It is clear that Kemal's programme of authoritarian modernization, despite its explicit and frequent evocations of the 'people', was permeated by a lack of trust in the latter. The Kemalist project was premised on establishing a relation of externality between modernity and Turkish society and attempted to regulate the propagation of the former to the latter. Turkey, according to Attaturk, should be forced to modernize through the – admittedly selective (Keyder 1997: 39–40) – suppression or uprooting of institutions, values, ideologies and practices that were considered anachronistic and regressive and the propagation or invention of alternative institutions, values, ideologies and practices that would serve the advancement of the principles of republicanism, secularism, nationalism, populism, statism and revolutionism which were central to Turkey's transformation.

## EUROPEANIZATION: SEMANTICS AND POLITICAL CULTURE

In view of this vision of modernity (and modernization) of the republican elite, it has become virtually commonplace to accept today that Atatürk 'believed that Turkey's future lay with Europe and the West' (cf. Müftüler-Bac 1997: 17). Indeed, this assertion can be supported by the fact that Western modernity, by which Atatürk was largely influenced, was in effect coterminous at the time with European modernity and that, therefore, the process of modernization he set in motion equals Europeanization.

However, such claims should be more closely scrutinized as they tend to conflate 'modernization' with 'Europeanization' or even 'Westernization' and to misread Turkey's domestic transformation as well as its foreign policy and international alliances. Although there is no doubt that Kemal was impressed and greatly influenced by the achievements of the French Revolution and the Jacobeans, it is equally true that Turkey's modernization necessitated, from his point of view, the adoption of a political system that drew considerably upon aspects and experiences of the Soviet experiment in political and especially economic modernization that was unfolding at that time. As one of the most eminent students of modern Turkey points out, the principle of statism (*devletçilik*), central in the ideology of Ataturkism (*Atatürkçuluk*), although never clearly defined, drew extensively upon the Soviet example of economic organization and Soviet practice (Zürcher 1997: 205–6). In effect, I would argue that the republican elite envisaged Turkey developing primarily into a modern (though not necessarily Western European) state, able to resist external military or economic threats and capable of being treated by other modern nations with respect and as an equal, in contrast to the Ottoman Empire which had been labelled the 'sick man of Europe'. It is true that the republican elite itself was divided into different factions of sympathizers of various European nations and the models of development they represented, including that of the Soviet Union. However, it was united in its determination to achieve the modernization of Turkey from above and the creation of a strong, modern nation state.

It is in the latter part of the twentieth century that Turkish foreign policy aligned the country with the US-led 'Western coalition', thus rejecting the Soviet model of development and integrating itself into the Atlantic political and military international networks, primarily through NATO membership (in 1952). Even in this new international environment, Turkey's European alignment was restricted initially to membership of the Council of Europe (1949). Then, especially in the late 1960s, Turkish elites started turning to the European Economic Community (EEC, eventually the EU). Turkey officially became an associate member of the EEC in 1964, in a decade when the latter replaced the USA as Turkey's most important trading partner (Zürcher 1997: 290–91). However, the EC–Turkey relationship was not a straightforward one.

Turkey's associate membership application in July 1959 was partly a result of the competitive character of Turkish–Greek relations of the period. Turkey's application was submitted 16 days after that of Greece and was prompted largely by concern that a successful Greek application might upset the delicate balance of power upon which the good and cooperative relations between the two south-eastern European neighbours had been premised since the 1923 Lausanne Treaty. In addition to this reactive dimension of Turkey's European policy of the period, Turkey's bureaucratic elite considered the country's EEC associate membership application as a further confirmation of the Western orientation of the Turkish Republic and as an act that would anchor it more securely in the institutional network of the Western alliance.

However, the fact that this application was dictated largely by external factors beyond the Turkish government's control meant that Turkey's policy towards the EEC had not matured at the time of the application and was marked by inconsistencies, ambiguities and contradictions which found their expression in divisions within the Turkish government. During the July 1962 negotiations between Turkey and the EEC, the division between two camps in the Turkish administrative and political elite found its official expression in the opposing views supported by the two main government departments involved in the formulation of the official Turkish position during the negotiations: the State Planning Organization (SPO) and the Foreign Ministry (Birand 1990: 165–7). The SPO, the agency responsible for central economic planning, had been established by the 1961 constitution and expressed the determination of part of the Turkish bureaucratic elite to abandon its unsuccessful experiments with Western-style liberalism and attempt to reintroduce a project of state-centred economic development along the lines of the Kemalist principle of statism. As Turkey's modernization was not seen as necessarily dependent upon the prospect of the country's association with the EEC and as disillusionment with liberal economic experiments had rekindled the appeal of a relatively autonomous development policy, it was no surprise when the SPO expressed its strong opposition to links with the Community. Its stance was premised on the grounds that 'any association [with the EEC] would hamper economic development in Turkey' (Müftüler-Bac 1997: 55). Consequently, the SPO accused the Foreign Ministry of selling out the country (Birand 1990: 165–7). Note that the organization's *dirigiste* approach to economic development was not formulated in a societal void, but had a sympathetic constituency in circles within the political and bureaucratic elite, which perceived the liberal economic principles underlying the economic dimension of European integration and the proposed association agreement as a threat to Turkey's interests.

On the other side of the divide, the Foreign Ministry represented another set of perspectives that prioritized Turkey's associate membership application. As was mentioned earlier, one of the reasons for this was related to the maintenance of geopolitical balance in south-eastern Europe. However, alongside this tactical concern, longer-term strategic considerations seem to have prevailed in the Foreign Ministry policy planners' thinking. Their perspective seemed clearly to link Turkey's development with the country's integration in Western in general, and west European in particular, institutions and processes. As a result, the Foreign Ministry strongly supported the option of association with the EC, arguing that this would accelerate Turkey's economic and political development (Müftüler-Bac 1997: 55). What is more, in an attempt to claim the political high ground in their skirmishes with the SPO, Foreign Ministry officials and their supporters mobilized the elements of Kemalist ideology that would legitimize their strategy of coming closer to the EEC. As Mehmet Ali Birand notes, the Foreign Ministry accused the SPO of religious fanaticism (Birand 1990: 165–7), implying that the latter was not in tune with Ataturkism's secular and modernizing heritage. Indeed, not surprisingly, both government departments justified their positions by referring to different emphases and interpretations of Kemal's political legacy as Turkey's decision to join the EEC or not had to be integrated, at least in terms of political rhetoric, into this modernizing project, with all the contradictions and ambiguities that this entailed.

From the EEC's point of view, although the Greek and Turkish applications of 1959 had officially been afforded equal treatment and the Council of Ministers had approved negotiations, reservations concerning Turkey's eligibility for EEC membership had been voiced early on. Müftüler-Bac (1997: 55) summarizes these reasons as follows;

> [T]he first reservation over Turkish membership concerned its Europeanness. The second involved cultural and social differences ... A third issue was Turkey's level of economic growth and development. Finally, there was concern over democracy in Turkey and the country's political structure.

Although one cannot dispute that all these factors have played a significant role in the formulation of European responses to the development of the EC/EU–Turkish relationship, it is clear that, as events unfolded at the time of the Turkish application for associate membership of the EEC, particular emphasis was to be put on the issue of democracy and human rights. The military coup of May 1960 brought about the suspension of negotiations in the short term, and propelled this dimension of Euro–Turkish relations to the top of the agenda in future negotiations. This development, in turn, has affected the particular way in which the EC/EU relationship with Turkey is 'domesticated'. In many quarters of Turkish politics today, Europeanization is treated as synonymous to 'democratization' or pressure to enhance and deepen liberal democracy and to activate appropriate citizenship rights.[2]

## DEMOCRATIZATION: CONCEPTUALIZING CITIZENSHIP AND POPULAR SOVEREIGNTY

One of the distinctive characteristics of the Turkish political system since the establishment of the Turkish Republic has been the particular way in which the principle of popular sovereignty has coexisted with a mistrust of the people crystallized in an authoritarian conception of the 'general will' (Mardin 1997a: 69). The imperative of building and consolidating a strong modern nation state as well as the negative experience of Ottoman experiments with parliamentary politics[3] tilted the balance decisively to a project of selective modernization from above. This envisaged the establishment of formally democratic, but in essence authoritarian, political institutions that would safeguard the unity and modernization of Turkey. According to Mardin, in Ataturk's thought, the Turkish people were to be educated and inculcated with an appropriate civic culture that would allow them eventually to gain full citizenship, through an apprenticeship of indefinite duration (Mardin 1997b: 121). This civic culture, however, incorporated a nationalist ideology of Jacobean inspiration that emphasized the unity and indivisibility, not only of the state and its territory, but also of the people. Ataturkism left no doubt that this unity and indivisibility was translated into popular homogeneity expressed in a single 'popular' voice and a sense of collective interest and purpose.

In practice, this process of authoritarian political modernization, combined with the economic modernization that Turkey has undergone, has not led to the development of individual autonomy or legal rights (Keyder 1997: 41). What is more, the bureaucratic and military elite has treated the modernization project of Turkey as one of indefinite duration, thus justifying their unwillingness to allow anything more than experiments with variants of tutelary democracy. This has contributed to the conceptual distinction between the 'people' and the 'nation' as opposed to the 'national' interest (usually equated with the preservation of the Republic and its Kemalist underlying principles). In this equation, 'national interest' takes precedence over particularistic interests, the expression of which has often been seen in republican Turkey as a threat to the unity of state and nation.

Turkish democracy was therefore established from above by a coalition of reformist bureaucracy and the military. It is in this context that the prevalence of the bureaucratic-military elite in modern Turkish political life is reproduced and that the prospect of activating citizenship rights is treated with suspicion. The Kemalist conception of the state (and therefore of its bureaucratic-military elite) as standing outside and above society and intervening to protect the national interest has often been used to legitimize authoritarian policies and military interventions 'with the armed forces claiming to be the embodiment of the state and the nation' (Ahmad 1993: 17). The military elite has used this assumption as the ideological cover for its interventions in social and political life and the overall powerful role played by the military even in periods of civilian control.

## BEYOND TUTELARY DEMOCRACY?

Turkey first experienced a process of transition from the Kemalist one-party regime to a multiparty system (officially inspired by the principles of Kemalism) in 1946. This transformation of the polity has been attributed to Turkey's alignment with the US-led coalition that emerged victorious after World War II and to its effort to achieve integration into the Western alliance (Hale 1990: 56–7). In this new international context, the republican elite deemed that embracing some form of liberal democratic system and experimenting with economic liberalism might facilitate Turkey's participation in the post-war international political and economic reconstruction and maximize the benefits this might entail. Although domestic pressures for democratization have not been absent in Turkish political life since the establishment of the republic, it could be argued that external factors and international relations have played a significant role in regime transformation and democratization in Turkey.

However, as has already been argued, the transition from one-party regime to a multiparty democracy was a restricted one in the sense that the guiding principles of Kemalism were posing a number of limitations on the political game, especially as far as the expression of opinions or political activity that might be perceived to threaten the secular or unitary character of the state and nation were concerned. Admittedly, restrictions to such activities have not always been implemented to the letter and political actors have managed to operate within the system, often bypassing official obstacles. However, since 1960 the military have intervened in Turkish politics through a variety of means on numerous occasions when they deemed that political developments were posing a threat to the state's Kemalist principles or were jeopardizing the country's political stability and social order.[4] The Turkish experiment with a limited form of liberal democracy was thus interrupted by direct military interventions in 1960, 1971 and 1980. In addition, the army retained different forms and degrees of presence in political life, even after handing power to civilians, through a variety of means, some of which are discussed later.

After 1983, the military once more initiated a process of cautious democratization. Initially this was mainly through the military junta leader, General Kenan Evren, who assumed the presidency of the Republic and thus maintained an institutionalized position in Turkish politics. In addition, in accordance with the 1982 Constitution the military retained some overseeing capacity through the constitutional role of the National Security Council as monitor of the country's political development. The Council proved to be an important instrument for the control of civilian political life, especially after Evren's retirement from the Presidency in 1989.

The disintegration of the Ottoman empire and of the (however imperfect) model of social symbiosis that its social and ethnic heterogeneity entailed (Mardin 1997a: 71) had left an indelible mark on the founding principles of Republican Turkey. In contrast to its Ottoman predecessor, the Republic was premised on the principles of social unity and indivisibility of the new state. These in turn went hand in hand with a mistrust of minorities among the bureaucratic and military elite, especially because, as Turkish historiography has argued consistently, these minorities and the protection of their rights were often used by various enemies as a means for the dismemberment of the Turkish homeland. In addition, note that this adhesion of Turkey's military and bureaucratic elites to the principle of national unity has often equated the perceived threat posed by ethnic or cultural minorities to the activities of political opposition parties and organizations and of non-state controlled Islamic institutions and organizations.[5]

This tradition of mistrust towards minorities was often translated into assimilationist and homogenizing policies, suppression of cultural and linguistic rights, denial of the existence of specific minorities, or physical extermination or expulsion.[6] One of the treaties upon which the modern Turkish state was founded, the 1923 Treaty of Lausanne, effectively 'forced' Turkey to recognize and protect a number of non-Muslim minorities (Armenians, Greeks, Jews), although in practice Turkey has strived to assimilate or, if assimilation proved difficult, uproot these minorities on a number of occasions. However, no treaty imposed any such obligation to Turkey *vis-à-vis* Muslim but non-Turkish populations such as Laz, Circassians, Albanians, Bosnians and, most importantly, Kurds (by far the largest non-Turkish ethnic group in Turkey), none of which were afforded any recognition of cultural difference and were subjected to intense assimilationist policies.

Indeed, this policy of non-recognition of such minorities in Turkey has persisted until today and has played a significant role in determining the parameters of political action in contemporary Turkish society. Although there seems to be a growing recognition of the existence of cultural, or even ethnic, minorities in Turkey, discourses of difference are still treated with suspicion or even not tolerated in some quarters of the political system. Admittedly, occasional public debates on the issue of minorities and minority rights have been part of the Turkish political process. In addition, the Kurdish issue has acquired a high profile since the adoption of armed conflict by the Kurdistan Workers' Party (PKK) in 1984, and more recently as a result of a number of successful arrests of leading PKK figures, including the capture of its leader, Abdullah Öcalan, in February 1999. However, the fact remains that the issue of recognition of modern Turkey's multicultural character is not officially acceptable.[7]

As far as the Kurdish issue is concerned, the official position has oscillated between non-recognition of the existence of a Kurdish nation or ethnic group and the adoption of policies that implicitly or semi-officially recognize their existence and afford them limited cultural rights. Examples of the former stance are more numerous. The Kurds have systematically been considered as 'mountain Turks' (Poulton 1997: 121) and have been put under pressure to assimilate, while the public use of their language was banned on several occasions since 1925 and yet again in 1983 in a drive (initiated by the military leaders of the regime established after the 1980 coup) to eradicate the country's Kurdish 'problem'. Kurdish or pro-Kurdish political parties and political personalities have systematically been prosecuted and persecuted on the grounds of promoting separatism, thus undermining the state's undivided and unitary character. Notable in this context was the Constitutional Court's 1993 decision to close down the People's Labour Party (HEP) because of its explicitly stated function as a Kurdish party, or the lifting of the parliamentary immunity of the deputies of its successor, Democracy Party, in March 1994 on similar grounds.

On the other hand, an alternative strategy, preferred by a minority faction among politicians, the bureaucratic elite and an increasingly vocal group of entrepreneurs, centres on some sort of recognition to Kurds as well as granting them cultural rights, or even limited autonomy in parts of south-eastern Turkey. This strategy has managed to find official, albeit limited and often temporary, expression. One of the most striking successes of this alternative stance has been the recognition of the right to use the Kurdish language in certain contexts and publications after the Turkish government signed the 1990 Paris Charter of the Conference for Security and Cooperation in Europe and thus undertook to respect minority rights. To this should also be added the repeated statements of the deputy prime minister Erdal Inonü in the period 1991–93 stressing the need for recognition and protection of Turkey's Kurdish citizens' cultural identity.

Yet progress on the Kurdish issue is precarious and often the introduction of positive measures is countered by measures of insufficient policy implementation. The paranoia that has marked political debate on the Kurdish issue has led to a state of political polarization. In such a climate the existence of an 'emergency' legal corpus and institutions that reproduce it and implement it exists alongside the constitution and legislation formally protecting a number of basic civil rights such as the freedom of speech, of expression etc. This fact effectively restricts the scope of these very rights on the grounds of national security and the prevention of terrorism. What is more, practices such as the notorious 'executions outside due process' (i.e. the police shooting suspects for allegedly resisting arrest or endangering police officers' lives) are not unusual and often bypass the 'due process' (Zürcher 1997: 329). This 'parastate' existence is not restricted to the confrontation of violent expressions of Kurdish separatism, but also extends to the monitoring, restriction and often persecution of human rights and Islamist activism and action or even the expression of views that are considered to offend or undermine the constitutional status quo or vaguely to threaten the unity of the state. Indeed, this is one of the grey areas in the Turkish legal and political landscape that have become the object of contestation both within Turkey and in Turkey's relationship with the EU, which has advocated consistently a political solution to the problem of 'terrorism'.

Although attempts to democratize Turkish political life and the country's legal system since the late 1980s have met with some success, the continued role of the military is linked inextricably with the ambiguous legal system and the reproduction of the parastate. Even today, 20 years after the last, and possibly most ambitious, *coup d'état*, civilian control of the military remains an unattainable goal for reformist politicians and human rights activists. Through the National Security Council (*Milli Guvenlik Kurulu* (MGK)), the highest informal decision-making institution in Turkey, the army's presence in political life is institutionalized and army interventions such as the 1997 ultimatum issued to the Welfare Party (*Refah Partisi*)-led government of the Islamist politician Necmettin Erbakan[8] are vested with legality. Thus, although the MGK is officially an advisory body and its recommendations are not legally binding, they are nevertheless influential in the formulation of the country's domestic and foreign policy.

The EU has expressed repeatedly its concern over the continued presence of the Turkish military in politics, even through this legal formula. Nonetheless, the latter would clearly be unwilling to see the MGK and its institutionalized participation in political life and constitutional control over civilian politics abolished. Some change is evident, as the last ten years have been a period of partial and selective army involvement in politics, as opposed to the repeated practice of staging *coups d'état* and freezing the political process that marked Turkish political life until the late 1980s.

## THE EC/EU AS PART OF THE TURKISH POLITICAL LANDSCAPE

After the 1980 coup, the EC prioritized the dimension of human and civil rights in determining the pace of the development of its relationship with Turkey, thus acting as an indirect force for democratization. Although the polyphony typical of the EC meant that mixed signals were often sent to

Ankara, it was nevertheless stated explicitly on many occasions by Community officials and politicians that one of the major factors inhibiting Turkey's accession to the EC was its perceived political backwardness – a polite term connoting Turkey's democratic deficit (European Commission 1978; Kramer 1996: 67–73; also Müftüler-Bac 1997: 74–6). Thus after the12 September 1980 *coup d'état*, the EC froze relations with Turkey. When, seven years later, Turkey officially applied for EC membership, the reaction of most member states was that Turkish democracy did not meet European standards. Similarly, at the December 1997 Luxembourg summit of the EU, Turkey's application was again declined, partly on these grounds. Even the markedly more positive Helsinki declaration of 1999 has stipulated that a 'road map' has to be set for Turkey (i.e. a process of reforms and transformations in which democratization and human rights occupy an important position).

To these, one should add the fact that in an era of increasing transnationalization, the EU has found that developments taking place within Turkish society are having significant effects in EU domestic politics. Several millions of migrants of Turkish or Kurdish origin reside in the EU and serve to increase the transnational flows of people, ideas and goods between Turkey and the EU. The eruption of the passionate demonstrations in protest against the arrest of the Kurdish leader, Abdullah Öcalan, by Kurdish residents of the EU in dozens of European cities in February 1999 has been a confirmation of this 'presence' of Turkey within the EU.

Yet in an attempt of reformist forces to reappraise the ideological foundations of modern Turkey (Pope 1993), the EU and its policy *vis-à-vis* Turkey has become a permanent feature of the public discourse in Turkey and a factor contributing to the legitimation or otherwise of political views, policies and action within the country. It is characteristic that various governments and parts of the political and economic elites in Turkey have been linking the need for liberalization with the process of integration into Europe. Thus democratic reforms in the political system have been either prompted by or justified on the grounds of the EU–Turkey relationship. Furthermore, a Human Rights Ministry was established in 1991 with responsibility for supervising Turkey's adherence to its international obligations regarding the protection of human rights and working towards meeting EU human rights standards. This, together with the redrafting of Turkey's penal code and the repeal of some of the most controversial and restrictive clauses of the constitution, was partly linked to Turkey's preparation of a membership application and the Customs Union that came into force in 1996.

As a result of the EU's potential role as a legitimizing factor in Turkish politics, Turkish civil society has shown signs of activation of social spaces the existence of which is premised on the adoption of a discourse of Europeanization and the Turkish political landscape is being slowly reconfigured. One of the most visible changes was the establishment of the now defunct New Democracy Front (*Yeni Demokrasi Hareketi*), initially a reformist society and later a political party founded by textile tycoon Cem Boyner. Boyner has attempted to intervene in the political debate by advocating extensive reforms, including the adoption of free market liberalism, full religious freedom, a political solution to the Kurdish problem and the expansion of political rights. Despite the limited success his party had at the polls during its brief life, Boyner's initiative encouraged other wealthy members of Turkey's civil society to become more involved in politics and express their support for reform. As a result, Turkish industrialists such as the Sabanci, Koç and Eczacibaci families as well as the chair of the Turkish Confederation of Industrialists, Halis Komili, have also engaged, directly or indirectly, in public debate, have been active in promoting democratization and education and have advocated the need for reforms, for political dialogue with the Kurds and for closer ties with the EU. It is clear that Turkey's industrial-financial elite (as well as those dependent on it) are supporting the removal of the last remnants of the *étatisme* that has characterized Kemalist ideology, the submission of the army to civilian control, transparency, an end to corruption and the 'normalization' of politics, and are no longer in favour of the maintenance of repressive state apparata. For this emerging alliance, the costs of the developmentalist state, its arbitrariness and its self-reproduction have become onerous. Businessmen strong enough to compete with and become part of the international corporate bourgeoisie opt for the rule of law, calculability and accountability. To these voices, for different reasons, are added the voices of moderate Islamic and ethnic movements which also express demands for promotion of political liberalism and basic rights. It is interesting to note that among the favourable reactions to the EU's December 1999 Helsinki declaration were those of some members of the Party of Virtue (*Fasilet Partisi*, the new Islamic party in the Turkish parliament), who saw in Turkey's EU membership the strengthening of democratization that would restrict the overbearing role assumed by the Turkish military.

In view of this increasing evidence of mobility, it has been argued that Turkey's European orientation is so strong and self-evident that there is a broad consensus – even among the military – supportive of Turkey's integration into the EU. To support this assertion, Müftüler-Bac (1997: 86) points out that '[o]n March 25, 1981, at one of the meetings of the National Security Council, the generals decided that once democracy was restored, Turkey should file an official application for membership'. Although such an assumption might bear some degree of truth, there is considerable evidence that the military in Turkey prioritize a stable political system as opposed to a democratic one and, in doing so, their interests and strategic choices are to some extent incompatible with the stated EU prerequisites for Turkey's eventual accession. It is characteristic that Prime Minister Turgut Özal's European strategy was premised on a programme of economic liberalization and a series of political reforms, such as the restriction of the army's role in the political process. However, Özal's attempts to bring the military under civilian control as well as to 'broaden' democracy were often met with pre-emptive moves by the military. Thus, his hint that lifting restrictions on the operation of communist parties was imminent was ignored by the military authorities who, in 1987, upon the arrival in Ankara airport of the leadership of the exiled United Communist Party of Turkey, and in front of a planeload of European journalists and MEPs, proceeded to arrest them. It would therefore be more sensible to argue that what is in fact emerging in Turkey today is an increasingly visible split of the country's elite into supporters of reform, often rallying around the banner of Europeanization, and supporters of a statist view of Turkey under the tutelage of a suspicious and possessive military elite.

This division is further reinforced and sustained by the influence of another important external player in Turkey's political affairs, the USA. Throughout the Cold War period and even after the collapse of Communism, the USA has emphasized consistently the importance of stability in Turkey as a priority over the country's democratization, and actively supported a controlled process of political transformation, whereby its main internal ally, the Turkish military elite, would retain a say and a presence in Turkish politics. This is indeed not a unique instance where European and American priorities regarding partner states diverge considerably in the Near East.[9] However, in the case of Turkey, this divergence reinforces the political divisions pertaining to the nature, extent and pace of democratization and, eventually, Europeanization of the country.

Frequent closures of political parties as a result of a restrictive constitution and an interventionist army, and the political instability this entails, have benefited parties that had until relatively recently sat in the margins of Turkish political life. As reform has been a quite slow and often reversible process, popular dissatisfaction with the continued corruption, with the limited prospect of change and with the frustration of the electorate's hopes for improvements in terms of income and welfare seems to find expression in 'third' solutions. These have comprised the more militant factions of the Islamist Party of Virtue, or more recently of the extremist Nationalist Action Party (MHP) which in the past election, having dissociated itself from its extremist youth wings (the notorious Grey Wolves) and fought an anti-corruption campaign, has emerged as a major government coalition partner.[10] The results of the two most recent general elections in Turkey indicate that the potential for populist politics with an 'intolerant twist' is all too present[11] and that general dissatisfaction with Turkey's political class might eventually lead to a radical transformation of the political personnel and the policies they represent.

## CONCLUSION

This article demonstrates that Turkey today is in search of a new social contract, premised on an extensive revision of the country's Kemalist inheritance and incorporating and institutionalizing the economic and political transformations that were set in motion in the Özal period and pursued by reformist governments of the 1990s, even though not always decisively. It also makes clear that this is not a straightforward task for the reformist forces in Turkish politics and civil society. Both the imperative and the nature of reform are the object of contestation between those factions within the bureaucratic and military elite that have associated their social supremacy with the maintenance of the Kemalist tradition and its preferred variant of modernization, and the emerging reformist forces who have tended to rally around the demand for Europeanization. This split is reflected naturally in the different ways in which these forces envisage dealing with ethnic separatism, human and civil rights and political Islam.

Central in the argument developed in the article is the exploration of the tensions between the Kemalist principle of modernization and Turkey's closer links with the EU, and their manifestations in the form of political crises and contradictions in Turkey's domestic policy. This is an element that is often neglected in analyses of Turkish politics as it has often been assumed that the modernizing 'camp' *a priori* accepts Turkey's European orientation. In contrast, it has been argued that the complex political and institutional landscape of Turkish society has been and still is informed by and has sustained two sets of competing conceptions of political modernization, one compatible to and one threatened by Turkey's European orientation.

In this internal struggle between the established model of authoritarian modernization and a more open modernist conception of political liberalism and citizenship, the prospect of a deepened relationship between the EU and Turkey has played a significant role in domestic Turkish politics during the past two decades. The economic transformation required for Turkey to adapt to the market liberalization necessary for membership, combined with the EU prerequisite of democratization for such a development, is in the process of undermining the authoritarian, paternalistic culture of state intervention. Turkey's political dilemma may in this sense be yet another example of the effect that EU-inspired deregulation has had previously in societies sharing a southern European state tradition. However, the intensity of the dilemmas faced by Turkish society as far as its modernization (and Europeanization) is concerned is in some ways unique. The country's European identity has often been questioned in view of its geopolitical position and interests – both Near Eastern and European – and of the influence of Islam in Turkish culture and identity. What is more, the divisions in Turkish society are deep and reform often proves an extremely precarious enterprise. However, the pace of transformation of Turkish society and economy is such that the imperative of political modernization and Europeanization has now acquired a new sense of urgency.

## NOTES

1. A number of issues are raised by this association of Europeanization with democratization: I would argue that the insistence of the EC and later the EU on the attainment of specific (yet vaguely defined) standards by candidates for membership or even for partnership (such as the Euro–Mediterranean Partnership Initiative which focuses partly on the democratization of partner states) is driven partly by the need of defining the EU as a transnational or post-national entity characterized by its democratic traditions and practices. In other words, I would consider democracy as an indispensable element in the process of construction of a European institutional and post-national identity.
2. The incorporation of European settlers in the networks of the empire's cities, however imperfect and incomplete, indicated that European modernity was not seen as something to be imposed on the empire, but as a presence that was in dialogue with Ottoman society, through everyday exchanges, from the mundane to the official level. Tolerance, if not acceptance, of diversity and the other was an important element of this synthesis while it was highly incompatible with the Kemalist modernization project that was marked by a retreat from these loci of coexistence and exchange.
3. I am referring here to the inability of the post-1908 Ottoman parliament to operate because of what Mardin has described as 'ethnic/ideological' gridlock (1997b: 121).

4. Military interventions varied in terms of their ideological backgrounds, their type and their duration. Thus, the 1960 military coup has been seen as a 'democratic' intervention, whereas the 1971 and 1980 coups have been seen as 'anti-democratic' by some analysts. Although I would not dispute the different ideological and political premises of these interventions, this is not the place to enter such a discussion. Suffice it to say at this point that what is important here is the establishment of a tradition of military intervention in political life.
5. As early as 1925, the introduction of the Law on the Maintenance of Order and an extensive policing and justice framework in order to confront the Kurdish insurgency in South-eastern Anatolia was also used for the suppression of conservative, liberal and Marxist opposition. Similarly, the strong anti-terrorist legislation introduced in the 1980s and 1990s in order to confront the Kurdistan Workers' Party (PKK) was also used often for the suppression of political dissent.
6. On the fiscal, linguistic, education and nationality-related policies of the Kemalist state *vis-à-vis* its ethnic and religious minorities, see Poulton (1997: 114–29).
7. Having said that, it is important to recognize that among the younger urban educated social strata there is a widespread acceptance of, or even interest in, the cultural diversity and different ethnic origins of modern Turks. This interest does not have to do with any discourse of cultural or political separatism, or of minority rights, but is part of a less nationalistic attitude on the issue of cultural and, more generally, social diversity. However, there is little evidence that such an outlook has filtered through to the bureaucratic and military elite that determines policy on these issues.
8. Cf. *Radical* (National Political daily) 2 March 1997. This ultimatum is a case in point of the way in which the military are in a position to influence, if not dictate, political developments. Already in 1996 military members of MGK expressed concern at the expanding influence of Islamist organizations in state apparata. By early 1997, the military's warnings became more explicit. The Army's seriousness and determination was also shown in February 1997, during a demonstration in support of the introduction of *Sharia* (Islamic law) as law of the state in the suburb town of Sincan, just outside Ankara. The Army leadership temporarily stationed a number of tanks and personnel carriers in the town to indicate the military's disapproval and decisiveness. Eventually, in an MGK meeting on 28 February 1997, the military leadership presented the then Prime Minister Erbakan with a list of 20 points on government policy and requested its implementation within two months. A political crisis was precipitated and Erbakan resigned in what the Turkish and international press called a postmodern coup. In January 1998, the Welfare Party was banned by the Constitutional Court, its assets confiscated and many of its activists were arrested and prosecuted.
9. A first systematic attempt to chart this divergence of US and EU policy objectives in the 'Greater Near East', including Turkey, after the collapse of the Soviet Union can be found in Blackwill and Sturmer (1997).
10. However, just as in the case of Italian former neofascist leader Gianfranco Fini and his party, Alleanza Nazionale, it is unclear if this transformist strategy is sincere. Ultra nationalist and populist statements and mobilization of the public during the Öcalan trial in the summer of 1999 have marked the MHP's first months in government, while continued intolerance of social and political opponents can be seen in everyday life contexts. The MHP's policy on human rights and democracy is still unclear, although, despite its participation in government, the party has been fairly reserved and a tacit supporter of government policy.
11. It is also quite significant that both the Islamists and the MHP have attracted younger voters than other parties (Cornell 1999: 230). Both parties are engaged in a process of achieving hegemony over the younger generation by organizing at secondary school level.

## REFERENCES

Ahmad, F. (1993): *The Making of Modern Turkey*, London: Routledge.

Birand, M.A. (1990): *Turkiye'nin Ortak Pazar Macerasi* [Turkey's Common Market Adventure], Istanbul: Milliyet.

Blackwill, R.D., and M. Sturmer (eds.) (1997): *Allies Divided; Transatlantic Policies for the Greater Middle East*, Cambridge MA: MIT Press.

Cornell, S.E. (1999): 'Turkey: Return to Stability?', in S. Kedourie (ed.), *Seventy-Five Years of the Turkish Republic*, London: Frank Cass.

European Commission (1978): *Turkey and the European Community*, EC Background Report, 4 June.

Hale, W. (1990): 'The Turkish Army in Politics 1960–73', in N. Sirman and A. Finkel (eds.), *Turkish State, Turkish Society*, London: Routledge.

Kasaba, R. (1988): *The Ottoman Empire and the World Economy*, New York: State University of New York Press.

Keyder, H. (1997): 'Whither the Project of Modernity? Turkey in the 1990s', in S. Bozdogan and R. Kasaba (eds.), *Rethinking Modernity and National Identity in Turkey*, Seattle: University of Washington Press.

Kramer, H. (1996): 'The EU–Turkey Customs Union: Economic Integration amidst Political Turmoil', *Mediterranean Politics* 1/1, pp.XX–XX.

Mardin, S. (1997a): 'Projects as Methodology: Some Thoughts on Turkish Social Science', in S. Bozdogan and R. Kasaba (eds.), *Rethinking Modernity and National Identity in Turkey*, Seattle: University of Washington Press.

—— (1997b): 'The Ottoman Empire', in K. Barkey and M. von Hagen (eds.), *After Empire: Multiethnic Societies and Nation-Building*, Boulder: Westview.

Müftüler-Bac, M. (1997): *Turkey's Relations with a Changing Europe*, Manchester/New York: Manchester University Press.

Pope, H. (1993): 'Turks Question Ideological Foundations of the State', *The Independent*, 21 July.

Poulton, H. (1997): *Top Hat, Grey Wolf and Crescent: Turkish Nationalism and the Turkish Republic*, London: Hurst.

Sunar, I. (1987): 'State and Economy in the Ottoman Empire', in H. Islamoglu-Inan (ed.), *The Ottoman Empire and the World Economy*, Cambridge: Cambridge University Press.

Zürcher, E. (1997): *Turkey: A Modern History*, London: I.B. Tauris (rev. edn).

## OTHER SOURCES

Hale, W. (1994): *Turkish Politics and the Military*, London: Routledge.

Heper, M. (1985): *The State Tradition in Turkey*, Huntingdon: Eothen.

Kasaba, R. (1997): 'Kemalist Certainties and Modern Ambiguities', in S. Bozdogan and R. Kasaba (eds.), *Rethinking Modernity and National Identity in Turkey*, Seattle: University of Washington Press.

# The Europeanization of Malta: Adaptation, Identity and Party Politics

MICHELLE CINI

## INTRODUCTION

Malta's road to EU membership has so far been a rather bumpy one. Yet with an application for membership submitted in 1990 and a cautiously positive Commission Opinion issued in 1993, it looked for a time as though Malta's pre-accession experience would be relatively smooth. The election of a Labour government opposed to EU membership in 1996 changed all that and seemed to put paid to any notion that Malta would enter the EU with the 'first wave' of mainly central European applicants. But in yet another turnaround in 1998, early elections brought in a new Nationalist government and the reactivation of the Maltese application. Malta's pre-accession experience thus far is undoubtedly unique and is for that reason fascinating. But despite the proliferation of academic writing on EU enlargement, relatively little (outside Malta at least) has been written on the island's bid for membership. This little country of around 370,000 inhabitants usually has to make do with a paragraph or two in the key texts. And while this short article can do only a limited amount to redress this deficit in the enlargement literature, it does seek to review some of the key debates surrounding Malta's prospective accession to the EU. It does so by focusing on the theme of Europeanization and, more specifically, by addressing the relationship between the reform (or adaptation) process in Malta and the conflicting conceptions of Maltese national identity.

While the topic of 'Europeanization' is a relatively new research focus, the beginnings of a 'literature' on the subject is gradually emerging (see e.g. Ladrech 1994; Schmidt 1998; Knill and Lemkuhl 1999; Lavdas 1997; Olsen 1995). Yet as this body of work deals almost exclusively with the impact of *membership* on existing EU states, one might question whether it can feasibly be appropriated by those working on enlargement and applied to countries that are still outside the EU.[1] The article begins, therefore, by offering a suggestion as to how Europeanization might be defined when applied to states that are not (yet) EU members. Thus, Europeanization is conceived of as a process of institutional and policy adaptation on the one hand, and as a (re)statement of national identity on the other. The article then reviews Malta's relationship with the EU, paying particular attention to the events of the 1990s, before considering in the third section Malta's adaptation to EU norms and rules and the extent of consensus that exists over this form of Europeanization. Finally, two rather different conceptions of Maltese identity are outlined, suggesting why Malta's two largest parties remain divided over the issue of EU membership.

## DEFINING EUROPEANIZATION

There are of course many different ways of conceptualizing and defining 'Europeanization'. Ladrech, for example, says that it is 'an incremental process reorienting the direction and shape of politics to the degree that EC political and economic dynamics become part of the organizational logic of national politics and policy-making' (1994: 69). By contrast, Featherstone focuses his attention on how, in the case of Greece, Europeanization has been attributed a meaning synonymous with that of modernization, though '[i]n another sense, it simply masks a more common, general question: what is the impact of the EU on its member states?' (Featherstone 1998: 24). In a useful overview of the Europeanization literature, Colino (1997) has identified four broad categories: Europeanization as 'Communitarization' (i.e. as a competence shift from the national to the EU level); as 'Eurostandardization' (i.e. a convergence of policy in a particular sector); as 'Euroadaptation' (i.e. as an adaptive response by national institutions and actors to European initiatives); and as 'Euroentropy' or institutional convergence (in terms of governance systems and institutional designs). However, all of these, as Colino admits, are 'closely related in most cases' (1997: 7).

It is not self-evident that such definitions and categories, which in the main have arisen out of empirical research on the impact of EU membership, are helpful when applied to applicant states. At the very least it is important to be selective and to think through what precisely is meant when the Europeanization of, say, Estonia, Hungary or, in the case of this article, Malta is discussed. This article takes as its starting-point a twofold definition of 'Europeanization'. This is much more than just identifying two discrete ways of defining the concept; rather, it suggests that there might be different processes of Europeanization coexisting, competing or complementing each other: in other words, it suggests that we might more correctly speak of Europeanizations in the plural. Thus one aim of this article is to raise questions about the conceptual relationships that might exist between different definitions of Europeanization, definitions which could shed light on the actual processes of change taking place in states striving to become full members of the EU.

The first definition sees Europeanization as a process of adaptation. This inevitably begs certain questions – adapting to what, and how? It might be added, therefore, that the adaptation process is one which revolves around EU norms and rules (e.g. legal, economic, administrative). But more than this, it also revolves around certain conceptions of what it means to be a modern state, that is, around assumptions about modernization (Featherstone 1998). The practice of Europeanization is likely to involve a process of internal reform, usually guided and assisted by the European Commission. This process can take many forms, the most obvious of which is the establishment of institutions and the promulgation of new laws. This type of Europeanization tends to be practical and rational in application, leading to concrete reforms which impact to a greater or lesser degree upon national systems of governance.

By contrast, the second definition sees Europeanization as a restatement or redefinition of national identity. Europeanization in this sense is concerned with the affirmation or construction of a collective state of mind. It is an intersubjective process which is more emotive than rational. It is about the nation's or the state's place in the world as it seeks to answer questions such as 'Who are we?', 'Who are they?' and 'How do we all relate to one another?' While the first form of Europeanization involves adapting to Europe and 'acting European', the second requires a country (both elites and publics) to identify with Europe and to 'think European'. But before applying these two definitions of Europeanization to the Maltese case, the discussion begins by considering Malta's relations with the EU to date.

## THE EVOLVING EU–MALTA RELATIONSHIP

Ever since Malta was granted independence from Britain in 1964, the island has both sought out and shied away from direct involvement in the European integration process. The Nationalist Party (PN), which has traditionally been the party of the middle class, business and the Church in Malta, has consistently sought closer relations with the Community;

the Maltese Labour Party (MLP), Malta's class-based socialist party, has always been reluctant to be drawn into too close a relationship (Fenech 1988). Not surprisingly it was the PN leadership that signed the Association Agreement with the European Community on 5 December 1970 (Council of Ministers 1970). And while they oversaw its coming into force on 1 April 1971, a Labour victory in the June elections of that year meant that the Agreement's original ambition – to establish a customs union over two five-year periods – was never implemented, even though the Agreement itself remained in place.

With the MLP in power for 16 years, there was little prospect that closer political relations with the EC would be sought. The MLP government did cultivate good relations with the Italians, however, and the agreement signed between the two countries in September 1980 guaranteeing Maltese neutrality is evidence of this. The development of strong relations with the southern Mediterranean, and particularly with Libya, also dominated Maltese foreign policy to the extent that it is even claimed that when the US bombed Tripoli in April 1986, the Maltese provided the Libyans with some advance warning of the attack (Bin 1995: 14–15).

In 1987, after an extremely confrontational electoral campaign characterized by sporadic violence (Howe 1987: 243), the PN were elected on a liberal, non-interventionist but 'socially conscious' platform (Fenech 1988). But rather than reactivating the Association Agreement, the new government decided to go for membership, submitting to that effect an application to the EU's Council of Ministers in 1990. The European Commission's Opinion in 1993 which followed from this application was cautiously favourable to Maltese accession while pointing at the same time to fundamental reforms that would have to be implemented. The European Council's positive conclusions at the June 1994 Corfu Summit led the Council on the 10 April 1995 to agree to open accession negotiations (with both Malta and Cyprus) six months after the end of the 1996 Intergovernmental Conference. This suggested a start date of early 1997.

Such steps encouraged the Nationalist government to initiate a series of reforms which were highly controversial in Malta, but which the government argued were necessary – with or without the accession motive. However, the 'government was ... accused of having pursued economic policies designed to impress Brussels but detrimental to national competitiveness and of causing a fall in tourist numbers (the backbone of the Maltese economy together with industry)' (European

Parliament 1999). Particularly contentious was the introduction of a value added tax (VAT) at the start of 1995. Moreover, the political scene after the election was dogged by accusations of corruption within the PN ranks (Fenech 1997b).

In the elections called by the Nationalist Government on 26 October 1996, the MLP were returned to power with a majority of three seats (Fenech 1997b).[2] Led by Alfred Sant, they were elected on a platform of opposition to EU membership, even though they claimed that theirs was also a pro-European stance – that they nevertheless wanted close relations with the EU. However, they immediately 'froze' the Maltese application, removed Malta from NATO's Partnership for Peace (PfP),[3] and ended the political dialogue with the EU. They also scrapped the new VAT introduced by the previous government, replacing it with their own rather complicated version. The one area the new government did not touch, however, was the Euro–Mediterranean Partnership (European Parliament 1999: 6).

Thus the MLP began a process which would reformulate Malta's relations with the EU: first, negatively, through withdrawal from existing structures; and secondly, more positively, through the construction of a new relationship with the EU, one which was to rest on the establishment of an industrial free trade zone, increased cooperation in a number of key areas and dialogue on security concerns (European Parliament 1999: 10–11). The Commission's new framework for relations, outlined by the Commission in February 1998, detailed some of the steps that would have to be taken by the Maltese government to implement this new relationship.

Despite their opposition to EU membership, the Labour government acknowledged that Malta was in dire need of economic reform and industrial restructuring. Thus a series of austerity measures were introduced which sought to reduce the public deficit. These were extremely unpopular. As a result of these policies and because of internal strains within the Labour Party elite, early general elections were called on 5 September 1998 (Calleya 1999). Despite opinion polls predicting a Labour victory, the elections resulted in a majority for the Nationalists led by Eddie Fenech-Adami.[4] Along with the arrival of the new government came the 'reactivation' of the membership application and the recommencement of steps which the new government hoped would lead to Malta's eventual accession to the EU.

For the Commission, the 'thawing out' of the old application meant reassessing Malta's position in the light of developments since 1993.

Rather than issuing a new Opinion, an update was produced in February 1999 (European Commission 1999a). The February report led to a decision of the General Affairs Council in March which initiated the screening process. This began in the last week of May 1999 and came to an end early in 2000 with the agriculture chapter the last to be closed. The Maltese government are keen to 'catch up' with the other front-running applicant states (Borg 1999b) and for that reason negotiating positions were to be submitted to the Commission in a number of areas early in 2000, with a view to membership at or after the start of 2003. This opened the way for negotiations to begin, a decision agreed at the Helsinki European Council in December 1999. Thus in February 2000, discussions began on eight chapters of the 'acquis'. In October 1999, the Commission issued both a Regular Report which provided updated information on the Maltese reform process (European Commission 1999b) and an Accession Partnership which spelt out what Malta should do to adapt to EU rules and norms in the short and medium term (European Commission 1999c). This latter forms the basis of a National Programme for the Adoption of the Acquis which was completed by the Maltese government in September 2000.

This short introduction to Malta's recent relations with the EU serves to highlight the rather shaky foundations upon which the Maltese membership bid rests. With Malta's two parties split over whether the island should join the EU, and with public opinion on the island also divided, the future of Maltese 'progress' towards accession is uncertain. An MLP victory in the next general election, which will probably take place in 2003, could mean withdrawal from the accession process at a very late stage, or even from the EU itself should Malta have joined by this point. Yet with both parties committed to a referendum, it is popular sentiment which might ultimately decide the issue. The extent to which this will simply reflect the party political split on the island remains to be seen.

## ADAPTING TO EUROPE

Despite the upheaval of the freezing and then the reactivation of the membership application, Malta has already gone some way towards adapting to European norms and rules. All the same, the Commission's assessment, based on its own Copenhagen criteria (which focus on political and economic factors, as well as on Malta's capacity to take on membership obligations), demonstrates that while some progress has been made, there is still a great deal that needs to be done before Malta can accede to the Union. While the Maltese government is keen to set itself a deadline of January 2003, precisely how long it is likely to be before Malta can accede to the EU is still unclear.

First, on political grounds, the Commission has confirmed that Malta meets EU standards, particularly in respect of human rights, though this does not mean that other political questions are irrelevant. The challenge for the Maltese government is one of convincing the Commission that its constitutional neutrality is no barrier to the implementation of the EU's Common Foreign and Security Policy. This is important as a revision to the Constitution in 1987 formalized Malta's non-aligned status, confirming Malta as a neutral state (see Bin 1995; Redmond and Pace 1996). The Constitution states that Malta must not participate in any military alliance and that no foreign military base can be located on the island. It also places limits on the use of Maltese military facilities by foreign forces (*Constitution of Malta* 1992). There is, however, some disagreement over whether constitutional neutrality is really likely to prove a threat to Malta's accession to the EU. The PN line has consistently been that there is no contradiction between Maltese neutrality and EU membership (Fenech 1988). Yet the Commission is not so sure of this, having stated that a revision of the Constitution might be necessary, something which could be difficult given the two-thirds parliamentary majority needed and the almost certain opposition of the MLP. While the latter also see the Constitution in potential conflict with EU membership, their solution is, of course, not to join in the first place.

Secondly, both economically and industrially, the Commission has confirmed that the Maltese meet the Copenhagen criteria, even if there is still some way to go before the island would be allowed to join the Union. Here the situation at the end of 1999 was very different from that at the start of the 1990s when the Commission stated in no uncertain terms that

> The reforms which imply Malta's adoption of the acquis communautaire affect so many different areas (tax, finance, movement of capital, trade protection, competition law, etc.) and require so many changes in traditional patterns of behaviour that what is effectively involved is a root-and-branch overhaul of the entire regulatory and operational framework of the Maltese economy (European Commission 1993: 13).

Perhaps the greatest challenge that remains, however, involves the resolution of the budget deficit problem (at around nine per cent of GDP) and the overhaul of public finances (government debt is around 95 per cent of GDP) that is necessary to accomplish this (*Financial Times*, 6 October 1999). The challenge is both a technical and a political one, as the effects of the austerity policies implied in such a reform are likely to be unpopular. The opening-up of the Maltese economy provides another challenge, as not only will cutting subsidies and removing customs levies, planned as a rolling programme over the period 1999–2002, threaten the survival of many of Malta's small firms, but it will also leave a large hole in the government's finances, a hole the government hopes to fill from taxes. It is not clear that the new VAT introduced in January 1999 and the measures being taken to tighten up tax collection will compensate adequately for the loss of revenue (*Financial Times*, 6 October 1999).

Finally, the Commission's recent reports chart the progress that Malta has made towards adopting the Union's *acquis*. Here, too, progress is variable, and there still remains much to do. In the short and medium term the recommended steps towards adaptation on this front are listed in the Commission's Accession Partnership (European Commission 1999c). One particular concern, however, relates to whether Malta would be able to cope administratively with EU membership. There was some disquiet over this in the Commission's 1993 Opinion (European Commission 1993: 14), and only recently have new structures been put in place. Horizontal coordinating bodies were set up in 1999, but the Commission's October 1999 Regular Report also points to sectoral weaknesses, such as the need for new regulatory bodies in sectors covering such areas as energy policy and intellectual property (European Commission 1999b). Neither is it clear that Malta has an adequate number of diplomatic staff with international experience which would enable it to cope with the obligations of EU membership.

But perhaps the greatest challenge to the adaptation process arises out of the lack of party political and societal consensus on the issue of EU membership itself. While party/societal consensus on accession is not part of the Copenhagen criteria, Commission statements in the past suggested that adapting to Europe might also, ideally, involve the forging of at least a cross-party consensus on EU membership. In Malta no such consensus exists. Much of the debate about relations with the EU over the past few years has taken the form of competing arguments about what is or is not in the national interest. Both parties have claimed that they represent the interests of the Maltese people (Fenech 1988). The Nationalist line is that

EU membership is unequivocally in the Maltese national interest. By contrast, in 1998, the Labour Foreign Minister was arguing that 'The Government of Malta believes that membership of the EU is not in the best interests of either the EU or Malta' (Vella 1998b; see also Vella 1996). He claimed that there are two reasons for this: that it is not feasible for Malta to implement the *acquis*; and that the neutrality clause in the Constitution would prevent Malta playing a full role in the Union. More recently, it has been suggested that there are two strands to the MLP's position on EU membership: the first arguing that it is not appropriate for Malta to join because of the island's unique social, political and economic situation; and secondly, that Malta cannot afford to carry out the economic and social changes needed at the speed demanded by the Commission. While the first suggests a position of principle, the second, it is argued, leaves open the possibility that the Opposition could temper its anti-EU stance, although there is no evidence that this is likely to happen in the short term (*Malta Independent on Sunday*, 24 October 1999).

To place too much emphasis on the absence of consensus is to ignore the quite phenomenal convergence that has taken place programmatically between the two main political parties (see, however, Hirczy 1995: 260). Politicians on both sides of the political divide have recognized this, to a greater or lesser degree. For example, in 1998 George Vella, then Labour Foreign Minister, noted that 'Although much is made about the lack of consensus in Malta when it comes to discussing relations with the EU, there is no doubt that consensus does exist on the fact that the Union is our most relevant partner, both in political and in economic terms' (Vella 1998a). More stridently, however, in 1999 the Nationalist Prime Minister was adamant that 'While there are many views on the tactics to be adopted ... the broad strategic direction towards a more competitive, less insular Malta in close partnership with her European neighbours is one around which a nucleus of national agreement can be seen to have grown' (Fenech-Adami 1999). The Nationalist government has used the distinction between means and ends to highlight the specific characteristics of this national consensus. It has argued that development, reform and modernization is the government's ultimate goal, whereas EU membership is merely a means or a strategy for achieving that goal (Fenech-Adami 1999).[5] As Howe (1987: 236) has said, 'Much contemporary Maltese political debate reflects sharply opposed *strategies* for modernization' (my italics).

This is more than just the political rhetoric of politicians talking the language of consensus. There has been a massive policy change undertaken by the MLP since the mid-1980s and the departure of Dom Mintoff, the charismatic Labour leader who led the party for most of the post-war period. Since the MLP's defeat in 1987, there has been an increasing recognition in the Party's speeches and documentation that Malta has to modernize and that trade liberalization is the way to do this (*Malta Sunday Times*, 17 October 1999). Fenech (1997b: 442), for example, notes how the MLP shed its interventionist policies, making the distinction between left and right in Malta less marked, and as we have seen it was at least in part the outcry over the austerity measures introduced by the MLP government in 1997 and 1998 that led to the premature election and the PN's victory.

The success of the Nationalist government in handling both the practical and technical aspects of the adaptation process, in tempering the potentially painful economic impact on the Maltese small business community, and in continuing to place themselves on the political high ground when it comes to arguing for EU membership, will be important in shaping the interests and expectations of both the Maltese electorate and the Maltese elite towards European integration. While the MLP seemed rather vulnerable on the issue of EU membership in 1999 (*Malta Times*, 23 October 1999), this could change should Nationalist policies be seen, for example, to be driven solely by a set of criteria decided in Brussels (and not in the interests of the Maltese themselves).

## IDENTIFYING WITH EUROPE

While perceptions of interests are extremely important, so too are constructions of Malta's identity. Malta is a very young state. Independence was granted only in 1964 and it was not until 1979 that the British navy finally left the island. Both colonization and geography have left their mark on Maltese culture. Thus it is hardly surprising that since the mid-1960s, as in the case of many post-colonial developing states, the question of national identity has become a major preoccupation. As Caruana (1992: 19) suggests: 'Malta was only recently made. Perhaps the Maltese are still in the making.' However, even before World War II, questions of identity dominated Maltese politics. At the time these took as their focus the language issue (Howe 1987: 236), even if:

> [o]nly superficially was it a struggle between tradition (Italian) and utility (English). It was a clash of visions for Malta: between those

> who envisaged Catholic Malta as their Latin Mediterranean patria, enjoying a high degree of autonomy, perhaps in some loose federation with Italy; as against those who, while also advocating representation, firmly believed that Imperial and Maltese interests were one and the same thing, that true patriotism meant consolidating Malta's fractious ties with Britain (Caruana 1992: 19).

While this 'clash of visions' has meant an inability to 'reach a consensus on self-identity' (Frendo 1994: 14) and even though this no longer takes the same form in post-independence Malta, echos of it still remain today, particularly within the two dominant political parties (ibid.). Indeed the island (and its inhabitants) 'feels itself ambivalently situated, in a number of key areas, between the apparent "modernity" of the European world, and the traditional societies of what one might want to call the Mediterranean' (Mitchell 1996: 147). This has been reflected in an academic (and particularly an anthropological) interest in Maltese culture and identity (Boissevain 1965, 1977; see also Mitchell 1996) which has itself provided 'the raw material to fuel the fires of identity politics' (Mitchell 1996: 142).

From these studies can be seen two constructions of Maltese identity. The first might be called Malta's 'non-aligned Mediterranean identity'. This is associated on the one hand with the island's neutral and non-aligned status, and on the other with an anti-clerical tradition. Here, Malta is constructed first as a Mediterranean state and only second as a European one. The Mediterranean ties are paramount, as they acknowledge Malta's unique geopolitical situation. Important also is a recognition that while Malta's links with the rest of Europe (and Italy in particular) are important, so too is the relationship that Malta has with the Arab states of the southern Mediterranean and particularly with Libya (Fenech 1988). The metaphor of Malta as a bridge between the northern and southern shoreline of the Mediterranean (Mitchell 1996: 142) has found its concrete expression in the proactive role that the island has played and continues to play in promoting Mediterranean cooperation. The examples of the CSCE and, more recently, the Euro–Mediterranean Partnership are often recalled in this context (de Marco 1999).

A second construction of Maltese identity views the island as a European and indeed as a (prospective) EU state. This identity is a Christian Democrat one, tied closely to the pro-clerical tradition within

Malta. The Mediterranean perspective is important here too, but is of secondary relevance as it is claimed that it is only by tying Malta firmly into the northern Mediterranean camp and by joining the EU that Malta's bridge-building potential will be strengthened. References to Malta's 'European vocation', though often left undefined, epitomize this version of Malta's identity, even if at times Maltese European identity does seem to be more of an aspiration than a reality. Take for example the current Foreign Minister, Joe Borg's words when he claimed that the inevitable changes that come with being members of the EU call for 'the dynamic *reinvention* of both the Maltese people as individuals and Malta as a nation' (Borg 1999a; my italics).

There can be no surprise in discovering that the first 'version' of Maltese identity is that which is pushed by the MLP, while the second is associated with the PN. For the MLP, this construction of Malta's place in the world is wholly consistent with its line on EU membership. The same can be said of the PN's interpretation of Maltese identity. Yet what is not clear is which came first. Did the PN decision to apply for EU membership follow logically from their understanding of Malta's identity, or is the rhetoric about Malta's European vocation merely a *post hoc* justification of a policy line based more on an understanding of Malta's (or possibly the PN's) interests? Likewise, one might ask whether the Labour position has now more to do with the party's desire to differentiate itself from the Nationalists than with a particular understanding of who the Maltese are and what their place in the world should be.

## CONCLUSION

So what does all this tell us about the Europeanization of Malta? We have seen above that Malta currently is engaged in a process of Europeanization in that it is adapting to EU norms and rules. But even if the *Financial Times* (6 October 1999) is confident enough to claim that the 'Maltese people seem increasingly convinced that their future lies with Europe', it is more difficult to say whether Malta is engaged in a process of Europeanization in the second sense (i.e. in a redefinition of Maltese identity). What can be said on this score is that Nationalist elites have actively been involved in constructing a pro-European identity for Malta, even if the existence (or construction) of a competing national identity favoured by the MLP means that the 'victory' of a European identity is no foregone conclusion. On this basis, one might assume that the relationship between the two definitions of Europeanization (i.e.

between adaptation and identity redefinition) is that the former impacts upon the latter. In other words, it might be hypothesized either that the adaptation process in which Malta is engaged will help to forge a new European identity for the island, or conversely that it will not (possibly as a result of a backlash against EU-inspired reforms). Such hypotheses seem reasonable on the basis of the Maltese experience thus far.

However, it might also be reasonable to hypothesize that particular understandings of Maltese identity will either inhibit or assist in the adaptation process, that is, that identity impacts upon adaptation. This seems to be what Mitchell means when he hints that it is how the Maltese perceive themselves (in answer to the question 'Who are we?') that shapes attitudes to EU membership:

> [The] Maltese themselves fall into a model whereby the ideal of bureaucratization, ultimately based on an image of European rationality, is held up as a future hope. This ideal would play Malta into a northern and western politico-cultural sphere. Once more, conflict emerges between the interests which herald this rationality as an attainable ideal for future Maltese politics, and those which are more sceptical – whether European identity should be sought in political life, or whether the Maltese 'Mediterranean' character makes this impossible (Mitchell 1996: 145).

If this accurately reflects the relationship between adaptation and identity change, it can be assumed that Europeanization not only implies a process of institutional and policy adaptation on the one hand and a process of identity redefinition on the other, but also an *interplay* of adaptation and identity change, with each feeding off and feeding into the other. How this interplay affects outcomes (e.g. whether Malta will or will not remain in the EU) is an empirical question. And while in the case of Malta it is too early to predict just how the island will be Europeanized, the next three or four years should provide at least an interim answer.

## NOTES

1. On eastern Europe, however, see Schimmelpfennig 1999.
2. The MLP won 50.7 per cent of the votes, and the National Party 47.8 per cent, with around two per cent going to other parties. As a result of the 1987 constitutional reform, this led to the National Party being given an additional four seats (out of a total of 65) in the unicameral House of Representatives.
3. Malta had joined PfP in April 1996 under the PN government. Thirty Maltese soldiers were sent to Bulgaria in June 1996 to participate with six other countries in the 'Cooperation Determination 96' exercise.
4. The new parliament comprises 35 Nationalists and 30 Labour members. This gives the Nationalists (in Maltese terms) a huge majority. The PN obtained 51 per cent of the votes and the MLP 47 per cent. Alternativa Democratika won two per cent.
5. Fenech-Adami also says that EU membership can be a goal too in its own right as it fulfils Malta's European vocation. This is dealt with below.

## REFERENCES

Bin, A. (1995): 'Security Implications of Malta's Membership of the European Union', *The International Spectator* 30/3, pp.5–26.

Boissevain, J. (1965): *Saints and Fireworks: Religion and Politics in Rural Malta*, London: The Athlone Press.

—— (1977): 'When the Saints go marching out: Reflections on the Decline of Patronage in Malta', in E. Gellner and J. Waterbury (eds.), *Patrons and Clients in Mediterranean Societies,* London: Duckworth.

Borg, J. (1999a): 'The Challenge of the EU and the Public Service', speech by the Minister of Foreign Affairs as part of Public Service Week, Mediterranean Conference Centre, Valletta, 14 May.

—— (1999b): Speech by the Ministry of Foreign Affairs at the EU-Malta Joint Parliamentary Committee, Brussels, 8 Nov.

Calleya, S.C. (1999): 'Early Elections in Malta', *Mediterranean Politics* 4/1, pp.113–18.

Caruana, P. (1992): 'From the Kitchens to the Courts', Review of H. Frendo (1991), *Party Politics in a Fortress Colony: the Maltese Experience*, 2nd ed (Malta: Midsea Books) in *Administrative Review* 1, pp.18–19.

Colino, C. (1997): 'The Manifold "Europeanization" of the Audiovisual Sector: Expanding European Initiatives and German Domestic Responses', paper presented at the Final Workshop on 'The European Policy Process' organized by the Human Capital and Mobility Network, University College Dublin, 8–10 May.

Council of Ministers (1970): 'Agreement establishing an association between the EEC and Malta', *Official Journal* L 61, 14 March 1971.

*The Constitution of Malta*, English Language Version (1992): including amendments of 1994 and 1996 (downloaded from http://www.geocities.com/CapitolHill/3355/cont-text.html, 11 Nov.).

de Marco, G. (1999): Speech by the Deputy Prime Minister and Minister of Foreign Affairs at the Conference of the Chairpersons of Foreign Affairs Committees of the Member States of the EU, Bonn, Germany, 9 March.

European Commission (1993): 'The Challenge of Enlargement. Commission Opinion on Malta's Application for Membership', *Bulletin of the European Communities, Supplement* 4.93.

—— (1999a): *Report Updating the Commission Opinion on Malta's Application for Membership*, COM 69 final, Brussels, 17 Feb.

—— (1999b): *1999 Regular Report from the Commission on Malta's Progress Towards Accession*, 13 Oct. (http://Europea.eu.int/comm/enlargement/index.htm, downloaded 3 Nov. 1999).

—— (1999c): *Malta: 1999 Accession Partnership (Commission Proposal)*, 13 Oct. (http://www.magnet.mt/press_releases/1999/october, downloaded 12 Nov. 1999).

European Parliament (1999): 'Malta and Relations with the European Union', Briefing No.5, PE 167.350/rev.2, Luxembourg, 2 Feb.

Featherstone, K. (1998): '"Europeanization" and the Centre-Periphery: the Case of Greece in the 1990s', *South European Society and Politics* 3/1, pp.23–39.

Fenech, D. (1988): 'The 1987 Maltese Election: Between Europe and the Mediterranean', *West European Politics* 7, pp.133–8.

—— (1997a): 'Malta's External Security', *GeoJournal* 41/2, pp.153–63.

—— (1997b): 'Malta' *European Journal of Political Research* 32, pp.439–45.

Fenech-Adami, E. (1995): 'Mediterranean Security: a Maltese Perspective', *Mediterranean Quarterly* 6/1, pp.1–9.

—— (1999): Speech by the Prime Minister at the Federation of Industry Annual Conference, 'Shaping Up for Europe', Qawra, 17 Feb.

Frendo, H. (1994): 'National Identity', in H. Frendo and O. Friggieri (eds.), *Malta. Culture and Identity*, Malta: Ministry of Youth and the Arts.

Hirczy, W. (1995): 'Explaining Near-Universal Turnout: the Case of Malta', *European Journal of Political Research* 27/2, pp.255–71.

Howe, S. (1987): 'The Maltese General Election of 1987', *Electoral Studies* 6/3, pp.235–47.

Knill, C., and D. Lehmkuhl (1999): 'How Europe matters. Different Mechanisms of Europeanization', *European Integration Online Papers* 3/7 (http://eiop.or.at/eiop/texte/1999-007a.htm, downloaded 15 Nov. 1999).

Ladrech, R. (1994): 'Europeanization of Domestic Politics and Institutions: The Case of France', *Journal of Common Market Studies* 32/1, pp.69–88.

Lavdas. K.A. (1997): *The Europeanization of Greece. Interest Politics and Crises of Integration*, Hants: Macmillan.

Mitchell, J.P. (1996): 'An Island in between: Malta, Identity and Anthropology', *South European Society and Politics* 3/1, pp.142–9.

Olsen, J.P. (1995): 'Europeanization and Nation-State Dynamics', *Arena Working Paper* 9, Oslo, March.

Redmond, J., and R. Pace (1996): 'European Security in the 1990s and Beyond: the Implications of the Accession of Cyprus and Malta to the European Union', *Contemporary Security Policy* 17/3, pp.430–50.

Schmidt, V.A. (1998): 'Loosening the Ties that Bind: The Impact of European Integration on French Government and its Relationship to Business', *Journal of Common Market Studies* 34/2, pp.222–54.

Schimmelpfennig, F. (1999): 'The Double Puzzle of Enlargement. Liberal Norms, Rhetorical Action, and the Decision to Expand to the East', *Arena Working Paper*, WP 99/15, Oslo.

Vella, G. (1996): Address by Deputy Prime Minister and Minister of Foreign Affairs and the

Environment at the General Affairs Council of the EU, Brussels, 25 Nov.
—— (1998a): Statement by the Deputy Prime Minister and Minister of Foreign Affairs and the Environment at the 10th Meeting of the EU–Malta Joint Parliamentary Committee, Strasbourg, 2 April.
—— (1998b): 'Malta on the Road to a Free Trade Area within the European Union', lecture by the Deputy Prime Minister and Minister of Foreign Affairs and the Environment during 'Malta Week', Hamburg, 22 April.

# ABSTRACTS

**Southern Europe and the Process of 'Europeanization'**
KEVIN FEATHERSTONE and GEORGE KAZAMIAS

This article introduces the theme of 'Europeanization' in the context of the focus on contemporary southern and Mediterranean Europe. In applying the term 'periphery' to the region, it argues that the major contrasts that exist between it and the 'core' EU states serve to highlight in stark terms the challenges endemic within the Europeanization process. It explores the different meanings of 'Europeanization' and argues that it necessitates a broad focus and a complex ontology. The case studies that follow are placed within the perspective of domestic institutional adaptation, albeit in multi-tiered, core-periphery setting. The southern experience highlights the dynamism, asymmetry and fragmentation of the Europeanization process. These attributes are of increasing significance both to an understanding of the patterns of change underway in the region and to the future stability and cohesion of the EU itself.

**European Policy-Making and the Machinery of Italian Government**
DAVID HINE

This article analyzes Italy's attempts to adapt its central government machinery to the demands of European policy-making since the mid-1980s. It shows how the introduction of a more complex and articulated form of cross-departmental coordination at both the policy formation and the implementation stages of the policy cycle was affected by the Italian institutional culture. Institutional adaptation did come, but was delayed and often distorted by uncertainty over the broader changes to the machinery of government which were taking place over the same period, and by a culture in which cohesion and purpose in public policy goals tended to be sustained more through formal legal definitions of the policy process than through the development of shared attitudes towards the role of programmatic political leadership.

**Europeanization and Italy: A Bottom-up Process?**
MARCO GIULIANI

This article offers a synthetic review of the domestic effects of the EU integration process on Italian politics and policy. Although Italy has recently undergone a process of rapid transformations, the overall account of these changes is far from clear. It is argued that the Europeanization process passed through the window of opportunity opened by the crisis of the entire party system, but it affected the internal arena by changing the attitudes of domestic policy actors rather than by imposing reforms on the political structures. The dynamism of certain policy arenas may even alter specific institutional relationships, but it cannot be assumed that some peculiar features of the present Italian political system will clash against the EU's potential evolution towards a power-sharing configuration.

**The Europeanization of Greece: An Overall Assessment**
P.C. IOAKIMIDIS

The aim of this article is to examine the general pattern of Europeanization in Greece. 'Europeanization' is seen here as a process that is transforming the domestic political system in the direction of weakening the position of central state institutions, while strengthening decentralization and civil society. Europeanization is to be understood as a process that is experienced differently by member states and applicants, affected by a range of factors connected to the state, policy-making and political culture, as well as by how a state views EU membership. Greece, like other south European states, has embarked on a process of 'intended', rather than 'responsive', Europeanization.

**Multilevel Governance and Europeanization:**
**The Case of Catalonia**

QUIM BRUGUÉ, RICARD GOMÀ and JOAN SUBIRATS

The article aims to explore the patterns of multilevel governance in Catalonia in the context of a process of Europeanization. Catalonia is no longer a simple sphere of linguistic and cultural identity deprived of political expression. Nor, however, is it a political reality with the structures of a nation state. Today, Catalonia is a country with a considerable degree of self-government, but whose place within Europe for the most part continues to be articulated through its political dependencies on the Spanish state. At the same time, it is a country with an internal network of strong local identities – municipalities and *comarques* (or counties) – and a capital, Barcelona, with its own extraordinary projection: all of which is also expressed in the political sphere. To explore the complexities of Catalan governance, first we develop a framework of analysis; secondly, we examine the multilevel distribution of public resources; and finally, we investigate the framing, at multiple territorial levels, of policies that handle these resources.

**The Transformation of the Portuguese Political System: European Regional Policy and Democratization in a Small EU Member State**

JOSÉ MAGONE

This article highlights the EU's importance in the development of the Portuguese political system. European public policy in general and European regional policy in particular have become important packages of administrative modernization in the Portuguese case. Indeed, in the past 15 years the democratic structures set up after the 1974 Revolution have not only been consolidated, but they have also been given a new qualitative dimension. The article concentrates on what is by far the most important area of European public policy in this context, European regional policy, and assesses how the Portuguese political system has absorbed the rationale behind the EU's policy-making and implementation.

**Cyprus and the Onset of Europeanization: Strategic Usage, Structural Transformation and Institutional Adaptation**

KEVIN FEATHERSTONE

This article analyzes the EU's impact on Cyprus during its 'pre-accession' phase. The processes of Europeanization are considered in terms of the structural transformation of state–economy relations (in which 'empowerment' is diffuse and differentiated among domestic actors); and the adaptation of the state administration (to the demands of coordination; readjustment of competencies). Across a range of domestic reforms, EU pressure has been crucial to its pace, if not also its content. With the exception of the events of 1974, the stimulus from the EU represents the most far-reaching transformation of Cypriot society in four decades of independence. Europeanization also plays a major role in the discourse of key actors on foreign policy (where the EU is seen as a vital foreign policy lever). Yet the high expectations of the EU to 'unblock' relations with Turkey poses important strategic risks for the EU should it fail to deliver.

**Managing the Spanish Economy within Europe**

CARLES BOIX

This article explores the economic policies developed by the Spanish socialist government from 1982 to 1996, particularly with an eye on the impact the process of European integration had on them. The introduction of stable macroeconomic policies, in the form of high interest rates, is traced to the interaction of three factors. First, an increasingly internationalized economy, reinforced by the European single market and monetary union projects, forced the Spanish government to fight inflation and deprived it of the possibility of using currency depreciations. Secondly, a radical and fragmented union movement made it impossible for the González cabinet to rely on stable corporatist pacts to achieve wage moderation. Finally, intense pressure to build a welfare state and miscalculations about the direction of the economic cycle led to loose fiscal policies that had to be compensated with tight money measures. To compensate for its incapacity to establish a social democratic corporatist regime, the PSOE engaged in an active industrial policy geared to a restructuring of the publicly owned enterprises, expanded the Spanish public stock of human and physical capital, and increased social spending to compensate the unemployed and the losers of the transformation of the Spanish economy.

**Economic Adjustment and Financial Reform:**
**Greece's Europeanization and the Emergence of a Stabilization State**
GEORGE PAGOULATOS

In a brief part of the 1980s and throughout the 1990s, Europeanization, more in the nominal-macroeconomic than in the structural sense, was the most pronounced economic objective of Greek governments. This objective was pursued mainly through extensive reliance on monetary austerity predicated upon financial liberalization, and through the transformation of the growth state into a stabilization state. Macroeconomic policies were aimed at triggering the disciplinary mechanisms that would facilitate structural adjustment by eroding domestic sociopolitical resistance. A principal strategy employed for transforming a growth state into a stabilization state was one of surrendering government control over finance to the regulatory authorities of an increasingly autonomous central bank and to the allocative functions of a rapidly internationalizing market.

**Europeanization and Convergence via Incomplete Contracts?**
**The Case of Turkey**
MEHMET UGUR

The formal link with the EU was expected to reduce the probability of Turkey's deviations from its declared European orientation and make Europeanization less costly. This article argues that such expectations have been too optimistic. Both EU and Turkish policy-makers have continuously ignored the 'control-reliance' and 'muddling through' aspects of the Turkish policy-making process and the incomplete nature of the contracts expected to lock in Turkey's European orientation. Consequently, Turkey's European orientation has lacked credibility, its convergence towards EU standards has remained suboptimal, and Turkey has become economically integrated with but politically detached from the EU. The article examines these anomalous results with respect to economic policy, human rights and the Cyprus problem. Based on this analysis, the article concludes with an assessment of the Helsinki decision confirming Turkey's candidacy and explores the conditions that must be satisfied to ensure that the road from Helsinki leads to Turkey's integration with the EU.

**Reluctant Europeans? European Integration and the Transformation of Turkish Politics**

SPYROS A. SOFOS

Turkey is in search of a new social contract premised on an extensive revision of the country's Kemalist inheritance and incorporating the economic and political transformations set in motion in the Ozal period. This is not a straightforward task for the reformist forces in Turkish politics and civil society; the imperative and nature of reform are the object of contestation between those factions within the bureaucratic and military elite that have associated their social supremacy with the maintenance of the Kemalist tradition and its preferred variant of modernization, and the emerging reformist forces which rally around the demand for Europeanization. In this internal struggle between the established model of authoritarian modernization and a more open modernist conception of political liberalism, the prospect of a deepened relationship between the EU and Turkey has played a significant role in shaping Turkish politics during the past two decades.

**The Europeanization of Malta: Adaptation, Identity and Party Politics**

MICHELLE CINI

This article reviews Malta's engagement in a process of Europeanization. 'Europeanization' is defined in two ways: as the process of adaptation to European rules and norms; and as a redefinition or restatement of national identity. In the case of the first definition, we find evidence that Malta is indeed Europeanizing. However, in the second sense, the coexistence of two conflicting 'versions' of national identity contributes to the party political and societal divide that exists between those supporting EU membership and those opposing it. In this latter sense, there remains a degree of ambivalence surrounding the Europeanization of Malta.

# INDEX